'*The Crossway* is in many ways classic travelogue, so classic indeed that early admirers have drawn parallels with Patrick Leigh Fermor . . . Stagg allows an emotional honesty to filter through the golden prose, a willingness to lay himself bare in front of his readers as he is struggling psychologically to understand himself at the same time as struggling physically to put one foot in front of the other'

PETER STANFORD, *Observer*

'Having finished this account of a 5,500km pilgrimage, on foot, from Canterbury to Jerusalem, I felt dazed. Dazed at the thought of all that I'd learnt from its pages about 2,000 years of Christianity, dazed at how immediate its author had made so many centuries-old stories feel, and dazed at the strangeness and brilliance of this extraordinary travelogue.'

REBECCA ARMSTRONG, *i*

'The author combines an eye for the landscape and the architecture of the towns and villages he passes through with an ear for history and the conversation of the people he encounters . . . a formidable achievement . . . his sensitivity enhances the experience of his readers as well as his hosts. This secular pilgrimage is a lively read'

JOHN URE, *Country Life*

'The journey as redemptive recovery is a well-worn trope, but there is no glib ending here. I really enjoyed this book.'

SARA WHEELER, *Spectator*

'Such pitch-perfect prose that he has already attracted comparisons with Patrick Leigh Fermor's celebrated accounts of his youthful travels'

The Tablet

'A gripping pilgrimage through faith and doubt . . . his trip offers little in the way of facile pseudo-spiritual uplift. It is much richer, deeper – and more valuable – than that . . . A first-rate writer, and a tough-minded one, Stagg . . . writes with a sort of rapturous exactitude about the peoples, climates and landscapes he meets'

BOYD TONKIN, theartsdesk.com

'Stagg's walk, and the book that has resulted from it, is a brave, even bravura, performance'

Catholic Herald

'There have been some excellent footslog memoirs in recent years . . . but none describing as marathon a trek as Stagg's'

BLAKE MORRISON, *Guardian*

'Stagg *notices* people . . . such attentiveness is a rare gift. So, too, is his sure sense of the right few words to portray those he meets . . . With Stagg, we are enchanted'

Church Times

'Stagg poignantly recounts not just his own journey as a spiritually-charged Paddy Leigh Fermor but that of the saints, soldiers and pilgrims who trod the path centuries before him'

New Statesman

'It is epic but it always feels intimate . . . There is poetry in Stagg's depiction . . . he offers us descriptions of landscapes dripping with lush musings, novel analogies and striking metaphors, taking us to places populated with strange, amusing, humbling monks, nuns and fellow searchers'

Literary Review

'A beguiling portrait of one young man's search into the hidden corners of Europe'

Sunday Times

'Poignant and poetic . . . an extraordinary journey . . . much of the book is taken up with absorbing accounts of saints and pilgrims, crusaders and revolutionaries . . . the narrative contains some captivating imagery'

TLS

'A sublime, intense, and intimate account of a journey . . . Beautifully written, filled with strange encounters and extraordinary language, *The Crossway* is a meditation, an escape, a confrontation, a losing and a finding. It is a timely antidote to our disconnected times.'

PHILIP HOARE, author of *Leviathan*

'The extraordinary story of a pilgrimage to find out the meaning of pilgrimage. Completely absorbing, personal, often funny, and full of fascinating encounters – an enlightening book from an exciting new writer.'

SARAH BAKEWELL, author of *At The Existentialist Café*

'The journey is remarkable – a hike of thousands of miles across Europe, undertaken with rare bravery and stamina. But what is really extraordinary about Guy Stagg's *The Crossway* is the writing – acutely sensitive, hyper-alert and unflagging in its exploration of the strange depths and by-ways of human belief.'

PHILIP MARSDEN, author of *Rising Ground*

'Guy Stagg makes a pilgrimage across Europe, into history and, most powerfully, the (troubled) interior of his soul. He takes us on a journey full of wonder and woe, poetry and pain; writing in prose that's as sure-footed as it is unsettling in its honesty. A brave and beautiful account of a man's search for meaning.'

RHIDIAN BROOK, author of *The Aftermath*

'A marvellous book. There's a lovely plainsongish immediacy to the telling that I found hugely beguiling, and (unusually) Stagg is as effective on people as he is on place. It's also a generous piece of self-reckoning.'

WILLIAM ATKINS, author of *The Immeasurable World*

'Stagg's fabulously open hearted account easily bears comparison with the great walking and monastery books of Patrick Leigh Fermor except he goes further in revealing the damage, and how it might be repaired'

ROBERT TWIGGER, author of *Red Nile*

'A gorgeous and moving book.'

JAMIE QUATRO, author of *Fire Sermon*

'I loved it. Odd that a journey made to find salvation (a kind of 5,500 kilometre Stations of the Cross taking almost a year to walk) should turn out to be such a page turner. The reason is Stagg himself – an engaging, challenging, endlessly interesting companion who just happens to write formidably well. Travel writing has a bright new star.'

ALEXANDER FRATER, author of *Chasing the Monsoon*

'*The Crossway* is moving and unique . . . At the book's heart is Stagg's own story; troubled, he seeks redemption and hope. Does he find them? He makes his search into a story that is gripping and uplifting.'

MAX EGREMONT, author of *Forgotten Land*

'What a privilege it's been to read this compelling and moving book, to travel with a writer who records everything he sees and feels with such care and passion. The writing is beautiful and his voice so engaging, so unflinchingly honest, throughout. I finished *The Crossway* and just wanted the author to keep walking.'

JAMES MACDONALD LOCKHART, author of *Raptor*

Guy Stagg was born in 1988 and grew up in Paris, Heidelberg, Yorkshire and London. *The Crossway* is his first book.

GUY STAGG

THE CROSSWAY

PICADOR

First published 2018 by Picador

First published in paperback 2018 by Picador

This paperback edition first published 2019 by Picador
an imprint of Pan Macmillan
20 New Wharf Road, London N1 9RR
Associated companies throughout the world
www.panmacmillan.com

ISBN 978-1-5098-4459-3

1 3 5 7 9 8 6 4 2

A CIP catalogue record for this book is available from the British Library.

Typeset in 10.7/13.04 pt Stempel Garamond LT Pro by Jouve (UK), Milton Keynes
Printed and bound by CPI Group (UK) Ltd, Croydon, CR0 4YY

Visit **www.picador.com** to read more about all our books
and to buy them. You will also find features, author interviews and
news of any author events, and you can sign up for e-newsletters
so that you're always first to hear about our new releases.

THE CROSSWAY

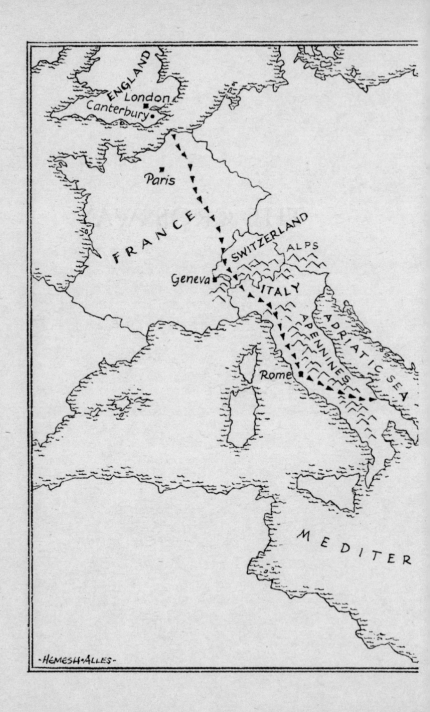

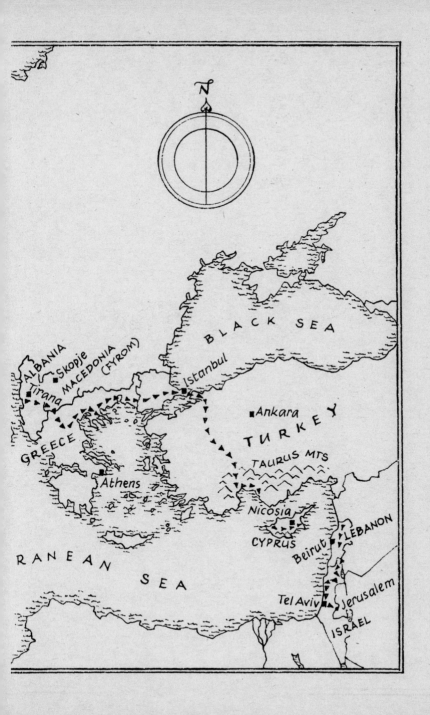

Prologue

It was late afternoon when I reached the saint's house. From a distance the building seemed hidden in mist. Closer I could piece it together: white walls, a low door, a tiled roof and shuttered windows. One of the shutters was loose, its catch bent out of shape. The room through the window was unlit, but I kept looking until the darkness came apart. A wooden chair leant against a wooden desk in the middle of the floor. Two crutches hung over the hearth, a giant rosary tied between them, its cross the colour of bone and each bead a knuckle. Dust on the floor, on the chair, the desk. Dust like vapour on the windowpane glass.

I tried the door and found it open. Inside the house was still, with a frosted, sour taste. A guestbook lay on the desk, the last entry dated eight months ago – twenty names in children's handwriting, from a school trip that visited in the spring. Under the book was a homemade board game, the pieces three model pilgrims, the board a winding road. Square number one was a drawing of this house. Fifty-five squares on was a box labelled Rome.

Signs were fixed to the walls, the printed card grey with damp. Here the saint helped his mother cook bread. There he played with his brothers and sisters. Upstairs was the room where he prayed.

Dropping my rucksack, I climbed the staircase. An attic ran the length of the house, with a brick chimney in the middle and bare cob at both ends. The roof tiles were bare too, the roof beams exposed. These beams were the same pale shade as the rosary downstairs, turning the attic into a skinned ribcage.

Past the chimney was a whitewashed alcove containing a cot with a chicken-wire mesh, a waist-high statue of a starved young man, and a stone slate engraved with the words *Merci à St Benoît*. The crucifix above the cot had Christ lying on his side with face serene, as if the cross were a bed and the body only resting.

Here the saint slept each night.

The previous evening, staying at the Abbaye Saint-Paul de Wisques, I had been told about this place – the childhood home of the patron saint of pilgrims. When the brothers learnt I was walking to Jerusalem, they urged me to stop by. Now, standing in the saint's bedroom, I tried to remember the rest of his story.

Benoît-Joseph Labre was born midway through the eighteenth century. His father was a tradesman, his uncle a priest. His mother gave birth to fifteen children: five sons, five daughters, and five that never lived. The children were raised in Amettes, a farmers' village seventy kilometres south of Calais. As a boy Benoît-Joseph was quiet, devout, and at sixteen he decided to enter a monastery. But, when he went to the Carthusians at Longuenesse, they turned him away. The Cistercians at La Trappe did the same. He was too young, they said. Too frail. He did not know plainsong. He had not been taught philosophy. The boy wanted to withdraw from the world, yet every time he tried it ended in failure. Instead, he cast himself out.

Aged twenty-one, Benoît-Joseph left home, promising to return for Christmas. His mother, his father, his brothers and sisters – none of them saw him again.

For the next seven years he wandered Western Europe. This was the early 1770s, and the pilgrim tracks that once connected the continent had fallen into disuse. Benoît-Joseph Labre lived nearer to an age of steam than an age of sacred travel, yet he journeyed on foot between Einsiedeln and Rome, Loreto and Santiago de Compostela. The boy too weak for the monastery covered thirty thousand kilometres with no money in his pocket and no cloak for his back.

His days were endless hardship. He ate dry bread or the herbs that grew wild by the roadside. He slept on the ground or, when offered a roof for the night, refused a bed and slept on the stairs. Imitating the Fools-for-Christ – those medieval mystics who behaved like lunatics and animals – Benoît-Joseph made himself wretched for fear of pride. According to his confessor, Fr Marconi, this humility was born of love. The pilgrim so loved his fellow men that he hoped his austerities might atone for their sins. But was it love that first pushed him away from home? Looking at the cot where he slept, I could think of another reason. Ever since he was a boy, Benoît-Joseph had dreamed of life in a monastery. The adult world rejected him, thus he decided to live always as a child, a pilgrim Peter Pan.

Well, perhaps. Or perhaps I wanted the saint's journey to explain my own somehow. For Benoît-Joseph Labre was the patron not only of pilgrims, but also of vagrants, unmarried men and the mentally ill. And, standing in his bedroom that afternoon, I felt his story had something to teach me.

The alcove was dim now, and there was not one sound in all the house. No creaking doors, no heaving floors, the whole place made mute by dust. Yet I had a vague sense that I was no longer alone here, so I left the attic and ducked down the stairs. Then I slipped out into the mist.

*

My first pilgrimage started on a midsummer morning six months earlier. I set off from the flat where I was living in London, followed the Thames east, and joined the medieval route to Canterbury. It was a surprising thing to do, as for much of the year I had been afraid to leave my room.

When I was twenty-three I had a nervous breakdown. Afterwards I was frightened of the city, of lunchtime crowds and rush-hour trains and the angry, anxious streets. I went to work and sat senseless at my desk. I went to doctors and psychiatrists, counsellors and therapists. Otherwise I lay in bed, turned from the window, my thoughts hurting.

One year on, the fear was lifting. In early summer I was taken off antidepressants. As the days got warmer, I wanted to go outside, and that June I decided on a walk. Canterbury was a whim – the walk at the beginning of English literature. The forecast was good, meaning I did not think to bring a waterproof jacket. Or buy maps, trusting my phone instead. That Wednesday was the solstice. Perfect.

Everything went wrong. For two days I marched from dawn until dusk, covering almost a hundred kilometres – a grim total for someone who last hiked at school. On Tuesday I went so far off course that I had to catch a train to my hostel. On Wednesday I was soaked and sunburnt in the space of an hour, and spent the entire afternoon trudging down the A2, eyes harsh from exhaust fumes. When I got to Canterbury my heels were bruised and my socks clotted with blood. Yet I do not remember the pain. I remember lying on the grass beneath the cathedral, watching the daylight last into night, with a sense of relief so complete it was like healing. For a long time my world had been closing in, smaller and smaller, until it was no bigger than a cell. Walking made the world wide again.

A figure carrying a staff and scrip was etched onto a stone by the cathedral's southern porch. Around him was written, *La Via Francigena / Canterbury – Rome*. At that point I knew nothing of the holy road to St Peter's, but as I lay on the grass an idea took shape in my mind. Why not keep walking? Why not leave England and walk to Italy? And then keep going, to the edge of Europe, on and on to the world's most sacred city.

The following day I learnt what I could about the Via Francigena. One website listed the names it had been known by: Lombard Way, Frankish Way, Chemin des Anglois, Via Romea. A second website listed the Anglo-Saxon kings who travelled its length – Caedwalla and Coenred, Offa and Ine – as well as Alfred the Great and King Cnut. A third explained how, in the year 990, the Archbishop of Canterbury also travelled the Via Francigena, to collect his pallium from the pope. On the return journey a scribe noted every town and city where they stopped. An image of that manuscript showed a page of numbered Latin names, some of which I recognized: *I Urbs Roma*, *XXVI Luca*, *XXXVIII Placentia*, and *LIV Losanna*. Although the Via Francigena was the major pilgrimage in northern Europe, this itinerary was the only one to survive from the period, and when the pilgrimage was revived a millennium later, it formed the basis of the modern route.

The Via Francigena also continued south beyond St Peter's. In Albania it became the Via Egnatia, a Roman road across the Balkans. From Turkey a patchwork of crusader paths led all the way to the Holy Land.

Rome, Istanbul, Jerusalem. That was it. That was my pilgrimage.

If people asked about the plan, I told them I wanted to explore the major crises in Christianity: the collapse of belief in Western Europe and the exodus of Christians from the Middle East. It was true, but it was not the truth. It was not reason enough to wander out of my life. There was another reason, though one I kept to myself. That time of unhappy confusion was over, but I was not better. Or rather I was better, yet less, much less, than I had once been. Brittle now, and hollow too, and knocked down by the slightest of blows. I thought the journey might build me up again. I walked to mend myself. But this reason I was ashamed to admit. I do not believe in God, do not believe in miracles, and do not believe that a sacrament can cure a sickness. Therefore, when friends wanted to know about the journey, I said that I needed some exercise, that I could not drive, that I didn't own a bike and was afraid of flying. They laughed and wondered if I would ever return.

I said little more to my family, only that I was going on pilgrimage and would be home before the year's end, as Benoît-Joseph had done.

Three months after that midsummer hike I handed in my notice. Three months after that I moved out of my flat. New Year's Eve I spent at my parents' house, staying up late to repack a rucksack, fitting in a sleeping bag and tent, waterproofs and notebooks, six pairs of socks and a mouth organ for when I was bored. My mother made sandwiches, wrapping them with the last of the Christmas cake, and next morning my father drove me to Canterbury.

We arrived at the cathedral for matins, the sun rising in the crypt windows and fraying the stone tracery. When the service was done, the dean gave me a blessing in the Trinity Chapel. Then my father said goodbye and I began to walk.

Off to Jerusalem on the first day of January, a flawless Tuesday morning. I strolled along beneath clear skies and wondered if this was providence. But the boat from Dover crossed into cloud and ever since the mornings had been foggy. In those early weeks dawn was at nine, dusk at five, and my progress slow on muddy footpaths. Heading south-east from Calais, I often had to run to cover the day's distance before nightfall.

By Friday I was trekking past fields of blue loam. The air was bitter, like a bonfire after rain, and the fog thick as smoke.

When I got to Amettes the daylight was ebbing. I ambled around in the half-dark, trying to imagine the village 265 years ago. This was not hard, for its barns and stables were centuries old, its streetlamps smudged and hazy. The Labre house, however, was a disappointment. I expected signs, tour groups, perhaps even a gift shop. Instead I found a sullen set of rooms decorated with a few dusty mementos.

A church stood on the hill above the house. Inside it smelt of candle wax and wet copper coins – a cold and settled smell. Mist drifted through the doors and hung in the nave like incense.

The church interior was devoted to Benoît-Joseph. There were banners embroidered with his portrait, the golden brocade turning green with age, and paintings of a hollow-cheeked figure staring at the heavens. His biography was told three times over: on laminated boards, illustrated posters, and in the stained glass of the windows. Circling the aisles, I tried to work out why the story bewitched me so.

Aged twenty-eight Benoît-Joseph ended his pilgrimage in Rome, living in the Colosseum and spending his days among the destitute. Rome's citizens were soon telling stories about the young man. How he knelt in church and floated from the ground, or burnt with a faint lustre as he prayed. How, in his hands, a single loaf of bread became two loaves, ten loaves, twenty, and he would give the bread away until there was nothing left for himself. Benoît-Joseph wanted to break free from desire, from need, but it made him frail. His knees swelled from praying the Forty Hours without rest. His stomach distended from constant fasting. On Holy Wednesday, aged thirty-five, he collapsed during mass at Santa Maria ai Monti. He was carried to a nearby house and given the last rites. That evening children ran through the streets shouting, 'The saint is dead!'

His body was returned to the church and laid in repose. The crowds that gathered to mourn him were so large, a guard had to be posted at the door. And every day another miracle: those who were sick and dying, who had lost their minds, prayed to the young man and were cured.

Accounts of these miracles spread round Europe. Within three months the newspapers in Paris and London were reporting on the beggar whom Rome was calling a saint. Finally the Labre family learnt what had happened to their son.

Early in the nineteenth century the church at Amettes acquired several cast-offs associated with the pilgrim. Some were on display in the north transept, including the font where he was baptized and the straw mattress on which he died. The rest I discovered in glass cabinets near the entrance. A leather shoe in a giltwood box. A plaster mask on a bed of purple silk. A crumbling pair of knee-caps. Taken together, they gave the impression that Benoît-Joseph was not an eccentric child of the Enlightenment, but a great martyr of the Middle Ages.

In the year 1881 the pilgrim was made a saint. On the date of his canonization, Paul Verlaine, the most popular Decadent poet, wrote a sonnet to celebrate. Looking back at the era of Voltaire, Rousseau and Robespierre, he claimed that Labre was 'the only light in France from the eighteenth century'. Jules Barbey d'Aurevilly, the dandy novelist who influenced Proust, called him 'a sublime vagabond'. André Breton, founder of the Surrealist movement, described him as a 'glittering beggar'. Germain Nouveau, another poet, who had once shared a flat with Rimbaud, visited Amettes during a fit of madness and vowed to live the rest of his life in poverty. He then walked twice to Santiago in imitation of the saint.

It's no surprise that these *fin de siècle* writers were enchanted. Benoît-Joseph's humility was in part a performance, his devotion shot through with pride. Perhaps I was captivated by the saint for the same reason, but looking at that shabby collection of relics, I realized there was something pitiful in the slow suicide of his piety.

A park covered the hill between the church and the house, its grass grey and its flowerbeds black. Fourteen stations ringed the grass, each station shaped like a gravestone, with scenes from the Passion sculpted in bas-relief. They showed Christ dragging his cross, Christ crucified, Christ's broken body laid upon the tomb. The names of the donors were carved beneath: *La Paroisse de Marville, La Comtesse de Bryas,* and *La Famille de M. Labre Laroche*. A few names were blotched with lichen, and one of the shrines, number thirteen, had lost the pinnacle from its cap.

The stations dropped in the direction of the house and rose on the far side of the hill. Before leaving the site I decided to complete a circuit. As I paced round the park, the same phrase kept playing in my thoughts. *Chemin de Croix, Via Crucis. Chemin de Croix, Via Crucis.*

The Way of the Cross is the blueprint for Christian pilgrimage. By walking in Christ's footsteps, a pilgrim shares in his sacrifice. If any man will come after me, Jesus told the disciples, let him deny himself, take up his cross and follow me. Benoît-Joseph Labre felt called by this command, starving himself that he might be saved, and his story would haunt the rest of my pilgrimage. Not because it was frightening, but because it was familiar. To feel drawn across a continent by a longing that has no name. To feel drawn towards sacrifice. These things I knew.

At the top of the park, beyond the fourteenth shrine, three crosses were staked into the earth. Each cross held a spotlit body, and beneath the crosses were three women with covered faces, spotlit also. One of the women, Christ's mother, was bowing at the feet of her child. When I glanced up, a fault trembled the lights, and for a moment the statues were in shadow, as though something moved unseen among the display.

By now the sky was turning over and darkness falling. I kept walking, past the final stations, until the saint's house was hidden in the mist below. Trees scratched the undersky, their branches sharp like thorns. High above was Calvary, bright against the coming night.

PART ONE

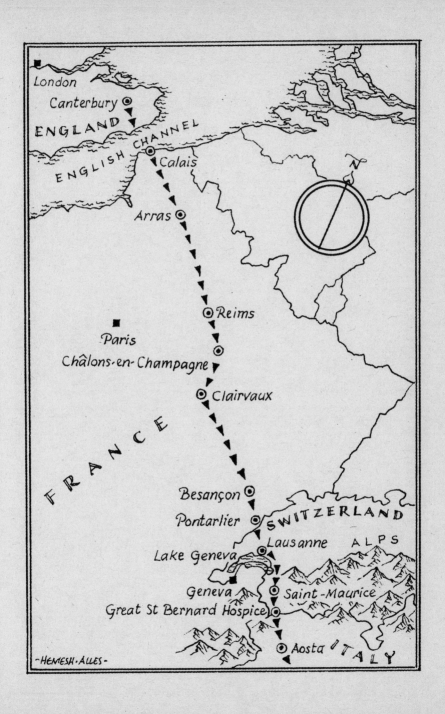

London

Canterbury

ENGLAND

ENGLISH CHANNEL

Calais

Arras

N

Reims

Paris

Châlons-en-Champagne

Clairvaux

FRANCE

Besançon

Pontarlier

SWITZERLAND

Lausanne

ALPS

Lake Geneva

Geneva

Saint-Maurice

Great St Bernard Hospice

Aosta

ITALY

-HEMESH-ALLES-

École Saint-Jean-Baptiste-de-la-Salle was a bungalow. Three bungalows, forming three sides of a courtyard. The yard's surface was decorated with a circle, a star, a shield and mantling – the school crest, maybe, or a playground game chalked onto the concrete. Beyond was a porch, enclosing a locked set of double doors. Round the back I found more bungalows, as well as a dining room and a chapel. I also found a nativity scene with three wise men the size of schoolboys and a manger trussed in fairy lights, blinking onto the lawn.

I had been given this address the previous morning. It was a boarding school run by the Society of St Pius X, and the priests were happy to host pilgrims – or so I was told. However, I was given no phone number, meaning I could not ring ahead and ask to stay. Now I worried that nobody was home.

Eventually a young priest came out to meet me. I tried to explain myself, telling him that I left Canterbury four days ago and was following the Via Francigena across France, Switzerland—

The priest cut me off: 'You want somewhere to sleep?'
'Please.'
'To stay for how long?'
'One night.'
'Tomorrow our students return.'
'I leave in the morning.'
'We have mass in the morning.'

'After mass.'

The priest folded, unfolded his arms. He was tall and lanky, breathing loud through his nose. 'You are alone?' he asked.

'Yes.'

'All alone?'

'All alone.'

His name was Fr Robert. He thought there were some spare beds in the infirmary. There. I could sleep there.

The double doors opened onto a hall with paper chains tied to the ceiling and a Christmas tree sagging in the corner. The infirmary was on the far side. Fr Robert gave me the key and made me promise to lock up when I left. Otherwise the boys would steal the medical supplies.

Two beds ran the length of the infirmary. One of them looked like an operating table, its head fixed at an angle. The other bed had a rubber mattress, elastic-edged sheets and a *Quick & Flupke* duvet cover. Garlands of tinsel hung from the shelves, and the whole room had the greenish tang of antiseptic mixed with floor polish. A shower two-thirds the size of a normal unit stood at one end, its panels not glass but tinted plastic. When I tried to wash, I banged my elbows and shins.

An hour later Fr Robert was back. Dinner time.

The priests lived in an apartment off the entrance hall. Two more were waiting for me in the kitchen. Fr Joseph was a shy man with a shy smile, bending over the oven in a blue apron. Fr Jean was a small, stubbed figure with a yawning mouth, who sat at the table discussing which of the school's students would go to seminary, how well Arras were performing in the local football league, and what day the baby Jesus was circumcised. When I asked about the menu for the evening, Fr Joseph placed a tray in the middle of the table, its contents hidden under a drying-up cloth. Then Fr Jean drummed on the tabletop and Fr Joseph whipped the cloth away, revealing a basket of bread, a bowl of oil, and four pots of tapenade – green olive, black olive, aubergine and chickpea.

'Caviar!' said Fr Joseph.

'Caviar for the peasants,' said Fr Robert.

'For the priests,' said Fr Jean. 'For the pilgrim.'

Once Fr Jean had recited grace, we all sat. My hosts kept passing the tapenade round the table, each priest trying to serve himself after the rest. When everyone was eating, Fr Robert said, 'Like the Last Supper, no?' I asked what he meant, and he explained that this weekend was the end of the Christmas holidays. Lessons began on Monday.

And what subject did Fr Robert teach?

'Anything. Whatever you want.'

Fr Joseph pinched his lips into a pained smile. 'You understand if I say teaching is not Fr Robert's vocation.'

'My penance,' said Fr Robert, making a snorting noise to show that he was joking. 'This school is my exile.'

Fr Jean wanted to know how long I had been walking. I told him I had started on Tuesday. And what route would I walk across France? I listed the cities I could remember: Arras, Reims, Châlons-en-Champagne, Besançon, Pontarlier, and then over the border to Switzerland.

He nodded. 'And you walk to Rome?'

'To Jerusalem!' said Fr Robert.

Fr Joseph clapped his hands and began asking questions. No, I wasn't a student. No, not an academic. Not studying to be a priest, not training to be a missionary, not walking to find my faith. Yes, this was my first pilgrimage. No, never before. Not Santiago. Not Assisi. No, not even Lourdes. With each answer Fr Joseph looked more and more embarrassed. Eventually he asked: 'But why are you walking?' I told him that, although I was raised an Anglican, as a teenager I stopped believing, and now I had little idea what faith felt like. But I thought the best way to learn about religion was by taking part in a ritual. And, if I walked to Jerusalem, I would also learn about the Christians living along the route. It was a speech I had written down in French and learnt by heart on the ferry from Dover. The priests' responses were a frown (Fr Robert), a yawn (Fr Jean) and a nervous grin (Fr Joseph).

'And how will you walk in winter?' Fr Robert asked.

I shook my head, confused.

'If there is nowhere to stay?'

'I have a tent and a sleeping bag—'

'Or you lose your way?'

'And I have maps from here to Italy.'

'The Alps!' cried Fr Jean.

'I go over the Alps,' I replied, becoming more and more flustered. 'At the Great Saint Bernard Pass.'

Fr Robert was still frowning. 'In the snow? You will climb two thousand, three thousand metres in the snow?'

'I can wear snow shoes.'

Fr Robert made another snorting noise. Fr Jean added his own barking laugh.

'Your first time?' Fr Joseph asked again. 'Your first pilgrimage?'

I went to bed early, but could not sleep, the rubber mattress yelping whenever I turned and Fr Robert's questions nagging in my mind. I had expected bad weather – my rucksack was fat with waterproofs and thermals – but never thought snow might make the pilgrimage impossible.

As I lay in the infirmary, I watched headlights from the road outside spilling between the curtains and illuminating the bookshelf above my head. I spotted a pocket catechism, a cartoon account of the lives of the saints, a solve-it-yourself mystery set in Venice and a pamphlet about sex called *Jésus et son corps*. On the shelf below there was a crèche, the ox and ass replaced by a toy safari. Two lions, three antelope and a carved elephant crowded the manger. A few strands of tinsel had fallen onto the crèche like straw upon the stable floor, made golden that night of a miracle. Cradled by this Christmas scene, my worries began to calm.

Next morning was Epiphany. Mass was held in the school chapel, an A-frame building with cream-coloured hangings. The priests wore chasubles of white brocade, the choristers wore surplices of white silk, and the altar was decorated with winter roses, arranged by an elderly woman wearing a veil of white lace.

It was my first Sunday in church for six or seven years. The rest of the congregation – families from local villages – knew when to stand, when to kneel and when to run a thumb down their face like a thread of oil, a stitch over the forehead, the lips, the heart. Though I copied as best I could, I was often out of sequence. The Latin liturgy was new to me, likewise the hymns and prayers, but I recognized the Gospel reading: a passage from Matthew telling the story of three wise men, a star shining in the east, a child born in Bethlehem, and gifts of gold, frankincense, and myrrh.

Fr Jean gave the homily. He talked about eating too much at Christmas and drinking too much at New Year. And he talked about his resolutions: to pray more, telephone his sister more, and go jogging twice a week.

Then he talked about the three wise men. 'St Melchior, St Gaspar and St Balthazar. From all the Orient – from India, from Persia, from Arabia. Travelling thousands of kilometres in the winter just to visit a baby.' Fr Jean looked towards me, his expression almost benign. 'The first pilgrims to visit Our Lord.'

After mass the priests sold cakes in the church foyer. Earlier that morning the baker had delivered eighty-four *galettes des rois* to the school gates, and now they were stacked in tray racks, the whole congregation queuing to buy one. The queue kept stalling as each customer swapped gossip with a favourite priest. With Fr Robert, who boxed the cakes in a single sweeping motion; or Fr Joseph, who bent over a ledger and copied out receipts; or Fr Jean, who circled the hall with a sack, collecting the chocolate and sweets that every family had brought as a gift.

When I returned to the infirmary, sunshine filled the room, colouring the plastic shower panes and blazing off the tinsel. I stripped the rubber mattress and folded the cartoon blanket before packing my rucksack and locking the door behind me.

It was almost eleven. Fr Joseph was sitting in his office, counting the money from the sale. The sack of treats bulged at his feet, and when I knocked he dipped his fingers into the sack, removing a handful of sweets. 'Please,' he said, gesturing for me to take them. 'The women of a certain age, they think we have no fun. Christmas, Easter, always the same: *Have them, Fr Joseph! They tempt me, Fr Joseph! They're the devil, Fr Joseph!* We give them to our students, and they eat and eat until they are sick.' Thanking him, I wondered whether this much kindness was waiting for me at every stop. If so, I had no need to fear the winter.

Fr Robert was tidying the hall with the help of some choristers. One boy wrapped decorations in bubble wrap, while another stuffed paper chains into green Galeries Lafayette bags. A third boy lifted the Christmas tree onto the priest's shoulder. 'The next time maybe I walk with you, eh?' Fr Robert shouted as he carried the tree away, leaving a trail of dead needles behind him.

Fr Jean was dismantling the nativity scene on the lawn. When I said goodbye, he raised two fingers to my face –

up and down, left and right – quivering the shape of a cross. Then he went back to work, laying the statues of the wise men in wooden crates. He worked with such patience, such care, as though the statues were made from ceramic, or glass, or he was holding the relics of the saints themselves.

A week later the weather turned. It was Sunday again, my last evening in Reims. I had spent the weekend at a convent near the city limits, an orange-brick building that resembled a fitness centre. All afternoon the earth gave off a cool, aching odour, and around seven the first flakes fell. That night I sat by my window and watched the snow coming down like stars dropping from the sky. Next day I walked out into the cold.

The morning was quiet, with the muffled hush of blanket snow. As I moved into the suburbs of Saint-Léonard and Sillery, there was no traffic, nor any footprints on the powdered pavement. I crossed a canal, a river, a motorway and a train track, and then entered the Champagne region, where the hillsides looked like scattered sheets of music. Snow had turned their terraces into pages, strung with wire staves, and every vine was a note and every vineyard a melody. The corners of the pages were not numbered, but stamped with little badges – Lanson, Veuve Clicquot, or the gilded arms of Charles de Cazanove. A path led through the terraces, but it was hidden by snow, and I spent most of the morning tramping down rows of vines. Yet I did not mind. Instead I felt that childish glee at the year's first snowfall, when everything is padded and thrilling.

Villages huddled above the vineyards, beside a range of hills called the Montagne de Reims. One of the villages,

Verzenay, was home to the miniature mansions of a dozen champagne houses, a concrete lighthouse containing the local champagne museum, and a wooden windmill flying the red-sashed flag of G.H. Mumm.

I was aiming for Trépail, another village some twenty-four kilometres south-east of Reims. The cathedral office had given me the address of a farm with a room for pilgrims, ringing ahead to find out if I could stay. I could.

That afternoon I met a boy and a girl making angels in the snow. When I asked for directions, they pointed at the wooded slopes of the Montagne de Reims. A dirt track led into the woods, the ground rising on the right and on the left sinking back towards vineyards. The track ran past oak and ash and dwarf beech with twisted branches – a fairytale forest. On my map it edged the eastern corner of the Montagne de Reims and exited a short distance from Trépail, but the route was criss-crossed by dozens of trails and I quickly lost the original. For a while the air was flushed; then the temperature dipped and the daylight faded. I could not guess the shape of the landscape through the thickening trees. Nor, once the light had dimmed, could I guess my position on the map.

After an hour in the woods my fingers and toes felt wet, felt sharp. Checking my compass I saw that I was moving west – a quarter-turn off course. Ahead, the ground climbed steadily. Behind, fresh powder covered my footsteps. I was lost, and soon it would be dark. Yet I felt no alarm, only a dismayed acceptance: how easy it was to walk into a crisis.

I stopped moving. Sat on my rucksack. Listened very hard. The quiet was heavier here, the snow dampening any sound. A minute passed, another minute, and then I heard a noise like static: a car driving on fractured ice.

Run. Down the sloping hillsides, over the snow-combed bracken, under the twisted beech trees – my rucksack catching on branches, my trousers tearing on brambles. With each pace I grew more and more panicked, at one point tripping and tumbling onto the floor, my mouth filling with peppery snow grit. But I kept running, because I could see the jangle of headlights through the trees and hear the flash of wheels on frozen mud.

The ground lowered fast and levelled as I stumbled onto the road. Puddles of ice pooled on either side of the tarmac, while the road's surface looked black and greasy. I was just in time to watch the car I had been chasing speed away, taillights flaring into the distance. Then I was alone again, lungs clawing for breath in the cold night air.

Seven minutes later a second car set me right for Trépail.

Spring is the season to walk in. Or summer if you don't mind the heat. The end of summer, stretching into autumn. There are not enough hours of light in the winter, never mind the weather. Few youth hostels are open, few *gîtes d'étape* or *chambres d'hôte*, and none of the campsites. I could not afford hotels, so I went to churches and asked for shelter. Sometimes there was a guestroom attached to the presbytery, or a camp bed in the parish office. Once I was lent a church hall, my fleece folded up for a pillow and my sleeping bag rolled out beside the radiator. If there was no monastery or convent, no presbytery or parish office, a stranger would take me in. The first time, this seemed a miraculous thing. Here's what happened:

After the vineyards I walked alongside a canal, Canal latéral à la Marne. The water was high against the towpath, with the clouded shine of tarnished silver. Ash trees grew on the opposite bank, their branches bobbed with mistletoe, and birch trees thin as needles, gathered in thousands and shuttering the sun.

At teatime I reached Châlons-en-Champagne. The cathedral was closed, but nearby stood a Gothic church built from slush-coloured stone, Notre-Dame-en-Vaux. The church shop sold postcards of nuns, and three women sat behind the counter. One of the women took my hand and started talking very fast. I was young! I was alone! I was travelling in winter! 'But how will you find Rome in the snow?' she asked.

Her name was Colette. She had brown eyes and coiled brown hair. She let go of my hand and drew a picture in blue biro – a wintery scene with peaks, pines and bauble-shaped stars. Underneath she wrote a prayer like a song lyric – *No matter how long the route, no matter how hard the journey*, etc. Then she popped the prayer into my jacket pocket and zipped the pocket shut.

When I mentioned I was looking for somewhere to stay, the women started ringing round town. Their calls were answered with polite refusals or the automated apology of a disconnected number. '*La Maison Diocésaine?* . . . *L'Auberge de Jeunesse?* . . . *Camping Municipal?* . . . *Hôtel Moritz?* . . . *Presbytère Saint-Jean?*' After ten minutes they were out of places, until Colette had an idea – '*Tiens! Dr Cuvelette! Rue Garinet!*' – and marched me into the street.

She led the way through Châlons, telling me how she used to import British cars to France and had once driven – that's right – a Triumph Stag. Her movements were wound tight, as if trying not to skip, and when we passed a sports shop she darted inside, pouncing on a pair of ice soles. A gift, she repeated, a gift, but I said no, it was too kind, she mustn't spend money on me. However, I did not ask what became of her business. Nor did I ask about the prayer she zipped into my pocket, whether she heard it at a wedding or a funeral, or taught it to a child, or recited the words in the dead of night when she woke rigid with fear.

These were the things I never learnt about Colette.

No. 14 Rue Garinet was a three-storey townhouse with two front doors. Its walls were panelled, each panel painted a different colour, giving the house a nursery feel. Downstairs the rooms were full of shrubs, which Dr Cuvelette moved around in intricate patterns, protecting the plants from phantom draughts. The doctor was a prim, precise man, his hair growing over his ears. When I asked what kind of doctor, he said that he was retired, yet still he worked.

In the evening Dr Cuvelette cooked two minute steaks for supper. We did not speak during the meal, but listened to a radio report on France's invasion of Mali. When the main course was done, he brought out the cheese on a tray, but somehow it slipped from his hands and fell to the floor. Then he looked down for a long time, too embarrassed to tidy.

At nine o'clock we heard a knock at both front doors. Colette was back, carrying a pair of ice soles. 'I don't drink. I don't smoke. How else shall I spend my money?' she asked.

This was not a one-off. Night after night strangers would welcome me, feed me and find a place for me to sleep. At first I was surprised by this hospitality, for it seemed like a practice left over from another century, but soon I came to rely on it. Although the temperature stayed near zero, people were kinder in the cold, and I walked with a warm sense of gladness, for it seemed possible to cross an entire country on charity alone.

From Châlons I left the Champagne region and spent three days hiking on prairie. Each evening the same sort of family took me in. The husbands were farmers with red hands and weathered cheeks. They would spend half an hour making the fire, weighing every piece of kindling in their fingers. When I asked about their jobs, they would answer my questions without looking up. More weather coming, they warned. Coldest January since eighty-five. Their wives were employed by the *mairie* or the local farmers' association and wanted to know about my parents, my siblings, asking their names, their ages, where they lived, where they worked. They also wanted to know about my route – Over the Alps? On foot? – and wrote long lists of telephone numbers for me to take: the emergency services, the gendarmerie, the village mayor, the parish priest, a nearby hospital, three or four government offices, and a last number that had something to do with helicopter rescue.

I would be given a son's bedroom to sleep in, the wallpaper printed with motorbikes, desert buggies and the logo of the Paris Dakar Rally. There would be teddies at the bottom of the wardrobe and boxes of Lego under the bed. The owner of the room had already grown up and moved out, and that evening his parents would tell me that there were no jobs in the countryside, that the public services were shutting down, and that France was now full of foreigners.

During the daytime I marched on the plains of southern Marne. In summer this would have been the dullest part of the Via Francigena, but winter turned the acres of crop and forage into an arctic desert. There was no colour in the sky, nor in the bedded fields, nothing but starched sheets of white stretching from track to horizon, shapeless except for the earth's own contour, like the mound and fold of a human body. Occasionally I noticed a jeep, or an electricity substation, or a spread of farm buildings, but they seemed too small to be real: toy things, crushed by the great expanse of snowflat.

One of the villages was full of decaying houses. They

had stripped walls, exposed rafters, and bedrooms sat on scaffolding. The last house boasted a new door and a new doorway, but everything else was rubble, as if the earth had flinched and levelled it. For a while I explored the debris, stepping over a drawer of baby's clothes and a tractor buried in breezeblocks, until a chained Alsatian began barking at me and I turned away.

Later that day I passed a wind farm. From far off the turbines resembled trees struck by lightning, with bleached and barkless trunks. Closer, I heard the air dragging through their blades like the cry of geese. As I approached, the sun emerged from between the clouds and angled shadows spun the snow. Watching the fields turning, I felt the sunlight cold against my skin and the jagged edges of the wind. So I stood there with hands on hips, the breath pouring stunned from my chest. Then I went south from the Marne and left the plains behind.

That sense of wonder could not last: it soon gave way to drudgery. When I came to the hill country above the River Aube, I found a forest being cut down. My route followed a logging trail wide as a dual carriageway and the rutted remains of a footpath. The slopes were pitted with tree stumps, sawdust and woodpeel mixing in the sodden earth to make a black mud that swallowed the boots from my feet.

Around teatime, as the sky grew heavy with snow, I passed an old hunting cabin that smelt of moss and turf, lumber and mould. Then I joined another logging trail, this one sinking towards the Val d'Absinthe.

It was early evening when I reached the valley floor. The trail ended with a brick wall, worn away in parts. Beyond I could see sentry posts and chain-link fencing, barbed wire and concrete cellblocks, and beyond that a vast abbey, its buildings low, its windows barred. Although my map called this site L'Abbaye de Clairvaux, the last monks left two centuries ago. Clairvaux was now a prison.

The abbey was once the leading religious house in France, but under Napoleon it was turned into a work camp for thousands of common-law criminals and a high-security jail for the country's political prisoners. Since then its cells have hosted militant socialists, far-right radicals, anarchists, terrorists and revolutionaries. Which is why, in the second half of the nineteenth century, Clairvaux was home to Prince Peter Kropotkin.

Kropotkin was born in Moscow in 1842, a minor member of the Rurik dynasty – the kings of medieval Rus. In his twenties he became an officer in the Imperial Army, carrying out surveys of Siberia and Manchuria, and exploring Scandinavia for the Russian Geographical Society. Aged thirty he declared himself an anarchist and joined a socialist literary society known as the Circle of Tchaikovsky. Two years later he was imprisoned for spreading revolutionary propaganda and locked in a fortress outside St Petersburg. He escaped and fled to Geneva, where he lived until 1881. Then he was expelled from Switzerland and shortly after, in France, was arrested for his membership of subversive organizations and sentenced to five years in Clairvaux.

Kropotkin's memoir, *In Russian and French Prisons*, gives a detailed account of these experiences. During his stay the former abbey contained between fourteen hundred and two thousand inmates. The main compound was crowded with metalworks manufacturing iron beds and iron furniture, looking glasses and picture frames, as well as workshops for weaving velvet, broadcloth and linen, gristmills for grinding grain, and yards for cutting limestone, sandstone and chalk. Four steam engines powered the site, running day and night, filling the valley with the noise of machinery and the smoke from a hundred chimneys. Kropotkin likened it to an industrial town.

What's remarkable about this description is how closely the inmates' lives mimicked those of monks. Prisoners slept in dormitories, wore identical grey clothes, ate mostly bread and vegetables, and worked six days a week – with breaks for prayer and study. They even followed a rule of silence.

All this had existed at Clairvaux from the start.

The abbey was founded in 1115 by a young nobleman called Bernard, the star monk of the Cistercian Order. Bernard was famed for his fanatical austerity, and he shaped the abbey in his image. Set in a remote valley, surrounded by fen and forest, the architecture was stark, the discipline harsh, and the daily routine relentless. Monks woke at four, worked six or seven hours a day, spent the same amount of time in worship, and often went without food or sleep.

Severe though it sounds, this mixture of contemplation and manual labour was popular. Before Bernard, the Cistercians were begging for alms, but by the end of his life they were the fastest-growing order in Europe. The order's emphasis on self-sufficiency turned its brothers into craftsmen, livestock breeders and engineers, while their monasteries became thriving farms and factories. Some used waterwheels to crush wheat, sift flour, full wool, tan hides and cut wood, while others contained mines and smelting works, with blacksmiths to cast lead piping and lead roofing, or forge iron tools, iron fittings, kitchenware, horseshoes and ploughshares.

For Bernard the work had a clear moral purpose. Manual labour kept the monks humble and the cloister cut off.

And, by forsaking the world, the Cistercians set the clearest course for salvation.

Peter Kropotkin believed the opposite was true. Deny freedom of choice and you do not encourage virtue, but destroy it. In a pamphlet titled *Prisons and their Moral Influence on Prisoners*, the prince wrote that 'in prisons, as in monasteries, everything is done to shut down a man's will'. His memoir went further, comparing the prisoners at Clairvaux to machines. It's an acute metaphor for the circumscribed life at a nineteenth-century jail or a medieval monastery, with their industrial output and mechanical approach to morality, yet there is an important difference between the two institutions. True, by joining the Cistercians a monk was giving up his will, but unlike a prisoner, he had chosen to do so. Circling the prison walls that afternoon, I could not understand why anyone would make this choice. Nonetheless, as I discovered during my stay here, pilgrimage was part of the answer.

Kropotkin was released from Clairvaux early, thanks in part to a young radical called Georges Clemenceau. He ended up living in the London suburb of Bromley, where he wrote a series of books making the scientific case for anarchism. Then, following the February Revolution of 1917, he returned to Russia. After forty years in exile he was greeted like a hero – flags flying, crowds cheering and a job offer as minister of education. However, believing a stateless society was at hand, he said no.

A few months later the Bolsheviks seized power and Kropotkin's life work was, in his own word, 'buried'.

It took half an hour to reach the prison gates. The facade was dressed stone, cut crudely like an army barracks or the stables of a stately home. There was no light from the windows of grey glass, but a house on the opposite side of the road gave off a warm glow. This was a hostel for the visiting families of prisoners. Inside I found a guestroom with low ceilings and exposed brickwork, where a woman sat watching television. She wore a glossy shell suit and her right leg was resting on a chair, the ankle bandaged.

I put down my rucksack and explained why I was here. The woman made a face. 'Jerusalem? Stop it! For how many days?'

'Three weeks.'

'On foot? All on foot?'

'Canterbury, Calais, Arras, Reims, Châlons-en-Champagne—'

'I don't believe you.'

'Do you want to come with me?'

She gestured her ankle. 'Stop it!'

Her name was Eva. She had bleached hair and bright make-up that made her whole face look puffy. When I asked about the injury, she explained that she was dancing, she was drinking, she was an idiot. Eva was here to see her son, Mathis. He was almost my age, she said, almost my height, and had been training as a mechanic until he was sent to Clairvaux. While Eva told me this, she held a hand to her mouth. At first I thought she was surprised by the coincidence, upset even, until I realized with a sting of embarrassment that she was smirking. I had arrived at the hostel dressed for skiing and claimed to be walking to Jerusalem. She was not hiding tears, but laughter.

'You want the nuns?' Eva asked, lifting herself from the sofa with a crutch. 'Next door. They live next door.' She removed a pack of cigarettes from her bag. 'Just to smoke they make me go outside. Like a prison. Every time I want a cigarette: *Outside Eva. Go outside!*'

The nuns were waiting for me in the kitchen, a

cramped room with a wood-burning cooker taking up most of the space. They were both small, both plump, and both generous to the point of recklessness. They reminded me of doves, feathered in grey wool and white blouses, fluttering round the room and cooing at one another.

Sr Marie-Bertille was in her seventies, with fluffy hair and a pointed mouth. She had been in charge of the guest-house for twenty-eight years. 'We've never had a pilgrim in winter,' she said, removing jam jars and biscuit tins from the cupboards.

'There was one,' said Sr Anne-Christine, who was warming a pan of milk on the hotplate. She was younger, gentler, and when she spoke she slowed her sentences as if talking to a toddler. 'Last year. Or the year before. In November.'

'I remember!' said Sr Marie-Bertille. 'He was following Joan of Arc through France.'

'Joan of Arc?' I asked.

Sr Marie-Bertille nodded. 'She came here. Dressed as a man.'

'She stopped at the abbey on her way to meet the king,' said Sr Anne-Christine.

'But,' Sr Marie-Bertille continued, now emptying plates from a cupboard, 'I think our pilgrim was mad.'

'They called La Pucelle mad too,' said Sr Anne-Christine.

I asked if any other famous pilgrims had visited the abbey.

'Everyone came to Clairvaux,' said Sr Anne-Christine. 'Popes, princes, saints.'

'They never wanted to leave,' said Sr Marie-Bertille, now removing apples and oranges from the fruit bowl. 'They came here to die.'

At last Sr Marie-Bertille found what she was looking for: a tin with a picture of a lemon tree on the outside and, on the inside, a lemon cake wrapped in parchment paper. She cut three slices of cake, Sr Anne-Christine mixed three mugs of cocoa, and then we sat together at the kitchen table. However, the cooker's fire must have gone out, because the milk was barely heated and chocolate powder clumped on the surface. Sr Marie-Bertille wailed at each lukewarm sip, until Sr Anne-Christine bundled the mugs into the microwave, perching on the edge of her seat as she waited for the chime.

'Is it difficult running the guesthouse?' I asked when the cocoa was ready.

'We try to welcome everybody,' said Sr Anne-Christine. 'Also, we try to keep a Christian house. Sometimes, to have both, it's very difficult.'

'We are always full at the weekends,' said Sr Marie-Bertille. 'Friday to Monday, no space anywhere. Children on the beds, children on the sofas, I open a drawer and – my goodness! – more children.'

'Sometimes our guests are angry. Sometimes they argue, or they ask for too much.'

'This weekend the families came from Tunisia. All afternoon their mothers were cooking in the kitchen, and then they laid down blankets and sat on the floor, eating with their hands.' Sr Marie-Bertille lifted a piece of lemon cake from her plate. 'With their hands!'

'Why don't you live in a convent?' I asked. 'No guests, no prisoners.'

Sr Anne-Christine shook her head. 'When I have a holiday, I make a retreat. Five days, six days, and I am bored. It's tranquil, yes, but my calling is here at Clairvaux.'

'And the pilgrims!' cried Sr Marie-Bertille. 'Every summer more pilgrims! Last year seventy, seventy-five – from France, from Italy, Belgium, even Canada.' They were groups and couples mostly, walking the Via

Francigena in two-week sections, or four-week stretches, or walking the whole thing in a three-month slog.

I asked the reason more people were going on pilgrimage.

'Perhaps they want to meet strangers,' said Sr Anne-Christine. 'Or perhaps they want to be alone.'

I tried again: 'But fewer people go to church. Fewer people become priests or nuns.'

Sr Marie-Bertille sealed the cake tin and put the jam jars back in the cupboard. 'Pilgrim, monk, they are all the same. They want to learn what they believe.'

They want to learn what they believe. That phrase stayed with me for the rest of the evening. As I sat with the nuns and listened to stories of pilgrims past. As I sat with Eva and listened to the weather forecast (roads, railway lines, schools – all closing down in the snow). I was still thinking about it as I stood by the door, watching fresh powder brush the prison walls with white. The idea made me feel vulnerable, as if testing some unspoken motive.

Clairvaux's entrance was lit from every angle. Leaving the hostel and approaching the abbey, I tried to imagine a route over the high walls, through the locked gates, into the great silence. And I tried to imagine the sounds beneath the silence: the hum of a generator, the shudder of plumbing, the insect buzz of a sodium lamp, and a prayer whispered along a corridor like sand on a flagstone floor. And the footsteps of monks, echoing round the courtyards. And the plainchant etched into the ancient air.

Eight hundred and eighty-four years before me, one spring afternoon, an English pilgrim called Philip arrived at Clairvaux. He had recently left Lincolnshire, where he was a canon, to journey to Jerusalem. At this point the abbey was little more than a collection of wooden huts, and Philip planned to stop for just one night. Instead he abandoned his pilgrimage and joined the monks.

To understand why, we need to go back another century.

At the end of the first millennium, the last pagan power in central Europe – Hungary – converted to Christianity. In 1018 the country's king, Stephen I, opened his borders to pilgrims. Around the same date the Balkans were conquered by Byzantine forces and, for the first time since the Roman Empire, there was an overland route to Jerusalem. Until this point only those who could afford to travel by boat were able to visit the Holy Land. Now people from any class could make the trip. Mass pilgrimages began leaving from France and Germany, journeying to Jerusalem on donkey, horseback and foot. By the end of the century entire armies were setting out for the city, and once the crusader states had been established, the pilgrim traffic was constant.

Religious travel within Europe was also on the rise, thanks to the growing number of Benedictine monasteries. They provided the infrastructure for popular pilgrimage and encouraged the practice among the laity. Cluny, the most important Benedictine foundation, even used its network of religious houses to promote routes such as the Camino de Santiago.

These two callings still resembled each other. Before leaving home medieval pilgrims would prostrate themselves at the altar of their church, lying face down in the exact pose that a novice adopts when taking his or her vows. While on the road every hour was spent in walking or worship. They kept to the liturgical timetable, owned only what they could carry, and gave up all domestic responsibility. Obedience, poverty, and chastity.

Bernard of Clairvaux claimed that monastic life was

also a pilgrimage. Even though a monk's body remained in one place, he travelled with his heart. And a monastery was a prison with open doors, he wrote, where the brothers were held by their love of God.

Penance was what linked all this together. Cluniac monasteries encouraged lay pilgrimage by emphasizing the penitential rewards of a trip to Santiago or Rome. Cistercian monasteries went one better, insisting that life in the cloister brought the best chance of salvation. However, facing the abbey entrance that evening, I struggled to imagine the savage sense of guilt that drew medieval monks to this place. Even if pilgrimage and monastic life were two expressions of the same impulse, as Sr Marie-Bertille claimed, I was no closer to understanding that impulse. Instead I was standing before a locked gate, shivering and confused in the winter dark. So I turned indoors, said goodnight to Eva and went upstairs to bed.

My room was on the second floor, high enough to see over the prison walls. A prayer card had been placed on the pillow, with an image of Bernard kneeling beneath the Virgin Mary. Standing by the window, I watched snowflakes drifting onto the prison's watchtowers and cellblocks, onto the church, chapter house and cloister. The flakes twinkled as they fell, yellow and red, copper and brass.

After Philip cut short his pilgrimage, Bernard sent a letter to the Bishop of Lincoln explaining what had happened. He joked that the canon reached his destination sooner than expected: 'He has entered into the Holy City [. . .] This is Jerusalem.'

The abbot's argument was borrowed from St Augustine, who was in two minds about pilgrimage. On the one hand, Augustine understood life as a spiritual voyage. His *Confessions* is filled with images of exile and homecoming, while *City of God* argues that man is a stranger in this world, finding rest only when he returns to heaven. On the other hand, Augustine believed that we approach the divine with our hearts rather than our feet. Worship, not wandering, brings us closer to God.

At Clairvaux every moment was spent in worship. Not just the time in church, or at study and prayer, but the long hours of chopping wood, tilling fields, cleaning, mending and building. Even the monks' austerity was a form of devotion, channelling their desires towards the divine. Bernard once wrote that, through constant discipline, he had freed his soul – *liberavi animam meam* – but it was the liberty of surrender rather than strength.

For Peter Kropotkin, to efface the will was to bind a man. For Bernard it broke the chains. He taught that a monk could see the City of God without ever leaving the cloister: *This is Jerusalem.* Which is why Dante chose the abbot as his final guide in *The Divine Comedy*, leading the pilgrim poet through the highest realms of heaven. And why, on coming to Clairvaux, young Philip never went anywhere else again.

My own journey had given me some insight into this idea. I hiked eight hours a day, six days a week, sleeping wherever a room was offered and rarely leaving the Via Francigena. The weather was a trial, yes, but that night in the prison guesthouse I felt like my life was somehow lighter. As if I had given up control over the course of my days. As if the pilgrimage was carrying me through the winter.

Next morning the snow had settled.

The nuns began the day with a service in a cupboard chapel off the guestroom. While Sr Marie-Bertille and Sr Anne-Christine recited prayers, Eva clattered round the kitchen, swearing and dropping things.

When we left the chapel, the guestroom was in disarray. There were dirty plates on the table, dirty pans in the sink, and the sideboard was slopped with cereal. A suitcase had been tossed onto the carpet: T-shirts from Miami, branded tracksuit bottoms, and bras and socks in fluorescent shades of pink. Meanwhile Eva sat in the middle of the room, her head thrown back, letting out a noise half scream and half whimper. I could not tell whether her suitcase was broken, or her food was burnt, or her ankle was hurting, or she missed her son. I could not tell who was free, who chained, and who was bound by love. But, as I stood in the doorway, I felt a deep pull of pity, like these three were family now.

'Every week,' said Sr Marie-Bertille, stepping over the strewn clothes. 'Every week this is what she does.'

'We agreed today, Eva,' said Sr Anne-Christine, standing in the doorway with folded arms. 'You cannot stay past today.' The whimpering scream became a sob, and Sr Anne-Christine put her hands to her ears. 'If you need money, we will pay for your ticket.' The noise stopped. 'But this is the last time. Please, the last time.'

I'm not much of a walker. My legs are short, my stride hurried – an anxious, wasteful gait. And I have not spent most holidays since childhood rambling round the Lake District. A few weekend hikes in the months before the pilgrimage were little preparation for twenty-five, thirty-five kilometres a day. By the third week, heading south-east towards Besançon and the Swiss border, my spine was aching and my shoulders welted. Then there was the twinge in my left ankle, the snag in my right calf and the popping in each knee. As the temperature sank deeper, my early exhilaration flagged. The winter had become haunting.

After Clairvaux I spent the night in a fortified town

called Châteauvillain, waking early and leaving through a deer park. The sun did not rise that morning, but bled into the clouds, and the colours in the park were subdued, like light at the bottom of a lake. The air was grey, the fallen leaves were grey, and the mud a pallid grey that was sometimes green. Mist hung in the tree branches, a dirty mist gathered in parcels. Once or twice I saw it twitch, but the deer remained hidden. Walking down avenues of elm, I tried to conjure their shapes from the haze. No animals, alas, but I glimpsed other figures in the veiled air. At times the cast of a costume drama seemed to be wandering the park with me: musketeers in feathered hats, maids in dragging skirts, and altar boys carrying candles and crosses in gloved hands.

Eventually I spotted a herd of fallow deer in a thicket of hawthorn. Two of the deer, two fawns, watched me with eyes of button black. A third, a buck, strutted by without turning his head. I stood with my arm half-raised, until a doe with a speckled coat crept out from behind the hedge, her lips pouting, head cocked. She moved forwards, one pace, two, but a stray scent must have startled her, because then she ran from me with puppet steps, quickening into the mist.

There were more ghosts in Langres's old town.

The old town was set on a hill above the rest of the city, its narrow streets lined with eighteenth-century mansions. As I wandered those streets the following afternoon, I kept hearing music: strains of violin from a boarded house, folk songs down a deserted alleyway, and choirs practising in the cathedral, even though the stalls were empty.

My boots were coming unstitched, and I needed to repair the seams. Though I passed workshops selling trays of elegant, impractical cutlery – forks the size of paperclips, or sewing scissors with jewelled handles – it took an hour to locate a cobbler. The shop's window contained row upon row of antique shoes, as well as riding boots with steel spurs and turned leather tops. It was four o'clock, but the place was still shut for lunch. When I returned thirty minutes later, it had vanished entirely.

The Langres presbytery was a grand building with an iron gate that locked at nine each night. Next to the presbytery, upstairs from the chapel, I found a flat for pilgrims. Its roof was damaged and its rooms being renovated, but I did not mind, because there were duvets on the beds and radiators on the walls. In addition, previous pilgrims had left packets of pasta and rice in the larder, along with tea, coffee, and energy drinks in disco colours. I took comfort in this hint of community, as if a distant stranger had remembered me.

All night the wind cheered round the attic. The curtains shivered, letting in tremors of streetlight, and the radiator tick-tocked, tick-tocked, heating the building by some marvel of clockwork. At midnight the ticking ceased. Shortly after, I heard footsteps climbing the stairs to the flat and a hand beating on the door. Thinking it was one of the priests, I called out, but there was no answer. Instead a chair scraped along the landing, stopped, scraped again, and went rattling over. I called out a second time, and a second time there was no answer. Then I heard a sound I could not name: the swishing of Bible pages, or the coughing of a baby. Then: nothing.

For the rest of the night I lay awake, too frightened to move. I kept telling myself that I was imagining this presence, even though my breath was short, my throat choked. Once I heard voices – In the street? In the chapel? – but otherwise the presbytery was taut with silence.

At first light I left Langres. It was Saturday 26 January: the coldest day yet. Walking from the old town, my sleeves and collar frayed white with frost, and I could feel the chill in my eyelids, my jaw.

Footpaths dropped through formal gardens, off the hill and into the woods. Two men were out working that morning, one choosing trees to fell and marking them with a cross, the other cutting the trees down with a chainsaw. When the trunks hit the earth they threw up ice like smashed glass.

Around midday I came to a medieval refuge with walls of beaten stone and windows bricked shut. Close by was a pond frozen hard in the night. Although I was hungry, it was too cold to sit and eat – my face sore, my lips splitting.

Later that day I entered the department of Haute-Saône and the grassy flats of the Saône Valley. Rash-red hedges divided the pastures, and the valley was fringed with woodland. A twisted road led between the woods, the roadside littered with rubbish. In a couple of hours I counted seven vintage porn films, twelve packets of cigarettes, four cans of Kronenbourg and a tankard made from punched tin.

Most of the villages on the road to Besançon contained *lavoirs* – brick or stone structures with public washbasins, where I sheltered from sudden showers of hail. Otherwise I sheltered in churches with domes of enamelled tile, their coloured squares laid out in lattice patterns. A few had posters of a boat pinned up inside, its mast a cross, its sails shaped like the sun, and the words *Annus Fidei* printed beneath. I would stare at the poster until I was bored with waiting, and then march into the hailstones with eyes to the ground. Twinge and snag. *Pop, pop.*

The few people I met in that last week of January wanted to know why I was walking in winter. I told them that I planned to make Rome by Easter. Had I waited until spring to leave, some small excuse would have delayed me – three months, and then another three, and then another. But I worried I had started my journey too soon, without enough training and into the worst of the weather. Though I still asked strangers to house me each night, the assurance of those early weeks was gone. After Besançon the Via Francigena climbed the Jura Mountains on hiking trails, which I realized now would be buried in snow. And, even if I made it to Switzerland, I still had to get over the Alps.

Madame Lucas was spindle thin, her face made up of angles. I had been given her address at the parish in Langres and was hoping for a bed that night. 'Do you have cancer?' she asked when she answered the door. 'Most pilgrims have cancer. In hospital they pray: please God make me better and I will go on pilgrimage. Then the tumour gets better and they have to walk.' She began to take off her cardigan. 'I don't have a tumour. But I don't have a shoulder. Look! It's made of metal. Of recycling.'

'No,' I said. 'I don't have cancer.'

'You're too young.'

'I hope so.'

'You have to wait a few years.'

Madame Lucas's sitting room smelt of hoovering, and her sofa was cluttered with cleaning products. She removed the carpet shampoo, motioned me to sit and placed a photo album on my lap. The first photograph showed my host standing outside Besançon Cathedral in a small group carrying rucksacks and trekking poles. The words *Le pèlerinage de Saint-Jacques-de-Compostelle* were written above the picture, the dates *11.iv.2010 à 6. vii.2010* below.

Besançon was a crossing place, a stop on both the Via

Francigena and the Camino de Santiago. During the Middle Ages, if the Italian city-states were at war, pilgrims hoping to visit Rome had to travel to Spain instead. But, after the Reformation, the route declined, and by the time of the Peninsular War it had fallen into disuse. When Spain joined the EU in 1986, fewer than ten people a year walked the Way of St James. Since then the pilgrimage has been brought back to life, and in the year of Madame Lucas's journey a quarter of a million completed the distance.

'Eight pilgrims. That's how many we were. All from Besançon. All retired. The youngest was sixty-one, the oldest was –' she scrunched her face as she tried to remember, balling her hands into two tiny fists – 'very old.'

Madame Lucas went through each member of the group, listing the medical crises they had recovered from. Breast cancer and lung cancer. Liver failure and heart disease and something wrong with someone's kidneys. Then she turned the pages of the album, past Chalon-sur-Saône (day six), Saint-Étienne (day fifteen) and Le Puy-en-Velay (day nineteen). More group shots, the eight companions feeding grass to a pair of ponies (Saint-Alban-sur-Limagnole, day twenty-four), or picnicking in a forest grove (the Dourdou Valley, day thirty-one), or posing next to a roadside shrine (Lauzerte, day forty-two, crossed out, day forty-three), or resting in the shade of a cloister (Abbaye Saint-Pierre de Moissac, undated).

When the route climbed into northern Spain, other pilgrims appeared in the photographs: a succession of strangers wandering west together.

'I talked to everyone,' said Madame Lucas. 'Sick people, old people, young people too! A boy from Greece, he was seventeen, eighteen, said he didn't believe in God. Said he was a communist. And a couple from Korea, they were on honeymoon, they hitchhiked the whole way to

Europe. And a woman from Argentina, she said she was leaving her husband, but I couldn't understand why, because she cried too much.'

So why did Madame Lucas walk?

'I'm old. I thought, if I don't go to Spain, I will stay alone in my flat until I die.'

And why was the Camino popular again? Was it, as Sr Marie-Bertille claimed, because people wanted to learn what they believed? No, no, said Madame Lucas, it was cheap flights, mobile phones, motorways, fitness fads and the internet. She thought the world was too fast. It's true. We need to slow down. We do.

Madame Lucas showed little sign of slowing down. Instead she moved in fits and starts, telling alarming stories that she kept cutting short to leave the room in search of props: a hiking boot with a hole through the sole, or a scallop shell tied to a ribbon. Once or twice she rushed off but returned empty handed, having forgotten what she was looking for. And, if she could not remember the name of a village or church, she would clench her fists and complain about being old. Or she would jump from the sofa and begin cleaning, or swallow a multivitamin tablet with a double espresso. Coffee to wake the dead, she called it.

Pamplona, Logroño, Burgos and León. Baroque monasteries and medieval hostels and beds laid out in barns. Towns of brown brick and red stone, hanging off the hillsides, and tableland and fallow fields and plains of yellow and dust. And always a line of pilgrims, lagging longer and longer.

'Most of them were tourists. They sent their rucksacks in buses and walked with nothing on their backs. They ate in restaurants and slept in *paradores* and never came to mass. And complained! All the time complained. It was too hot. It was too hard. I went slowly like –' she paused again, scrunched her face again – 'like a snail. And every

44

night I slept in the refuges. Every night sleeping in dormitories! But people leave old women alone in case they are crazy.'

At last the eight companions reached Santiago. The final photo showed Madame Lucas standing in front of the teeming cathedral, tanned and hunched and squinting in the sun. She looked very small, very happy.

'It's ugly! The ugliest cathedral in Europe.'

'Weren't you glad to see it?'

'I never wanted to stop. I wanted to keep going until the Atlantic—' She interrupted herself: 'Why don't you walk to Spain?'

This was not an easy question to answer, for in truth I was dismayed by the idea of the Camino. It seemed too crowded, too clichéd – filled with hotels, souvenir shops, and hundreds and hundreds of pilgrims. Of course, the medieval pilgrimage would have been just as busy, and I was often bored on the bare stretches of northern France. But, when I explained this to Madame Lucas, she looked bothered. Why didn't I walk with other pilgrims?

I told her that nobody else wanted to walk to Jerusalem – the answer I always gave.

'Of course! Nobody walks in winter.'

'And it means I talk to more people.'

'What people? There are no pilgrims on the Via Francigena.'

'Local people. The ones who take me in.'

'What if you are lonely and you want to give up?'

'This week was lonely,' I said, mentioning disturbed nights in tumbledown refuges and spooked mornings in misty parks. 'I'm learning to be lonely.'

Madame Lucas looked even more bothered. 'Tomorrow,' she said. 'Tomorrow we will find someone to walk with you.'

*

Tomorrow Madame Lucas had decided that she would walk with me. To Rome? Of course! And Jerusalem? Maybe. She would pray more about Jerusalem. As we ate breakfast, I tried to talk her out of it, describing the cold, the snow and the struggle for a bed each night. It was not until I mentioned hiking the Great Saint Bernard Pass on foot that her enthusiasm waned. On second thoughts, perhaps she would ask a priest to accompany me.

So we marched into Besançon to look for one.

The city's old town was wrapped in a dark bow of the River Doubs, its streets made up of grand Renaissance buildings. In the right light, their walls formed a glittering jigsaw of yellow and blue stone.

Madame Lucas crossed the roads without ever checking the lights – 'The drivers think I'm blind. They always stop.' If we passed an open door she took my arm and dashed inside. We saw a marble stairwell in a block of flats, the murals on the walls of a bank and a stucco ceiling in a hotel lobby. Sometimes the doorman or receptionist looked concerned, but nobody told us to leave. Nobody gets angry with an old woman, Madame Lucas claimed.

Then we visited churches. We visited the Cathédrale Saint-Jean, the Église de la Madeleine, and the Église Saint-Pierre. In each one my companion banged on the vestry door, but there was never any answer, and the secretary in the parish office looked puzzled when she was asked which priests were free for a pilgrimage. Nobody? What about a seminarian? None?

Next we tried the presbytery. We rang the bell and rapped on the windows, but again there was no answer. By this point I was keen to get away; however, Madame Lucas insisted we wait. A few minutes later the door opened and a priest with a fleshy face peered out. When he saw who was there, he attempted to close the door, but

Madame Lucas was too quick. 'I need a pee-pee,' she said. 'I'm an old woman.'

He sighed and let her in. She waved her arms around. 'To Rome! In the winter!'

The priest shook his head, puffing his pink cheeks. 'I cannot help you,' he said. 'Nobody can help you.'

Things got worse after that. Madame Lucas began asking people in the street to walk with me. She asked the till assistant in her favourite patisserie and a tour guide at the Musée des Beaux-Arts. Although I kept repeating that I was happier by myself, she seemed not to hear. Or she heard me, but did not believe me, for her desire to help was born of a biting loneliness that I could not console.

It was raining now. The jigsaw streets became a single shade of slate. When Madame Lucas suggested we break for coffee, I asked her to go home. She started listing the friends from her Santiago pilgrimage who might accompany me, but I told her no, no more, that was enough. Then I said goodbye and walked away.

The hills behind Besançon were covered in box. Paths led through the trees, between bungalows and cottages, statues and shrines. Climbing out of the city, my footsteps were urgent, as I tried to make up lost time. But then the sky darkened with storm cloud and the rain came down in sheets. Soon the paths were flooded, the woods becoming a house of horrors: a Virgin weeping raindrops, a lion with a roar like thunder, and a crucifix the size of a man, its body white as lightning. One of the bungalow gardens was hung with prayer flags, streaming purple and red, but when I stopped to look the rain fell so hard that it washed the sight from my eyes.

Chapelle Notre-Dame des Buis hung over the hillside in the shape of a lantern. Inside, a semicircle of chairs faced a stone altar with a single candle. The candle was lit, the whole room breathing in and out with the flicker of its flame. I sat and listened to the confused noise of the rain, until the storm passed and the chapel was quiet.

When I went outside again, clouds covered Besançon. I could not see the shining roofs of the old town, nor the hills gripping the city to the north and west – five hills, like the five knuckles of a fist – nor the monumental statue of the Virgin and Child towering to the east. But I could see the black mountains of the Jura rising to the south, and the black course of the River Loue carving a path into the range.

In the final days of January, I followed the river upstream. The water was high, with the rubbery look of storm surge. At one point I watched a school of plastic canoes pull loose in the current and wheel away. Otherwise I remember little of the drenched villages that lined the valley, but I remember how the hillsides became steeper and more thickly wooded, and how, when the rain ceased, the bare tree branches glistened.

Hiking to the source of the Loue I met no one and started talking to myself in strange accents, anxious to fill the quiet. I was in hermit country now.

The Jura have attracted solitaries since the earliest days of the faith. In the first century the range was home to St Beatus, the mythic apostle of Switzerland. In the fifth century it was the brothers Romanus and Lupicinus, known as the Jura Fathers. And in the seventh century saints Imerius, Ursicinus and Fromundus settled here. To the medieval mind the mountains were godless places, where creation had been rent open by the sin of man. And they were dangerous too, for despite the conversion of the local Alemanni tribes, the Jura still held pockets of witchcraft and heresy. But, by making a home in these mountains, the hermits made them holy.

Switzerland's most popular pilgrimage site – Einsiedeln Abbey – was founded on the cell of a ninth-century anchorite called St Meinrad. The country's patron saint, Brother Klaus, was also a solitary: a soldier and judge who left his wife and children in the year 1467 to live alone in the Ranft Gorge, where he preached peace to visiting noblemen.

Many of these hermits – Beatus, Imerius and Brother Klaus – realized their calling while on pilgrimage. As I walked through the Loue Valley, I began to understand why. Approaching the heights, my damp, despondent state turned into enchantment. In the early hours of the morning, I watched sunlight catch in webs of frosted bracken, while frozen puddles scattered the dawn like smashed gemstones. Later that day, nearing the Swiss border, I saw the snow layering into script, writing letters and words on the mountainside. If I stared at the inscriptions for long enough, they spelt out the names of people I knew. The winter was lonely, yes, but the solitude was also a spell, and deep in the mountains it consecrated the days.

Then I climbed into a snowstorm and these thoughts fled.

It was the first day of February, a Friday. That morning, when I left Pontarlier, the snow was falling fast. I walked on cross-country skiing routes, but made little progress in the knee-high powder. The stitching on my left boot was loose, the lip letting in water and the skin on my toes sponging. Also, my waterproofs were leaking where the fabric had ripped, back in the Champagne region.

After two hours I turned out of the woods and onto a road. The tarmac was gritted and the traffic light, but now there was no protection from the weather. As I approached the border, the snow came down harder, corridor villages of hotels and chalets disappearing in the flurry.

An empty road led to the border, where a sign

welcomed me to Switzerland. A second sign, an hour on, marked the highpoint of the pass: *Col des Étroits, Alt. 1153m.* Then the road dipped, the wind droned, and great bursts of powder filled the sky. What a storm it was, what a spectacle! Never have I seen the air so dense with snow, so many thousands of flakes, like a rabbling mob, like a revolution. L'Auberson, Sainte-Croix – where were these villages? I glimpsed only confused masses of grey, which I guessed were wide-roofed houses, and big, blurred outlines that might have been apartment blocks, and clocks with yellow faces beaming through the blizzard, and distant headlights moving this way and that – and otherwise nothing but the dancing air.

Beyond Sainte-Croix the storm lifted. As the weather cleared, the landscape reassembled. Six hundred metres below lay the Swiss Plateau, a patchwork of dark soil and green shoots. Two days' walk away the plateau sank towards Lake Geneva, but up here its chequered farmland seemed to hang from the horizon. Standing there, I felt a sudden rush of victory, as if I had triumphed in a race. France was finished. Nine countries to go.

A footpath led off the pass, switching back and forth as it descended through pine forest. Snow wadded the forest floor, which meant it was possible to slide between the switchbacks, catching at branches to slow myself. A few times I skidded and tumbled into the underbrush. Halfway down I tripped and had to run to keep my balance. Once I started running, I could not stop, so I ran and I ran and I ran off the mountain.

Midday. The churches in Lausanne rang twelve. I listened to the sound settle over the city: a thud before each strike, a high-pitched clanging, a clatter like falling crockery, and then the bass-note chime.

The city was built on the northern slopes of Lake Geneva, its streets sinking downhill in ridges and gullies and ending with a broad terrace that looked out onto the port. From the terrace I could see sailing boats moored in neat little lines, their tarpaulin deck covers coloured like bunting. Every boat seemed to shiver with the ringing of bells. The villages on the coast were also ringing, and I heard the churches of Saint-Prex and Saint-Sulpice, of Pully, Lutry and Bourg-en-Lavaux – a wall of bellchime sweeping across the water. Soon the water was quaking, its surface rippled with sound. When the chiming reached the far side of the lake, it echoed off the Chablais Alps, and they too seemed to quake, bells pealing from chambers deep inside each summit.

I remained on the terrace until the churches were quiet and the water at rest. Then I walked east along the shore.

The next two days were the most beautiful of the winter. The mountains surrounding Lake Geneva reminded me of theatre galleries: the scenery a painted backdrop, the water a polished stage. But, as I circled the lake, I grew more and more eager to start climbing. The Alps were near; Italy was near; I could imagine skipping the hundred kilometres to the border in an hour or so.

There were parks beside the port, their footpaths rimed and their playgrounds pillowed with snow. There were villas as well, mock-Second Empire mansions with clipped lawns gliding towards a beach or private jetty. Some gardens had pavilions for summer parties – brick cabins with leaded windows, or carved temples with fluted domes – but everything was shut for the off season.

Leaving the city, I rose into a steep region called the Lavaux. Nine centuries ago an army of Cistercian monks terraced these hillsides, creating the Swiss wine country.

In places the terraces were no wider than a double row of vines, clamped by walls of close-cut stone. Stone gutters carried the snowmelt off the upper slopes, and the paths between the villages were paved. The villages themselves resembled cakes, each house a slab of pink or cream sponge, their gables layered in icing and their windowsills dusted with sugar. A railway track divided the villages from the lake, and every fifteen minutes a train slid by in a puff of snow, robin red and quiet as a sleigh.

That afternoon I came off the vineyards and walked by the shore, stopping at the resort town of Vevey and sleeping in the basement of the Église Notre-Dame. Snow fell through the night, and it was snowing when I woke to leave, but at seven o'clock the sky cleared. Then I stepped out into a cloudless dawn. The air was so fine, the water so still, that the laketop looked like metal sheeting, while the mountains were shining plates of armour.

In Montreux old ladies wearing sunglasses and fur tottered down the promenade, past snow-blown palm trees and the forecourts of expensive hotels. The doors were locked at the Grand Hôtel Suisse-Majestic and the curtains drawn at Le Montreux Palace, but a woman in a blue gown stood on the balcony of the Hôtel du Grand Lac, staring at the silver light.

From here the Via Francigena turned south, leaving Lake Geneva on the banks of the Rhône. All day I followed the river, and by teatime it was snowing again. Come evening thick flakes battered my hood. The bursting impatience I had felt in Lausanne was now a reluctant resolve, pressing on in spite of myself.

Eleven hours after leaving Vevey, I limped into the abbey town of Saint-Maurice. The guest master, Fr Pélissier, greeted me in the abbey's entrance hall. He was tall and gaunt, wearing black robes and a braided belt. When I asked if I could stay the night, he winced and spoke in a whisper. The brothers were on retreat for the first weekend of Lent, he said. No one was allowed to stay. I told him that I was crossing the Alps on foot, hoping to make Rome for Easter. Just one night. Please.

He winced a second time and said that there might be a bed in the guesthouse.

I was given a small room on the second floor and went straight to sleep, but around eleven I woke to a brassy, woozy noise. An orchestra was tuning in the square opposite the abbey, and coloured lights teased my curtain. Looking from the window, I saw the town hall wrapped in banners and bows, and tables laid out below. Families stood at the tables, tubby in too many jumpers, their faces pinched with cold. Most of the children wore costumes, and I counted a fairy, a vampire, two princesses and a small team of superheroes. Then I remembered the date: Friday 8 February. This weekend was carnival.

When the orchestra started playing, I got dressed and stepped outside. Men with glowing cheeks stood in the streets. One of them – a middle-aged man in Alpine folk dress – took my hands and began mumbling. At first I thought he was speaking Italian. Then I wondered if it was Romansh. Finally I realized it was Latin.

I nodded and laughed, as though I understood, until the man smiled and sprawled off. When he came to a bench, he stretched out on the seat, pulling snow over himself like a blanket. '*In manus tuas, Domine,*' he repeated. '*In manus tuas, Domine.*'

Fr Pélissier did not believe my story about the carnival. Instead he glared at me without speaking. This was during breakfast, while we sat together in the refectory. Three or four abbey staff had gathered at the end of our table, but otherwise we were alone. Each time I finished a piece of bread, the guest master pushed one more towards my plate, a look of suffering on his face. The brothers were fasting for the day.

I was onto the last piece when a second priest arrived. He was the same height as Fr Pélissier, but twice the width, with squashed eyes and a teddy-bear grin. 'Fr Claude is ill,' he said, piling a tray with food. 'He is sick. He must have breakfast.' When the priest noticed me, he put down the tray and introduced himself. His name was Max. He asked where I was from and began speaking English with a regal accent: 'Welcome, welcome, how do you do? You are here to see our treasures, the secrets of St Maurice?'

'He's leaving,' said Fr Pélissier, standing from the table.

I asked if there was time to see the abbey treasures, but the guest master gave another suffering smile. Too hard, he thought. Not possible. Then, without waiting for a reply, he took my arm and marched me from the refectory.

In the entrance hall Fr Pélissier asked the weather forecast from the woman at the front desk. Snow today, snow tomorrow, perhaps snow all week, she replied. The guest master winced and warned that I would not be able to make Italy on foot. However, there was a bus twice daily through the tunnel under the pass.

I told him that I would wear snowshoes and use the ski routes instead.

'Too hard,' Fr Pélissier repeated, turning back towards the refectory. 'Not possible.'

When I opened the door, snow was frothing in the square outside. But, as I picked up my rucksack, I heard my name being called. It was Max, glancing over his shoulder and hurrying into the hall. Then he raised a finger to his lips and motioned me to follow, leading the way across a stone courtyard and up a stone staircase.

'I'm sorry about Fr Pélissier,' Max said when we came to his cell. 'He doesn't like guests.'

'I thought he was the guest master.'

'The abbot doesn't like guests either. So he puts Pélissier in charge – you see?'

Max made coffee from the chrome machine on his desk. It sat between a pair of designer speakers and an Apple desktop. More Apple products were stacked on a table, as well as a gleaming stereo and the breakfast tray claimed for Fr Claude. Meanwhile, gadgets blinked from the bookshelves of German literature and snow battered against the windows.

'This is my idea,' Max went on, handing me a cappuccino. 'You stay here until the storm is finished. You eat in my room, you sleep in the dormitories, and in the afternoon, when Pélissier is praying, then you can see the treasures.' His face ballooned into a smile. 'Take the day off! Rome will still be there tomorrow.'

So that's what I did.

Max's cell was a box of tricks. His bed folded away to give space for a kitchen worktop, with a microwave, fridge, and miniature hotplate. The members of St Maurice were canons rather than monks; Max insisted he had not taken a vow of poverty. Nonetheless, his deep-fat fryer was definitely against the rules. 'The other priests don't know! When they ask how I have chips, I say that I prayed very hard.'

The abbey was also a boys' boarding school, and the two institutions were connected by a glass passage. Half-term coincided with carnival, meaning the school was currently closed. After coffee we went to look for a bed, Max telling ghost stories as he tiptoed upstairs. When we came to a deserted dormitory, he whipped open the cupboards of clean sheets, shouting: 'Pélissier!'

At lunchtime my host fetched another tray of food.

Returning to the cell, his face was flushed. 'The guest master wants to know why Fr Claude is so hungry. He suspects!'

While I ate the meal, Max listed the abbot's injustices, complaining about how many classes he had to teach and how often he had to pray. He also asked me to say odd words in English – *mushroom* or *peculiar* – and, as I rolled my mouth round the vowels, his features puckered pink with laughter.

When lunch was finished, Max showed me round. We looked at the church, the cloister, the sacristy and the library, my guide pulling down pristine copies of Nietzsche and Marx from the restricted shelves. I learnt that the Abbey of St Maurice was the oldest religious house in the Alps, but in the seventeenth century it was flattened by an avalanche. Although a new abbey – the current one – was built next door, the remains of the original were still there, forming a maze of pitted foundations. Metal nets hung from the cliffs above, protecting the site from rockfall and forming a sheltered space, a no-man's-land, neither sacred nor profane. The plain of a thousand martyrs, Max called it, the earth flinted and full of bones.

At the centre of the site was a chapel to St Maurice. The saint was born in Thebes in the middle of the third century and commanded a legion of Christian soldiers in the Roman Army. The legion was posted to the Chablais Alps to drive out the local tribes, but before fighting they were ordered to make a sacrifice to the Emperor Maximian. They refused, because it was blasphemy, so as punishment the legion was decimated. The soldiers remained defiant, however, and so they were decimated again, and again – yet still they would not submit. In the end every one of them was executed.

Ever since, St Maurice has been popular throughout the Carolingian kingdoms. Holy Roman Emperors were anointed in front of his altar at St Peter's, while his sword and spurs were used in coronation ceremonies for Austria's royal family, and his lance was said to be the same spear that pierced the side of Christ – now lying on a crushed red cushion in Vienna's Hofburg Palace. A first abbey was established at the site of the martyrdom in the year 515, guarding a pinch-point in the Rhône Valley. Pilgrims stopped off here as they climbed towards the Great Saint Bernard Pass, the grandest bringing gifts. These gifts were now kept in a vault, along with the relics of the martyred legion.

'We are very proud of our treasures,' said Max, opening the cylinder lock and the metal-clad door. 'In September we parade them round the town and bishops come all the way from Egypt to join us. But each year they are disappointed, because there is no skiing in Saint-Maurice.'

Inside were ten or twelve display cases with glass screens. My host pointed out a jewelled pitcher given to the monks by Charlemagne, a thorn from Christ's crown left by the saint king Louis IX, a carved chest where St Sigismund's bones were preserved with those of his children, and a silver bust holding St Candide's skull.

Before we left, Max peered into the corners of the room. 'In case anybody is hiding,' he said. 'Once a man was locked in here and we forgot all about him.'

'He died?'

'Oh yes.'

'But that's terrible.'

'Oh no.' His face puckered pink again. 'You see, he was a martyr.'

That evening my host made too many chips. After the meal, while I sat around feeling fat and content, he searched online for video clips of the Proms. Then we watched recordings of 'Land of Hope and Glory', Max humming the tune and waving an imaginary Union Jack.

He had always wanted to see London, yet when I told him to visit me one day, he went quiet, saying that he was *un pantouflard* – a word I did not know. 'Here is my home,' he explained. 'I don't like to leave my home.'

At ten Max accompanied me to the dormitories. We did not risk the lights, using a torch instead. When I realized I had left my notebook in his cell, I jogged back to collect it, but on my return Max was nowhere to be seen.

The passage to the school was at the end of a corridor, forming a wing of the main courtyard. The moon was up, and panes of moonlight silvered the flagstone floor. Approaching the passage, I heard footsteps coming in my direction – not from the school, but from where the corridor turned a corner. At first I thought it was Max, though he moved with a bustle, and these paces were clipped. As I listened to the footsteps echoing forwards, my mouth dried out and my heart began to hammer. The closer they came, the more certain I was who they belonged to. Yet there was nowhere to hide, so I kept going.

The guest master moved out from the shadows, his face pale, his hands white. He walked forwards, wincing, but did not say a word, and we passed one another in silence.

My host had already crossed to the school. I found him in the games room, crouching behind a pool table. 'Pélissier is here,' he hissed. 'He's looking for us.'

'He saw me, Max.'

Max jumped to his feet and shuffled towards the abbey. Then he turned round and shuffled towards the school. Then he turned a third time and sat down.

'I'm so sorry.'

He began to giggle.

'Will you be in trouble?'

He kept giggling. 'The abbot is always looking for an excuse to excommunicate me.'

Next day we left the abbey together, still tiptoeing for fear of Pélissier. It was Sunday morning, eight o'clock, and the town was not yet awake. Carnival remains were strewn over the streets: ribbons and bottles and cannon-blasts of glitter. As I walked away, I looked back to see Max standing on the abbey steps. Then he waved, waved, and was gone.

I felt no safer as I entered the forested valley south of Saint-Maurice. There was something hostile about the snowbound landscape, unmarred by any sign of life. Hiking trails threaded the forest, and in summer these trails would have been the best of the pilgrimage: a shaded walkway above the River Rhône. In winter the powder on the paths was smooth, but the ground below was uneven, and I kept losing my footing. Soon I was wading through drifts – up to my thighs, my waist in snow. My boots split, my soles peeled, and though I had been travelling for forty days, I seemed little fitter than the first week.

A road and a railway line chased each other up the western flank of the valley. The railway was the St Bernard Express to Orsières, the last town before the pass. Above the track, the Scots pines were layered with snow like lace on a dark table. I walked on the opposite flank, but a few times I looked left and saw the train weaving a striped candy cane through the trees.

That afternoon I came to a mound of snow as tall as a house. I had never seen this before: the wake of an avalanche. It furrowed the face of the valley and then ploughed into the river a hundred metres below. There was no route round, so I went over on hand and knee. The powder on top was fresh, just two or three centimetres, meaning the avalanche was recent – last night or perhaps this morning. Beneath were chunks of ice with raw edges, branches shorn from trees, and snowpack solid as rubble. I crawled slowly, unbalanced by my rucksack, and toppled over every few metres like a clown in a slapstick show.

It took an hour to cover less than a kilometre of ruptured ground.

Somebody wearing a fluorescent waistcoat was standing on the far side of the barrow. When I clambered off, he ran towards me. The track was not safe, he shouted, the mountain unstable. Then he stopped shouting and his mouth hung open. Crouched low, breathing hard, trousers and jacket stuffed with snow – it must have looked as though I was pulling myself free from the avalanche.

'You are alive?' he asked. 'My God, you are alive?'

At Martigny the Rhône turned east, the road turning with it. The St Bernard Express went south, however, taking a curved course along a tributary called the Drance. The Via Francigena went south as well, climbing to the Italian border.

Next day I began walking on the west of the valley, but by midmorning I needed to cross over. When my path branched, I took the lower route down to the Drance. Although the route was cordoned off, the tape was loose, the knots undone, and I passed by without thinking.

Half an hour later I arrived at the water. There was more tape here, tying up a wooden footbridge. It was obvious why: the bridge's arch had cracked and its deck gaped wide.

My limbs were rigid with cold and my thoughts racing with frustration, so I jogged on the spot and tried to think of a plan. I needed to reach Orsières before the end of the day, and still had several hundred metres to climb. The channel was too deep to ford, the current too fast, and the only other footbridge was three or four kilometres off course. There were boulders above the waterline, yet too few to stepping-stone across. However, as I stared at my map, the gap in the deck taunted me. Surely it was close enough to jump?

Ducking the tape, I moved onto the bridge. The wood was planed with ice, and my boots stuttered for grip. I slipped once, once more, snatching at the handrail to keep upright, but after four paces the planking gave way and I plunged into the Drance.

As I fell, the weight on my shoulders pulled me back, rucksack smacking flat against the deck. I reached for the handrail, but it slid from my grip, fingers skimming off the rail, the balusters, the slatted deck. I reached out a second time, and the handrail came loose.

The stream was so cold that it skinned the tissue from my shins. Hamstrings tense and spasming. Thighs barbed with thorns. Penis stinging, gone numb. And a smell like stainless steel that was water a few degrees above freezing.

When my hips tipped off the bridge, my whole body wheeled round, legs swinging behind me, chest levering forwards. The weight of my rucksack pivoted, and rather than pulling me back, it threw me face-first into the Drance. But I did not sink. Instead, I hung there half-submerged.

It took a moment to understand what had happened. My rucksack was hitched on a kink in the balusters, its straps holding me above the torrent.

I was saved. I was stuck.

The bridge's wooden piers were still intact, and after splashing around for some footing, I dug my left knee into the girders, raised my right hand onto the trestle, one, two, three, lift – and I was out of the water. Then I hauled myself off the deck and onto the bank. For a while I tried to get warm by doing press-ups, but my arms were lame and I could do nothing except lie on my rucksack, gulping and heaving and feeling very ashamed.

The whole incident happened too fast for fear. Afterwards all I experienced was a desperate desire to try again. A short distance back the railway cut the valley on a bridge of poured concrete, and once I had changed from my soaking clothes, I scrambled up the path and dropped to the track.

Trains approached the bridge via a tunnel, its mouth in shadow. I could see nothing through the darkness, and though I listened for a few minutes, I heard only the urging of the rapids below. So I decided to risk it.

Stepping onto the bridge, I experienced that strange vertigo caused not by height, but by a sense of smallness. It was windy here, the air pressing at my legs, my pack, tugging my eyelids and blurring the forest scenery. The mountains were blurred too, like folded lengths of fabric, each pleat a gully and every crease a crest of white. The course was narrow, and if I set my sight on a fixed point – the workman's hut on the other bank – the gauge tapered to a single line.

A quarter of the way over, the track flexed. I wondered if this was the wind, but no, the metal was straining under an enormous load. Watching the rails tremor and pulse, I thought I could hear my heartbeat – *th-th-thump, th-th-thump, th-th-thump* – but then I realized the sound was coming from the tunnel.

I walked faster, counting the sleepers ahead, not daring to look round. Midway over, the tracks began vibrating. The trackbed was vibrating too, and the bridge's concrete arches. I started running, feet shambling in the snow, as the sound from the tunnel grew louder and louder. Soon I could not hear the wind, could not hear the rapids. Soon I could hear nothing but a heartbeat amplified a hundred times. *TH-TH-THUMP, TH-TH-THUMP, TH-TH-THUMP.*

Three-quarters of the way over, the riverbank rushed up to meet the bridge. By this point I was sprinting. Off the rails and off the sleepers, off the ballast and off the parapet and crash through the doorway of the workman's hut.

The train swept past, a red-and-white streamer with a cartoon St Bernard on the side. Two children, twin brothers, gazed from one of the windows, wearing blue blazers with striped bands, like naval cadets. Sitting up from the floor, I tried to salute them, but already the train was gone.

Fr Jean-Michel's hair was grey and his face dented into a frown. As we sat together in the Orsières presbytery, he asked the standard questions – Where was I from? How long had I been walking? Why alone? Why in winter? – without listening to my answers. Something was wrong, but I could not work out what.

'And Rome, you arrive in Rome when?'

'Easter.'

'For the new pope.'

'The new pope?'

'We must have a pope for Easter.'

I opened my mouth, closed it.

He went on: 'The Pope has resigned, you understand?'

'Pope Benedict?'

'He is not the pope any more.'

'No,' I said. 'I don't understand.'

Fr Jean-Michel told me what he could. Benedict was old, he said, and weak, and the problems in the Church were too much for one man. Previous popes had resigned – not recently – in the fifteenth century. It was an act of courage, of humility . . . His voice trailed off and he began to examine his coffee cup. After a minute's silence he asked if I was following the Via Francigena. I talked about leaving Canterbury six weeks ago, crossing the Champagne vineyards and the plains of southern Marne, the hills of the Haute-Saône and the mountains of the Jura, and then circling round Lake Geneva and into the Alps.

The dented frown became deeper. 'And tomorrow you take the bus?'

'Tomorrow the pass.'

Fr Jean-Michel shook his head. 'There's no path for hikers. If you fall, if you lose your way – it's too dangerous.'

'I can use the ski route.'

'You have skis? You have a guide?'

'Most pilgrims walk without a guide.'

'In April, May, summer – certainly – but not in February. We've never had a pilgrim in February, my whole time at the parish. Tonight you will sleep in the refuge. Tomorrow, the bus.'

Perhaps it was true that, since the Via Francigena's revival, nobody had completed the route in winter. However, prior to the opening of the tunnel, travellers had no choice. Medieval pilgrims used the Great Saint Bernard Pass throughout the year, with thousands making the journey in the snow. That is what I told Fr Jean-Michel.

The dent softened. 'Wilderness – you know this word?'

'Where Christ fasted?'

'Where he was tempted. Where he spoke to the devil.' The priest stood up. 'Now it is Lent. Now we are in the wilderness.'

I didn't know what to say. I said, 'Yes.'

'But when Lent is finished, we will have a new pope. And you will be his first pilgrim!'

The presbytery's ski gear was stored in an outhouse. Fr Jean-Michel let me borrow a pair of snowshoes on two conditions. First, I must leave them at the parish on the other side of the pass. Second, if the weather closed in before Bourg-Saint-Bernard, I must turn back.

The refuge was next door. Downstairs I found a kitchen and a dining room, upstairs an attic covered in rugs. Previous pilgrims had patched the ceiling with messages: good-luck letters, scraps of poetry, postcards and doodles and the first psalm from the Song of Ascents copied out in red crayon: *I will lift up mine eyes unto the hills, from whence cometh my help.*

I emptied my rucksack onto the dining table, looking for things to throw away. Among the rubbish I noticed a postcard of St Bernard, kneeling beneath the Virgin; a wintry scene drawn in blue biro, with a prayer written beneath; and three or four grubby sweets – all that remained of the handful given to me at the École Saint-Jean-Baptiste-de-la-Salle on a mild Epiphany morning 781 kilometres ago. I buttoned the gifts into my breast pocket and repacked the rucksack.

Tomorrow would be the hardest day of the pilgrimage. The pass was twenty-six kilometres from Orsières and fifteen hundred metres higher. And Fr Jean-Michel was right: it would not be safe to attempt the final ascent in poor conditions. But, even though the careless confidence of those early weeks had been punctured by a growing sense of danger, I knew that I would have a go anyway. Something stronger than me was pushing this pilgrimage forwards. The day's near-misses had been a reminder of what. Bridges, train tracks, sudden accidents: these were the images that had disturbed my mind during the dark nights of the depression.

As I unrolled my sleeping bag, I thought back to that time. Back twenty months, to a Friday at the end of May, when spring scrubbed clean the London streets.

That evening I walked home from work and closed my bedroom door. The room was not big: eight steps long, six steps wide, with a bed occupying much of the floor. Books were piled by the wall, and a picture hung over the doorway, showing a sailing boat on a calm blue sea. The window let in the noise; the curtain let in the light.

For the next few days I did not leave the room, but stayed inside, emptying out my life. From here every commitment I could think of was cancelled. Train tickets and theatre tickets. Birthday parties and house parties. An essay I was commissioned to write, a conference I was expected to attend, a pair of summer holidays and the interviews for a scholarship to America – I couldn't come, couldn't reschedule, couldn't explain. I wanted nothing to fix me to the future, a clear run at the horizon. You see, at some point that summer I hoped to kill myself.

The weekend was spent daydreaming – violent dreams from which I struggled to shake myself. Most were suicide fantasies: now opening my wrists in a bath, now tipping head-first from a rooftop, now jumping into the traffic, now falling, now falling. The rest were memories I had tried to bury, of a boy laid out on sleepers, left hand come loose, blinking the blood away. Yet it was not the dreams that troubled me, but the sensation of dreaming. Any movement in my mind was a slender, searing pain. I could not place the pain, as with a headache or wound, for it edged the limits of my awareness and made tender the space that I saw when I closed my eyes.

On Tuesday I went to the doctor. I told her that I felt defeated, and that this feeling of defeat was so overwhelming it made dying seem the simplest way to surrender.

The doctor sat on a yellow exercise ball. When she nodded, her whole body bounced.

I left the surgery with a prescription for antidepressants and a list of psychiatrists to visit. Over the following weeks I took assessments for depression and anxiety, for bipolar disorder and suicide risk. Each time I had to explain how my thoughts stung and reeled, how they hurt me, how they hurt.

Now, lying in the Orsières refuge and waiting for sleep, I thought about the months following the breakdown. What I remembered most clearly was a sense of stunned isolation, though in fact I was rarely alone. I worked in the largest open-plan office in London. I lived with my best friend, our flat midway between a crossroads and a railway. Our bathroom had a view of Victoria Coach Station, and all summer the pavements were busy with men and women about my age, dressed in sunglasses and wellies, taking coaches to Glastonbury or Latitude or a dozen other festivals. If the windows were open, I could hear their voices, their laughter.

Even after the drugs started working, the fantasies remained, but now I was helpless to realize them, my will made weak and fitful. Instead I kept to the flat, kept to my room. Eight steps long. Six steps wide. Curtain that let in the light.

I never took up those cancelled commitments. Ambitions, responsibilities – I let them all slide. The days were provisional, the future felt only as pressure, smothering any plans. But, after hiking to Canterbury, I began to believe that, if I made it to Jerusalem, then I would be well. This was the wager driving me through the winter. I could not turn round, or even slow down, for I feared returning to that room and those wrecking daydreams. I could only push on, push on, push on – until I walked free from the past. Yet I carried those memories with me, like the rucksack on my shoulders, the burden on my back. And the farther I hiked from home, the heavier they weighed me down.

There was a tiny shrine in the corner of the refuge: three candles, a rosary with plastic beads, and a carving of the Virgin Mary, gathered on a tea tray. I was too nervous to sleep, so I lit one of the candles and sat in front of the shrine.

As the flame cast its colour onto the ceiling, I read the names on the pilgrims' letters: Luca and Laurent, Hanna and Martijn, Ana and Judith and Jetta and Mark, Stef, Stéphane, Thomas, Simon, Marianna, Federica, Élisabeth and Eva. I wondered who travelled this route because they were lonely, or lost, or wanted to learn what they believed. Who was recovering from an illness, or seeking penance for past sins, or trying to mend what medicine could not cure. And I wondered if these were really the same reason, and we all walked in search of a miracle.

Closing my eyes, I could still see the candle, fluttering in the darkness, enfolding me with light.

I left the refuge at dawn. There was a church opposite the presbytery with granite columns vaulting the roof. The only colour came from a pair of lancet windows in the apse, their glass like an illuminated manuscript, and from an icon in the north transept showing a young man in loose robes, his right hand held up, held open. The gesture was not a blessing, but something simpler, a wave maybe, or a warning. Stand back. Stay where you are. His left hand carried a martyr's palm, the branch thin as a quill. *Bienheureux Maurice Tornay,* read the sign, *1910–1949.*

A door led through to a one-room museum, where I learnt the rest of the story.

Maurice Tornay was born in a hamlet near Orsières and baptized here in the Église Saint-Nicolas. The seventh of eight children, he was a restless, impulsive boy. On first hearing the legend of St Maurice, the Theban legionary, he promised his mother that he too would die for Christ, just like his namesake saint.

The boy spent each summer caring for the family's flock of sheep, but at fifteen he was sent to school at the Abbey of St Maurice. That year a French nun called Thérèse of Lisieux was canonized, having died of tuberculosis aged twenty-four. A memoir written during her sickness, *The Story of a Soul*, became a bestseller, and Maurice was bewitched by the book, writing: 'Death is the happiest day of our lives [. . .] our arrival in our true homeland.'

There were pictures of Maurice's schooldays on the panels in the museum. They showed a grinning boy with buck teeth and bottlecap glasses standing in the middle of his class photo, wearing a stiff collar, a striped tie and the peaked cap awarded by the Society of Swiss Students. There were also collections of relics in the cabinets around the room. One cabinet held a watch chain with no watch, a Latin exercise book with split pins and the peaked cap from the photograph, trimmed in a coppery thread that might once have been gold-plate.

In 1931 Maurice wrote a letter to the abbot of a nearby monastery, asking to join. The monastery was built at the highest point of the Great Saint Bernard Pass and had provided shelter to pilgrims crossing the mountains for centuries. Maurice found it hard to explain his calling, telling the abbot that he wanted to withdraw from the world, to be 'stripped of myself'.

The young man was accepted, and that August he travelled to his new home. His school uniform was swapped for the black gown hanging in the corner of the museum – a crumpled item, dulled with age. Other panels showed pictures from Maurice's time at the monastery, my favourite featuring nine novices on a hiking trip, wearing aprons and sunglasses, puttees and cloth caps, and posing like a band with instruments improvised from camping gear. One bowed a frying-pan violin, a second banged a cooking-pot drum, while a third played a piece of tenting as though it were a flute. Maurice stood at the rear of the group, lifting a flag to the camera.

There were more relics in the other cabinets: a chalice, a breviary and a pipe with a crooked bit. There were more photographs too, which showed a grinning boy grown into a stern man with sunken cheeks. The rest of the panels explained how this Swiss shepherd ended up preaching the Gospel in Tibet – but that part of the story would have to wait. It was time for me to follow Maurice Tornay onto the Great Saint Bernard Pass.

Outside, the snow was coming down in gusts. I stood in the church doorway, unsure which way to turn. On my left was the road to the pass, on my right the bus stop for the tunnel. Two hours from now I could be strolling off the mountains into Italy.

I looked south. In the distance the clouds were parting and the snow lay bright on the ridgeline. Pulling tight my rucksack straps, I started walking towards the sky.

As I went higher the weather lifted and the forest thinned, until only a few trees pierced the slopes, like splinters on pallid skin. By early afternoon everything looked clean, pointed. Liddes was a lonely village at 1,346 metres, Bourg-Saint-Pierre a stone hamlet at 1,632 metres, and Bourg-Saint-Bernard a deserted restaurant at almost 2,000 metres. The road disappeared here, one half burrowing into the tunnel, the other half hidden under several storeys of snow. The hidden half continued up a steep-sided passage with a penny-dreadful name – La Combe des Morts, the Valley of Death. This was the final ascent to the Great Saint Bernard Pass.

There was a clearing by the tunnel entrance, where three or four cars had parked. A couple with fair hair and silver jackets were putting on skis – the man called Alex, the woman Françoise. When I asked if they were skiing to the pass, Alex nodded.

How long would it take?

'Two hours, no problem.' He indicated the rising ramp of snow where the road ended. Plastic pennants signalled from the mountainside at thirty-metre intervals, marking a route for skiers. 'You go with the flags, right to the top.'

I watched the couple slip-step onto the ramp. 'Try to catch us!' Françoise called as they glided off.

Lengths of cirrus hung from the summits, but otherwise the day was clear. Two hours to the top? Of course I would have a go. I smeared my face with Vaseline, ate a block of Kendal Mint Cake, fastened Fr Jean-Michel's snowshoes, and approached the ramp.

The flags curved round a corner and mounted the Combe des Morts. Between each one the powder was worked into ruts – fresh tracks from Alex and Françoise, and frozen tracks from whoever had skied this way before. I moved slowly, clumsy in snowshoes, stopping every ten minutes to rest. By the first stop my lungs were tight and I felt a plucking pain in both legs. By the second my water bottle was iced shut. Yet I grew more determined with every step: a cheerful certainty that the walk was almost done.

Half an hour later I caught the skiers. Alex had a stitch and Françoise a problem with her binding. They sat on the snow and blinked, as if waking from a nap. I offered to help, but Alex shook his head.

By this point the peaks were hustled with cloud. When

I asked whether it was safe to keep going, Françoise took my hand in her silver glove.

'You are the leader now,' she said. 'Promise we don't get lost.'

I pushed on. The plastic pennants levelled and lifted again. To my right were the rugged walls of the Col des Chevaux, to my left the broad base of the Becs Noirs. A few times I looked back, but the skiers never moved, until I could not see them any more, until I could see nothing of the landscape below. The wind had risen and cloud was pouring into the valley. It was grey, ashen, black, and streaked with a violent blue. The slopes above were the same, the ridgeline coming apart.

I ran for the next flag, my feet paddling. Snow streamed off the mountain and powder filled the air. When I tried to breathe, swollen flakes caught in my throat. When I stopped breathing, I heard a flocking sound like a thousand flapping wings. Then the sky dimmed and the storm dropped.

I reached the flag, but the route ahead was rubbed away. Turning round, my route this far had also vanished. The route, the range, the arcing corridor of the Combe des Morts – the whole world spinning into white.

I watched the snow wipe clean the last of my footprints and then sat on my heels and wondered what to do. I was tempted to laugh at my own naivety, and the confident way I had marched into disaster. Instead I crouched down low, wrapping my arms around my chest and gasping hard in disbelief.

The Great Saint Bernard Pass was always the most dangerous part of the Via Francigena. Although a monastery was built at Bourg-Saint-Pierre in the ninth century, pilgrims often died during the final ascent. Pilgrims such as Aelfsige, an archbishop of Canterbury who vanished here in the year 959. Perhaps he was lost in a storm, perhaps he fell to his death, or perhaps he was killed by pirates.

For much of the tenth century the Pennine Alps were home to a roving band of Saracens. They sailed from Córdoba, the Islamic kingdom in Spain, seized the port of Fraxinet, close to present-day Saint-Tropez, and then charged into the mountains on the hunt for treasure, plundering the Abbey of St Maurice and sacking the monastery at Bourg-Saint-Pierre.

In 972 the pirates kidnapped Majolus, Abbot of Cluny, as he crossed the Alps on his return from Rome. The most senior monk in Christendom was ransomed for a thousand pieces of silver. Cluny paid the sum, but also lobbied the Count of Provence to clear Fraxinet. Within weeks the pirate port was under siege, and by the end of the year their Alpine Tortuga had been razed.

A new monastery was founded in 1049 at the highest point of the pass. Its founder was called Bernard of Menthon – another Bernard, born a century before the Abbot of Clairvaux. Since then the Great Saint Bernard Hospice has always hosted travellers. The monks also provided a rescue service, skiing out after avalanches to search for survivors. If they found a corpse – with the help of the famous mountain dog – it was taken to the morgue, for the ground was too hard to dig graves. In the cold the corpse's features remained perfect, until the whole thing crumbled. Frozen figures also lined the route to the pass, a grim sight used in a novel by Dickens, a poem by Longfellow and a series of sketches by Turner. Imagine! Pilgrims like statues, their bodies whole but their souls snuffed out, forming an avenue of martyrs on the road to Italy.

Each year one or two monks suffered the same fate. To the young Maurice Tornay they seemed heroic figures, risking their lives to rescue strangers. On joining the monastery he wrote to his sister Anna that, 'the more I live the more I am convinced that sacrifice [. . .] alone gives meaning to these days.'

Initially Maurice worried that he would feel trapped on the mountain pass, snowed in for six months of the year. However, he told his parents that he had never known such freedom. Yet it was not enough. In 1933 the Paris Foreign Missions Society asked the Abbot of the Great Saint Bernard Hospice if he could send some priests to Yunnan Province in south-west China, to evangelize the Tibetan borderlands. By September 1935 Maurice Tornay had made his vows of poverty, chastity and obedience, and within months he departed for Yunnan.

Before leaving, he asked his family to pray for him to become a saint. 'I want to use myself up in the service of God,' he wrote. 'I will never come back once I have gone away.'

I thought I could understand the young man's wish, yet when I tried to concentrate, the idea faded from me. Maurice was twenty-four when he left for China, the same age as Thérèse of Lisieux when she died. What was it he wrote? *Death is the happiest day of our lives [. . .] our arrival in our true homeland.* St Augustine again. I thought I could understand – but no, it was gone, and I was alone once more, squatting in a storm, and everything was white, everything havoc.

A few times I glimpsed one of the flags ahead of me, but never in the same place, and if I kept looking it would tatter into hundreds of pieces. A mountain mirage, perhaps. I also glimpsed a figure dressed in silver skiing through the blizzard. 'Alex!' I shouted, 'Françoise!' – but my voice strayed in the wind and the figure disappeared. Another mirage. Not to worry. Safer to stay here. Stay where you are.

The feeling was bleeding from my hands and feet. Footage from survival shows played in my mind, yet I had forgotten if I was supposed to pitch a tent, or get into my sleeping bag, or set fire to my rucksack, or dig a snow cave the size of a coffin. Or maybe I was meant to lie down. Lie down on the softened ground and sleep until the storm raged itself out. Sleep until the monks find me.

Stop it. Wake up. *You have to wake up.*

I opened my eyes. What time was it? The snow was dark and the daylight almost spent. Four? Four thirty? I needed to start walking, though my legs were seized and the route ahead still buried. If I kept waiting, I would doze off again.

Crouching a second time, I cleared the powder round the flag. As I brushed the fresh flakes away, my fingers pressed onto a seam where the snow was frozen in grooves. It was an old ski track. Whoever skied this way must have been guided by the flags. Keep with the track, and it would lead me to the pass.

I kept going, bending every few paces to dig for the frozen seam. The cold was like liquid, seeping through my clothes, seeping into my skin. My knees sored and went senseless. The wind bruised my face.

Eventually I saw the next flag flailing ahead of me, and the next one, and the next. By now my joints were stiff and my muscles biting. The higher I climbed, the heavier the snow, pelting against my jacket, my hood, and cymbal-smashing in my ears. The incline was getting steeper, slower – but then the ground began to flatten and there were no more flags.

In the distance I could make out the hull of a huge building, like some forgotten ski resort. Moving towards it, I saw a fracture of light from the front door. A man stood in the doorway, with a wooden cross at his neck. When I asked if I could come in, he laughed and laughed. The door had never shut, he said, not in a thousand years.

*

I was given a room on the top floor, a dormitory with eighteen bunk beds and a cupboard of blankets all to myself. Its walls were more than a metre thick, and the heat was turned high on the radiators. As the sensation returned to my fingers and toes, what I felt was something deeper than warmth – a padded comfort very close to consolation.

The room was boarded in pine, the corridors also, and that night the storm pressed against the windows, until it seemed I was bobbing below deck on an ocean liner. When I woke in the morning my legs listed as if too long at sea. Listed, and then buckled.

At midday I hobbled downstairs to have lunch with the dozen pious ski bums who volunteered here during the winter. They told me that, ever since the tunnel was dug under the pass fifty years ago, the order had been in decline. From ninety priests in the middle of the last century, there were now just three running the hospice, a few more serving the local churches, and no new vocations in a decade.

I was not the only guest. A group of skiers were also stuck on the pass. They sat around in the dining room, playing card games and staring at maps. It would have made for a promising whodunit: a doctor from Chile with a fondness for Kierkegaard, a Canadian defence analyst who made cryptic comments about Cold War Two, and a French entrepreneur who spent his twenties training to be a Jesuit, until one Wednesday morning he left the seminary and never went back. When I asked why, he mimed zipping his lips together. I liked to think that he had been hiding on the mountain ever since – not trapped but simply suspended, as if time were weaker here. I expected to see Alex and Françoise too, but they must have returned to their car before the storm set in. All the same,

I spent many hours in the cellar where the ski gear was stored, searching in vain for a pair of silver jackets.

I also spent a long time in the hospice museum. It contained a dingy mock-up of a monk's cell, an antique printing press with twenty-seven leather-bound books, the wooden sleigh used for carrying pilgrims' corpses, and various sizes of wooden ski. The photos on the walls showed life at the monastery in the 1920s and 1930s. I hoped to spot Maurice Tornay among the brothers, but I could not recognize him. Perhaps he was already in China.

Maurice arrived in Yunnan Province at the end of 1935. Within two years he was ordained and teaching at a town by the Tibetan border called Weixi, where he remained throughout the Second World War. When Japan invaded China there was famine in the region, and Fr Tornay – as Maurice was now known – had to beg for food, eating berries and bracken root so that his pupils would not starve.

In 1945 he was moved to Yerkalo, a village on a high plateau inside the Tibetan border. Three hundred Christians lived in the surrounding hamlets, but the nearest parish was eight days' walk away, over the border in China.

Tibet was one of the great prizes of Christian evangelization, and missionaries had been attempting to convert the country for centuries. Because of repeated efforts by Franciscan and Jesuit priests during the Age of Exploration, in the mid-eighteenth century it was closed to Christians. However, by the second half of the nineteenth century Tibet was under the supremacy of the Chinese emperors, and an 1860 treaty between France and China allowed Catholic priests to travel to the Chinese interior, prompting the Paris Foreign Missions Society to found a parish in Yerkalo. However, according to Tibetan authorities, the ban on missionaries remained.

In 1940 the priest at Yerkalo, Fr Nussbaum, was killed

by a gang of monks. Within six years his successor, Fr Burdin, had also died – this time of typhoid fever.

Maurice Tornay was chosen to replace him.

Fr Tornay made his way to Yerkalo in the summer of 1945. The local headman, Gun Akio, immediately tried to seize his church's land. Some months later thirty armed men attempted to ransack his presbytery. Finally, in January 1946, a platoon of soldiers marched Fr Tornay from Tibet with a gun to his neck, warning him never to return.

The priest spent his exile in the border town of Weixi. Merchants kept him informed about the congregation he left behind. Some had been forced to renounce their faith, others to donate their children to the lamasery.

Thirteen years after leaving the Great Saint Bernard Hospice, Fr Tornay decided to travel to the Dalai Lama and beg tolerance for Tibetan Christians. He shaved his beard, put on a kurta and baggy trousers, and joined a caravan of merchants making the two-month trip to Lhasa.

In early August the caravan entered Tibet. After a few days it halted at Tunto, where the merchants were searched and Fr Tornay ordered back. When he attempted to join the caravan a second time, soldiers escorted him from the country. He escaped the soldiers and began trekking towards the Mekong Valley, hoping to reach the mission house at Weixi. While he walked he recited a rosary, each footstep the line of a prayer – *Sainte Marie, Mère de Dieu* – a clearing in the forest, close to the Choula Pass – *Priez pour nous pauvres pécheurs* – four men, five men, the last one carrying a gun – *Maintenant et à l'heure de notre mort* – the guide killed first, and, as the priest knelt to perform the last rites, two shots.

He was hit once in the stomach and once in the temple. His body was stripped and left by the roadside. Three weeks later the Abbot of the Great Saint Bernard Hospice received a telegram. It read: *Tornay massacred*.

When I left the museum a bell was chiming for evening prayer. I went down to the crypt chapel and sat near the door. The chapel roof was pricked with lights, the altar hidden in darkness. No one here yet, so I closed my eyes and waited.

Sitting there, my mind filled with questions. Why was I haunted by these martyrs' stories? By Benoît-Joseph Labre, patron saint of pilgrims? By Maurice Tornay, the Swiss shepherd boy? Why, though I could not share their conviction, did their deaths make sense to me? Was it that they had freed themselves from society? Or given up responsibility for their lives? Or did I understand their fear at the wild freedom of the world? Did I feel it too?

In 1950 all Christian missions were expelled from Yunnan Province and the church at Yerkalo was abandoned. But Fr Tornay was not forgotten, and in 1993 he was beatified by Pope John Paul II. The Pope praised the former priest, who, 'in the spirit of his order, in which everyone risks his life to save people from storms, tried every means possible to rescue these pilgrim Christians in the Asiatic Alps'.

Walking through France and Switzerland, I kept encountering the idea of religion as sacrifice: in the monks at Clairvaux who died to the world, in the Jura hermits who made their homes in the mountains, and in the Theban legionaries buried beneath Saint-Maurice. They were all martyrs of a sort.

And they were almost all young men. There was an impatience to their faith, an adolescent recklessness, that I recognized. Take Maurice Tornay. As a student he was bewitched by the thought of dying for belief. As a missionary he travelled willingly into danger. He wanted to test his devotion, to prove it. Then he pushed himself so far from safety that he had little choice but to trust in God. Here was an opportunity found in no other context except war – to show courage, to show endurance and abandon himself to a single cause. More than that, Maurice Tornay wanted to tear down the veil between this world and the next, to reach out his hand and touch Paradise. A similar ambition moved me to walk in the depth of winter. I was drawn by the blank promise of the infinite. I wanted to test my recovery, prove it, to collapse the leap between faith and fact. Then I pushed myself so far from safety that I had little choice but to be well. However, though I was trying to walk free from my sickness, its memories still haunted me. And, travelling alone in the winter cold, I was helpless to defend against them.

Or perhaps I was reading myself into the saints again. In truth, the inner lives of these martyrs remained a mystery to me. And any comparison was melodramatic now that the most dangerous part of the pilgrimage was done. The longer I waited in the chapel, the more I felt glad about setting off in midwinter, because if a new pope were chosen for Easter, I would reach Rome at a moment of history.

There were windows on one side of the crypt, high enough to see over the snowline. The stars were rising and the moon shining off the snow. A few flakes cartwheeled by, but otherwise the night was still. The storm had ended; the crossing was clear. Tomorrow I would start walking again.

PART TWO

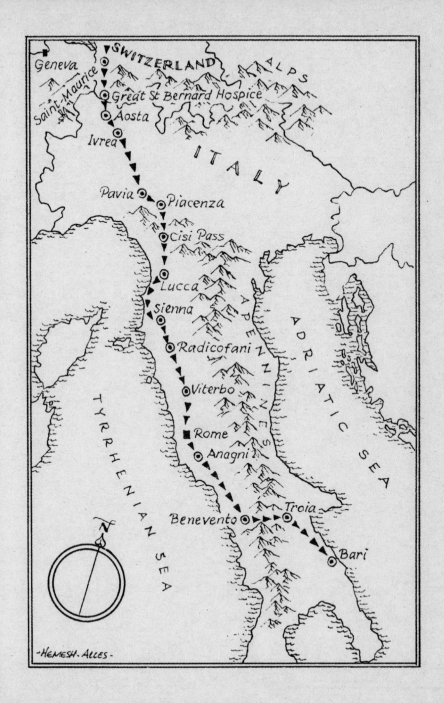

Six hot-air balloons, seven, eight, rising above Aosta. Some were ribbed red and white, some hooped yellow and green, like a packet of sweets spilled across the sky. They seemed to come from nowhere: launched off balconies, perhaps, or else shot from out of chimneypots.

It was Wednesday morning, the middle of February. Men and women in suits and skirts hurried to work in the streets below. On a whim one of them would look up, notice the balloons, and stop to watch. Then another would notice and start pointing. Soon groups of spectators were gathering in the piazzas, heads turned towards the sky. More and more people joined them, until it seemed the whole city was watching.

A breeze caught the balloons and carried them down the Aosta Valley. My own route ran along the valley floor, so I followed the parade east. Progress had been slow in the Alps, yet dropping from the mountains was effortless. My pack was lighter, my mood too, and the weather was mild below the snowline. Once more I felt the triumph of crossing a mountain border. Surely the walk would be easy from now on.

The hillsides lining the valley were terraced, each terrace framed with a trellis, each trellis rigged in vines. In summer their leaves might have shaded my path, but that winter the canopy was bare. I could still see the balloons through the gaps in the lattice. Sometimes they raced, sometimes drifted, sometimes gathered close together and scattered apart like billiard balls, splitting the felt-soft sky. Most of the morning they were in front of me, but a few times I glanced up to see one balloon bobbing above my head, its wicker basket ringed in a bulging collar of orange and blue.

By midmorning the orange-and-blue balloon was dragging. Just past eleven it slumped into a field on the far side of the valley, basket tumbling to the ground. I kept watching, waiting for the pilot to get out, but nobody stirred. Maybe it was unoccupied. A runaway balloon! Left behind, poor thing, as its friends fled towards Piedmont.

The valley cut south, ending with the medieval city of Ivrea. Its cobbled streets looked polished, but the cobblestones were threaded with pulp. Every year, to celebrate carnival, Ivrea's citizens fought one another with oranges. Though the mess had been cleaned several days ago, the air in the old town still carried a whiff of rotting citrus.

A cramped cathedral stood on a hill in the middle of the city. Nearby I found a slouching set of parish buildings. One of these buildings was a homeless shelter, where I was offered a bed for the night. Inside it smelt like a charity shop: old blankets, used books, and the rubbery smell of second-hand shoes.

In the last hour of the day ten more men arrived, greeting each other with nicknames. Although I hoped my walk would give us something in common, they responded to me with polite bemusement.

Stefano, the oldest, was known as Il Papa. His skin was loose and his teeth in pieces. When he asked my job, I said that I was a pilgrim. Stefano frowned. I said that I was hiking to Rome and then Jerusalem. He kept frowning. I explained my route from here to the capital: east across Piedmont and Lombardy, south over the Apennines, and then south-east via Tuscany and Lazio. He cut me off:

'You want to walk. Yes, we have a word for that. No, not a pilgrim. We say *un randagio*.'

I took out my dictionary and looked up the word. *Randagio* (nm), stray. So now I had a nickname.

There were twelve beds in the dormitory, with ageing frames that wheezed through the night. The bed next to mine was occupied by a middle-aged man wearing a leather jacket and a leather tie. His name was Aldo, his nickname Il Bagarino – the tout. Aldo had travelled round much of Britain and started listing cities to see if I had been too. His tone was earnest, severe, as if our whole conversation depended on my answer.

'Stoke? Blackburn? Huddersfield?' he asked.

I shook my head.

'Bolton? Luton? Wigan?'

I wondered which one was his favourite.

'London I did not like. My God, how I hated it. But Conwy? Conwy I liked.'

I kept asking questions and eventually learnt that Aldo's sister was married to a man from Yorkshire, a Sheffield Wednesday fan who had taken him to a half-season of away games. My neighbour's opinion of each place was based on the outcome of the match.

He went on: 'Preston? Ipswich? Barnsley?' Nope. 'Stirling? Sunderland? Leith?'

I told him I had spent a few summers in Edinburgh.

'Edinburgh?' He grimaced. 'My God, how I hated it.'

Aldo was puzzled by the pilgrimage. 'You want to drive?' he asked, unfolding my maps. 'Seven hours. You want to walk?' His finger traced the nine hundred kilometres between here and the capital. 'Two months.'

'I'm hoping to get there for Easter.'

'Easter?'

'The end of March. Five weeks.'

'Two months,' he repeated, now jabbing the map with his thumb.

Supper was at seven. The wallpaper in the kitchen had been stripped, leaving sheets of pockmarked plaster. We sat at a long table with a vinyl tablecloth, while Stefano served eleven plates of tortellini. Tomorrow Italy would choose a new prime minister, and everyone had an opinion about who should win. They all spoke at the same time, however, so I could not follow what was being said. But, as one man pretended to throttle the candidates and another mimed pulling out his hair, I began to guess their opinions. Yet the more they gestured and shouted, the less I could believe they cared. The whole debate had the sham urgency of a performance, making me wonder if their bluster and noise was simply evidence of helplessness. But, surrounded by this show of anger, I felt like a pretender for the first time on my pilgrimage.

During a lull in the argument I asked whether any of them would vote.

'Why do the politicians want us to vote?' Stefano shouted.

Aldo slapped the tablecloth. 'How many times have you voted?'

Stefano kept shouting: 'I tell you why. If I vote, and the man I vote for, if he wins, then what? Then I am to blame.'

'I swear to God Il Papa never votes.'

'Everything he does, I am to blame!'

'Never knows how to vote.'

Stefano folded his arms. 'So tomorrow I will spend the whole day in church, and nobody can blame Il Papa.' There was a moment's silence; then more shouts, more cries, and the whole performance started again.

Next day the country voted. The result was divided between the centre-left, the centre-right and a protest party led by a stand-up comedian. For the rest of my time in Italy the news was full of deadlock.

Into the Po Valley, the great plain that stretches the width of northern Italy. The Via Francigena crossed the plain at La Padana Bassa, its lowest and most fertile region. This was marshland once, drained by Cistercians in the fifteenth century and dredged into paddy fields. Strips of stubble ran from the track to the horizon, divided by dykes, ditches and concrete canals, which netted the ground in strands of silver water.

Entering La Padana Bassa I felt sure I was being followed. Whenever a breeze scuffed the path, I snapped round to see who was there. At one point I even climbed onto a sluice gate to scan for a figure in the distance. The sky was grey, and the earth was grey, and the waterways formed patterns like Nazca lines. Bleached light, starched soil and a vacant sense of space – of course I was alone. But, standing on the gate, I felt very small against the landscape, and the quick confidence that had carried me off the Alps became a prickling uncertainty.

Otherwise I walked fast with eyes to the floor. It was already the third week of Lent, and I needed to make up time. I did not believe Aldo's claim that Rome was two months away, but I fretted about the days lost to snow. Although the weather was dry now, I saw no sign of spring, only a dead still that reminded me of midwinter.

Each night I stayed in a presbytery or parish house. The priests who hosted me seemed preoccupied. They worried about Italy, worried about Europe, and worried about the Church, apologizing for the Pope's resignation as if somehow responsible.

The one exception was Fr Nunzio, whom I met at the

Abbazia di Sant'Albino. The abbey remains lay outside the town of Mortara: a Romanesque church in front, some Gothic ruins at the back and a barn-shaped hall between. Two caretakers looked after the place, a fidgety couple in their mid-fifties. The wife was called Gigi, the husband Francesco.

Antiques littered the hall's interior, either lying on the floor or balanced by the wall, waiting to be hung. It was a tatty collection: an icon inked onto a wooden board, a longsword flaking with rust, and a metal standard with the flag torn loose. When I asked what they were for, Francesco twitched. He could not explain . . . It was best that I waited . . . Fr Nunzio would be here soon.

The priest arrived that evening. He had sweeping eyebrows and a sagging smile, and when he spoke he flapped his wrists like a bird with a broken wing. We got to work: Francesco lifting the antiques to the wall, Gigi directing him with tuts and yelps, while I marked the place each one would hang. As we worked, Fr Nunzio invented stories about the items, telling us how the icon was marched through Lombardy by penitent processions and the standard carried to Jerusalem by crusader knights. And the sword? Why that was the holy blade of St Albino.

Then we ate together in the kitchen. During the meal Francesco and Gigi listened to a radio report on the favourites for the next pope. Afterwards they discussed the candidates, lighting cigarettes and stubbing them out half-smoked. I had heard some version of this conversation in half the Italian parishes I visited. It ranged from Vatican banking practices to the birth rate in South America, touching on the politics of more than a dozen prelates: the Archbishop of Milan, the Canadian Primate, a senior member of the Curia and an Austrian cardinal who was also a count. At first I listened with interest, but this soon turned into boredom, for the discussions never reached any conclusion and there seemed little comfort in worrying the questions again and again.

Eventually the caretakers went quiet and the priest spoke:

'Some of my parish, they say we must have a black pope, like the President of America. Some say a young pope – forty-five, fifty, no more. My nephew, he is not yet eleven, but this morning he says: *I will be pope! Me!* And every day we hear on the news that another candidate is *papabile*. Today a cardinal from Africa, tomorrow from Mexico, Brazil. Why is that? I tell you it is because the journalists want the election to be politics. Then they take all the problems of the world – not just the problems of the Church, but poverty and sickness – and they say: *Who will solve these problems? Who can fix the world?* But we are not choosing a politician. We are trying to learn the will of God.'

Francesco asked if there would be a new pope for Easter. Fr Nunzio's eyebrows danced, but he gave nothing away.

'Tomorrow we say goodbye to Benedict. We will have no pope, no prime minister, and no government. Italy will be like Belgium! Who can say how long it will last? You want to know my prediction? I predict God will surprise us.'

Gigi smoked. Francesco twitched. Fr Nunzio flapped his wrists. The radio was still playing, but the signal kept fading, so we sat and listened to the static, as if awaiting some fateful news. Again I had the sense that I was acting the part of a pilgrim, because the Vatican politics seemed silly to me. And, though I wanted to interrupt my brooding hosts, I knew that nothing I said could surface them now.

One day after the resignation I reached Pavia, a university town on the northern bank of the River Ticino.

Its buildings were a dull shade of orange, its piazzas a bright shade of brown. Although I was planning to visit Basilica San Pietro, where St Augustine lay buried beneath a sky of glazed gold, I could not find the place. Every church I passed looked the same – facades of burnt brick with sandstone buttresses clamping the corners – and I spent an hour or more wandering between Duomo di Pavia, San Michele Maggiore and Santa Maria del Carmine.

Eventually I came to a cobbled piazza north of the city centre and realized that the basilica was standing to one side, screened behind scaffolding. Its doors were locked, so I sat on my rucksack and waited. Three hours later I was still waiting.

Sitting there, I read a newspaper report on the Pope's last day. After leaving the Vatican Benedict was flown to Castel Gandolfo, where a crowd had gathered to wish him farewell. His words to the crowd were printed as a headline: *From this evening I will no longer be a pontiff. I will simply be a pilgrim who is starting the final stage of his pilgrimage on earth.* The newspaper also printed a profile of Benedict, explaining that, as a theologian, he championed the term *pilgrim people of God* for the Church. Then, as a cardinal, his coat of arms centred on a scallop shell, the pilgrim symbol. But my eyes kept catching on the date of Benedict's birth: 16 April, the feast day of Benoît-Joseph Labre. Pavia, the Pope, the patron saint of pilgrims – everything was linked, like the webbed waterways of La Padana Bassa, but I was not high enough to see the pattern. Instead, as with the homeless men in Ivrea, or the caretakers in Mortara, I could only wait for the future to reveal itself.

So then I hiked east along the Po. The earth beside the river was banked to protect from flooding, and my route ran over the embankment. Rough stone villages clustered on the hills to the north, but the floodplain was almost empty. Each morning began with mist, clearing by midday to reveal washed-out scenery like an abstract canvas.

On Sunday afternoon I stopped at a hamlet called Corte Sant'Andrea. Nearby, a weatherboard landing dipped down to the Po. The water seemed shrunken, with a greyish sheen that reminded me of the grease on boiled meat.

According to Fr Nunzio, pilgrims used to gather here to cross the river by boat, for there was no bridge before Piacenza. Fifteen years ago, after the Via Francigena was revived, a local boatman named Danilo Parisi began ferrying pilgrims across again. The priest had asked if I wanted a lift, but I told him I was supposed to be travelling on foot. However, he insisted this was the medieval route and rang the boatman to arrange my passage. At first Danilo was reluctant – Sunday was his day off – but eventually he agreed to meet me. Three o'clock. On the landing. Don't be late.

Danilo turned up around five. He was bulky and blushing, shouting apologies as he sped towards me in a dented motorboat. From the shouts I gathered that he had been hosting a lunch party which went on too long.

As the boat slowed near the landing, Danilo held out his hand. His arms were massive, the fingers callused and the palms chalky.

When I leant forwards, he pulled me on board. Then we swept into open water.

The river was so low that the boat seemed to be slipping along the skin of the earth. A depth counter showed how close we were to the riverbed, flickering from eight metres to six metres to three. Danilo veered between the shallows, cutting the engine every few minutes to announce that we had beached, that I must climb out and push. Each time I refused – growing more and more irritated behind a fixed grin – he would sob with laughter and speed on. The rest of the time he told jokes, or sang songs, or repeated stories about the pilgrims he had ferried across before me. He mentioned a film crew from the Netherlands, a unit of Swiss Guard, and another British pilgrim travelling alone. That pilgrim spoke like me, but was older, fatter – my father, perhaps? When I shook my head, the boatman looked disappointed. And, when I boasted about reaching Rome for the new pope, he looked dismayed. Benedict was gone! Berlusconi was gone! Danilo's heart was broken in two!

Trees dragged along the bank, and the sides of the channel blurred. The silt was the colour of putty, the shingle soft like clay, the water banded grey and blue, blue and grey. Above, the clouds reamed past and the sky stretched wide – as if the world was spinning faster, or the seasons streaming by.

Four kilometres downstream, metal rungs climbed onto the opposite shore. After we moored the boat, Danilo led the way up the rungs. A pair of terriers were tied near the top, yapping with boredom. My companion asked if I wanted to see his home and then shambled off without waiting for an answer, the dogs tripping at his feet.

The boatman lived in a bloated brick farmhouse crouched behind the floodbank. A bronze sign was pinned to the wall, smeared blue by the mist off the river. The sign gave estimated distances to Rome (588 km), Jerusalem (2,975 km), Canterbury (1,313 km), and Santiago (1,995 km).

As I put down my rucksack, Danilo counted off the

towns and cities before the capital: 'Piacenza, Fidenza, Pontremoli, Pietresanta, Lucca, San Miniato, San Gimignano, Siena . . .' He stopped speaking, started laughing. 'Maybe if you hitchhike. All alone – nobody will know!'

I laughed as well, but my voice sounded forced. Then I stopped laughing, because today was 3 March, the third Sunday of Lent. Twenty-one days until Holy Week. Six hundred kilometres to go.

Three middle-aged men were left over from lunch, sitting in the half-timbered barn and sharing a bottle of wine. On catching sight of Danilo they cheered. He motioned me to join them and then went into the house, returning with two more bottles and a red leather ledger, the words *Liber Peregrinorum* stamped on the cover. As I signed the ledger, Danilo offered me some wine. When I turned him down, he asked if I was fasting for Lent.

'I don't drink.'

'Not a Catholic?'

'Not a Catholic.'

'Maybe once you get to Rome—' Another sob of laughter.

I wanted to agree, but could not pretend that I was a believer. So I said that I was still getting used to the Catholic churches I visited on the route. At first I was put off by their gaudy interiors – the paintings and relics that decorated every altar, the statues and candles that crowded each chapel – until I learnt to see the longing in these displays, more sincere than the simple Protestant spaces I was used to. Yet I still felt wary of religion as spectacle, because the scale and splendour were proof not of truth but of power.

'No, no,' said Danilo. 'Religion has to be bigger than us.'

During lunch the three friends had decided on an

Easter pilgrimage to Bobbio, an abbey on the northern fringe of the Apennines. They started discussing the idea, while one of the three traced their route on my map. It meandered south from here for sixty-six kilometres, lifting into the Trebbia Valley.

'Why Bobbio?' I asked.

'There were pilgrims to Bobbio since before the Middle Ages,' the friend replied. 'It was founded by St Columbanus, the pilgrim saint of Ireland.'

'Francis of Assisi stayed there when he was a young man,' Danilo added. 'The monks showed him how to live in the forest and preach to the animals.'

At this point everyone started talking. No, no, claimed one, that was a local legend. But, claimed another, this region was where the friars were most popular. Mendicants, penitents, flagellants – Emilia Romagna was full of them, said Danilo. Then the friends began listing devotional movements. There was the Humiliati, a brotherhood of twelfth-century penitents based in Lombardy; and the Great Alleluia, a revivalist uprising that overwhelmed the Po Valley in the thirteenth century; and Venturino of Bergamo, who led a peace march to Rome in the early fourteenth century. Although I tried to note down their names, I soon lost track, becoming dizzy with each new detail.

One word was repeated several times: *jubileus*. I wasn't sure what it meant, so the youngest friend had a go at translating. 'It's Latin. It means no more debts, no more sins. You are set free, yes?'

No more debts, free from sin – was this the reason for their pilgrimage? It was hard to know what they believed behind the swaggering stories, the exaggerated laughter, and impossible to say whether they walked to find forgiveness. Yet I was glad for these rowdy exchanges, because they lessened the sense that my own walk was merely a stunt.

The men folded my map and finished their wine. When I asked how long their hike would take, Danilo marched me out of the barn and back onto the embankment.

'Bobbio,' he said, pointing south. 'Can you see?'

It was past six, but not yet dim, the daylight lasting late as a summer evening. To the south I could see a plain the colour of cloud, and beyond that I could see hills shaped like rippling water. Beyond that lay the rim of the earth, bruise blue where it touched the sky. Blue was the mountains. Blue was the Apennines.

Next morning the mist was too dense to see the far bank of the Po. I kept hiking east, approaching Piacenza through cloud thick as cloth, thick as ink. The smell of smoke lay on the river, and the air tasted black and bitter. Danilo's history lesson was still on my mind, his list of devotional movements repeating in my thoughts.

These were pilgrims too, of course, not solitary monks but mobs of pious laity. Yet I found their motives much harder to understand. I felt some sympathy for the missionaries and martyrs I had learnt about in Switzerland, but the popular side of religion inspired only bafflement and mistrust. It was easier to dismiss it as madness than work out why so many believers would willingly abandon themselves.

Most of these movements travelled via Piacenza. The city lay at a crossroads, where the Via Francigena joined the Via Emilia. This was another Roman road, linking Parma, Reggio, Modena, and Bologna, with Rimini on the Adriatic coast. Had I hiked its course in the autumn of 1260, I would have met an unusual collection of pilgrims. Penitents mostly, moving in shambolic groups –

sometimes a few hundred, sometimes a few thousand. I would have heard them first, for as they walked they chanted psalms. Closer, I would have seen the blood-black stains on their robes and the whips hanging loose from their hands. Closer still, I would I have smelt them, smelt sweat and salt and the reek of open wounds.

These were the first flagellants.

Flagellation had been practised in monasteries since the turn of the millennium. It was made fashionable in the late eleventh century by Peter Damian, a Benedictine prior who argued that a flagellant could atone for sin by whipping himself while reciting psalms.

The prior's most famous disciple was a monk called Dominic Loricatus. He was a champion flagellant, once managing three hundred thousand lashes during a quiet week in Lent. Following Damian's calculus, the monk performed a hundred years of purification. By my own estimate, he managed fifty blows a minute.

In the mid-thirteenth century the practice spread from the cloister. This timing was no coincidence, as Italian society was ringing with apocalyptic prophecies. The most famous was by a Cistercian monk called Joachim of Fiore, who was born in Calabria about a century earlier. As a young man he went on pilgrimage to the Holy Land and then devoted himself to reading the Book of Revelation. His commentary on the text forecast a third and final stage of history, a kingdom of the Holy Spirit that would be realized once the Antichrist brought untold suffering to the world. That dreadful reckoning was due in the year 1260.

Although Joachim died long before Judgement Day, his prophecy was not forgotten. The monk's followers were so numerous that Pope Alexander IV had to condemn his work in 1256. But it was too late. Next year, Genoa and Venice went to war, the year after there was famine in the Po Valley, and in 1259 a plague struck central Italy. Surely the Antichrist was on his way.

That spring a hermit living in the hills above Perugia received a vision. Because of mankind's sin, the vision revealed, God had decided to destroy the world. However, at the last minute the Virgin Mary stayed his hand. If we repented, we might yet be saved.

The hermit's name was Raniero Fasani. Like Joachim of Fiore, he was convinced of the coming apocalypse. But, like Peter Damian, he also believed that flagellation could lessen the penalty of sin.

Fasani went to the Bishop of Perugia with his vision. In order to be saved, he warned, the whole city must join in penance. The bishop was persuaded, and for six weeks the men of Perugia gathered outside to flog themselves, chanting, *'Misericordia, misericordia! Pace, pace!'* At home women and even children took part in the rite.

That autumn the ceremonies spread to northern Italy. The flagellants formed processions, tramping back and forth along the Via Emilia and attracting up to ten thousand penitents at a time. In 1260 they reached Rome and that winter copycat ceremonies sprang up in Bavaria, Bohemia and Poland. At first local clergy welcomed the movement, because the ceremonies were a chance for debts to be settled and feuds forgiven. That is the promise of penance: freedom from guilt, freedom from shame, the burden of sin shed from our backs. But it was heady stuff. As Peter Damian wrote, a flagellant 'bore in his body the stigmata of Jesus'. He need only look at his reflection, naked and bloody, to catch a glimpse of the crucified Christ.

Church authorities started to worry that the processions would descend into heresy, while civil authorities worried that they would cause riots. Flagellation was too popular, too unruly, and in January 1261 the Pope banned the movement. The bishops who had encouraged the practice now shut it down, and, as quickly as they began, the ceremonies died away. Or so it seemed.

After Piacenza I turned south into the Apennines, spending six days hiking across the range. In all that time I never once saw the sun. Sometimes, as my route rose through forested valleys, the showers would part to reveal hillsides of beech, their leaves dead but not fallen, gleaming like wet copper. Otherwise there were no colours, no shapes, no shining things in all the world, just the sodden vegetation, the smothered outlines of peaks, and the ceaseless sheets of rain.

Everything seeped. My waterproof trousers, my waterproof jacket and the waterproof cover for my rucksack. And the contents of the rucksack: notebooks, clothes, sleeping bag, food – all of them soaked through. My drenched boots weighed double and the skin on my feet blanched, the toes tender, rotting.

The Via Francigena lifted to the Cisa Pass and then lowered into Tuscany. For the first few days I climbed between hilltop hamlets unmarked on the map. To pass the time I sang to myself – thumping Victorian hymns half-remembered from schooldays – or else conjured lists of familiar items – every English county, every Shakespeare play. When my memory was exhausted, I became bored, and as the days dragged and the weather got worse, that boredom was edged with dread. How much longer could this weather last?

The third morning in the Apennines was stormy. Thunderheads streamed off the heights and fractus clouds tumbled over the road. The rain clattered on my hood – *pop* and *clink* and *thud* – while thunder played in the peaks above.

Around midday a pair of buildings heaved up out of

the storm. The first was a farmhouse, the second a shut-tered cafe. A sign on the corner of the house read, *Passo della Cisa*. This was it, the pass to Tuscany, 1,039 metres above sea level – dim as the deepest reach of a gorge.

Beyond the sign, at the highpoint of the pass, I found a chapel. On sunny days its tinted windows might let in a dusty disco light, but that morning the room was gloomy. Electric candles guttered against plastic icons and a glow-in-the-dark rosary dangled from a plaster statue. Chandeliers hung off the ceiling, their branches gilded, their bulbs gone. I could smell wet wool, damp stone, and the musty odour of compost.

I sat in a pew and waited for my sight to adjust. Silk flowers lay over the altar, the leaves a deep green, almost black. The storm made a flailing sound on the roof, but otherwise the chapel was quiet.

I was still thinking about the flagellants.

In January 1348, almost a century after Raniero Fasani's vision, an earthquake hit north-east Italy. Churches crumbled across the Po Valley and a stench of rotting eased from great rents in the ground. That spring the Black Death entered the country via the ports of Genoa, Venice and Pisa. Again it seemed the world was ending. Again the flagellants marched.

Their ceremonies soon spread beyond the Alps. By the end of the year they were taking place in Switzerland and Hungary, and come 1349 there were ceremonies in Flan-ders, Holland and Denmark too.

Flagellants in northern Europe modelled themselves on crusader armies. They refused to wash, shave or sleep in a bed, but dressed as knights and adopted ominous names such as the Brothers of the Cross. Their processions lasted thirty-three days – one for every year of Christ's life – and while they walked they chanted folk songs called *Geissler-lieder*, celebrating the Second Coming.

When the flagellants stopped at a church or cathedral, they would gather outside the entrance, while their leader, known as the Master, read a copy of a letter handed down from heaven. The pilgrims then marched in circles, leaping to the ground to confess their sins, before kneeling in ranks, stripped to the chest, and whipping their bodies with leather thongs, some flogging themselves for 6,666 stripes – the mythic number of blows suffered by Christ – and others studding their thongs with metal to scourge the skin from their backs, hacking away until the metal snagged on muscle and the Master had to kneel beside them, yanking the staple loose and causing gouts of blood to spray over the ground.

Because the flagellants claimed to be taking on the sins of the world, they were treated as martyrs. Crowds turned up to witness the ceremonies, the sick and dying collecting vials of blood, and the blind pressing stained robes to their eyes. In Strasbourg the penitents were even given a dead child to revive.

The movement was most popular in towns not yet afflicted by plague, where people hoped the ceremonies would protect them. When it became clear that they were helping to spread the sickness, local authorities cracked down. At this point the processions grew violent. Priests were stoned and Jewish neighbourhoods set alight, while in the forests of central Germany one flagellant Master baptized himself in the blood of his followers and vowed to march until Judgement Day.

In October 1349 Clement VI condemned the movement via papal bull. Although the Pope had patronized the early processions in Avignon, he now outlawed the practice, and once more the ceremonies were suppressed.

As I sat in the chapel, listening to the storm, I could not understand why anyone would join the flagellants. Histories of the Black Death treat the movement with a mixture of horror and fascination, as well as a few know-ing smiles. For some there might have been an erotic thrill, but the majority took part because they were ter-rified of pain. They were not trying to scar their bodies, but to free their souls from suffering. This paradox makes sense if you believe that death brings judgement. What was an hour or two of anguish compared with the howl-ing tortures of hell? Yet such arguments mattered less than the strange seduction of the ceremony, and this was what I struggled to understand: the giddy moment when the self was given up, the awful thrill of surrender.

I could still hear the rain on the roof, the tap and drum, the rattle and snare. It seemed to be leaking through the ceiling, dripping onto the twisted chandeliers and the pale skin of the statue. The altar stained, the fabric decayed, and the flowers bleeding black tongues of silk.

That afternoon I dropped seven hundred and fifty me-tres, back below the cloudline. Rain lisped in the trees and applauded against the cliffs, while the wind ransacked the villages, pulling chimneys and rooftiles apart. A motor-way hung off the western wall of the valley, the traffic making a shredding sound as it drove by, tyres skimming over plate water. Lower down, these sounds were lost to the rushing chorus of the River Magra.

Pontremoli was a cheerless town splayed above the river. I spent a night at the Capuchin monastery on its southern boundary. The walls of my cell were mottled with mould and none of the radiators worked. Although it was just gone seven, I had no choice but to strip my sodden clothes, spread them on the floor and slip naked under six woollen blankets. Yet I could not sleep, as every half-hour one of the friars opened the door to ask for money, because the brothers were so poor, so poor.

After four days of rain the forest paths were slipping away. I threw out my blotted maps and tried the road instead. The tarmac uncoiled along the banks of the River Magra – one side bordered with rock, the other side sunk under water. For much of the morning I hiked on the valley side, pressed into the rockface as trucks drove keen against the kerb. Otherwise I hiked on the river side, jumping the surf from cars as they ploughed through the flooded verge. Whichever side I chose, I regretted it.

Some of the cars slowed to offer me a lift. At one point a taxi stopped, the driver calling for me to get in. He said he would drive me for free, drive me to the steps of St Peter's, but when I told him I had to walk, he crossed himself and shouted that he could not help me.

The road veered from left to right, sinking through towns of gathered grey. In Villafranca I squatted in the wreck of a cement factory, eating clammy bread and cheese. In Lusuolo I sheltered beneath the concrete stilts of the motorway, in Masero under the crippled arches of a railway bridge. Otherwise I limped along, counting my paces – one *two*, three *four*, five *six*, seven *eight* – and with each pace grew more and more frustrated. *When I get to Italy the route will be easy* – that's what I had expected. But now I wanted to go home. Eight hours, ten hours of rain, day after day, my clothes never drying, my will drip-dripping away. Nipples chafing, skin shrivelled, sores lining my inner thigh. And then the doubt: why walk every step if you don't even believe?

Day five in the Apennines. The air dim and hurting.

Bodies lay by the roadside: a burst hedgehog, a maimed rabbit and a polecat turned inside out. And a heron with its wings fanned flat as a deck of cards.

Danilo's voice was scratching in my head. *Maybe if you hitchhike. All alone – nobody will know.*

When a car drove past, I tried to thumb a lift, but it did not even slow. The second car was the same, and the third car, the fourth. Then I withdrew my arm and trudged on, face hot with shame. I was sorry I had started this journey, sorry I ever left home, and wished now that the walk was over.

That afternoon the rain beat so hard I started laughing. Raindrops hammered the road, flying up like sparks. The sound grew louder and louder, building to a crescendo, never seeming to break. I could not stop laughing.

A deserted house stood on the verge, its upper storeys part-collapsed. Rain splashed through the door and spilled from the first-floor window. I went up to the house, took off my hood and stood beneath the stream. Water washed through my hair and trickled down my spine. There was water in my eyes, in the sockets, and water flooding my mouth. It smelt of iron, tasted of blood. Sharp, sharper – until I could not feel the water any more, until I felt nothing at all. But I stayed where I was, letting it pour from my fingers in strands of black silk. I stayed where I was, surrendered to the storm.

Sometimes the fear of pain is worse than the pain itself. Sometimes pain is a release from fear, frees us from our thoughts, keeps us close to the living moment. And sometimes, when we make our own suffering, the pain is a feeling like power.

On the sixth day I passed a roadside shrine tangled with gifts. There were toy lion cubs, a dinosaur from a Disney cartoon, and a baptism dress foaming with lace. Each one was labelled with a card, names and dates and messages of thanks written on the back. I wanted to read the messages, but everything was soaked, the gifts bleeding colour and the messages bleeding too, dyeing the card a watery blue.

A staircase led into the trees behind the shrine, rising towards a chapel. I began climbing, but halfway up I paused. To my right was a clearing, and beyond the clearing I could see the clouds part and the valley open wide.

As I watched the landscape compose itself, I felt a sudden swell of relief, like being lifted on a wave. Ahead I could see the empty sky, the flushed earth, the bits and pieces of rainbow – and a yawning space near the horizon which I guessed was the sea.

So now I had reached Tuscany.

Departing from Canterbury, I thought I was leaving the world behind. At first the solitude was exhilarating, because I did not know how I would cope alone. Walking in the Alps seemed heroic – the first winter pilgrim to cross the pass in decades – but the Apennines spoilt any sense of adventure. In the rain that same solitude was punishing, an empty space where my doubts could amplify, and I began to feel trapped by the very isolation that I once sought. Fortunately, at the mission house in Siena, I met my first pilgrims.

It was part of a convent – Convento Figlie della Carità di San Vincenzo de'Paoli – with a soup kitchen on the ground floor and bedrooms on the first. The walls downstairs were painted grey, and sacks of donated clothing sat in the corners. A group of single mothers lived upstairs, either looking for jobs or finishing college courses.

Sr Ginetta was in charge. She wore a blue fleece and a pleated blue skirt, and as we marched round the house she asked quickfire questions. How long had I been walking? What route did I take? All alone? All the way to Rome? You like walking? And Tuscany, you like Tuscany?

This, roughly, was how I answered:

After leaving the Apennines I went south along the Tyrrhenian Sea, past orange groves blushing with new fruit and marble yards stacked with uncut rock. The Apuan Alps rose to my left, quarries cracking the heights like still-lying snow. Strips of suburb bordered the mountains – towns, villages and coastal resorts sprawling into one another. Then I turned inland through a landscape of small valleys, small farms. The hills were hatched with cypresses, and the fields had the brushed look of suede. I packed away my gloves, my fleece, and walked upright into the warming weather, stopping each evening at the monasteries and presbyteries of medieval towns: Lucca, San Miniato, San Gimignano, and Colle di Val d'Elsa. Their buildings were stooped, their streets narrow, and their painted houses formed uneven ranks of amber and peach, ochre and cream. I told Sr Ginetta it was the most beautiful scenery I had seen this far, and just a little bit dull. She laughed and slapped her thigh.

One of the convent's first-floor rooms was a dormitory, with metal-framed bunk beds and starched sheets. Two pilgrims had already arrived, both dressed in Lycra sports gear. Giacomo was in his mid-sixties, a stocky man with a savage face. His left leg was kicked against the wall, while he massaged the hamstring between two balled fists. Oscar, his son-in-law, was about forty, his arms and chest fat with muscle. He lay on a bed, groaning and rubbing his eyes.

The two pilgrims left Lombardy a fortnight ago. 'We keep to the tarmac,' said Oscar. 'We don't stop to rest. Forty kilometres, forty-five, every day.'

'Why so fast?' I asked.

Giacomo swaggered towards me, standing too close and breathing in my face. His skin was red. His jaw bristled. The tendons on his neck stuck out like fiddle strings. 'Pilgrimage is not a holiday,' he said.

He started asking questions. With each answer I gave, his expression grew more and more contorted. No, I did not spend an hour a day begging for food. No, I did not recite a rosary while I hiked. No, I was not travelling as penance. No, I had not seen any miracles en route.

Oscar got off the bed. 'He's like me. He's an athlete.'

Giacomo scoffed. 'So why walk to Rome for Easter?'

I opened my mouth, shut it. My journey was neither a leisurely holiday, nor some marathon fitness session. Instead, as I tried to explain, I wanted to learn about religion by taking part in a ritual.

'No, no,' said Oscar. 'You're an athlete. You love to race.'

At that point a third pilgrim arrived. The pilgrim's features were handsome but damaged: his face long, his jaw strong and his broad nose broken several times. Grey hair spooled down from his nostrils, and his eyebrows were fringed with grey fibres. Meanwhile his rucksack was torn, the canvas sewn together with string, and another tear, in the left leg of his trousers, gaped to show a knee joint strapped in gauze.

When the stranger stepped through the door, Giacomo shouted: 'Lorenzo! We thought you gave up! We asked the hospitals, the police—'

It turned out that father and son-in-law had overtaken the new pilgrim earlier in the day. He walked too slowly, Oscar explained, much too slowly.

'An ordinary speed,' said Lorenzo, face creased with frustration. 'Four kilometres, five kilometres an hour.'

'We asked the nuns, the priests,' Giacomo went on. 'We thought maybe you turned back. Maybe you went home.'

'An ordinary speed,' Lorenzo said again. 'Not too fast, not too slow.'

The convent's dining room was downstairs. Three women stood round the table, laying out bowls of soup, pasta and salad, as well as plastic cutlery and paper plates. One was from Kosovo, another from the Ivory Coast, and the third from a village south of Naples. Ines, the African woman, spoke to me in French as she sliced her son's food. Meanwhile, her daughter skipped laps of the table, until Giacomo started conjuring sweets from behind the girl's ears. Oscar sat with the other women, telling stories about how far he had travelled, how fast. 'Look at my beard,' he said, raking his fingers through a fortnight's rusty stubble. 'Look at my feet,' he added, removing his socks to show pulped flesh. 'Two hundred and sixty kilometres to go!'

Lorenzo's expression was scornful. 'Why are you racing?'

'I don't have time to walk slow.'

'You have time.'

'I have a job.'

'Quit your job.'

'I have a family.'

'Take a bus to Rome.'

'I'm an athlete.'

'Or a bike.'

'A pilgrim has to walk.'

This went on for the rest of the meal. Occasionally Giacomo tried to interrupt, but the two men kept quarrelling, until they were simply parroting phrases at one another: *An athlete, an athlete ... Not too fast, not too slow ...* The three women were quiet now, and Ines's daughter had crawled beneath the table, hands to her ears. Then Giacomo rose from his chair to propose a toast. '*Habemus Papam!*' he cried, smiling his savage smile. Last week, on the second day of the papal conclave, white smoke had gone up from the Sistine Chapel. An Argentine cardinal had been appointed pope: the first pontiff from Latin America. But the decision was popular here too, because his family were originally Italian.

Oscar stood as well. 'Mario Bergoglio!' he shouted. 'From Piedmont!'

Lorenzo remained seated, muttering, 'Pope Francis, St Francis, the poor man of Assisi.' At the same time, the three women began clearing the table, their movements rushed as if anxious to get away. I hurried to help them, trying to distance myself from the other three pilgrims.

Every day the nuns provided lunch for 120 people. When our meal was over, Sr Ginetta brought out a plastic crate of lettuce and ham, and a bin bag full of buns. We formed an assembly line: Giacomo unpacking the ingredients, Oscar slicing the buns, Lorenzo layering each one with lettuce and ham, while I wrapped the whole lot in clingfilm. As we worked, the atmosphere in the room calmed. Oscar sang football chants, and Giacomo rushed ahead. Lorenzo took his time, counting out 120 parcels of food, until Sr Ginetta drummed the table and the children clapped him faster.

The athletes left Siena not long after sunrise. By nine o'clock Lorenzo and I were also away. Heading south from the Porta Romana, there was blossom by the roadside – pinkish petals lacing the cherry trees.

Lorenzo asked whether I knew the date. I wasn't sure. If we arrived in Siena on the fifth Sunday of Lent, today must be . . . Passiontide?

He shook his head. 'Today is the first day of spring. Today nature forgives our sins.'

Soon we were clear of the city, climbing onto dune-shaped hills of sandy yellow and corduroy brown. The grass on the hillsides waved in the wind, the dunes shifting over the earthbed. We followed a chalk path, a tarmac cycling track, and a potholed road between farm buildings converted into holiday homes. Swells of green lapped the road – moss green, olive green, mint green too, crested with strands of gold. Lorenzo was right. Spring was on its way.

Usually I walked quickly and stopped often. My companion walked at a steadier pace, breaking every two or three hours. I had no practice hiking in tandem and grew impatient trying to match him – my legs tense, muscles pent, movements crabbed as if cased in armour. Lorenzo showed no sign of moving faster, however, only muttered his favourite mantra ('An ordinary speed! Not too fast, not too slow . . .') and slapped at imaginary insects.

I was hoping that, after a few days together, we would be firm friends. One-on-one conversations, stretched out over hours, were what I liked best. But my companion spent the whole morning lecturing me on Movimento Cinque Stelle, the protest party that won a quarter of the seats at the last election. He told me that Cinque Stelle was against politicians, against lawyers, against armies and energy corporations and banks. The party's leader was a comedian called Beppe Grillo – 'A funny man for a crazy time!'

Was this the reason people voted for him? I wondered, but Lorenzo shook his head. 'Grillo speaks for us all. Like a prophet. Lorenzo is his number one fan. His number one fan.' Did I know that Cinque Stelle was founded on 4 October, the feast day of St Francis? And that the followers of St Francis were the first environmentalists? That's right, said Lorenzo, the best way to help the environment was to imitate St Francis. The mendicant life – travelling on foot, living off charity – that would save the planet.

'Is that why you're walking to Rome?' I asked.

'I walk as protest,' Lorenzo replied. 'Pilgrimage is protest.'

That afternoon he talked about motorway construction and industrial fishing, about tidal energy and the

Chinese space programme. Some vague conspiracy linked these subjects, but I could not follow its logic. Yet I understood where it was heading, because each time Lorenzo stopped speaking – when he checked his map, or admired the view, or paused to pee behind a thicket of laurel – he would murmur the phrase, '*Il Diluvio universale.*'

Around teatime the hills shrugged down to a winding stream called the Arbia. Our route slumped too, sinking between a railway track and a ditch slick with rainwater. Wildflowers chequered the sides of the ditch, teams of tiny frogs diving into the water when we passed. They left no wake as they slipped beneath the surface, only a faint pattern of hoops and coils. By now Lorenzo was rambling about the islands of plastic floating in the Pacific, while I nodded my head and longed for silence. Worried that I would have to listen to him the whole way to Rome, I also began plotting my escape.

At five o'clock we stopped in a village called Ponte d'Arbia, where the disused school had been turned into a pilgrim refuge. The assembly hall contained the remnants of a botched renovation: clotted paintbrushes, cracked tiles, scraps of carpet and scuds of Polyfilla, as well as sun-faded curtains and rubber bands stretched white with use. Upstairs, the classrooms were furnished with three beds each, their sheets clammy and the walls mildewed. Dust clumped the cobwebs, and a smell like damp towelling lingered in the air. I asked my companion if he wanted a room to himself, but he insisted we share.

Later that evening an odd thing happened. Lorenzo showered first and then wiped the bathroom with a mop. He asked me to do the same, so after showering I picked up the mop and began to clean. Its shaft was a tube of foil-thin metal with a welt across the middle, and when I pressed it to the floor, the whole thing folded.

Bother.

I went into the bedroom and asked Lorenzo if there was another.

'What's wrong with the mop?'

I tried to explain.

'You broke the mop?'

I tried once more.

'You think Lorenzo broke the mop?'

I tried a third time. It was no good.

'Why would Lorenzo break the mop?'

He seized the folded metal from my hands, knelt in the bathroom, and swabbed the floor. As he worked he muttered, '*Il Diluvio, il Diluvio.*' Then he got into bed and started reading the Bible, holding the pages very close to his face. When I offered to cook us a meal, he told me no, no food, he was fasting for the night.

That broad nose. That proud expression. Oh Lorenzo, I let you down.

Next morning I woke around five to the sound of packing. Sitting up, I saw my companion fastening his rucksack onto his shoulders. When I asked if he was leaving, he told me he wanted to walk alone. When I asked why, he barged out the door. I called after him, but heard no reply, so I turned over and went back to sleep. We were both glad to be alone again.

That was not my last encounter with Lorenzo. Two days later I reached a spread of clay hillocks called Val d'Orcia, where there were no trees, no grass, nothing but aged vines tying together the ruined earth. At the end of the valley a granite ridge rose to a thousand metres, marking the southern border of Tuscany. One of the peaks had a crumbling castle set upon its cusp. Below the castle stood Radicofani, a stone village facing south towards Lazio.

From here the even greens of Tuscany became a grey landscape of lakes and calderas and crests of volcanic rock.

Opposite the church I found a flat for pilgrims. The shelves were stacked with crockery and the cabinets crowded with games – packs of playing cards, boxes of draughts and a strategy game called *RisiKo!*, its broken board stuck together with tape. The dining table was long enough to seat twelve, the surface stinking of polish. A guestbook lay open at one end, containing entries from previous pilgrims. Lorenzo's was the first that I saw. He gave no address, only his name, his age, and a brief essay about *il Diluvio universale*. Oscar and Giacomo had stayed the night before, their message boasting that they would rise early and complete Lazio in a single dash.

I kept turning the pages, going back through the entries. Some of the messages I could translate, the rest only guess their meaning. A single word was repeated in every language: *Roma . . . Rom . . . Rim . . . Rome . . . Róma . . . Rzym.*

One pilgrim had been walking for seven years, ticking off half the shrines in Europe. He filled two pages with the list of towns and cities he had visited, but left no name or destination. Instead he left a drawing of a scallop shell and a single sentence: *30,000 chilometri per Christo.*

I flicked forwards to an empty page, wondering what to write. All winter I had travelled alone, and though at times I wished for company, I learnt to feel content by myself. Then I met three other pilgrims and that contentment came apart. My pilgrimage was not penance, not protest, not a race to Rome. And I was embarrassed by the real reason: a nonbeliever hoping a ritual would heal him. Yet, looking at the guestbook, I took some comfort from all the names. Hundreds of people must have hiked this way without knowing why. There was humility in this: setting off in the hope that the journey would make sense by the time you arrived. And honesty too, for who could travel all this distance without doubting their own motives?

Part of me wished Lorenzo was still here. I wanted to apologize, or else try to explain. But I knew we would never meet again, so I wrote my name at the top of the page and the words *thank you* in every language I could remember.

It was Friday morning. Holy Week began the day after tomorrow. Although I would miss Palm Sunday in Rome, I felt no disappointment as I dropped from Radicofani, only a restless anticipation. Entering Lazio, I stretched out my stride and gulped down the air, beaming at every person I passed. The capital was a hundred and seventy kilometres away, but I could count the stops between: Acquapendente, Bolsena, Viterbo, Sutri, Campagnano di Roma, and then the slow slog through the suburbs. So how long until St Peter's? A week? Less? Determined to make it in just six days, I walked hard all afternoon and that evening reached Acquapendente. Five days to go. One hundred and forty kilometres remaining.

On Saturday I was off early, hiking over deformed hillsides and through scraps of woodland. By mid-afternoon Lake Bolsena was in sight, the water wide as the horizon, like a second sky fitted beneath the first. A town extended along the shore, also called Bolsena, centred on a rambling church named Basilica di Santa Cristina. Its interior was pale marble, its ceiling braced with beams, and its tiles had the pinkish tint of scrubbed skin. A poster hung in the south vestry, showing an image I recognized from France: a boat, a cross, and the words

Annus Fidei printed beneath. The north vestry communicated with a chapel, a round Renaissance folly painted puffy yellow. After that came another chapel, and another, burrowing into the hillside, while the frescoed passageways weathered to worn plaster and raw tufa.

In the last chamber, a low catacomb, I found a statue of the saint laid on a bed of solid stone. The air was damp, the light dim, and my breath echoed off the ceiling. I thought of cells and crypts, of caverns and vaults, of sinking seven storeys into the earth. Then I closed my eyes and the tomb was dark. That was the fifth day.

I left Bolsena on Palm Sunday and climbed out of the lake basin. A road sign on the hillside marked one hundred kilometres to Rome. Then my path descended through fields of budding wheat.

Around six I stopped at Viterbo, a medieval town built from battered stone. One of the wall towers – in the gardens of an Augustinian monastery – had been converted into a pilgrim refuge. On the ground floor was a kitchen and a dining room, on the first floor a bank of showers. Two flights up was a dormitory containing eleven beds and a pair of west-facing windows. Through the window I could see the road to Rome scored with headlights.

I stood and watched the Sunday traffic rush towards the city. The capital was an hour's drive away, but the Via Francigena had another eighty-five kilometres to run. As evening deepened, the far-off lights became bright. One by one they blinked, flashed and fled into the dusk.

Then it was night. The fourth day.

Later I dreamed that I was bound in chains, that I was buried in a tomb. I dreamed that I was drowning and woke to the sound of rain.

It was still raining when I left Viterbo and headed south from the city. In the Cimini Hills I got lost in corridors of eroded sandstone. Every sign pointed the wrong way, every footpath sent me off course, and the urgency I had felt earlier in the week turned into a weary impatience. The rain retreated and the skies cleared, but I paid little attention to my surroundings, desperate now to reach the capital. So I did not notice the towns along the route – not Vetralla, not Capranica, nor the glistening lip of the Lago di Vico. Day three was done. Fifty-five kilometres to go.

On Tuesday afternoon I came to the town called Campagnano di Roma. The parish youth centre was a bare building made up of classrooms, changing rooms and strip-lit corridors. On the top floor was a gallery where pilgrims could stay – an altar at one end, hidden behind flax curtains, and foam mats piled at the other. Here I met a pair of women in their early twenties. Francesca was tall, her neck slender and her head floating loose like a balloon. Cecilia was smaller, hair cropped short except for a ribbon running down from the temple. Both women had graduated the year before last and drifted ever since – temping, volunteering, housesitting, babysitting and petsitting. One morning Francesca decided to come on pilgrimage. Of course Cecilia was free.

They left Siena a fortnight ago, covering twenty kilometres a day. 'But tomorrow we will be in Rome,' said Francesca. 'I don't believe it.'

An hour later we went to a cafe near the youth centre. Inside, the air was powdery, the smell mixed from baked dough and burnt sugar. Mirrors lined the walls, and when I caught sight of my reflection I felt embarrassed by the scruffy clothes, the patchy beard. All winter I had walked blind to my appearance, but that evening I felt self-conscious. Yet there was relief in this – in seeing myself through a stranger's eyes.

Cecilia scowled at her reflection, while Francesca ordered three plates of pasta and focaccia and chips. Then we ate together, the two friends telling stories from their journey. They talked a mixture of Italian and English, interrupting one another and laughing the whole time. Their stories made no mention of religion – not sin, not prayer, not the Pope's inauguration – and when I asked why they were walking, Francesca shrugged.

'Sometimes I think I could walk forever,' said Cecilia. 'Like the walking makes me free.'

They wanted to know about my own pilgrimage too. I explained that I had set off from Canterbury on New Year's Day and crossed the Alps in midwinter. I discussed the homeless men I befriended in Ivrea – Stefano and Aldo, Il Papa and Il Bagarino – and the boatman who drunk-drove me over the Po. Cecilia asked what was the worst part, so I mentioned the week of rain in the Apennines. Francesca asked what was the best, so I mentioned that same week, when the clouds lifted and I saw Tuscany for the first time.

She laughed. 'And why are you a pilgrim?'

I thought back to Giacomo's list of questions. Did I beg for my food? Did I pray while I walked? How many miracles had I seen along the way? Compared with Cecilia's more improvised approach, they seemed absurd. I was tempted to claim that method for myself, but instead I told the truth. I said that I had been ill and hoped the journey would help. As I spoke I realized my words had no weight, no stigma, no shame. I was afraid to share them, yet they could not hurt me.

When the cafe owner learnt that we were hiking to Rome, she would not let us pay, insisting we take away three little boxes of biscotti instead. Francesca clapped her hands, announcing that it felt like Christmas.

'I won't sleep tonight,' she said. 'I'm too excited for tomorrow.'

It was late when we returned to the youth centre. In the upstairs gallery Cecilia played with the foam matting –

making a fort, a wigwam, a temple – while Francesca leant from the window, rolling cigarettes and ringing her friends in Rome. I stood in the corner, grateful and amazed. This evening had been the most ordinary since Canterbury, yet that was its magic. Unlike the pilgrims in Siena, these women treated walking as something to be enjoyed rather than endured.

I laid out my sleeping bag and crawled inside, but an hour later I was still awake, listening to the two women's movements. I could hear them tiptoeing round the gallery, hear them whispering one another quiet, hear the gasps of stifled laughter. *Domani, domani*, I heard them say. Tomorrow was the last day.

Next morning I followed a strand of suburb into the city. My route skirted between pastures and paddocks, wild horses and farmed cattle, low hills, knotted woodland, bridges, underpasses, lay-bys and roundabouts, and by midday I was hiking on pavement. After twelve weeks of walking my heels felt flimsy, my shoulders raw, yet Rome was so close that there seemed no point in resting.

The villages on the outskirts were waymarked with little tags of gold, blue and white, sprayed onto lampposts and signs, guiding pilgrims for the final stretch of the Via Francigena. During the first two hours I counted the markings; after that I counted petrol stations; when the road ran beside a railway track, I counted train stations too. Yesterday evening Cecilia had told me that, once she and Francesca arrived at the track, they would take a train for the remaining distance. Nothing to see now, she warned, just a fifteen-kilometre traffic jam.

As if to prove her wrong, I began looking for evidence that I had finally reached the capital – a famous landmark or familiar street name. But all I noticed were the drab sights of the city's outer fringes: billboard posters advertising supermarket bargains; playgrounds set on squares of threadbare grass; apartment blocks crowned in satellites, aerials and air-conditioning units; vacant plots pieced with broken bottles and crushed cans; chains of wine bars and snack bars, of *tabacchi* and *panetteria*, of fruit stalls, fast-food outlets, and pawn shops swapping gold for cash, their slatted shutters spoilt with graffiti. Thirty, twenty, ten kilometres to go, and still I was walking, walking.

The architecture shifted back through the centuries. I passed an office block with a facade of fluted columns. I passed a house with chunks of masonry set into its base. I passed a church with a columned portico and walls of pitted pink. Since midmorning the route had been level, but around teatime it lifted onto the foundations of an older city.

By five o'clock the roads were clogged with cars. Commuters hurried along the pavement and my rucksack took up too much space. I kept following the waymarks as they skipped down a wall of stone slabs. Blue, blue, white. Blue, white, blue. White, blue, and a streak of gold – and then the markers ran out.

As the road tipped downhill, the pavement tapered away. Ahead the traffic was locked four lanes wide, but a yellow arrow at my feet pointed through a gate in the wall. So I opened the gate and went inside.

The wall bordered a park, with dust tracks ascending to a summit half-hidden by pine. I took the nearest track and started climbing.

Crossing the park, the noise from the road softened. As I rose towards the summit, the city's commotion was subdued. Then I reached the crest of the hill and the woods fell away. Beyond the sinking treetops I could see Rome clear in the evening light.

All day I had walked on the flat with no sense of scale. Now an entire capital was spread out beneath me. For some reason – the heat, the height, the fumes from a million exhausts – it looked as if the buildings were hovering off the ground. I could see apartment blocks shuffling over one another and streetfronts trembling like a curtain caught in a breeze. The roofs were a jigsaw of tile, slate and tar, of raised terraces and hanging gardens, of bell towers and clock towers and spires capped with crosses. Above them all was the shining dome of St Peter's, suspended from the earth.

I thought I should celebrate, clench my fists and pump my arms, or raise my hands and cheer. But the atmosphere in the park was tranquil – that brief interval between the end of work and the beginning of evening – and my excitement soon ebbed into relief. So I watched the buildings slow and settle, and then went down into the dusk.

It was past eight when I limped into Testaccio, a scruffy neighbourhood on the southern edge of the old city. In Siena I had been given the address of a local convent with a hostel for pilgrims, but I did not learn its name until I arrived, Spedale della Provvidenza di San Giacomo e San Benedetto Labre. Benoît-Joseph Labre. I shouldn't have been surprised: Rome was the city where he died. Yet I remembered how the saint's story had haunted me, that evening in early January, and wondered if I had walked nineteen hundred kilometres to brush up against the place where I started.

The convent had long windows, tall doors, and high stucco ceilings. Its walls were blanketed with white, giving the whole building a cushioned sense of calm. A few nuns floated in the corridors, but otherwise the place was still.

On the second floor was a set of dormitories with a kitchen next door, where a middle-aged woman was preparing food.

'Here at last, here at last! I thought you might never come!'

The woman's name was Gabriella. She had a golden face and a twittering voice. Gabriella was a volunteer, cooking meals for pilgrims when they reached Rome. First, however, she moved a chair into the middle of the kitchen and told me to sit. Then she placed a metal bowl beneath the seat, filling it with water from a stoneware jug. Finally she asked me to take off my socks. The knuckles were scabbed and the flesh flecked with dead skin, yet I did not feel ashamed, only the deep calm that lies on the far side of tiredness.

Gabriella knelt to wash my feet, rinsing them in the bowl, rubbing soap over the arches and soles, and cleaning the suds with more water from the jug. My toes prickled, stung, turned red, and went numb. At one point she asked whether I knew any prayers, and before I could answer she began to recite, *Padre nostro, che sei nei cieli* ... I murmured the words back to her, our voices falling into time ... *sia fatta la tua volontà, come in cielo così in terra.*

When the prayer was done she kissed my feet, dried them with a towel, and poured away the spent water. Then we ate together.

There was a poster on the kitchen wall, showing a boat with a cross-shaped mast – the image I had seen in a dozen churches since Calais. The words *Annus Fidei* were printed beneath. I asked Gabriella what it meant: a year of faith. It was the Pope's idea, she explained. Pope Benedict's. He wanted a year of evangelization, a year of renewal. 'If you make a pilgrimage to Rome, you are forgiven.' Gabriella paused. 'Like a jubilee.' Another pause. 'You know this word: jubilee?'

What was the term Danilo had used? *Jubileus*. I could not remember the translation, something about thanksgiving, or peace, or debts being forgiven.

I shook my head.

'OK,' said Gabriella, 'so I will explain.'

On the first evening of the fourteenth century a small group of pilgrims gathered in St Peter's Square. They were sent here by a wandering preacher who claimed that anyone visiting Rome for the New Year would have their sins absolved. The story spread, and by the end of the week thousands stood outside the basilica.

Vatican officials were surprised by the sudden crowds. However, rather than turn the pilgrims away, they put the Veil of Veronica on display – the cloth that wiped the blood from Christ's face during the Passion.

Two weekends later, as Pope Boniface VIII watched pilgrims processing past the Veil, he noticed an elderly gentleman carried on the shoulders of his family. When the Pope asked the man's age, he replied that his first visit to Rome was a century ago, in the year 1200, when he was carried on his father's shoulders. On that occasion, the man claimed, every pilgrim to St Peter's had their sins absolved.

Scholars were sent to the archives to confirm the story, but no evidence was found. Yet the Pope did not want to disappoint his visitors, so that February he proclaimed an *annus jubileus*. From now on the first year of the century was a holy year. All pilgrims to Rome would be granted a plenary indulgence.

The theology went something like this:

Because of original sin, no amount of virtue can earn us a place in heaven – only God's grace does that. However, to reward good behaviour the Church encouraged belief in Purgatory, an intermediate stage of purging between this life and Paradise, where earthly offences were punished. It was a compromise between two competing visions of the divine: a just God and a merciful one. But it also allowed penitents to quantify their sins, even price their guilt. Time in Purgatory could be reduced through acts of penance such as prayer, fasting, almsgiving and pilgrimage. This remission, measured in years, was called an indulgence. A plenary indulgence cleared the entire penalty; a lifetime of wickedness wiped clean.

The papal bull announcing the Jubilee claimed that Boniface was reviving an ancient tradition. In fact nothing like it had been seen before. Although a previous pope, Urban II, offered a similar indulgence to knights on the First Crusade – to spare them from sins committed while fighting for the Church – that was a one-off. Boniface's Jubilee was open to anyone and was repeated every hundred years.

Come the spring, ten thousand pilgrims were pouring into the city each day: noblemen and merchants, clergy and laity, artisans, labourers and beggars. The walls of Vatican Hill were broken open, and the Sant'Angelo Bridge – the pinch-point over the River Tiber – fractured.

On Maundy Thursday Pope Boniface greeted the pilgrims from the balcony of St John Lateran, reading out a list of Church enemies who were forbidden the plenary indulgence. This included supporters of the White Guelph faction in Florence, such as Dante Alighieri. The poet was among the pilgrims to Rome in the Jubilee year and later set the opening of *The Divine Comedy* on that same Maundy Thursday. Unsurprisingly, his poem criticized the growing scope of papal indulgences. Canto XVIII of

Inferno even compared the pimps and seducers thronging the eighth circle of hell to the Jubilee pilgrims mobbing the Sant'Angelo Bridge.

It's true that the event helped re-establish Rome's status as the capital of Christendom, but this was evidence of weakness as much as strength. Given that Jerusalem was no longer in Christian hands, there was something desperate about the celebrations, because the papal city was a poor substitute for Palestine. However, nine years after the fall of Acre – the last crusader state in the Holy Land – the Jubilees gave Europe a new pilgrim centre.

In the following centuries the Pope's festival was revived many times, becoming the greatest spectacle in a golden age of pilgrimage. His indulgence was also recycled for scores of major and minor feasts – this was the *Annus Fidei* I had seen advertised on all those posters. And, said Gabriella, as we sat together that first evening in Rome, seven centuries later the Holy Year was still popular.

When I woke the morning after arriving, my legs were stiff and my feet bruised. It took several hours to leave the convent, and several more to find the guesthouse where I was staying that weekend. The guesthouse was attached to a monastery, Monastero di San Gregorio al Celio, which overlooked a broad road running from the Circus Maximus to the Colosseum. I got there at twelve, went back to bed, and slept almost twenty hours – a plunging sleep so deep that I woke with no memory of where I was, but stepped from my bed feeling reborn.

Next day was Good Friday. In the afternoon I went to buy a second pair of boots and a second set of maps. That evening the road outside my monastery was lined with pilgrims: old men from Mexico with trimmed beards and baggy suits; young women from the Balkans with patterned scarves wrapped round their heads; a family from Poland with seven children in blazers and skirts; and another family – French, I think – their sons in matching football strips.

The evening was overcast, but the clouds drew away with the edges of the day until there was nothing left in the sky except a taut, twilight blue. The air cooled, the traffic thinned, and then I stepped outside to join the pilgrims.

Everyone was queuing at the Arch of Constantine. Police patted down the queue, except for a group of German nuns who were waved straight on. Then they spread out in the Piazza del Colosseo, on the far side of the arch. To their right was the Colosseum, a great cliff of chambered stone lit by the gentle pulsing of lamps. To their left was the Palatine Hill, with a ruined Roman temple at its base. A stage had been built on the temple's foundations: a throne in the middle and twin rows of torches stage right, fixed to form a burning cross. More torches crazed the lip of the stage, above a bank of decaying brick. Below the bank, near the foot of the hill, security barriers kept back the crowd. Children stood beneath the barriers, their arms looped through the rungs, holding leaflets and rosaries and candles in coloured cups – all waiting for the Stations of the Cross.

Night fell. The piazza filled. Choristers and priests circled the stage. The rest of the audience was in darkness, a pool of shadow lapping against the Colosseum walls. I stood between an elderly couple dressed for a funeral, reading tiny black Bibles with tiny black torches, and a pair of men dressed for the beach, shaking their shoulders and rubbing their hands. It was too dim to follow my order of service, and I was too nervous to talk with these strangers, but soon I grew tired from waiting and my thoughts began to drag.

After two hours the audience went quiet, as a police light flashed from the road and a convoy of cars approached the Palatine Hill. When a limousine parked beside the stage, the two men nearest me started shouting: *Viva il Papa! Viva il Papa!* Others joined in, now cheering, now clapping, until the mood in the square swayed from mourning to celebration. *VIVA IL PAPA! VIVA IL PAPA!*

It was nine o'clock. Pope Francis had arrived.

Over the top of a few hundred heads, I saw a figure dressed in an ivory frock coat, stepping out from the car and mounting the steps to the stage. As he reached the throne, the shouting grew louder, the young men in front of me whooping and whistling. I wanted to join in, but when I opened my mouth no sound came out, and once more I felt like an imposter.

Eventually the figure raised his arms and the audience was quiet. He began to speak, his voice weaker than I expected, welcoming us with a few exhausted phrases. Then a pair of actors started reading the fourteen stations, every station followed by a commentary, a selection of prayers, and a chorus of the Stabat Mater. At the same time, cinema screens on either side of the square cut between the faces in the audience. When Jesus fell for the first time, the camera jumped to a woman who had been crying. When Simon of Cyrene lifted his cross, to a man with eyes squeezed shut. When Veronica wiped the blood from Christ's face, to a line of children tugging their parents' clothes, desperate to leave, desperate for the loo.

Each commentary was written by a member of the Maronite Church, linking Christ's Passion to the persecution of Eastern Christians. A few Lebanese flags flapped above the audience, red and white and wagging in the breeze. As the evening deepened they drooped towards the ground, the fabric seeming to wilt.

My fingers were cold, and the backs of my knees pinched and pinged. I kept staring at the cinema screens, watching coverage from inside the Colosseum. A wooden cross was being marched round the theatre's fourteen shrines, every member of the procession holding a flaming torch and jagged light clawing open the arched passageways. At each shrine the cross was handed on, to a woman from India in a saffron sari (Station III), to a priest from China in a crimson-trimmed cassock (Station VI), and to a nun from Nigeria wearing a leather jacket over her habit (Station X).

By now I was jogging my heels and counting down the stations. The bluish scent of night filled the square, made acrid by the smoke off the torches. Nearby the young men shivered and the elderly couple yawned, their eyes fixed on the stage, waiting for something I could not see.

Jesus fell for a second time. The procession stepped out into the piazza. He fell for a third time. They paced through a parting in the audience. Candles starred the darkness, the crowd quivering in the candlelight. The procession mounted the steps to the stage. Christ's clothes were stripped from his skin. They paraded before the throne, the Pope, the temple columns. Christ's hands and feet were nailed to the cross. Flags fell from the sky. Stars fell from the night. Christ cried out. Christ gave up his life. Silence. All the stage silent and the body of God laid lifeless on the ground.

It was late when we left the piazza. The motorcade went first, followed by a busload of nuns. Otherwise the roads were closed, so we walked in wide ranks down the middle. Parents carried sleeping children and couples went hand in hand, their expressions a mix of exhausted patience and solemn relief. After standing so long in the crowd, my own mood was flattened out, senses blunted by so much spectacle.

When I got back to the monastery it was almost mid-night. The courtyard, the guesthouse – everything was still. No light in the corridors, no voices on the stairwell. For a moment I thought I heard chanting inside the church, but when I tried the door it would not give. Locked, of course, and the tabernacle bare, and the great tomb sealed shut.

The Stations of the Cross narrate Christ's journey to the place of crucifixion. In Jerusalem's Old City a series of chapels mark the sites where, according to custom, each station took place. The tradition of pilgrims walking the Via Crucis began in the same century as the Roman Jubilees. After the loss of the Holy Land, Franciscan friars were given custody over the region's Christian sites by its new Mamluk rulers. They started conducting tours of the Old City, and later built shrines in Europe modelled on the Via Crucis. These shrines were copied in cathedrals and churches across the continent, while the fourteen stations became the focus of Good Friday worship.

As with the friars' more popular piece of devotional theatre – the nativity crèche – it was a way of bringing the Holy Land home. And, as with the Jubilees, it used the rituals of pilgrimage to shift Christendom's spiritual centre from the former crusader kingdoms.

This was important as, soon after the first Jubilee, Rome lost its status at the centre of the Latin Church. Pope Boniface was partly to blame. He kept falling out with European monarchs. Thanks to a feud with the King of France, in 1303 Boniface was locked up in his palace at Anagni. He soon died of a violent fever, inspiring rumours that he had gnawed off his hands and brained himself against the bedroom wall. His successor, Benedict XI, died eight months later – this time it was rumoured to be poisoning – and by the end of the decade Pope Clement V was established in Avignon.

Pilgrimage to Rome declined in the following decades. Petrarch, the leading poet of the period, explains why: 'All France, the Low Countries, and Britain, are engulfed in war; Germany and Italy are crippled by civil strife, their cities reduced to ashes; the Spanish kings turn on each other in armed combat, and throughout Europe Christ is unseen and unknown.' In 1341 Petrarch was made the first Roman laureate since Antiquity. He joined a diplomatic mission to Avignon, trying to convince the current pope, Clement VI, to proclaim a second Jubilee. The original jubilees – Jewish festivals of forgiveness recorded in Leviticus – were held every fifty years, so why not call a second to mark the half-century?

Although Clement refused to leave Avignon, he gave his permission, and the proclamation went out that winter.

By 1348 the Black Death had reached Europe. Next year, in September, Rome was hit by the worst earthquake in its history. Thousands were killed or injured, with thousands more left homeless. Petrarch again: 'The houses fall down, the walls collapse, temples are overthrown, shrines are wrecked, the laws trodden underfoot. The Lateran Palace is razed to the ground and its basilica, mother of all churches, stands roofless, open to wind and rain.'

Pilgrims who completed the journey to Rome were appalled. Churches were draped in tapestries to hide the damage, but worshippers kept injuring themselves on the cratered floors. Meanwhile, sick and dying citizens littered the streets.

Historians of pilgrimage often compare the ritual to tourism. They emphasize the pleasures of travel, the temptations of the route, and the celebrations on offer at the major shrines. But hike a few hundred kilometres and what you notice are the hardships. For a medieval traveller there were the added risks of war, disease, and roads made dangerous by bandits. The Jubilees give us some idea why anyone would endure this ordeal, because the festivals made Rome feel like the centre of the world again, and salvation seem near at hand. Yet they also exposed the mindlessness of collective devotion, for as Dante suggested, they were displays not of piety but power. Ringed round by believers, all doubts were quelled, all fears quieted. It was the same draw as those flagellant ceremonies: the hope and fear and the awful thrill of surrender.

In 1350 up to a million pilgrims came to the city over the course of the year, and when the Veronica was displayed on Sundays and feast days, the crowds were such that four, six, even twelve people were trampled to death at each gathering. On that occasion the Basilica of St John Lateran was added to the churches pilgrims must visit to receive the indulgence. Petrarch was one of those pilgrims and his account of the visit shares in their sense of excitement. The basilica's Sancta Sanctorum housed the most prized relics in the Roman Church – Jesus' foreskin and umbilical cord – and for Petrarch this was the climax of the journey, proving that Rome was no longer the city of martyrs or apostles, but home to Christ himself. Forget the crusader states: here was the New Jerusalem.

Ironically, the 1350 Jubilee was also a swansong for Rome's status, as over the coming decades rival popes split the Latin Church.

In 1378 a new pope, Urban VI, was elected in Rome. However, an antipope remained in Avignon, dividing Catholic nations. The kingdoms of France, Castile, Aragon and Naples were loyal to Avignon; those of England, Poland, Hungary and Sweden sided with Rome; and the Holy Roman Empire shifted between the two.

Once again, pilgrim numbers declined. In response,

Urban proclaimed a third Jubilee for the year 1390, but died eleven weeks before the event. The year was a flop anyway, with those who supported the antipope forbidden from attending. Yet Rome's next pope, Boniface IX, could not announce an additional Jubilee for the expected date – the year 1400 – without discounting the last.

In the final summer of the fourteenth century another penitent movement sprang up on the Ligurian coast. Its followers were known as Bianchi because they dressed in white and performed ceremonies mixing flagellation and forgiveness. While one branch of the movement pinballed across the Po Valley, a second branch marched south through Tuscany. By September they had reached Rome, and that autumn they processed round the capital, chanting the Stabat Mater and calling for peace.

Rome's citizens welcomed the penitents, but Church authorities were unsure how to respond. One of the Bianchi claimed that he was John the Baptist reborn, clearing the way for Christ's return, and there were reports of all-night processions filling the city with flagellants.

Boniface IX was a weak pope. The Bianchi made him nervous. Soon a rumour started that he had put the movement's leaders in prison.

The Pope could have suppressed this sudden outburst of piety, but instead he decided to reward it. When a second flock of pilgrims showed up in the late autumn, these ones hoping for a Jubilee, Boniface let the celebrations go ahead. Though no proclamation was made, the Holy Door at St Peter's was opened and the relics of the apostles put on display. Once more the pilgrims processed in front of the Veronica; once more the plenary indulgence was granted. Thousands came to Rome over the course of the year and the Jubilee tradition was saved.

*

Easter Sunday. I left the monastery at daybreak. All week the streets had been busy, but that morning they were bare. The buildings on the Campo de'Fiori shifted from deep blue to dull silver, and when I crossed the Tiber a porcelain light parted the clouds, paling the river water.

It was still early when I reached Via della Conciliazione, the arcade leading from Castel Sant'Angelo to St Peter's Square. A porter waited at the doors of a hotel, and three vendors laid out racks of plastic souvenirs: spangled crosses, gaudy icons, and keychains stamped with pictures of popes. Otherwise the arcade was empty, its rows of palazzos – schools, embassies, Vatican headquarters – shut up for the day.

At the end of the road a cordon of police stood smoking and drinking coffee. There were more police inside the square, along with camera crews and workmen wearing fluorescent waistcoats.

As I approached St Peter's, the great colonnade arced out on either side, a vast basin formed by twin trains of fourfold pillars. An altar stood in the middle of the square, wrapped in woven gold. Behind it, the basilica was decorated with flowers, with lilies and forsythia swagged yellow and white, as well as ranks of tulips stepping down from the Holy Door, palm fronds plaiting the columns, and crates of mixed gerberas circling the plinths, a pell-mell pattern of cream and orange and candyfloss pink.

Soon the Easter pilgrims would be here. Before they arrived, I tried to imagine the square already filled, populating it with the crowds from the fourth Jubilee.

By 1450 the schism had ended and Rome was the uncontested capital of Western Christianity. That year, roughly forty thousand pilgrims showed up each day, with a million gathering in the city for Easter. Every inn, hostel and guesthouse was occupied, forcing the poor to camp in church porches. Supplies ran low, prices soared, and the streets were choked with people. On Sundays, when Pope Nicholas V greeted visitors from St Peter's Basilica, he drew such crowds that the guards had to beat them back with sticks.

The Pope cut the amount of time pilgrims needed to stay in Rome to receive the indulgence, eventually reducing it to a single day. However, their numbers only diminished after a plague that summer.

Come autumn, the worst of the epidemic was over and the pilgrims returned. Once more the inns were occupied, the supplies ran low, and the poor camped out in church porches.

During the run-up to Christmas, a final surge of visitors arrived in the city, hoping to catch the closing weeks of the indulgence. On 19 December, the last Sunday of Advent, St Peter's Square filled as usual, but for some reason the papal blessing was delayed and then abandoned. In the late afternoon the audience was sent away. Daylight failing, they moved towards the Sant'Angelo Bridge, and even though vendors and carts obstructed their path, thousands filed onto the crossing. Meanwhile a small party approached from the opposite side, led by a Venetian cardinal who would one day be appointed Pope Paul II. Despite the mass of people coming the other way, the cardinal pushed on and the bridge was blocked.

As I stood in the square that morning, trying to imagine the medieval crowds, I heard voices behind me. Looking round, I realized I was no longer alone. It was eight o'clock and the first pilgrims were arriving. I could see a line of seminarians in brand-new vestments, movements poised like children in their parents' clothes; and a line of scouts in shorts and socks, marching upright with puffed chests; and a family dressed for a wedding, the

men wearing fawn-coloured waistcoats, the women in mantillas of black silk.

By nine o'clock the new arrivals were joining queues. By ten o'clock those queues had become entire pitches of people, surrounding the altar and spilling out to the colonnades.

The steps of St Peter's were bustling now. There were bands of cardinals in scarlet mozzettas and rochets of white lace. And there were bands of bishops in purple cassocks and tufted birettas. And rows of choristers in gowns of the same shade, standing without moving, wondering where to put their hands. A garrison of Swiss Guard formed up at the base of the steps, wearing blue capes and starched collars, striped tunics and striped breeches, golden-corded armour and boots of mirror-black, their helmets plumed with feathers, their halberds hung with flags. Organ music swelled from the basilica, but pilgrims were still entering the square. Pilgrims in tailored suits and designer dresses, in stiff uniforms and dark robes. Pilgrims carrying embroidered standards, painted banners, printed signs and collaged pennants. Pilgrims wearing badges and brooches and pins tipped with holy insignia: the medals of chivalric orders, or the five-fold cross of Jerusalem, or the scallop shell from Santiago. Voices in a dozen – two dozen – languages, shouting and cheering and squealing with excitement. Tens of thousands, hundreds of thousands, more people than I had seen in the past three months put together – and then something split. I could feel the weight of the sky and the texture of the air. I could feel the morning on my face, but harsher now, as if a layer of skin had been peeled from my body, or the lids had been sliced from each eye. The people near me were swarming, jostling, wrestling. They were pressing at my mouth, dragging at my throat. We were too many. We were too close.

The panic came in waves. Fat colours. Blunt noises. Swells of confused movement. My breath was short – the ribcage clamped, the pressure lost from each lung – and my vision tunnelled, until no space remained in that vast square. It was as if the atmosphere had collapsed – the air rushing out, the clouds dropping down – or the heavens were falling on our heads.

We were too many. Too close.

I slipped between a set of barriers and walked up one of the aisles. The choir had started to sing, but already I was pushing through the police cordon that sealed St Peter's Square, not stopping to listen as the chorus cried out, nor pausing to watch as Pope Francis approached the altar – no, turning my back on the cardinals and bishops, the priest and guards, on the brutal splendour of the basilica and the great basin flooded with people, turning away and hurrying down Via della Conciliazione, past the succession of grand palazzos, past the souvenir vendors, hotel porters, and tourists arriving late for mass, pacing the whole length of the street until I reached the Sant'Angelo Bridge.

Soon I was standing on the bridge, leaning against the balustrade. A breeze came off the river, brushing against my palms and cooling the sweat that filmed my face. The Vatican was behind me; the palaced streets of Ponte were in front. The Tiber turned at my feet, with no waves except the crease of the current. Then the sun showed between the clouds, stunning the surface of the water, and a bell began chiming from the far bank, another bell, another, the sound cascading together.

They were still chiming as I stepped off the bridge, arms stretched wide for balance. And as I sat in the doorway of a nearby church – Santi Celso e Giuliano – counting my breaths to keep calm.

I could picture it now, that dreadful Sunday evening.

December, bitter cold, a few days shy of the solstice. Dusk when the pilgrims began crossing the river, their shoulders hunched, their heads bowed, footsore from standing all afternoon. The bridge packed with stalls, selling rosaries and *ex-votos* and badges of copper and tin. And the cardinal coming the other way, painted and jewelled and sat fat on his horse.

The light was failing, so nobody leaving the square could see what was happening ahead. Restless with waiting, they pressed forwards, meaning those on the bridgehead were crushed against the bank. Meanwhile, those on the bridge were jammed in place, and as the pressure increased, they started to suffocate. Some tried to jump into the Tiber, others tried to crawl away, but most were smothered where they stood.

When I closed my eyes, I could hear it too. Hear shouts going up in French and German, Spanish and Italian, English, Armenian, and Greek. Hear flesh pressed into flesh, hear skin beginning to burst. Hear collarbones popping, ribs cracking, and the bridge's fracturing foundations. Up there – Can you see? – a man crawling on the heads of his neighbours. Down there – look, look – a woman kneeling as if praying, her body balled up and trampled into the floor. Limbs pulled loose, clothes torn away, and flagstones wrenched from the floor. Men throwing themselves off the parapet, their arms wheeling, their legs flailing, round and round and – smash! – against the water.

Eventually the castellan of Sant'Angelo sent in his guards. Bodies were carried off the bridge one at a time, with more bodies dredged from the river. In the end two hundred dead were counted. Three horses, also crushed, completed the toll.

The dead were taken here, to Santi Celso e Giuliano. That evening, families knelt in the church, raising cupped candles to each tortured expression in turn. When it lit on the face of their brother or sister, their parent or child, they would cry out and let the candle flame drop to their feet.

At midnight the corpses were placed in St Peter's Square. Some could only be identified by their clothes, the features bruised beyond recognition. Others remained anonymous: cloaks ripped and tunics bloodied. How did Dante describe the eighth circle of hell? A chasm filled with new anguish, new torment – *nova pieta, novo tormento* – and sinners swimming naked in its depths – *Nel fondo erano ignudi i peccatori.* That circle was where Dante housed the simoniacs – all those who sold Church offices or profited from spiritual favours – and where he reserved a space for Pope Boniface VIII, father of the first Jubilee. As the grandest spectacle of medieval pilgrimage descended into tragedy, his words now read like prophecy. And, moving away from that monstrous pageant, I felt hollowed out by its history.

Come midday I was on the Via Appia Antica, the old road south from the capital. I was leaving Rome.

The road began at the Porta San Sebastiano and cut through the wide expanse of the Caffarella Park. From museums and townhouses to fields of grazing animals – a groove scored straight out of the city. The paving was a soft purple shade, rutted by the wheels of carts and carriages. Stone slabs lay along the edge, their corners black with lichen, and sunken tombs sat on the grass, beside toppled pillars and capsized watchtowers. In the distance I noticed the remains of an aqueduct, its arches fallen in like the broken links of a chain.

At lunchtime the park was full of joggers and cyclists, but during the next hour their numbers thinned, and by early afternoon I was alone again. Planes shrieked from an airport behind the treeline, while from far off I could hear the low rumble of a motorway.

Around teatime the paving ran out and puddles dashed the path. Then I reached a grove of trees and a wooden footbridge. Its deck was snapped in two, the gap a metre at most, but I hesitated as I came nearer. Although the water under the bridge was in shadow, I could just see my reflection on the surface. Below that I could see darkness like the night, see bodies massing in the cold, see the clotted grey of exposed skin—

I took a deep breath and jumped.

Sinking onto the opposite side, the weight of my rucksack carried me down, and with a sudden feeling of release, I ran.

Anagni was a hilltop town seventy kilometres east of the capital. When I arrived on Tuesday afternoon the place was awash with rain, streets streaming and gutters flooded. On my first night in Rome, Gabriella had given me the address of a convent here with a bed for pilgrims. Asking directions, I was pointed towards a house on the fringes of the old town. Its lights were off, its curtains drawn, but I kept knocking until a woman about my age answered the door. Her hair was cropped and messy, her eyes full of light, and she wore a zipped black hoodie with sleeves twisted into her palms. Her name was Giulia.

Giulia invited me inside and brought out coffee and cake, apologizing for her fluent English. She had been a novice at the convent for two and a half years, and in six months' time she would take her vows.

When Giulia asked what I wanted, I gave the standard answer – that I left Canterbury in January, hiked to Rome for Easter, and was pushing on to Jerusalem. But, when I said that I was hoping to stay the night, she shook her head.

'In Rome I was told you had a room for guests—'

'Not us. Maybe the Sisters of Charity?'

'The Sisters of Charity?'

'Next to the palace. The pope's palace. They have a room for pilgrims.'

Realizing my mistake, I began to apologize, but Giulia cut me off: 'I'm happy you came to us. You are the first person I ever met who is walking to Jerusalem.'

At that point the front door opened and four nuns stepped in from the rain. Now there was confusion: more coffee, more cake, a tour of the convent, a visit to the chapel, a goody bag filled with fruit and nuts, and a copy of a travel diary written by an Italian priest – *Diario di Terra Santa*. The photo on the dust jacket showed a handsome chap standing in a desert, wearing a safari suit, dog collar and cowboy hat.

Giulia offered to take me to the Sisters of Charity. Sharing her umbrella, she led the way into Anagni's medieval centre. Water splashed down the road, while a cobblestone sky closed over us. More water pooled in the piazzas, their buildings blotted out.

As we crossed the crooked passageways of the old town, Giulia asked questions about my journey. How many days, how many countries, and how many kilometres? And please, was I in Rome for Easter? All her life Giulia had lived near Rome, but she had never been for Easter. Maybe I saw Pope Francis? Or the Way of the Cross? Or maybe I went to Sunday mass at St Peter's?

I said that I went, but had to leave.

Giulia looked disappointed. 'Why?'

I ran through the reasons in my head. None of them answered her question. What did it matter if I was overwhelmed by the crowds, or if I doubted my pilgrimage could heal anything? In the end I did not reply, until Giulia suggested: 'Maybe there were too many people? Or maybe, how do I explain, because everyone else was a pilgrim, you were left out?'

Maybe. At the beginning of the pilgrimage I hoped that, by taking part in Christian rituals, I might better understand the beliefs. On Sunday morning that hope had faltered. Here was the resurrection, the miracle on which the entire Church was founded – yet I could not believe that death was defeated this day. For others in the crowd the ceremony meant salvation, but for me it was just a show, a sham. So I quit Rome and started walking again, but my sense of purpose was gone. If the ritual had no meaning, why keep going? Why not give up?

That was what I asked Giulia.

For a long time she was quiet. Then she said: 'A few years ago I never went to church. I went to parties, went dancing – same as all my friends. I had a boyfriend – the same. But one day, I can't say why, one day I wanted to go to mass. Like I had to go. In the church the priest said: *Do you know that Jesus suffered on the cross so you could live? He died so you could live.* And those words broke my heart. They broke my heart. Not where your feelings are, somewhere deeper than that. Jesus gave his life for me. What could I give for him?'

The summer before, Giulia had volunteered at a school in Albania run by nuns. The simplicity of their lives seemed beautiful to her, and now the memory of that summer returned. 'No way I wanted to be a sister. I wanted a normal life, a normal job. I wanted a family – normal. But every time I prayed was the same: Jesus gave his life for me. It took a long time – a lot of tough conversations with God – until I realized what I want is not the most important. What He wants is the most important.'

We came to the gated entrance of a submerged

courtyard. A palazzo stood at the far end, the loggia stained black by the rain. The stone archway on the left-hand side enclosed a wooden door.

Giulia rang the bell and we stood watching raindrops riddle the puddles. While we waited, she said, 'When I was twenty, if anyone told me: Giulia in five years' time you will be a nun, I would call them crazy. Now it's the opposite. If I make a plan for five years' time, I'm the crazy one. I don't know what will happen in five months. Maybe I will be a nun – but God decides. I have to trust him.'

Then she said, 'Sometimes I think it's a mistake. I wish I was certain, like I always knew the future, but that means I wouldn't need God. He makes me brave when I'm afraid what happens next.'

Finally she said, 'Or maybe that sounds crazy.'

It did not. It sounded hopeful and full of humility. As Giulia spoke, it seemed possible to doubt, possible to despair, yet still believe. This was far from the triumphant spectacle I had seen in Rome – a longing faith much closer to loyalty. There was courage here, born not from self-confidence but from living small before the world. I wanted to tell her this, yet I struggled to find the words. I could not explain how her story moved me, nor confess my fear that the pilgrimage would heal nothing. Moments later the door opened and another nun invited me inside. Then my guide was gone, dancing through the puddles with umbrella held high.

As you go south from Lazio, the architecture ages, Classical and Baroque churches replaced by Romanesque and Gothic. The landscape ages too, the plains weathering away and the mountains bowing down. Their summits were now topped with a scree of chopped-up rock, while their slopes were crude slabs of granite and lime. The pastures had also gone, replaced by fields of dust and the fretted canopies of olive groves. Farm workers stood in each grove, either pruning the trees or raking the felled branches into piles, before setting each pile alight.

Although I was glad for the turning weather – the mornings milder, the evenings lighter – there was little warmth in the sun, as if the season was still making up its mind. Hiking east through the upper corner of Campania, I noticed only a few signs of spring: the primroses spotting a building site by Alife, or the almond blossom brushing the scrubland outside Telese, or the string-thin saplings in the low growth near Solopaca.

Ten days after leaving Rome I reached Benevento, a crumbling city built from stone. An arch in the city centre marked the start of the Via Traiana, the Roman road to the Adriatic. I was planning to follow its course as far as Bari, where I would catch the boat to Albania. From there another Roman road – the Via Egnatia – would lead me through Albania, Macedonia and Greece, all the way to Istanbul.

The Dauni Mountains lifted up beyond the city: a hinge of sandstone ridges marking the border between Campania and Apulia. The foothills were the colour of leather, and the grass on the summits made a scraping sound in the wind. A new road led into the mountains, but the work was not finished yet: in places I found asphalt, in places gravel, and in places a sandy track hacked from the hills. Discarded furniture lay by the roadside, mostly cabinets with charred panels or sofas with rotted stuffing.

There were no cars on the upland roads, no people in the hilltop hamlets, only flat-roofed houses yellowing with age and fallow plots where the earth was clumped like rubble. Though I had been walking for a hundred days, my shoulders were still tender, my rucksack still heavy. And the new boots were a poor fit: their soles rigid, their toes cramped.

My thoughts kept returning to that Easter weekend, trying to work out what went wrong. Aimless, left out, nagged with doubt – these were the reasons I had given Giulia for leaving Rome. True, after the giddy achievement of reaching the city, the Holy Week celebrations left me hollow. But this did not explain the panic I felt in St Peter's Square. Although similar fits of anxiety – the weighted sky, the textured light, the voices piercing the air – had troubled the years I spent in London. And before that too.

The fits began in my early twenties, when I was living in Buenos Aires. Walking into the Dauni Mountains, I was reminded of that city. The loneliness of the mountain range recalled those isolated months in the capital: no escape from the solitude, no distraction from myself. And, as I climbed towards the pass at Masseria San Vito, my mind tunnelled back to that time.

Even now I cannot explain why I went to Argentina. I had vague plans to learn Spanish, to write a novel, to tour round Patagonia. I hoped to find some sense of purpose too, but instead I fell apart.

I was staying in a studio flat on the fifth floor of a modern block. The bedroom was bare, with a plastic table and fabric blinds. Its windows faced a cemetery, Cementerio de la Recoleta, where the country's grandest families were buried beside soldiers and politicians and scientists. Their graves were a mix of Classical and Gothic, Art Deco and Art Nouveau, Neo-Babylonian and Byzantine Revival. Each day I looked down on a riot of statues, domes, cupolas and spires, some shining, others polished, but most a polluted grey.

My first weeks were spent exploring the neighbourhood. It was late August, early September, and though traffic jammed the roads, the cafes and restaurants were empty, the parks and plazas deserted. Whenever I got lost I grew frantic, walking faster and faster, trying desperately to retrace my steps. I struggled to ask directions or follow maps, struggled to use buses, taxis or the metro. A few mornings I struggled to leave my room, standing by the door and inventing reasons to remain inside.

The real reason was simple: I was afraid of the city.

I drank to calm the fear, every day a little more. Since university I had drunk too much and over time the habit hardened, until it was no longer a pleasure but a compulsion. Yet I was only twenty-two and assumed I was too young to have a problem. Besides, my evenings had an ugly glare that I mistook for glamour. One evening was spent sipping whisky with an American congressman and his favourite pair of prostitutes; another evening it was cocktails with a princess from one of the smallest kingdoms in Europe; and in the cigar room of the Alvear Palace Hotel I met polo teams and pop stars and the nephew of a general who commanded the Junta.

No matter how late these evenings lasted, they always ended the same way. Alone in my flat. Sat at the table. Drinking until I fell to the ground.

When the weather warmed, tourists filled the cemetery below my window. I watched them wandering between the graves, photographing carved angels and embossed plaques, or queuing to leave flowers at the tomb of Eva Perón. Soon I was going outside again, visiting museums and bookshops and attending mass at the Catedral Metropolitana. The archbishop was presiding, one Cardinal Bergoglio.

That was the month of the first attack. It was the end of October, shortly after the death of the former president, Néstor Kirchner. I was crossing the Plaza de Mayo, a paved space at the centre of the city, where men and women queued to see the president's body lying in state. Halfway across the square I felt the air tighten. I could hear my breath grating, hear the blood in my ears, see the buildings shiver, the paving sharpen. With each step I took, the noise in the square became louder, the contrasts violent, until I thought my eardrums would burst, my eyes burn white.

This lasted maybe three minutes, maybe ten. Then I walked away feeling thin and brittle.

A few days later it happened again, as I roamed round an antiques market in San Telmo. And again, as I watched a student protest in Avenida Córdoba. So I went back to my room, locking the door and staying inside. But after that things went wrong very fast. I drank and drank until my liver ached and bloated, until my feet puffed and went purple. I came to with wrists trembling, hands trembling, with fingers bruised and knuckles sheared – forgotten accidents from the lost hours of the night. The tremor lasted until I drank again, the glass rattling in my mouth as I tried to bite the rim.

I had never known such isolation. Despite thousands of lives crammed close on every side, I experienced only the vast indifference of the city. The solitude became a cell, my thoughts hemmed in by the activity all around. I sought comfort in drinking, company too, and before long I was getting through a litre of gin a day.

Climbing into the Dauni Mountains, those memories weighed on my mind. Rising towards the barren heights, I grew more and more angry with my younger self. What a waste! How willingly I let myself drown! But at the time I felt helpless to prevent it, for the drinking was something stronger than will, something animal and raw. Like the savage calling that inspired those pilgrim mobs. Like surrender.

I never learnt Spanish, never finished the novel, never

travelled outside the city. In all those months I never once visited the cemetery opposite the flat. During the last month I rarely left my room, though there was vomit in the sink, vomit in the bin – spirits mixed with stomach acid and the tin-tasting scum of blood. Though the air was yellow and reeking, the bedsheets stained with piss. Though there was ash on the tiles, on the tables and blind, ash on the windows, ash scattering the cemetery, on the domes and statues, spires and plaques, and ash on the angels' faces. Yet no matter how much I drank, I could not leave my mind, nor dissolve the memories that were gathering there. Memories I had hidden; memories I had lied and lied to keep secret ... A boy standing above a bridge. Darkness beneath like a pool of water. A train screaming through the darkness. And now the jump ...

By Christmas I was back in London, but I struggled to leave Buenos Aires behind. I panicked on buses and tube trains, on busy streets and congested roads. I went sober for one week, two weeks at a time, and then I would drink until I wrecked myself. I tried to forget, tried not to think, but my mind was wayward now.

Six months later I was lying in bed, turned from the window, dreaming of suicide.

Approaching Masseria San Vito, I thought I could walk out the anger, but soon my heels were blistered, my legs burning. That anger was for the present as much as the past, because I knew this pilgrimage was no less childish: a wanton risk with my own well-being. Nearing the pass, I began muttering to myself in mocking phrases – *clever boy; clever, clever boy* – for what I had called healing was in fact a kind of punishment. Perhaps I never even wanted to recover, but simply to mask my suffering, to endure in silence.

As I neared the abandoned summits, my mind bobbed up from the past. Downy oak lined the road near the crossing, their trunks black and their branches scarred. They emerged from the splintered earth like the remains of bombed-out buildings.

Masseria San Vito consisted of a fortified farmhouse and a ruined chapel, the roof gone and the roof beams collapsed. Each piece of timber was sheathed in tarpaulin, resembling the ribs of an upturned umbrella. Outside the chapel a fountain flowed into a trough, water slopping over the edges and onto the ground. The damp earth smelt like a wound.

After two hundred metres the road topped the ridge-line. From here I could see the mountain range reaching north, and the slopes to the south stitched with wind-mills. Though the wind was relentless, the turbines did not turn, standing still as sentries. A shining lake of solar panels lay at the base of the range, and beyond that was the Tavoliere Plain: green fields of tomato and wheat, grey terraces of walnut and almond, and then acre upon acre of olive grove, stretching towards Bari.

Somewhere past the sweeping cloud shadows and the heat-hazed plain, much farther than I could see, was a pale stripe of light where the earth met the sky. It was the Adriatic – just six days' walk away. After that the land tapered into a narrow finger of rock, pointing towards Jerusalem.

I walked on the flat with the wind in my face, staring at the stark blue sky. Spring was here, yet the sunlight was stale, and warm gusts grazed the back of my throat. Salt flavoured the air, along with the smell of stagnant water, and the sea flashed in the distance. It was Wednesday 17 April. Twelve kilometres to go.

At midday I skirted an industrial estate made up of

storage units, kennel cages and rows of ageing warehouses. Their windows were fixed into frames, but the glass was so scoured with sand that it looked opaque, like a cataract clouding an eye.

Next came a set of skips brimming with junked electronics. After that was more rubbish: shrivelled cartons and plastic casings, heaped in bluffs or spread on the ground. Five caravans formed a half-circle in the middle of the dump, with a woman squatting beside them, rinsing clothes in a red tub. Behind her a group of men lifted a crank generator from a wooden crate. They stopped work as I walked by, watching me with fists on hips.

Three or four children played football in a clearing beyond the caravans. Two more children stood in the road: a girl aged ten or eleven, her black hair tied in bunches, and a boy – her younger brother, perhaps – holding a teddy to his cheek. The girl was carrying a sack so heavy it tilted her to one side. As I approached, she let go of the sack and tins of food spilled onto the tarmac. Then she started asking questions. No, I wasn't American. No, not Albanian either. English. England. It's north of Italy. Go over the Alps and – never mind. No, I wasn't married. No, I didn't have any cigarettes.

The girl kept miming cartoonish puffs to make sure that I understood. Eventually she said, 'You're a priest. You have to give me something.'

'I'm not a priest.'

'Fr Tomasso always gives me something.' She kicked the sack. More tins fell onto the floor: tinned pork, tinned tomatoes, tinned beans. 'Fr Tomasso will be angry if you don't.'

She held out a hand. Her arms were tanned and scratched and thin as twigs.

'It's a sin,' she said.

I gave her a packet of dried fruit – what remained of

the goody bag from the nuns in Anagni – and she stuffed it into her sack. Then she collected the tins from the ground and disappeared between the bluffs. I was hoping for some gesture of thanks, but her face showed only scorn, and I turned away feeling cheated.

There was more rubbish spread on the streets of Bari.

Franco worked in a sweet shop opposite the Cattedrale di San Sabino. He had a ragged beard, wore ragged robes, and when he smiled he turned his face to the sky. This shop was owned by the parish, its sweets piled in chests like pirate treasure, while a gang of eight-year-olds ran circuits round the room, snatching at rainbow lollipops and bowls of sugared almonds.

The cathedral office had sent me here because Franco was in charge of pilgrims. I told him that tomorrow I was catching a boat to Durrës and walking to Istanbul – any chance of a bed? He crossed his arms and clucked his tongue, before taking my arm and marching me out of the shop.

Parish buildings lined the piazza, my host leading the way into a tangle of corridors and courtyards. Sometimes he opened the door on an unlit chapel or a lightless cupboard, glancing inside before moving on. Eventually we stopped at a dingy room containing two beds and a desk covered in aftershave bottles. The scent of sandalwood filled the air, and the bottle caps glinted in the half-light. There was a suitcase under one of the beds and three polo shirts arranged on top in electric shades of orange, pink and green.

'You can share with Jacopo,' said Franco. 'He is a good man. An unlucky man. So maybe keep your passport in your pocket – understand? Jacopo is a good man, but he is unlucky.'

Jacopo arrived that evening. He was in his late thirties, skinny and pasty, his black hair glossed back with gel. He had been living in the parish for almost a month.

'Thank you for sharing,' I said, as we shook hands. 'Only one night.'

He gripped my fingers. 'Stay longer. It's better not to be alone.'

There was a television above the desk, the aerial wired through the window. Jacopo fiddled with the control panel, trying to fix the static, but could not make the picture work. After a few minutes he gave up and played music on his phone instead – East Coast rap two decades out of date. He knew the lyrics by heart, without understanding a single word.

Sitting opposite, I wondered if Jacopo was trying to impress me. And there was something dignified about this little man, with his folded polo shirts and bottles of scent. Maybe the rest of his life was chaos, but here he was lord and master.

It was still early when Jacopo put on pyjamas and got into bed. I suggested we turn off the light, but he shook his head. Then he began telling me about his marriage. Each stage of the story had a prop: a photograph of a child – a girl aged six or seven – that was torn at the corner where his wife had ripped her face from the frame; a box file of letters from lawyers and priests, from welfare officers and child protection charities, and from family members related in ways I could not follow; texts his wife had sent, asking for a laptop or a washing machine or a car, because the last one was towed, crashed, broken beyond repair; as well as letters Jacopo had written in marker pen, begging to see his child – letters she returned without ever reading. And there was more. Answerphone messages left late at night, the voice sodden and screaming. Trousers and shirts with blue holes bleached into the fabric. At one point Jacopo lifted his pyjamas to show a greasy scar on his ribcage, claiming this was where she stabbed him. When I asked why, he told a confused story involving a birthday party, his wife's best friend and a visit from the police. Watching him arrange the props with practised gestures, I wondered how much to believe. And, as his tone of wounded pride became pleading, my sympathy gave way to suspicion.

The cathedral chimed ten, eleven, but Jacopo kept talking. A few times he suggested we escape to the Balkans, as if he had guessed my real motive for walking – seen through the rucksack and boots, the unkempt clothes and uncut hair, and glimpsed a reflection of himself. I stopped trying to tell him otherwise. I stopped even trying to listen. Finally, around twelve, I asked if we could turn off the light.

My companion sighed and switched on a desk lamp. The bulb was covered in cloth, glowing rash-red in the corner.

'It's better, yes? Like a chapel, yes?'

Later that night I heard Jacopo calling out in his sleep. There were no words, just shapeless sounds escaping his throat, but I could guess what he was saying. It was a pained and frightened noise. It was confession.

Next day we went for a meal together. The parish served lunch to fifty or so unemployed men in another building off the main piazza. Franco stood by the door, dividing the queue in two: Italians this way, foreigners that. I sat with three men from Ghana – Emmanuel, Stephen and Daniel. They spoke English mixed with an Akan dialect and wore suits that looked as if they were made from carpet. They were discussing visas: applying for them, renewing them, buying, selling and losing them. Daniel, the one on my left, had a leather briefcase balanced on his lap. When a nun said grace, he crossed himself. When the students serving food asked if anyone was Muslim, he raised his hand.

Our first course was pasta soup. After the plates were cleared, Franco came over, grinning at the ceiling. Each day one of the tables remained behind to help tidy, he explained. Today was our turn.

Emmanuel frowned. Stephen frowned. Daniel covered his face with his hands. 'I never should have come,' he said. 'I never came here before.'

The three men began to mutter objections, but Franco was firm. Today.

Daniel stood to leave. Franco asked him to sit. 'I can't understand a word you are saying,' Daniel cried, hugging the briefcase to his chest.

'He says you stay,' Emmanuel explained.

Daniel started shouting. 'Can't you see I'm sick?'

Franco asked him to sit a second time, but he kept shouting – 'Speak English! What's the matter with you?' – so Franco asked me to translate.

'He wants to leave—' I began.

'Tell him I'm sick!' Daniel cried. 'Tell him I never came here before!'

'He says he's sick.'

Franco's shoulders slumped and the expression melted from his face. Watching his features droop with disappointment, I felt as if I were to blame. I wanted to apologize – wanted somehow to rescue the situation – but already he was stepping back to let Daniel go, murmuring *'Basta, basta.'*

After lunch the students threw wet rags onto the ends of brooms and raced them across the floor. Two of the volunteers, two brothers called Nico and Bruno, wondered why I was here. When I mentioned the pilgrimage, they looked anxious. Nico started listing reasons why it was too dangerous to hike in Albania. Bruno began telling stories about hold-ups in hotel rooms and murders on mountain roads. But, when I asked how many times the two brothers had visited the country, they laughed.

'No, no,' said Bruno. 'We're not stupid.'

I returned to the room and packed my bag. Jacopo was waiting for me, stretched out on his bed. When I wished him luck, he clutched my hand, asking if I would buy him a ticket to Albania. As I made excuses, he nodded his head, for he already knew my answer. I felt ashamed that I could not help him, after so many strangers showed trust in me. It seemed the pilgrimage was making me no kinder, but grasping as that gypsy girl outside Bari, or impatient as my neighbour at lunch. And the humility I had learnt over the winter was giving way to harshness. However, it was too late to repair the mistake, so we shook hands a second time and I left him alone.

In Bari's old town every street looked the same. The houses were built from pale stone, draping the pavement in blue shadow. Teenage boys sat on their heels in the shade, selling phone chargers and used handsets, while old women haggled in the doorway stalls, faces wrapped in black headscarves. That afternoon, exploring the old town, it was as if I had overstepped the Balkan Peninsula to arrive in a crusader port on the shores of the Levant.

Basilica di San Nicola stood in the northern corner of the old town. The church resembled a Norman fort, straddled by a squat pair of towers. Its exterior was made from plain slabs of sun-bleached stone; its interior was antique white. Three arches crossed the nave midway up. Above that a tier of round-headed windows let in a dazed afternoon light. Above that the wooden roof was inlaid with canvasses, showing a heavenly host descending from the clouds. Intricate foliage framed each painting, the whole ceiling frothing with gilt. It was a gorgeous sight, like a box of jewels spilling from the sky, but utterly out of place beside the bare granite masonry.

Downstairs I found a crypt chapel. The saint's tomb lay at the back, dressed in a gleaming necklace of oil lamps. Nicholas was the gift-giving bishop who inspired Santa Claus and a favourite wonderworker of the Eastern Church. In the late eleventh century Italian merchants stole his relics from Myra, southern Turkey, and brought them home to Bari. Yet pilgrims from the East still visited the saint, praying at the Orthodox shrine on the far side of the room.

I went over to the shrine, an alcove half-hidden behind a wickerwork of candles. Angels decorated the iconostasis, their heads ringed in haloes no bigger than penny pieces, with portraits of saints embedded into the wood.

The basilica seemed tethered between the Eastern and Western churches, pulling both ways at once. Its ceiling recalled a Venetian palace, its crypt a Byzantine sanctuary. But, as I stood among the gilded darkness, I felt no thread connecting these two, only a daunting sense of the distance covered.

How long had I been walking? Sixteen weeks ago I left Canterbury and caught the ferry to France. Calais, Amettes, and the little house where the patron saint of pilgrims was born: I struggled to remember them now. Yet I remembered that Benoît-Joseph Labre stopped at this tomb while he wandered Italy. Bari was the farthest he ever went from home, the edge of Latin Europe. I also remembered the excitement of those early days, when I first realized that I could cross a continent on foot. That excitement soon turned to anxiety as I struggled into the mountains, the snow mounding higher, my thoughts beginning to stray. Reaching Italy, I felt confident once more, until that sodden week in the Apennines when

I wanted to hitchhike. And again, in Rome, when I could not cope with the Easter crowds. Despite Sunday mass at St Peter's, the draw of mass devotion – of flagellants, of Jubilees – remained a mystery to me. Maybe faith was fear turned inside out, or hope spread wide among strangers, but collective ritual seemed oppressive. Next I would travel to a region where I spoke none of the languages and knew little about the local religion. After two thousand four hundred kilometres I felt more removed than ever from the faith I was trying to understand, but closer, much closer, to the depression I was trying to escape.

I wanted to remain in the crypt a little longer. I thought some epiphany might be waiting for me, if only I were patient. Nicholas was the protector of orphans and scholars, travellers and thieves, and all those who journey by sea. I stood opposite the shrine where he was buried, watching the candle flames knit and fray, but it never came. So then I left the basilica and went down to the port.

PART THREE

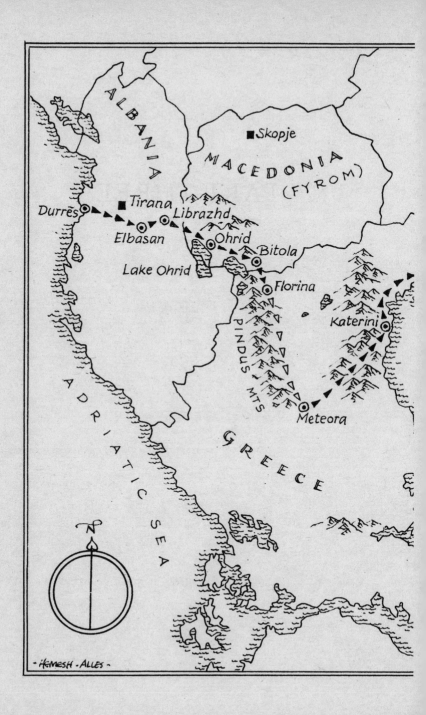

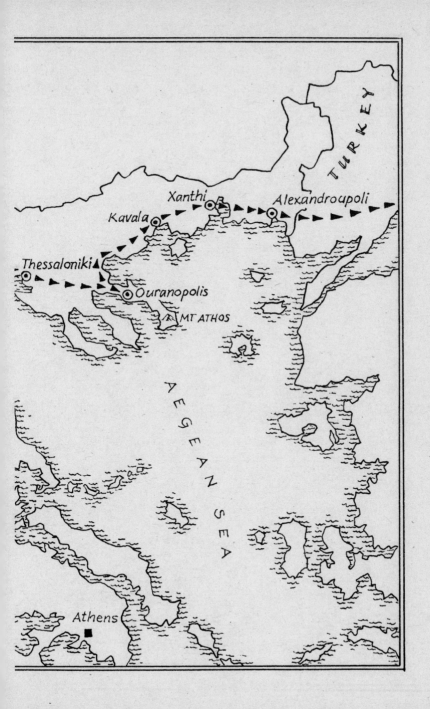

At first I found no shelter in Durrës. Neither at the white wedding cake of the Orthodox cathedral, where the gardening priest bowed his head and repeated apologies. Nor at the Catholic church in the narrow alleyways of the old town, where the doors were locked, the windows dark, and the presbytery long abandoned. Nor at the Missionaries of Charity mission house, where a nodding nun explained that their beds were reserved for pregnant women, or homeless women, or women escaping their husbands. But eventually I had some luck at the Dominican church, a breezeblock hangar with a concrete dome, a tapering bell tower, and a disused hall next door. Dust filmed the floors, and the walls were florid with damp, but there were three bunk beds in the back room and the priest said I could stay as long as I wanted.

I spent all weekend in the city, buying maps and asking for advice. My plan was to head south to the River Shkumbin and then follow the river east until the border – a week's walk across the country's waist. However, the idea met with little support. It could only be done by car … It was impossible by car … Three days … Ten days … There were bad men … There were bears … There were no Christians past Elbasan …

Most people wondered why I had come on holiday here. I told them about the Via Egnatia, the Roman Empire's trunk road, which scored a line through central Albania, southern Macedonia, northern Greece and western Turkey. This was the road the Apostle Paul travelled to Rome, and a thousand years later it carried half the armies of the First Crusade to Constantinople. But, when I said that I was hiking its length, my listeners looked alarmed.

Hiking? In Albania? No, no, there was no hiking in Albania.

I left Durrës on Monday morning and marched down the coast. My boots were still sore – soles bruised, toes crushed – and I had only a road map to guide me. Banks of pastel-painted hotels faced the road: Hotel Bonita, Hotel Dolce Vita, Tropikal Resort and Grand Hotel Pameba. No blossom in their gardens, no flowers in their forecourts, and their pastel paint dissolving in the drizzle. Between each hotel I glimpsed a strip of beach: grey sand, grey sea and a great grey sky.

At lunchtime I stepped onto the beach. There was a restaurant near the water with walls of clear plastic and a corrugated roof. Inside, three men in checked jackets sat toasting one another with shot glasses. Round the back, a waiter stood under an umbrella, grilling crabs on a barrel barbecue. The crabs made a creaking noise as they cooked, the flesh steaming and the shells cracking.

Seawashed rubble clustered on the beach. Oil-slick puddles made rainbows in the sand. Dilapidated breakwaters lay out among the surf, and the waves flopped, flopped against the shore. Breakwaters, rubble, puddles, waves – and the smell of industry clogging the air. What a dismal place.

Behind the beach a railway skirted a row of rough-sawn cliffs, with concrete bunkers sprouting from the heights like monstrous mushrooms. I followed that railway for much of the afternoon, as it curved onto the coastal plain. Grass grew up between each sleeper, but the track was still busy: men on scooters, boys on bikes, and an ageing couple dragging a carthorse. The only surprise was the diesel engine that trembled past around teatime, dragging three striped carriages and a wagon of freight.

Grey skies gave way to diluted sunshine, and the seaside resorts became drab little towns. Villas styled like gangsters' palaces bordered the towns – a mess of rococo gates, mansard roofs, Classical porches and Gothic turrets – standing among skeleton building sites. These sites were made up of twisted iron frames packed in concrete and balanced on precast columns, the whole structure then stacked three or four storeys high, its ground floor bricked and mortared, plastered and carpeted – becoming a family home, say, or a restaurant with a lino floor – but its remaining storeys left undone, with rusted strands of iron poking up from the concrete. A few of these shells housed crates of tools, or dismantled cars, or toddlers asleep under tarpaulin tents. The rest were littered with rubbish, with polythene bags and aluminium cans and hessian sacks of sand. But my entire time in Albania I never once saw a builder at work.

I stayed on the plain all that day, and the next day, and the next, hiking along the hard shoulder. Old men sat by the road, selling engine oil and tiny pots of polish. As I walked past, they would tweak their thumb and forefinger together, gesturing a question: Where was I going? What was I doing? Sometimes men with shaved scalps drove by in pristine Range Rovers, shouting offers of a lift, while at other times tractors little bigger than armchairs overtook me – Massey Fergusons six decades out of date – the farmers waving from behind shuddering engines. Every second car was a Mercedes, a boxy number from the 1990s painted beige, fawn, camel, buff, khaki, pewter or tan. Although these drivers honked their horns as they passed, I never could tell if this was encouragement, or surprise, or some kind of warning.

I was following signs for Elbasan, a small city eighty kilometres east of Durrës. I had expected the used cars, the unfinished architecture and the signs of discarded industry, but I had not expected the cheerful bemusement that greeted me by the roadside. And, as I neared the city, I began to share in this confusion. What *was* I doing here?

Learning more about Orthodoxy. That, at least, was what I told myself. Although I could remember that the Christians in Eastern Europe, Russia and the Balkans had split from Rome in the eleventh century, otherwise I knew little about this branch of the faith. However, I avoided most of the Orthodox churches, because the priests were forbidding figures and the services left me baffled – endless hours of standing, bowing, kneeling and chanting.

On the third morning I entered the Shkumbin Valley, a narrow passageway cutting into the mountains. Each day in Albania had been warmer than the last, and now the sky was spare with light. Farmland flanked the road and allotments lined the river, with elderly couples kneeling in the soil. When I waved they stopped their work to stare, watching me without expression. I kept waving until they went back to work, bending once more to the ground.

Next day I reached Elbasan. Here the trouble started.

Esme had green eyes and blonde-brushed hair that fell from her head in spirals. I was already besotted with her. 'Peel-grim,' she said, as her friend Arjana nodded along. 'Yes, in Albania we have a lot of peel-grim.'

It was late on Friday afternoon. We were sitting in a fifteenth-century fortress in the centre of Elbasan. Earlier that afternoon Esme and Arjana had taken me on a tour of the city: the state hospital, the state university, the open-air markets and the Rinia Park. We even went on a ride at the funfair, a metal pirate ship that squealed as it swung back and forth.

Elbasan Castle was the final stop. Its outer walls were still standing – a square of mounded masonry with watch-towers capping each corner and ivy overwhelming the battlements – but the space inside was now a complex of hotels and apartment blocks, with gardens, an amphi-theatre and a restaurant on propped terraces. We sat on the top terrace, looking out at the city's muddled rooftops, at sagging tiles and slanting shingles and sheets of pitch-black bitumen.

Esme kept speaking: 'In Laç – you have visit Laç? Drive to Tirana, drive to Lezhë, next is Laç. In the hills there is a church, Shën Antoni. Every summer peel-grim are coming to the church. From Albania, from Kosovo, from Greece. Everywhere. A lot, a lot. Ten thousand maybe. Everyone is coming for a miracle.'

'Do you believe in miracles?' I asked.

'Yes. I believe.'

'Have you ever seen one?'

'Once I have.'

'Go on!'

Esme looked embarrassed. 'My family is Muslim, but everyone is coming to Laç – Christian, Muslim, everyone. When I was eighteen we went for peel-grim-edge. Inside Shën Antoni I prayed to meet a man who I will marry only for love.'

Earlier that afternoon Arjana has explained how most of her friends were already married, the matches chosen by their parents, the weddings held within weeks of leav-ing school. However, because these two were nursing students, they had earned a little time. Esme wanted to choose her own husband.

'I prayed with all my heart,' she went on. 'One month after, my prayer comes true.'

By this point the restaurant was filling up. Groups of middle-aged women wearing too much make-up were joined by sleek young men in chrome-coloured shirts. Sitting beside them, it was easy to forget about the walk and imagine that I was here on holiday.

I asked Esme how they met. She looked embarrassed again and motioned typing. Facebook. First he sent her messages. Then they spoke on Skype. Finally they went for coffee, and Esme fell in love. To begin with she kept the relationship secret, because her parents knew nothing about the boy's family. However, one day her mother heard her whispering down the phone, and soon the whole story was out. That was when Esme decided the two families must meet. But they needed somewhere special. Somewhere neutral. So, back to Laç.

'We were late when we arrive to the church. My parents thought I was sick because I was too nervous. But when my father sees I am in love, he cannot be angry.'

'And now Esme is engaged!' Arjana added.

Heart breaking, smile fixed, I asked when she would marry.

'He is in Manchester. You know Manchester? For two years he has been working there. For two years I have not seen him.'

'He cannot come home,' Arjana explained, 'because there are no jobs in Albania.'

Arjana was smaller than Esme, with tiny hands and a tiny face. Her expression was earnest, but when she smiled she showed every one of her tiny teeth. A few hours ago, looking round the hospital, she had talked about work. The medical staff never had enough doctors, Arjana told me, but too many nurses. This was worse, because none of the nurses were properly trained, and elderly patients would often turn up with their wife or daughter, refusing to let anyone else care for them.

The hospital consisted of lightless hallways and cluttered corridors – a mess of blue binbags and beds on casters. Patients lay in the wards, the family members at their sides looking out with startled eyes. One of those patients, an old man tied up in plastic tubing, wanted to speak with me. His mouth was folded in, as if he had swallowed his lips, and though the jaw moved up and down, no sound came out. I tried to listen for his voice, but heard only a hollow *pock*, *pock*, like the bouncing of a ping-pong ball.

Esme and Arjana had lessons in the hospital; however, they were both studying at a private college called Università Cattolica Nostra Signora del Buon Consiglio. The college was run by nuns and classes took place in three or four languages. After qualifying, most of the students looked for jobs in Italy or Switzerland, but Arjana was different. She wanted to stay.

In the late afternoon, as we sat in the restaurant, she tried to explain why. 'Esme says I am scared to leave home, but if everyone leaves, who will make our country?' Arjana asked, holding out two tiny hands. Shadows crept through the gardens below, and buried lamps lit the grass in shifting constellations. Over the ramparts groups of men drifted along an avenue of reddish tile, while in the distance I could make out the funfair, its twists and slides and spinning tops shaped like giant toys. When the blue faded from the sky, the fairground lights began to dance, ribbons of neon wheeling round and round. For a moment I understood what kept Arjana here, because in a single day the country had opened up to me, and it seemed now like a precious place.

'There's nowhere the same as Albania,' she added.

Esme hoped to find a job in Manchester. 'Last year

I apply for a visa. Not to work, only to visit, but they tell me no visa.' She tugged at a spiral of hair, trying to remember the word. 'I know why. Is because I did not go on peel-grim-edge. So next month I will apply again, but first I will go to Laç. I will pray with my whole heart. And then maybe another miracle.'

That evening the nuns at Nostra Signora del Buon Consiglio hosted a dinner party. There were four of them: Sr Louisa Antonia, who took countless photographs on a digital camera; Sr Olga, who held a napkin to her face whenever she was in frame; Sr Alessandra, who kept rubbing her eyes as if the whole world was a surprise; and Sr Shalom, the mother superior, who talked less than the others, and smiled less too, but when she laughed she waved her arms like a conductor. The rest of the sisters would always join in, whether or not they heard the joke.

The nuns shared an apartment on the top floor of the college. It was rather smart: wax candles, embroidered tablecloths, silver picture frames and polished floors. The air smelt of crushed lavender and chopped herbs, with the ticklish afterscent of icing sugar. I turned up carrying a bunch of tulips and expecting three hours of strained conversation, but by the end of the evening I wanted never to leave.

Although the nuns' dining table was only big enough for eight, they had invited all the teachers – doctors and lecturers come over from Italy for a term. And, once everyone was squeezed into their seat, the room filled with a shared sense of anticipation, like a surprise party awaiting its final guest.

On my right sat a lecturer called Andreas. He wore expensive glasses, which he kept pushing up his nose with the tip of his finger. As a child Andreas had spent three years living in Nottingham, and now he spoke English with a Midlands accent. As an adult he had trained to become a criminal psychiatrist, but changed career after profiling too many paedophiles.

I asked if he was happy teaching here.

'The first time? No way. I left within three weeks. I couldn't cope with the atmosphere. The last mother superior, Sr Benedetta, was impossible. For the nuns, for the students, even the teachers. You know what she said to Sr Alessandra? Said she was too stupid to work here. Sat through her lessons. Made her take the students' exams. Sr Alessandra passed, but afterwards she was so depressed she couldn't leave her room for a year.'

'A year? Poor Sr Alessandra!'

He leant towards me. 'One day the governors decided to move Sr Benedetta to a college in Tirana. That's when Sr Shalom asked for her to be sent elsewhere. Albania is too small, she said. The other sisters would never escape. So Sr Benedetta was taken out of the country. Where? I don't know where.'

I started talking about my journey, and about the monks and nuns who had taken me in, trying to describe the fascination of their solitary, surrendered lives. 'But it must be odd working in a place where half the staff take a vow of obedience,' I added.

'It's like being dead. But that's the culture here: repressed.' He leant closer. 'There are young men in my class who are clearly gay, but cannot admit it. They will get married, have children and never understand their own sexuality.'

When Sr Shalom said grace, Andreas stopped talking. From that moment on, the discussion reeled round the table without settling. I remember Sr Olga explaining that, although this was a Catholic university, they taught students from all religious backgrounds. Albania was the most tolerant country in the world, Sr Louisa Antonia added, because every religion was persecuted during Hoxha's dictatorship. Yet Sr Shalom worried that Europe was becoming less tolerant and that her students would struggle to find jobs. But perhaps this was a blessing, Sr Alessandra suggested, as the university was meant to train the next generation of nurses, not send them away. At that point the other sisters nodded in tandem.

There was wine and music and too many courses. I kept turning down carafes of red and extra helpings of food. By the end of the first course, Sr Shalom's cheeks were shining. By the end of the second, Sr Olga had given up hiding from the photographs. Midway through dessert, while Sr Alessandra talked in tottering French about her favourite Father Brown mysteries, Sr Louisa Antonia ran from the room, returning with a bottle of homemade limoncello. She poured the liqueur into ten tiny glasses, reciting the recipe to herself – white spirit, sugar syrup, six peeled lemons – as the rest of the table simmered with laughter. Then Sr Shalom proposed a toast, wishing me luck for the rest of my trip. Listening to her speak, I realized that today had been my favourite of the whole pilgrimage. In my mind, fantastic plans were forming: I would stay in Albania, live in Elbasan, and marry Esme. (Those green eyes! That spiralling hair!) Now Sr Shalom was raising her glass into the air, the drink honey-bright in the candlelight. I raised my own and took a sip. Another sip. A third and the glass was finished.

Finally Sr Alessandra opened a box of After Eights, shaking them onto the table. 'My gosh,' said Andreas, watching plastic wrappers gem the cloth. 'English chocolates!'

Sr Shalom began to laugh, waving her arms in a figure

of eight. The other sisters joined in: an orchestra of nuns, laughing in harmony.

My holiday mood lasted all week. It was the feeling of restless possibility that comes with the spring, as each evening stretches longer than the last. Past Elbasan the valley narrowed and the fields bunched into steep slopes of pine. Plane trees knitted their branches above the road, while the colours in the woods became dense. Rich greens. Richer blacks. My boots were looser now, the soles beginning to soften, so I slowed my pace and dropped down to the river, picnicking by the bank or washing my feet in the water.

The upper valley was sparsely populated, but there were villages with children playing in the street. As I walked by they would call out in the few English phrases they knew. *Hello how are you I am fine*. Sometimes they ran towards me, shaking my hand and pulling my rucksack straps. *Hello what is your name please*. Long after I left their villages, one or two would still be skipping at my side, wittering away in a dozen words of English. *Hello how are you goodbye*.

Later, as I hiked on the gravel banks above the river, a man cycled up behind me and got off to walk. He was wearing white trousers, white shoes, white socks and a white T-shirt. His hair was powdery grey, and dry spittle flecked the edges of his mouth. The man's name was Mehmet.

Mehmet told me that he was once a wealthy engineer with a house in Elbasan, a flat in Tirana, and one, two, three Mercedes to drive between them. 'But then Jesus Christ, Son of God, gives me a vision.'

'What kind of vision?'

'White light. Like soap. It washes the buildings, washes the streets, washes the sun. Everything clean after that. All the sin washes away.'

'Are you sure it was from Jesus?'

'Jesus Christ, Son of God, was the most clean man.'

'I see.'

'Now Mehmet has no car. Now Mehmet cycle everywhere. Kukës to Vlorë. Shkodër to Sarandë. Everywhere cycle. Everywhere tell the good news.'

He asked my job. I told him I didn't have one. 'Keep walking – that's my job.'

'You must pray!' he announced. 'Every morning, when you get out of bed, you must pray: Please God to give me a job.'

'Haven't got a bed either.'

'You must pray! Every morning pray: Please God to give me a bed.'

'I used to work for a newspaper.'

He paused a beat, two beats. 'When I went to Greece, to tell the good news, I met a journalist of the BBC. He say: Greece will fall out of Europe. I say: Greece will not fall out of Europe. Every morning Mehmet pray to God that please Greece will not fall. Yes?'

'If you say so.'

Patches of grey grew in the pits of his T-shirt. Leaves of paint peeled from his bike. His shoes made a snarling sound on the gravel, and his voice never dipped below shouting.

I walked more quickly. Mehmet matched my pace.

'Where is your wife?' he asked.

'No wife.'

'You must pray!'

'Did you pray for a wife?'

'Mehmet prayed. Now he has too many.'

'But I can't afford to get married.'

'God will make you rich. You must—'

'Yes, I get the idea.'

Mehmet licked his lips. The skin was chapped and chalky. 'Every morning you must pray: Please God to make me rich. Then you must give everything away to charity and God will give you ten times more, twenty times more.'

I told him I didn't want to be rich, but it was too late.

'If you give ten euro to charity, God will give to you hundred euro. If you give hundred euro, God will give to you thousand euro. Mehmet is charity. Every day Mehmet tell the good news. Give hundred euro to Mehmet and God will give to you thousand euro.'

I stopped moving. 'I haven't got a hundred euros.'

'Give fifty euro to Mehmet and God will give to you five hundred euro.'

'I want to walk alone now.'

'Give Mehmet thirty euro—'

'Go away!'

He licked his lips a second time. His mouth was clenched, hungry. Then he got onto his bicycle and rode off, tyres grinding over the gravel.

That was on Saturday morning.

On Saturday afternoon I entered the lower slopes of Mt Jablanica – a ridge running down the eastern edge of Albania, forming the main border with Macedonia. The road tracked an antique railway as it burrowed between boulders, cliffs and buttresses of rock. Though my path kept climbing, I seemed to rise no higher, but grew dizzy following its twisted course, tramping hour after hour in the sun.

Eventually I came to Librazhd, a town forty kilometres west of the border, set in the fold of a hill. Mismatched buildings lined the streets, their walls made of brick and mortar, plaster and glass, the corners chipped and the colours muddied. Red balconies, blue porches, green shopfronts and pink awnings – all of them grimed with age. Here and there I noticed wooden gables or tiled roofs, but I saw no church, so I went into a grocery shop and asked for a priest.

The owner of the shop had a frowning face and a schoolboy haircut. He motioned me to wait and called for his son, Aleks, who swaggered downstairs and started to translate. Yes, there was a church in Librazhd. There, in the hut opposite the shop. The Antiokia Evangelical Church. That's right, a Protestant church. England was a Protestant country, yes? Good. Aleks's father was the church pastor. Tonight I would stay with his family, and tomorrow we would go to church.

Aleks showed me upstairs. Above the shop was a flat with rooms of blond pine and a smell like warm bedding. The furniture was pine too, and the shelves decorated with religious memorabilia: plastic-framed postcards of Jesus, or passages from Scripture carved in stone. Yet the place was too new to feel welcoming, and so tidy that I was reluctant to put down my rucksack.

The windows in the sitting room faced east towards the mountains. Aleks made a bed for me on the sofa. 'My father built this house,' he announced, as he laid out the blankets and sheets. 'He built it with his hands. I am very blessed; I know that I am very blessed.'

Aleks was twenty-two. His head was shaved and his movements abrupt, but he spoke softly, his English ornamented with polite turns of phrase. When Aleks was a boy, Peace Corps volunteers visited the town each weekend. Librazhd had the only Protestant church in the region and they came for the Sunday service. They would often spend the night, meaning Aleks could practise his

English. One of them married his sister, and now she lived in America. 'In summer I will go stay with her. When I am done studying, maybe I will move there. I am studying to be physiotherapist. Truly it is my dream, but in Albania there is no money for physiotherapist.' He shook himself and lit a cigarette. 'Come, you will meet my friends.'

Outside, the *passeggiata* had begun. Groups of boys and groups of girls flocked from one end of the high street to the other, from a fast-food restaurant with ketchup-red booths to a pizzeria with a purple floor. They were teenagers mostly, the girls wearing fluorescent eyeshadow and perfume scented like sweets, the boys wearing squeaky trainers and T-shirts decorated in album covers.

Aleks's friends were waiting for him at the top of the street. For the next half-hour we strode around, strolled around, stood around, and finally sat in a terrace cafe with lighted globes strung from each corner. My host told a confused story from last summer about crossing into Greece illegally, finding work at a holiday resort, falling for a local girl, and getting banned from the country for the next three years. But, when I requested more details, he rushed off to find his cousins.

Forty-five minutes later he had not returned. I asked the friends whether he was coming back, but they simply shrugged. Otherwise they ignored me, except to play-punch my arm and ask for a passport or a job. When I tried to answer they laughed and told me it was a joke, only a joke.

One of the friends wanted to know how long I had been walking. Three months, three weeks, and sixteen days, I answered. And how many women had I slept with in that time? None? Surely not. 'Man, if I was travelling that long,' he said, 'it would be all the countries.' 'I tell you,' said another, 'I can't sleep if I don't have sex.' Soon everyone was talking at once. 'You have a girlfriend?' 'You have a wife?' 'Who makes your food?' 'Who cleans your clothes?' 'You don't like women?' 'You like men?' 'Like boys?' 'Want to be a monk?'

I explained that I stayed most nights in churches and monasteries, which made meeting young women a bit tricky. And that, if I had been in a relationship, I might never have left home. But no matter what I said, I could see they were disappointed. In Italy, spending time with pilgrims and priests, I had forgotten how strange my journey might seem. Now I struggled to justify the walk, and after mumbling a few phrases about the crises in Christianity, I turned away to search for my host, cheeks hot with humiliation.

Eventually Aleks returned to the cafe looking glazed. 'I met my cousins,' he told me, as we hurried back to the house. 'They buy me shots.'

'It's no problem,' he went on, his voice slack, his feet stumbling. 'My parents never notice. They never drink.'

Aleks's mother had made stuffed peppers and pilaf. She was a quick, nervous woman, serving the food with quaking wrists. When we held hands to say grace, it was like holding a sparrow.

I spent the meal asking questions about their church, which Aleks translated. With each question his father grew more and more quiet – a stiff, furious quiet. He said: 'No Protestants in Albania before communism.' He said: 'In the nineties the missionaries arrive from America.' He said: 'The churches, the mosques, every year their numbers are smaller, except for the Protestants . . .'

Silence. The pastor stood, his cutlery clattering to the floor. Then he walked from the room, slamming the door behind him.

Aleks's mother was still sitting beside me, her eyes

squeezed shut. She was trying to swallow a mouthful of rice, but her throat had stopped working. I watched her jaw jut, watched her cheeks bulge, until finally she gulped it down and the tears ran from her eyes. Then she got up and shuffled through the door. Aleks went crashing after her.

I stayed at the table, eating alone. Although I heard muffled sounds of argument behind the door, I could not guess what they were about. Streetlights blared through the window, but the streets were quiet now.

When Aleks came back his eyes were red-rimmed. He scoffed the remains of the rice and began to tidy the table. Once it was clear he set up a backgammon board. Half-way into our first game, he said: 'I know my father wanted to talk to you. Truly he wanted to tell you about our church. He founded it from nothing. He built it with his hands.'

We kept playing. Aleks kept winning.

'My father is my hero. It makes him angry when I smoke.' He blinked hard, his voice unsteady. 'But this is the last time, I swear.'

I was confused. Aleks had been smoking all evening without ever trying to hide it. There was a cigarette lodged behind his left ear and an ashtray on the balcony outside. Then I remembered his stumbling steps home and the reckless way he finished the leftover food. Of course. He did not mean cigarettes.

At last the evening's stifled collapse made sense to me, and the smothered frustration between father and son was explained. Yet the jagged atmosphere in the house remained, as if nobody had been forgiven.

'I know that I am blessed,' Aleks said again. 'But sometimes it's hard. Truly it's hard.'

*

Next morning we went to church. The Antiokia Evangel-ical Church was a pair of low rooms with plaster walls and a polystyrene ceiling. There was no altar, pulpit or pews, but six rows of six chairs facing towards a stage. By ten o'clock the chairs were full of women in colourful skirts and men in baggy jackets. Children sat on the floor or crowded round the stage, shouting one another quiet. Aleks's father stood at the front, his arms crossed, his head bowed.

To begin with we sang hymns, the words projected onto the wall. Four teenage girls stood on the stage to lead the singing, their clothes copied from a music video. During the chorus they would swing their hips and raise their arms into the air, and when the oldest girl stepped forwards for the descant, the one on her left burst into pantomime tears. I tried to join in the singing, but felt so out of place that my voice choked and I could only mouth the lyrics.

Between each hymn one of the children gave a reading, racing through a passage from the Gospels. Then Aleks's father improvised a prayer, his pauses punctuated with the words: *Hallelujah* and *Amen*. These words were echoed back by the congregation, becoming louder at every response. The pastor also delivered the sermon, and though it lasted almost an hour, I was never bored. As he spoke he knelt to the floor, or stood on tiptoe crying, 'Amen, Amen!' Meanwhile the congregation clapped and cheered and broke out in spontaneous prayer, their faces thrown back, their palms turned skywards. His sermon was in Albanian, but one section was made up of English loanwords, and these I could recognize. No more computers – *Amen!* – No more internet – *Amen!* – No more show business – *Hallelujah!* – No more rap music – *Hallelujah! Amen!* While the pastor spoke, Aleks lurched from side to side. *Hallelujah! Amen!* His mother was babbling, her tongue spilling loose from her mouth. *Hallelujah! Hallelujah!* Every hand was raised, the whole church swaying. *Amen! Amen! Amen!*

Noise – there was so much noise in that little room.

After the service I helped stack chairs at the back of the church. Photographs were pinned to the walls, showing the pastor waist deep in the River Shkumbin. The rest of the congregation were watching from the shore, dressed in robes and waiting to be baptized. I recognized some of the younger members: the tearful girl from the choir and two of the friends from last night, gasping as they were lifted out of the water, sunlight splashing on their faces.

One of the photographs featured an older woman rising from the river. Her eyes were open, her mouth wide open, and sunshine seeped through her pale clothes, her papery skin – the whole body made bright by the sodden light. It was a frail body, the edges blurred as if quaking in fear. It was Aleks's mother. I kept looking at the photograph, pierced by a sudden sense of recognition, for I realized that the babbling noise she made during the service was tongues. She was speaking the language of Pentecost.

Half an hour later pastor and son escorted me from Librazhd. As we marched past the fast-food restaurant with ketchup-coloured booths and the pizzeria with a purple floor, Aleks began to translate.

'My father says: Jesus has taught us to love strangers. Truly, it makes us glad to help you, because that is what Jesus has taught. But my father does not understand why you are walking. He says that Jesus suffered on the cross so we do not have to suffer. Also he says that in every country there are Christians, there are Muslims, and there are people who do not believe. In every country there are proud men and wicked men, injustice and sin. Everywhere the same. So why walk?'

I gave no answer. After a while Aleks added: 'But that is only his opinion. If I could, I would walk like you. If I could quit this town, I would do it.'

Come with me, I wanted to say. Leave Albania and walk with me to Jerusalem! But I did not speak, because I knew that Aleks would remain here, and so we went the rest of the way in silence.

The high street swung out of Librazhd, crossing the River Shkumbin and rejoining the road. I stopped to thank my hosts, before they turned towards the town, father leading son, back to the house he had built with his hands.

I left Albania on a clean and cloudless Monday. A wall of rock ran south from Mt Jablanica, and for the first hour of the day I hiked up its side. The sun was rising behind the mountain, tipping peak-shaped shadows over the valley floor. As it lifted higher, the peaks folded in on themselves, a sweep of shadow racing me onto the ridgeline.

A winding road tacked towards the border. Garages edged the road, each one with a hose in front. Their spouts were fixed at an angle and set to full strength, the water arcing out to catch the bright rim of the morning, before splashing to the ground with a sound like dropped coins.

By eleven o'clock I was on top of the ridgeline. The guard at the crossing wanted to know where I was going, so I took out my map and explained.

My route started from Lake Ohrid, near the Albanian border, and led to the Pelagonia Plain, on the border with Greece. The plain was divided from the lake by a narrow mountain range draped in black pine: Mt Galičica. A single road skirted the range, ending some seventy-three kilometres later in the city of Bitola. Few settlements lay between, so I had decided to cover the whole distance in a two-day trek.

The guard grew bored as I explained my route, waving me on without another word. I kept to the ridge for the next hour, rounding soft-headed summits of fern. Macedonia was below me, the whole country covered in cloud. Whenever the clouds parted I saw splayed hills with great scoops of grass at their base. Lake Ohrid lay beneath the hills, the sunlight spread on its surface like sequins sewn into the water. Each time I glimpsed the lake, I felt a surging sense of achievement. Despite the warnings in Bari, I had crossed Albania without trouble, and felt now as if I could hike through a war zone.

Eventually the road dipped below the cloudline, past orchards of apple trees, timber-framed houses and meadows flecked with alpine flowers. By lunchtime I had reached the lake. It was thirty kilometres long, with forested slopes enclosing a clear palette of sky. The water was lucid blue that day, and flawless as if sealed beneath enamel. Six or seven fishing boats winked on the far side.

All afternoon I circled the shore, approaching a fortified city on the eastern edge. The old town stretched halfway up the headland, its houses white boxes topped with terracotta tiles. This was Ohrid – once the holiest city in the Balkans.

It was evening when I arrived in the city and dark by the time I found somewhere to stay. Later that night I left my room and went down to the lake.

Guesthouses were gathered near the port, with restaurants and bars opening onto the waterfront. Russian tourists strutted between them, wearing backless dresses and high-heeled boots. More Russians smoked on the quayside, flicking their cigarettes into the water. They were late twenties, early thirties, paired off in gorgeous couples. Listening to the laughter in their voices, I was reminded of Aleks's friends and their mocking questions, of Aleks's father and his polite disapproval. I began to feel embarrassed by my journey, for its hardships seemed pointless, its motives confused. Then I remembered Elbasan, remembered Esme and Arjana, and the nuns' dinner party, and the limoncello thick as honey. Absurd drink. My first in two years. With that my embarrassment became something else: a sudden desire to get drunk. I felt it rush my thoughts, quicken my pulse, felt my cheeks pinch and my lips quiver – until I turned away from the lake and went up into the old town.

Cobbled streets rose through tiers of Ottoman houses. The upper storeys of each house jutted over the ones below, their wooden cumbas and projecting eaves closing out the stars.

Eventually I came to a grand church near the top of the hill. It was built from uneven squares of stone and inlaid with arches of patterned brick. The corners were spotlit, giving every surface a dim, dimpled, orange-peel shine. Approaching the gates, I could see gilded icons above the doorway and ceramic tracery in the windows, their designs made molten by the light.

Behind the church lay a set of upright columns and sunken foundations. A sign by the gates announced that these were the remains of the Ohrid Literary School. St Clement, patron saint of Macedonia, was buried inside.

Had I returned the following day, the tour guide would have told me the rest. He would have explained that Clement was a Bulgarian missionary who started the famous school in the ninth century. The school taught theology in local languages, rather than the Greek used by clerics, and according to some scholars it was the first university in Europe. Its students, the guide might have added, established monasteries all round Lake Ohrid,

turning this city into the spiritual centre of the western Bulgarian Empire. But one thing the guide would not have mentioned: within a century of the saint's death, the whole region was a nursery of heretics. Because the mountains east of Ohrid were the heartland of the Bogomil Church.

About a hundred years after the establishment of the Ohrid Literary School, a new heresy arrived in Macedonia, founded by an enigmatic figure known as Bogomil. His followers practised total simplicity, refusing to eat meat or drink wine, and remaining celibate their whole lives. Most of their time was spent praying or begging for food, which to some people looked like piety. However, according to one influential sermon, they also worshipped the devil, calling him the creator of the sun, the sky, the earth and all mankind.

This sermon was written by a Bulgarian priest named Cosmas. It portrayed the Bogomils as freakish figures with wasted bodies and colourless skin, who laughed at icons, barked at priests and muttered blasphemies at the Virgin Mary. In addition, the heretics rejected churches, sacraments and the entire Orthodox hierarchy, making them dangerous radicals: 'They teach their people not to submit to the rulers,' Cosmas claimed, 'they blaspheme the wealthy, hate the king, ridicule the elders, reproach the nobles, regard as vile in the sight of God those who serve the king, and forbid servants to obey their masters.'

Why Macedonia? Actually, it's hard to imagine a better location. The country was protected on all sides by mountains, but the Via Egnatia brought merchants and missionaries through its south-east corner. Sheltered from Constantinople, unorthodox ideas could flourish.

Thanks to the Ohrid Literary School, the region surrounding the lake was still a centre of monasticism.

However, there was also a strong spirit of rebellion here. In the early eleventh century, once the Bulgarian Empire had come under the influence of Byzantium, the peasants were Slavic, the ruling classes Bulgar, and the priests Greek. Joining the Bogomil Church – a homegrown movement that spoke the local languages and adapted native rites – was a protest against colonial rule.

Looking at Cosmas's sermon a second time, it's easy to guess the reasons for the heresy's popularity. The Bogomils lived among the people, praying, fasting and doling out forgiveness. So why did Cosmas call them devil-worshippers?

To make sense of that accusation, we need to go back another six centuries. Before Christianity was adopted by the Roman Empire and its fundamentals fixed in the Nicene Creed, the eastern edge of the Mediterranean was a spiritual Silicon Valley, crowded with mystics, hermits and start-up sects. Many of these sects followed a dualist offshoot of the faith known as Gnostic Christianity. They believed that the angry, jealous Yahweh of the Old Testament was a demiurge, or devil, and that the material world – full of anguish and grief – was the devil's domain.

Although the distinction may seem abstract, its consequences were profound. Creation was no longer a gift to be enjoyed, but a purgatory to be endured. And, if flesh was wicked, the concrete side of Christianity – the churches and sacraments, the festivals and rites – no longer made sense. So they were replaced by endless rounds of mortification and prayer.

What drew people to this bleak worldview? Well, for many, dualism helped make sense of suffering. The cruelty of this life cries out against a loving God, as an all-powerful deity is behind every hurt, every tear. Conventional theodicy struggles with the problem of evil, having to excuse the creator responsibility for his work.

However, if this world has been hijacked by the devil, God is off the hook. Therefore, though dualist teaching seems bizarre, it avoids one of the central paradoxes of monotheism. For the charge still stands. The suffering remains.

Among the most influential of these sects were the Manichaeans, who counted a young Augustine of Hippo among their members. But, once Nicene Christianity became dominant, they were hounded beyond the borders of Byzantium.

Over the next few centuries dualist teaching was revived several times in remote corners of the empire. During the Early Middle Ages a sect known as the Paulicians appeared in Armenia, rejecting the Old Testament, the incarnation, icons, relics, crucifixes, and the whole structure of the Orthodox Church. Contemporary accounts linked their beliefs back to the Manichaeans, and also accused them of devil worship – the origin of Cosmas's claim.

In 871 the nascent Paulician kingdom was destroyed by the Byzantine Empire, and its priests went into exile. As a result, dualism moved west along the Via Egnatia, turning the Roman road into a highway for heterodox teaching.

Prior to the invention of the printing press, the best way to propagate a new idea was via an itinerant preacher. For a religious idea, vagrancy was also a seal of authenticity – if not orthodoxy. When Paulician preachers showed up in Macedonia around the tenth century, they found a willing audience, and the Bogomil Church was born.

Which brings us back to Cosmas. Even though his sermon was written to warn against the heresy's rapid expansion, Bogomilism soon spread throughout the Balkans. By the beginning of the twelfth century the heretics were established in Constantinople. Their leader was now a tall, withered figure named Basil, a former physician from Bulgaria who, according to one rumour, learnt medicine in Ohrid after being expelled from a monastery. Basil was so popular with the city's nobility that Alexios Komnenos, the Byzantine emperor, invited him round for supper. Convinced the emperor was about to convert, Basil shared his secrets. He explained how his followers would pray seven times a day and five times a night; fast on the second, fourth and sixth days of the week; and observe bans on meat, alcohol, sex and Church sacraments.

Komnenos listened to everything that Basil told him. When the meal was over, he called the guards. Soon each one of the city's heretics had been rounded up.

In the *Alexiad*, an epic account of the emperor's reign attributed to his daughter Anna, the trial of the Bogomils occupies several chapters. Basil's execution forms perhaps the most vivid passage in the entire chronicle. A massive bonfire was built in Constantinople's hippodrome, its flames stretching thirty metres into the air. The heresiarch was given one final chance to repent, but instead began to rant and rave, boasting that God would reach down from the clouds and rescue him. His cloak was thrown onto the fire and flared up at once, but no, shrieked Basil, look how it floats through the sky, soaring towards heaven!

At this point the audience grew nervous. Some had visions of the cloak ascending like an angel; others were convinced that demons protected the master Bogomil. Eventually the guards lost patience:

> Then they [. . .] took him and pushed him, clothes, shoes and all, into the middle of the pyre. And the flames, as if deeply enraged against him, ate the impious man up, without any odour arising or even a

fresh appearance of smoke, only one thin smoky line could be seen in the midst of the flames.

I left the lakeshore, heading east up the side of Mt Galičica. Half an hour after setting off, I realized my water bottle was almost empty. Overgrown gullies sank from the road, with streams rustling along the bottom, but I was confident I would pass their sources higher up and did not climb down for a refill. Yet higher up the noise of the water became faint, until I could hear nothing except the heaving wind and the whisper of my stepcount. *Five thousand five hundred and twenty-two. Five thousand five hundred and twenty-three.*

Heretics were on my mind that morning. This was the first day of real heat, and there was something menacing about the dry air, the brindled black of the forest – it was easy to picture a starved preacher hefting round some forbidden text. As I rose through the trees, my feet became swollen and my shirt damp. Also, the water in my bottle stewed, its plastic cap hot to touch. And, when I looked up midmorning to see the crags smoking ahead of me, I immediately thought of bonfires.

Closer, I could make out domes of rubbish, heaped high and set alight. Plastic crates, fabric furnishings, scrap packaging and mounds of books – hundreds of volumes, centuries of work, their pages flaking into the air.

Smoke billowed onto the road. There was smoke in my eyes, smoke in my mouth, and the smoky fumes were greased with heat. I opened the water bottle, tipped it back, gulped once, twice, and the whole lot was gone.

After that the road veered between dense forest and overgrown heathland. The air was warm, and I walked fast, hoping for a house where I could ask for water. *Nine thousand four hundred and seventy-six.* My mouth was dry, my tongue thick. *Nine thousand four hundred and seventy-seven.* Points of pain edged my skull. *Nine thousand four hundred and seventy-eight.*

Nine thousand four hundred –

Nine thousand –

I gave up the count.

Twenty-three kilometres from Ohrid, at the highest point of the road, there was a clearing. A log cabin stood in the middle, the windows boarded up and the walls swarmed with graffiti. Behind, I could see a brick out-house with its door ajar. Holding my breath, I ducked through the doorway. Shit was smeared on the walls and floor, like markings for some strange ritual. Flies screamed above the toilet bowl, but I found no sink, no tap, nor any sign of running water.

Beyond the clearing the road sank through slopes of alder, oak and ash, descending into the Prespa Valley. This was a basin midway between Mt Galičica and Mt Baba, a checkwork of low hills and terraced orchards, tipping south towards Lake Prespa. Surely I would find a drink soon.

Thirty kilometres from Ohrid I passed sluice gates and sewage pumps. Irrigation ditches divided the orchards, their channels dry but for a brackish residue resembling drool. By now my tongue was rough and the saliva sticky in my cheeks. I thought of fasts, of ascetics, of wandering holy men living off air. Surely I would find one.

Thirty-two kilometres from Ohrid I saw an orchard with rubber hoses netting the trees. One of the hoses was leaking, a clear liquid spilling from the rubber and muddying the ground. When I bent down to collect some, the warm earth crumbled like biscuit. The liquid had the same flavour as metal, as mould – the same temperature as blood. After just one mouthful I poured it away, but now my gums tasted singed.

Thirty-five kilometres from Ohrid and at last I came to a stream, a shallow trench with sides of pebble and turf. Silt clouded the water, but I filled and emptied my bottle twice over. Then I lay on my back and listened to the current giggling past. The ground seemed to sway beneath me, and the braced impatience I had felt since Ohrid relaxed. Lying beside the bank, I realized why the Bogomil Church still haunted my thoughts.

Pilgrimage had shown me what was radical about the wandering life, as on the road all tokens of status were left behind. Food and shelter were riches enough, while possessions were excess weight. This made it easy to sympathize with preachers and cults on the fringes of the faith. They resembled the penitent movements I had learnt of in Italy, without the power and pageantry of mass devotion. But perhaps my sympathy was really uncertainty. Unlike with Catholicism, I could not fake any familiarity with Orthodoxy. Instead I was drawn towards its outcasts, for they seemed to endorse my growing sense of exile.

Thirty-eight kilometres from Ohrid I stopped at a clay-coloured town called Resen. The convent of Sveta Bogorodica lay in the hills above the town. At six o'clock I reached its gates and lowered my rucksack to the ground.

The convent was set in a grassy bowl collared by woodland, its church and chapter house whitewashed halls. The cellblock was whitewashed too, with a veranda of timber beams and sculpted banisters. A pair of Alsatians were tied to the veranda, and they started barking when I let myself in, straining at their chains and scratching the earth. Although I called out, I heard nothing over the baying dogs. I knocked on the chapter house door: no response. I circled the courtyard – flowerbeds, herb gardens, and a chicken coop on a balding lawn – but nobody was home.

As I turned back towards the gates, a woman stepped from the cellblock. Black clothes hung loose off her body, and a pair of half-moon spectacles made her whole face peer.

I explained that I was walking to Jerusalem and looking for somewhere to spend the night.

The woman crossed her arms, uncrossed them. Her gaze was pained, as if trying to place some dreadful memory. 'Only Sr Paraskeva can give you permission,' she replied in Australian-accented English. 'Sr Paraskeva's away.'

I asked if I could camp on the grass outside the convent. No answer. Or was there a priest in Resen I could stay with? Again, no reply. Had the woman spent time in Australia? I wondered. No, nothing.

Thanking her, I lifted my rucksack onto my shoulders. As I moved off, she spoke once more. 'You know, I've been on pilgrimage. A few times I slept in parks. And a bus stop too, but that was just one night.'

'Where was this?'

'You know Fruška Gora? It's in Serbia. It's this mountain with all these monasteries. Or Asenovgrad? That's Bulgaria. That's mountains too, but with chapels. Or Meteora, you know Meteora? Hold on, I've got a picture somewhere.' She searched her pockets, handing me a postcard of a monastery balanced on a slender stump of rock. 'That's Greece. That's the Pindus. Meteora, like meteorite. Are you travelling there?'

I gave the photograph back, promising to try.

'It's tough when you're travelling alone, when you haven't got anywhere to sleep – I know it is! There's only me here at the moment, so it's not proper for a man to stay. But if it's just one night, I guess you could use the guestroom.'

'That's very kind.'

'Except, if someone comes to visit, someone from the village, you have to keep out of sight until they're gone. All right?'

'Fine.'

She held out her hand. 'I'm Anna.'

Sveta Bogorodica was built on terraces. A brick chapel occupied the top terrace, a brand-new building with marble offcuts lying by the door, navy and white like little fragments of the night. The main church stood on the next terrace down, its piecemeal walls constructed from brick and stone, its roof tiles blotched with lichen. Inside, the ornaments were sooty and the icons masked in smokestain.

Another terrace down was the cellblock. My room was up a wooden staircase, along a wooden gallery, and through a wooden doorway at the far end. It was a modest space. Unvarnished timber floor. Unpainted plaster wall. Three mattresses piled to one side. Three rugs folded on top. Yet the effect was somehow comforting, for unlike the monumental austerity of a Cistercian monastery, the simplicity at Sveta Bogorodica seemed improvised. Maybe the nuns were also guests here, making their lives as small as possible and leaving no trace behind.

While Anna showed me round, I asked questions about her pilgrimage.

'I didn't have much money,' she said. 'That's why I slept out. In Croatia the police took me to a hotel, said otherwise they would arrest me. There were plenty others sleeping in the park – local people, local men – but because I was foreign they thought I was rich. All I had was fifty euros – for emergencies! And I gave that away – to a homeless man! He didn't have any money, any coat, nothing to eat. I knew that, even if I gave him all my money, I was still much richer than him. Then I went to a church to ask for some bread and you know what happened? The priest gave me a hundred euros. Like that, a hundred euros. I said: I want your address! I want to pay you back! But he said: It's a gift. Keep it. Then I started laughing, like maybe God was playing a trick on me.'

Once I had unpacked, we sat in the kitchen. Glass jars crowded the shelves, containing vegetables preserved in oil or pickled in brine, as well as jams, jellies, marmalades and chutneys, with plastic containers of spices and pots of herbs labelled by hand. The whole collection twinkled like a bag full of marbles.

Anna made grilled-cheese sandwiches with a roast-pepper paste called *ajvar*. 'It's special cheese,' she told me, 'Lent cheese.' This year Orthodox Easter fell five weeks later than the Catholic festival, which meant Anna was still fasting. No meat, no dairy, no oil, and only one meal a day. 'We can eat soya and quorn, but the shops always run out. I tell them: Buy enough! Stock enough! Then Sr Paraskeva changes what days we fast, how many meals we have—'

'So there's only you and Sr Paraskeva living here?'

Anna nodded. 'Macedonia has all these empty monasteries, and the Church wants to fill them up. Problem is: no vocations. Except for the big places, most have one monk, one nun, and plenty are empty.'

'Is it difficult, just the pair of you?'

'I guess we argue.' She paused. 'You could say I'm used to it.' Paused again. 'See, Paraskeva's actually my mother.'

'Sorry?'

It went like this: Anna's parents were originally from Macedonia, but they emigrated when she was a child. Anna and her sister grew up in Australia, until their father died and their mother decided to become a nun. So she gave away her possessions and bought a one-way ticket home. 'My sister was pregnant. Paraskeva left the week before the birth. My sister thought she was losing both parents, one after the other. But a nun gives up everything for God. Family, everything.'

'Her name – what does it mean?'

'St Paraskeva! She was a pilgrim. She ran away from home. Went all round the Balkans, went to Jerusalem, lived right next door to the River Jordan. But when she knew she was going to die, went home again. I call the nun here Paraskeva because, see, she isn't my mum any more.'

'Even though you came with her?'

Before Anna could answer, the dogs started barking. My host moved to the window and then ducked down with her hands to her mouth. 'Hide!'

Out of the kitchen, up the staircase, along the veranda – crawling on hands and knees. Then into the guestroom, into the corner, flat behind the mattresses. Stay still. Try not to breathe. Listen to the cheerful shouts coming from the courtyard. Glance through the door at the middle-aged man waiting by the gate. Notice the baseball cap, the waistcoat, and the cardboard trays stacked in his arms. What's he carrying?

I turned back, holding my breath. It was almost eight, and a lazy light clouded the convent. My shins were scraped, my elbows sore, but when I closed my eyes the pain subsided and I felt very far away – exiled from all I had known, hidden in this half-wild place. Lying there, I could smell grass and pine and the hazy scent of pollen. I could smell spring falling fresh through the air.

When I opened my eyes the sun had set and the room was gloaming over. The voices outside were quiet now, but then Anna called my name.

'It was Kiril,' she said as I emerged. 'He was worried

I might be lonely. I told him: Don't worry! Don't come here all the time! I told him, but he won't listen.'

The trays contained about ninety eggs. Anna asked me to carry them into the kitchen. 'I have to paint them in time for Easter – every one!' she said, adding: 'If you wanted to give me a hand, I guess you could stay another day.'

I did want to stay. Stay tomorrow and the rest of Holy Week. Stay long enough to see spring bursting from the hills around Resen and summer shimmering on the Prespa Lakes. To see autumn burning in the forests of Mt Galičica and winter smothering the Pelagonia Plain. I was tired of travelling and sick of being a stranger, so why not leave off walking and rest here for a while?

However, I had promised a friend I would reach Greece for the first week of May. So I thanked Anna and explained that I must push on.

A few hours later, back in the guestroom, I was woken by a noise from outside. The moon was very bright and the convent buildings luminous. My host was wandering around on the terrace below, talking to herself in broken sentences. Her voice sounded fitful against the immense silence of the valley. I watched her locking and relocking the gates, and for a moment it seemed she was trying to open them, trying desperately to escape. Then she turned away, muttering to the dogs in the mad midnight light. I wondered what calling had taken Anna from her home and what loyalty kept her here. And I wondered if she would wait out her life in this place. Who was she waiting for?

From Resen my route climbed again, circling the Baba Massif and the border with Greece. All morning I roamed among high meadows and mixed woodland, a warm breeze teasing the back of my neck. That afternoon I made my way down onto the Pelagonia Plain, approaching the city of Bitola.

It was May Day. There were hundreds of clouds in the sky. There were hundreds of fields at my feet. There were thousands of families out in the fields, picnicking in the long grass or playing games on the ochre earth. Waves of tobacco and wheat washed towards the River Crna, while the smoke from barbecues scrolled the summit of Mt Baba.

I hiked hard all afternoon, and after thirty-seven kilometres I reached Bitola. On the edge of the city I stopped at a grand church in a grove of fruit trees. Its caretaker, Goran, lived next door. His cottage had a bedroom, a kitchen, and a bathroom no bigger than a cupboard, with toilet, sink and shower fitted one on top of the other. Goran was child-thin, his beard too bushy for the rest of his body. Earlier that day, when giving directions to the church, Anna told me that he had wanted to be a priest ever since he was young. After seminary Goran came to Bitola to look for a wife. Ten years later he had not found one.

Although the caretaker spoke no English, his friend Damjan was here to translate. Damjan was paunchy and pug-faced, with muscle-packed shoulders and hands the size of shovelheads. He had a degree in civil engineering and a diploma in transport infrastructure, but worked as a taxi driver.

When I asked whether Goran could become a priest without a wife, Damjan bit his cheeks. 'We are a poor country,' he said. 'The priest is a well-paid man. Many women want to marry the priest, but nobody marries Goran.'

'No girlfriend?'

'Too shy! Ten years, not one.'

Goran was fasting, so I ate with Damjan. We opened the windows and doors and sat in the kitchen, sharing plates of sausage, gherkin and bread. My companion talked for the whole meal, the chewed food falling from his mouth. At one point he tried to sell me a holiday home in the hills above Bitola, at another point he lectured me on Yugoslav nationalism, and several times he suggested I marry his niece. Although I nodded and laughed as he spoke, I struggled to read the furious glee in his features.

Then we discussed heresy, Damjan beating the table while he talked. Again, I could not say whether this was anger or delight.

In the late eleventh century Pelagonia was thick with heretics. When Bohemond, Prince of Taranto, marched his army along the Via Egnatia to join the First Crusade, he stopped off here for supplies. The *Gesta Francorum*, an account of the campaign written by one of his knights, records how the army laid siege to a heretic town near Bitola. Once the citizens surrendered, the whole place was set on fire – buildings, livestock and every last inhabitant. Who were these poor unfortunates? Bogomils, perhaps, although the *Gesta Francorum* does not say. Nor does it provide any detail about their profane practices. Of course, it's unlikely that a crusader army could tell the difference between a community of Orthodox ascetics and a sect of Byzantine heretics. And Damjan argued that there was no connection with the dualists of the Early Church anyway.

Most accounts of medieval religion give the impression that, wherever you find a pious cult preaching devout simplicity, a chain of influence leads back to Gnostic Christianity. According to my host, this accusation was simply an excuse for persecution, used first by the Byzantine Empire, and then by the crusading forces of the Catholic Church.

'Is like Iraq!' (Here Damjan slapped the table.) 'The Americans want a war, so they make up reason for invasion.' (Here he smacked his lips.) 'Before Iraq, there are no terrorists.' (He slapped and slapped.) 'But after Iraq, everyone terrorist.' (He smacked and smacked.) 'Read the history. Is certain.'

The most infamous of all medieval heretics were the Cathars, who emerged midway through the twelfth century in the region ruled by the counts of Toulouse. Preaching a familiar mix of the popular and the puritanical, they soon rivalled the local Catholic Church. In response, Innocent III called a crusade – the first ever against a Christian country – and in the spring of 1209 a band of noblemen from northern France marched their armies south to conquer the heretic city of Albi and the dissenting towns of the Languedoc. There they uncovered widespread rejection of the clergy and sacraments, as well as sectarians who refused to swear oaths or abide by the law, and deviants who took part in orgies and infanticide.

It was the Bogomil Church reborn, carried west in the wake of the crusades!

Recent scholarship has cast doubt on all of this. Fasting and intensive prayer were common devotions in the High Middle Ages, and it would have been easy to recast regional customs as profane rites, thus gaining papal sanction for a violent power grab. The King of France was keen to assert his authority over the counts of Toulouse, and looking at the range of names given to the heretics, you can glimpse the paranoia that inspired his campaign. Although widely known as Albigensians, the heretics were also called Bougres – the French for Bulgars and the root of the English word 'buggers' – Poplicani – a mangling of the name Paulician – and Manichaeans. In the nineteenth century this deviant reputation was seemingly confirmed when historians settled on the term Cathars, from *katharos*, the Greek for pure – a word originally used to describe the ascetics of the Early Church.

When I mentioned the Cathars, Damjan started shouting. 'Bogomils the same!' *Smack*. 'The Greeks invent the heretics to make excuse for empire.' *Smack, smack*. 'Then they burn anyone who tries to start rebellion.' *Thump*. 'Is certain.'

Well, it was certainly possible. And, as we sat in the kitchen together, it was not hard to believe. Outside, the moon bathed the grove in a fragile light, blue and green and sometimes silver. I watched shadows seeping through the plasterboard walls and Damjan's face becoming drawn, as if he had aged half a century while we spoke. I was no longer confused by his cartoon expressions, but enchanted, for it seemed he was not telling me the history of the High Middle Ages, but a piece of folklore handed down through the generations: the story of a few believers who held onto their faith despite doubts, despite fears, despite wild cries of condemnation. Who lived brave and lonely before the world.

And perhaps he was. Because an almost identical argument was first put forward a century ago, and printed in the most unlikely place.

The eleventh edition of the *Encyclopædia Britannica* is the collector's favourite, a grand summary of global knowledge published just before the First World War. It contained, for the first time, an entry on Anarchism. If you ever have all twenty-nine volumes to hand, flick to the end of the first book and you will find the article between Anapaest and Anastasius. Its author tracks the theory's origins to the Greek philosopher Zeno, the sixteenth-century poet Bishop Veda, and to 'several early Christian movements beginning with the ninth century in Armenia'.

Which movements? The author does not say, nor does he give any evidence for this astonishing claim. However, it's possible to work it out.

Run your finger down to the article's last paragraphs and you will see the term *Christian anarchism* introduced, with Leo Tolstoy's *The Kingdom of God is Within You* given as the guiding text. Find a copy of Tolstoy's book and turn to the opening chapter, where he discusses the work of a Bohemian revolutionary called Petr Chelčický, who believed the Gospels commanded pacifism and the renunciation of political power. This is the line to look out for: 'Chelčický taught what has been taught until the present by the Memnonites and Quakers, and what in former years was taught by the Bogomils, Paulicians and many others.' Here, surely, is the source of the encyclopedia's unlikely taxonomy. The early Christian movements that inspired anarchism were the Paulicians and the Bogomils. But, Tolstoy argued, this interpretation of the Bible is likely to be met with persecution. 'All such books, which are called heretical, have been burnt together with their authors.'

Tolstoy was convinced that real Christianity meant political radicalism. Funnily enough, the Bogomils thought the same. Cosmas's sermon noted how the heretics claimed to be true believers. However, by the standards of the Orthodox hierarchy they were anarchists. *They teach their people not to submit to the rulers,* his sermon warned. *They blaspheme the wealthy, hate the king, ridicule the elders, reproach the nobles . . .*

The eleventh edition of the *Encyclopædia Britannica* was published in 1910, the year that Tolstoy died. This particular article became one of its most widely read entries, reprinted in books and pamphlets for half a century. The author was even described as the 'father of modern anarchism'. Like Tolstoy, he was a Russian aristocrat who gave up his wealth to live by radical principles. Unlike Tolstoy, he was exiled from Russia and spent his life wandering Europe, even serving a short spell in Clairvaux Prison. His name, of course, was Prince Peter Kropotkin.

A gun tower painted like a Greek flag guarded the border near Bitola. I crossed over at midday on 2 May. I was worn out from racing through Macedonia, and reaching Greece brought no sense of achievement. But that Sunday was Easter again. Time for a break.

When I reached Florina, the first town after the border, I took a bus south and spent the weekend with a university friend and her family. When the weekend ended, I caught another bus back to Florina, intending to rejoin the Via Egnatia. However, midway up Thessaly we passed the Pindus Mountains, and, remembering my promise to Anna, I stopped to visit Meteora.

It was a deranged landscape, where the lip of a plateau had splintered into a canyon of stone pillars. Sometimes they were smooth, sometimes wrinkled, and sometimes scarred with black gullies, or streaked with granite bands, or pitted with sandstone caves like the howling sockets of a skull. The first hermits came here in the eleventh century, climbing the pillars to live as stylites at the top. Over the next five hundred years they built a chain of monasteries on the stacks. However, from the sixteenth century their numbers declined and now only six foundations remained, with a tiny staff of monks and nuns.

I arrived on Tuesday morning and tramped up through the canyon. The heat was thick and the air stuffy. All weekend I had been feeling unwell, and the higher

I climbed the more feverish my symptoms – face hot and throat gagging. I only made it to one monastery: a Byzantine fort perched on a monolith of golden-grey conglomerate. From below it looked as delicate as honeycomb, but within the corridors were close and the courtyards cramped. And each room was packed with people, with hundreds and hundreds of pilgrims.

Otherwise I remember little of Meteora, except for the ranks of coaches crammed with tourists and the school trips crowding the footpaths. And the hermit caves teeming with climbers. And the canyon forest foaming like a jungle canopy.

That evening I stayed at a campsite in the village of Kastraki. From midnight until dawn I threw up every half-hour, until my stomach was empty and I dry-heaved onto the grass. Then I lay in my tent, too weak to leave.

The day was warm, the weather humid, and by midmorning the tent's fabric had turned fluorescent in the sun, the putty odour of new plastic mixing with the fetid tang of half-digested food. Lying there, I knew my journey was becoming drudgery, yet I remained anxious about falling behind, twitching and trembling with impatience. I was convinced that I should never have left the route, never have come to this pilgrim playground, and I decided that, if I wanted to get better, I must start walking again. Not take the bus back to Florina, but hike out of here at once. By heading east across the Olympus National Park and north up the Aegean coast, I could rejoin the Via Egnatia at Thessaloniki. This would add a hundred kilometres to the distance, but I told myself it was penance. It would cure me.

Later that afternoon the heat became close, smothering. Eventually the sky clouded over and rain fell. Each raindrop made a puncturing noise as it landed on the tent, and all evening the valley was loud with thunder.

Next morning I packed away my sodden kit and marched into the hill country of central Thessaly.

I threw up again as I climbed out of the valley, but after a few kilometres my stomach settled. Rising higher, I noticed thistles growing tattered by the roadside and rainclouds gathering on the horizon. I walked. Kept walking. Pushed on. Once more. Well done.

But I was not better. The following afternoon I arrived at the village of Krania, on the northern edge of Thessaly. The weather was damp, so I went into the church for shelter. Rain pattered on the windows and plashed against the roof, while a priest recited prayers in the choir. When he was finished, I asked if there was anywhere I could stay. He did not answer; instead he took my arm and walked me to the cafe opposite the church, pointing at the drunkest man in the room. The drunkest man in the room stood to shake my hand, but collapsed before he reached me. By the time I had helped him back into his seat, the priest was gone.

My new companion spoke a little English. As I explained why I was here, he slurred something about a spare room, gesturing for me to sit and muttering the phrase: 'You are welcome.' On his table there were two bottles of wine, one bottle of ouzo, a jug of water, a jug of ice, a plate of half-eaten pastries, an ashtray full of cigarette ends, three or four shredded napkins, and ten or twelve empty glasses.

I pulled up a chair.

The man was called Christos. He had skinny arms and a perfect pot belly. His face was knotted, each expression formed from a twist in the mouth. Another man sat opposite him, stubbing out cigarettes in the leftover food.

This man was slimmer, the tissue pulled tight across the skull. His name was Kyriakos.

'Today is special day,' said Christos, motioning towards his friend. 'Today is birthday.'

I wished Kyriakos a happy birthday, but Christos shook his head.

'Understand,' he went on, 'Kyriakos have three sons. One policeman, one lawyerman and one dead in a car crash. Today his son is twenty-one, but he is dead!'

When I realized what he was saying – that the two men were drinking in commemoration – I apologized and tried to leave. However, when I stood from the table, Christos gripped my wrist. His eyes were blank and blazing, his breath aniseed bitter. 'You are welcome,' he said again, tightening his grip. Then Kyriakos began to sing, swinging his elbow to keep time.

Standing there, I tried to imagine drinking away the evening with these two. It was the kind of traveller's tale I had hoped for in Greece, but now it seemed wretched. Yet the weather outside was no better and I still needed a bed for the night, so I sat once more.

Kyriakos wore rimless glasses, the lenses smudged with prints from his fingers. He was a maths teacher and had spent two decades working in German primary schools. That was the language in which he spoke to me, mixed with the odd word of Italian. 'Dresden, München, Stuttgart,' he repeated, *'piccolos, piccolos.'*

Christos had been a sailor. For thirty years he sailed container ships down the western coast of Africa, across the Indian Ocean, to Singapore and Shenzhen, to Jakarta and Shanghai, and Mother of God how he missed the sea. He was also a communist and believed every man had a right to a job, a house, a car— At this point Kyriakos interrupted to order more wine, offering me a glass. I told him that I had been ill, but Kyriakos insisted the wine would help. I explained that I did not drink, so he nodded and called for ouzo.

There was a mobile phone in the middle of the table. Each time it rang, Christos covered the handset with his fingers. 'Nobody home!' he told me the first time. 'Joke telephone!' he said the second. By the fifth or sixth call he was tired of the game. 'My wife,' Christos admitted. 'She comes from Thailand. Says I drink too much. Never understand Greek culture.' His mouth twisted into a sorry smile. 'Only time I drink is because I miss the sea.'

The afternoon was draining away, and a sloppy yellow light filled the square outside, while inside the windows were steaming over. When I reminded Christos that I needed a place to stay, he returned to politics: 'I am communist. Every man must have room to live.' Worried that I had misunderstood his original offer, I asked again about a bed. Before he could answer, Kyriakos launched into another song. I repeated my question, but now Christos was singing too, marking the tempo with a glass of ouzo.

Part of me wanted to laugh. Part of me wanted to shout, or shake my host by the shoulders. If there were no beds in Krania, I needed to leave. Already the sky was dusky, the evening coming on. Cigarettes smouldered in the leftover pastry. Backwash bubbled in the dirty glasses. The rain pattered, clamoured.

I stood from the table.

As I lifted my rucksack, Kyriakos raised another glass of ouzo towards me. In the flurry that comes from a decision finally made, I took the drink and swallowed it. Turning, I saw an Asian woman with fragile features waiting in the doorway. Of course: Christos's wife!

My host lurched forwards and started gurgling in her ear. He must have explained my story, because she left the cafe and moments later returned with a key. Then she led me across the square into an apartment building opposite.

It was so sudden, so unexpected, that I never even thanked her. Nor did I thank the two men who rescued me from the rain, or apologize for ever doubting them.

The flat had white walls, white furniture, and bedsheets of crimped white cotton. Its windows faced the square, and, unpacking my rucksack, I glanced up to see Christos leaving the cafe. His arm was draped along his wife's shoulder, neck hanging back, mouth open wide. He looked like he was trying to taste the rain, or rinse the tears from his eyes.

I had no map of the Olympus Range and found my way using a compass. Whenever I came to a hilltop, I would take a bearing off the crushed cone of Mt Olympus, but then drop into another valley and zig and zag off course again. The mornings were wild with birdsong, but the afternoons felt heavy and still, and the canopy thickened overhead until it seemed I was sinking below ground. Clouds of flies hovered around my face, catching in my nose and mouth, while the path disappeared beneath the swollen foliage.

All weekend I walked with my eyes to the floor, trying to remember a few phrases of Greek, though there was nobody to ask for directions. In fact, the whole area had an atmosphere of sudden desertion. On my first afternoon the tracks were covered in cowpats, yellow butterflies dithering over the fresh faeces. An animal smell ripened the air, but the cows had all disappeared. That evening, as I descended into a seething green valley, I heard the echo and clang of goatbells. I stared through the thickening darkness, yet I saw no goats, nor sheep, nor shepherds hurrying home for the night.

Crossing the range, I started making lists again: ancient philosophers, Attic tragedies, and every member of the

Classical pantheon. But I was too agitated to remember much, my thoughts flustered with frustration.

I could not understand my decision to walk from Meteora. It meant I had to improvise a route and kept going astray. I felt guilty about leaving the Via Egnatia, for though I hoped to follow an unbroken chain of Roman roads and medieval trails, now my plan was disrupted. And I felt guilty about the glass of ouzo, too – my second drink of the pilgrimage. But I told myself it was a mistake, no more. It would not happen again.

Mt Olympus marked the upper edge of Thessaly, where the Pindus punched east towards the Aegean. A road wrapped round the mountain's southern flank, rising through forests of pine, cresting a thousand metres, and then coiling down towards the coast. On Monday afternoon I joined its course and around teatime came to a parting in the trees, catching sight of the Aegean fifteen kilometres away. The sea shone hard as hammered bronze, tilted in the light, with the Thermaic Gulf arcing away to the north. Looking out, I imagined I could see across the gulf and glimpse the pale sprawl of a city on its farthest rim. Thessaloniki.

It took me a week to reach the city, stopping each evening at a roadside chapel. Since Meteora my confidence was shaken, so I did not seek permission from the local priests. Instead I passed fretful nights under flickering oil lamps, waking before dawn to hike off with my head bowed. Although I had given up learning about Orthodoxy, it was easier to sleep in these bedroom-sized shrines than ask around for a host. During the daytime I held long conversations with imagined figures from the past, or dreamed up fantasy versions of my future. But, when strangers called out to me, I pretended not to hear. So I never found out the names of the Bosnians who shared their lunch with me in the plantations below

Olympus, before buttoning down their denim shirts to lay tobacco seeds in the midday heat. Nor the middle-aged men who bought me lemonade in the cafes near the coast, exchanging newspapers and asking over and over why Europe was punishing the Greeks. And I ignored the Arab children squatting at a junction outside Thessaloniki, who waved as I walked by and then ran into the road to swab the windscreens of the waiting cars.

I became convinced that I was safest alone. This was my mistake.

Thessaloniki's old town was huddled on a hillside north of the city centre. The sloping streets were quiet – few cars, few restaurants or shops – and the stone houses painted in chalky yellows and pastel reds.

My hostel was a modern building with a garden out front, the flowerbeds a mess of juniper and broom. There was nobody here, except for a small lady napping on the common-room sofa. When I entered the room, she sprung off the sofa and began tidying. She was in her early sixties, but reminded me of a baby, with chubby cheeks and unblinking eyes. Her name was Dora.

I explained why I was here. 'To Istanbul?' she asked, so I replied, 'Yes, Istanbul.' 'And Jerusalem?' she asked, so I replied, 'Yes, Jerusalem.' 'With foot?' she asked. 'All alone?' she asked. 'How many kilometres a day?' I began to answer – 'Twenty-five, thirty,' – but was cut off: 'Not enough.' 'Well, more if I have to,' I said, but again I was cut off: 'You have to.' She went on, 'When I was a girl my school was twenty-three kilometres from my home. In Kavala. If our car was broken, I went with bicycle. If our bicycle was broken, I went with foot. One day I walked all the way to school in the morning and all the way home in the evening. In Kavala. Yes?'

Dora thought that, from Istanbul, I should fly the final leg of the journey. 'Not safe,' she told me. 'Syria, Lebanon, Turkey – not safe.' I asked why Turkey was unsafe. 'The Turks are very hospitality, yes, but you cannot trust them. My mother always say: You can eat with a Turk, but you cannot sleep with a Turk. My mother. Yes?'

I laughed and promised I wouldn't forget.

'No,' she said. 'We never forget.'

Dora was very hospitality too. She referred to the hostel guests as her children and boasted about who was staying: an academic and an architect from Italy; a Dutch father and son on a cycling holiday; a Cypriot woman studying to become a doctor; and a Marxist activist named Michael. He was from Middlesbrough.

That evening Dora cooked for her children ('Turkish food. It's true. Greek food is Turkish food.') We ate on the patio, the academic lighting candles and the architect opening wine. Dora sat at the head of the table, urging us to try different dishes, or else arguing that the Greeks should leave the eurozone and return to the land, to the fields and farms and olive groves. As she spoke, the two cyclists nodded along, their blond heads bobbing in the candlelight. Sitting among these strangers, the blind determination that had carried me across Greece began to calm, for here I was just another tourist.

After the meal Dora cleared the table, refusing all offers of help. When Michael asked where she found her energy, she replied that God gave her strength.

'God never gives me strength.'

'How many times have you asked him?'

Michael hesitated. 'Actually, I'm an atheist.'

'No, I know there is a God.'

'How?'

'When I gave birth to my son, I have a thrombosis. The doctor said, Dora you must have surgery, but I said, No surgery. In my room was an icon of Theotokos, the Mother of God, and when the doctor left I began to pray. Please, please, let me be a mother to my children. So I stay in the hospital and after two months the thrombosis is gone. Two months. Yes?'

Michael did not answer. Dora tried again. This time she told the story of a couple she knew who waited thirteen years for a daughter. Shortly after the child was born, Dora's son crashed into their car and the girl was injured. While she was in hospital, the son stayed in church, praying for her recovery. Once the girl was sent home, he remained in church to give thanks. 'Even now he visits three times, four times a week. Even now he gives thanks she is alive.'

The table was quiet. I could not tell if this was embarrassment or surprise. The academic frowned, her lower lip stained with wine, and then stretched and sighed and moved off into the night. The rest of the table followed, the cyclists bickering with Dora over the washing-up.

When Michael was the only person left, he took out a tin of tobacco and started rolling cigarettes. His skin was pale and pinched, his manner polite to the point of surprise.

Michael had been living in Thessaloniki for several months, working with local communists to free Greece from the hated Troika. He used that phrase – *the hated Troika* – often. *Pose the question of power* was another favourite, turning up in sentences like: 'Call a general strike, demand an end to austerity, and pose the question of power. See? It sounds so easy.' By *it* Michael meant revolution. He was optimistic about *its* chances in Greece. 'I'm fifty-five,' he told me, 'and never have I seen so many of the right conditions in a single country.' At that point his eyes lost focus and his voice became quiet. I caught only fragments of what followed – 'The purpose of politics is a world without want . . . Democracy can never be an end in itself . . .' – until he started discussing online activism and his voice was loud: 'People think because I'm working class I don't understand collateralized debt. They think because I swear on Twitter I didn't go to Oxford. And suddenly it's three in the morning and I've written two thousand words under a *Daily Mail* article and I can't sleep for all the hate.'

It was not hard to imagine Michael plotting revolution from his laptop, but I struggled to picture him marching in the streets. However, when I learnt that he had been an alcoholic for five years, I experienced a tug of remorse. It was not pity so much as recognition, for he had the stunned shyness of one still wounded and the quiet mania of the unconsoled. And, when he said that he would never return home, that he would lose his life for this cause, I thought of Lord Byron, coming to Greece to fight for independence and dying before he reached the battlefield.

'Sounds so easy,' Michael said again. 'Easy-peasy.'

I left him rolling cigarettes and went down to the shore. It was late on Saturday, and I wanted to walk the promenade before bed. There was relief in wandering alone through the warm evening, no bag on my shoulders, no boots on my feet. I felt the unhurried ease of a Mediterranean holiday, as if the boundaries of the day were looser now, or time had relaxed its grip.

The centre of Thessaloniki consisted of monumental squares linked by wide avenues. Its Neoclassical office blocks and Art Deco hotels resembled cruise ships parked up beside the pavement. Near the port I found an older neighbourhood, the houses converted into bars. There were wooden tables and wooden floors, metal chairs and metal lamps, music pumping from speakers and rainbow colours projected over the cobblestones.

One of the bars faced the promenade. I sat outside, angled towards the sea. Though I was planning to order coffee, when the waiter suggested ouzo, I paused.

Thessaloniki was halfway to Jerusalem. My sickness from Meteora was gone. Tomorrow I would take the day off. So why not say yes?

The ouzo came in a frosted bottle. It tasted sweeter than I expected, and thicker too. As I drank I watched the city lights reflecting on the water. Out in the gulf the waves glittered like burning oil, distant flares.

When the first bottle was finished, I ordered another, and another. Then I wandered the cobblestone streets with a swelling sense of purpose. The buildings rose and fell around me, as if the tide had drawn in over the land, or we were drifting out to sea. I kept circling the neighbourhood, stopping at half the bars I passed, until the last one closed and there was dawn in the sky.

For the next few days I was drunk the whole time, roaming round the city and feeling sorry for myself. Everything had gone wrong in Greece: leaving the pilgrimage route, falling ill in Meteora, and now this spree in Thessaloniki. I regretted coming to the Balkans, because I had lost all sense of purpose here. And I regretted the rest of my journey, too, for I had not healed during the walk, but spoilt any chance of recovery. As I circled the city, my self-pity became despair. I wanted to cry out – A mistake! A mistake! I did not mean to drink again! – but instead my thoughts collapsed into a single desire: to push myself past rescue.

The Via Egnatia ran down the middle of Thessaloniki. On my second evening in the city, I tripped while crossing the road.

As the ground swept up towards me, I tumbled back through time, back to the earliest days of the depression. Before I lay in a London bedroom, turned from the window. Before I hid in a Buenos Aires flat, frightened to go outside. Back to the summer I left university. Back to the night of the fall.

It was the end of August. I was walking between parties on a road in south-west London. At one point the houses lining the street became a brick wall, separating the pavement from a railway cutting. The wall was low enough to climb and coped with slabs of stone. For some reason I was wearing a suit, and, when I lifted myself onto the wall, a button snapped off the cuff. Then I stood over the cutting with arms spread wide and eyes turned down. Streetlamps traced the tracks below, a gleaming seam two or three storeys down.

I was planning to jump into the path of a train, but once I had climbed onto the stone slabs, my plan seemed ridiculous. When a set of carriages screamed by, I laughed as I pictured myself bounding onto the back like an action hero. A man in a suit, alone in the world, running from his life – no, I would not jump.

Instead I waited for the train to pass and stepped out into the empty air.

I remember the sound of rushing all around me. And the night slipping by like spilled ink. And fast, how fast my body fell.

The second I stepped out was the second I crumpled onto the track. That was the sensation. That was the sensation which returned to me in Thessaloniki, as my hands slapped hard against the tarmac. A fall faster than thought.

It stayed with me as I crawled off the road. As I limped along the pavement. As I sat in a bar, picking grit from my palms and ordering ouzo in confused Greek. As I sipped the glass with thick lips and stinging fingers. I could remember it now, that wretched London night. Remember coming to with blood on my face, in my mouth and my eyes. Remember the numbness all over, the taste of my teeth, and the pressure gone from both ears. My ribs were sore, the lungs seizing each time I inhaled, so I lay on my back without moving. The sides of the cutting framed the night, making the clouds seem very close. But, when I tried to touch them, I realized I could not lift my hand. The left hand – I could not even feel it.

Later I found a route up from the cutting. Later still I found directions to a hospital. I told the nurse who stitched my forehead together that I had been mugged. To the doctor who fitted my arm in a cast, I said that I was beaten up. My family heard that I was thrown down some stairs, for wearing the silly blue suit.

I stuck to this story because I was ashamed of what had happened. I thought that, by telling the lie often enough, it might undo the truth. This was easier than trying to make sense of my behaviour, for there was no hurt which could explain the attempt, nor any disappointment that might justify it. Yet I did not realize how the depression had warped my thoughts, turning every doubt into a defeat and every slight into a reason to fall free from this life. Nor did I realize how my deceit was making worse the damage, the lie becoming its own dreadful burden. But, wandering through Thessaloniki, I felt no sympathy for my younger self, only an appalled sense of shame. I wanted to fix it, wanted to be rid of it, wanted to rewrite the past.

In the months that followed the fall, though my injuries healed, the secret stayed sharp within me. I could not forget the thrill of holding tight to a life and then letting go. Or a decision that was no decision at all, but something deeper, like surrender.

It felt this way to drink again. A letting go. And the

more I drank, the more vivid the memories of that London night. Everything I saw in Thessaloniki reminded me of the attempt – of a road crossing over a railway, of a fall faster than thought. The crooked trunk of a palm tree was the kink in my sleeve from where the wrist had snapped. The grating sound that the waves make was the fizzing of blood as it pushes through sheared skin. The sky was a purple-stained jacket, the cobblestones polluted clouds. Exhaust fumes clotted in my mouth, and a cupped glass weighed no heavier than a human heart. Yet I kept drinking until the two cities blurred, until the unlit avenues were a railway cutting, and the shimmering promenade was a train track, and the newspapers by the roadside were a body shrouded in a blanket – a tramp maybe, or a pilgrim, or a corpse wrapped in white like the one that was crucified.

We were on a boat, sailing down the eastern leg of Chalkidiki, a sixty-kilometre peninsula which ended in the limestone peak of Mt Athos. On the upper deck a bearded Russian and his son let seagulls swipe pieces of bread from their fingers, three teenage boys posed for photographs with a priest in a ragged cassock, and an elderly beggar laid out prayer beads on a black cloth – six euros each, ten for a pair. But there was no theme to them, the pilgrims on that boat, except that not one was a woman. Women were forbidden from the Holy Mountain.

The coast skimmed by on our left, a thin strip of sand with wooded hills above and forest-green water below. Two buildings crouched at the water's edge, beside a jetty of yellow concrete. I looked for the monastery these buildings belonged to, but it was hidden among the hills.

However, as we approached the jetty our driver called out its name: 'Zographou!'

There were twenty monasteries in total, housing some two thousand monks. Otherwise the peninsula was deserted, except for an ever-changing population of pilgrims. Although an isthmus connected Mt Athos to the mainland, its border was closed, and the only access by boat. A place on the boat required a three-day pass stamped with the triple seal of the monastic republic. Before leaving England I had applied for a pass, and in Thessaloniki I realized it was dated Friday 24 May. This was what brought my binge to an end. I packed my rucksack, paid my bill and walked hard across Chalkidiki, arriving at the ferry port of Ouranoupolis late on Thursday afternoon.

Next morning, sailing down the coast, I watched the hills grow steeper and more thickly wooded, studded with the remains of hermit cells. By now the teenagers had joined the seagull game, while the bearded Russian was haggling over some prayer beads for his son.

Then I saw the monasteries.

The first one looked like a castle, topped with towers and cupolas and cellblocks painted nursery blue. 'Dochiariou!' the driver cried. The second resembled a fort, its stone buttresses and timber balconies stretching along the beach. 'Xenophontos!' The third was a great white palace, its copper roofing a tarnished green, its domes and spires gilded. 'St Panteleimonos!'

Our ferry slowed to let the father and son off. 'St Panteleimonos!' the driver shouted again. 'Rossikon!'

Rossikon. The Russian Monastery. At the end of the nineteenth century a third of the monks on Mt Athos were Russian, and for many St Panteleimon was their home. The monastery also hosted the Holy Mountain's most infamous visitor: a *strannik*, or pilgrim, who had hiked here from Siberia.

A decade after that visit, in May 1907, the *strannik* published an account of his journey titled *The Life of an Experienced Pilgrim*. It records how he used to walk forty to fifty versts a day (a verst is just over a kilometre) and once marched the whole way from Kiev to the Siberian capital of Tobolsk – a distance of roughly 2,500 versts – without ever changing clothes. He also claims to have worn chains, prayed bare-chested in swarms of mosquitoes, and been chased by wolves and would-be murderers.

The Life of an Experienced Pilgrim does contain some useful tips. It recommends going on pilgrimage for months rather than years and wearing a hat while worshipping in the snow. It also warns against evil spirits that cause depression and disease, or inspire dangerous feats of endurance. And it's not all hardship. The author mentions the farm workers who gave him food and shelter, and the holy men who cured his insomnia and chronic bedwetting. He treats travelling as an education, delighting in everything he learns. And at times his experience mirrored my own, as when he recalls that living wild 'was my bliss and consolation. I walked outside and found consolation in nature.'

Our experienced pilgrim was illiterate. His account was dictated and makes for a difficult read. And, once you know a bit more about his biography, the gaps begin to show. The author expresses doubts over the value of monastic life, but never admits that he joined the monks at St Panteleimon, until he witnessed an older brother abusing one of the novices and left in disgust. He recommends humility when being introduced to senior members of the clergy and nobility, but never explains how his own travels so impressed the Bishop of Kazan that he was welcomed into the highest reaches of Russian society. He even refers to an audience with Tsar Nicholas II, but brushes over the meeting's remarkable outcome. Yet the *strannik*'s reputation for holiness was such that he was invited to heal the emperor's haemophiliac son.

All the same, Rasputin's rise through the Romanov court only makes sense when you take into account his pilgrim past. Wandering was a sacred calling in Russian Orthodoxy, because the scale of the country placed a unique demand on roving preachers. Thus the very qualities which should prevent a Siberian peasant from befriending the royal family – modest background, minimal education, coarse manners, odd habits and total lack of ecclesiastical status – became his proof of piety.

I knew nothing about the contemplative tradition from which the *stranniki* emerged, but that tradition was called Hesychasm, and Mt Athos was its home. As our ferry eased into the peninsula's main port – a cluster of red-roofed buildings with a jetty of piled rubble – I began jotting down questions. My hope was that, by learning more about the practice, I might bridge the distance I felt from the Orthodox faith.

'Orthodoxy's not a philosophy; it's not a theory; it's a way,' said Johnny. 'It can't be explained, only experienced.'

Johnny was in his early twenties, with freckled skin and the reddish beginnings of a beard. His definition was, I suspect, learnt by heart, because it sounded stiff even in a Glasgow accent.

We met in Karyes, the village capital of Mt Athos. He was bent over a map of the local hiking trails, while a friend marked out their route. Although a few battered minibuses taxied pilgrims between monasteries, most people travelled on foot. These two were aiming for Iviron, on the peninsula's eastern coast, which was my own destination that day. When I asked if I could join them, they seemed reluctant. Perhaps it was embarrassing to meet someone from Britain, because their pilgrimage no longer felt secret, but after a pause they invited me along.

Leaving Karyes we passed groves of walnut and hazel and entered the woods. The air was green here, the sunshine filtering through the canopy and the greenish shadows warm. A few shafts of light parted the branches, catching on the split cobbles and shining streamwater at our feet.

The friend was called Stephen. He had massive forearms, stamped with tattoos, and a chest shaped like a steamer trunk. At first I found him daunting, for his features were set in an ugly grimace, but then he started telling me about his wife. Stephen explained that he used to be an atheist, until he married a Cypriot woman who wanted to raise their children Orthodox. Soon they were attending church together. 'Half the time I'd no idea what was happening. Eventually I stopped trying to understand, just followed everyone else. That's when it started to click. All the history, tradition, weird bits – only make sense during the services.'

'Those are the best converts,' said Johnny. 'Take a rational decision and you're doing it wrong. The point of Orthodoxy's not understanding: the point is union with God. You can't think your way into that.'

Was Johnny a convert too?

'Religious vagrant, that's what I am. Church of Scotland, Church of England – until one Sunday I went to the Divine Liturgy and thought I was in heaven.'

As we descended to the shore, my companions kept talking. They were an unlikely pair: two sailors who had served together in Portsmouth and the Clyde, off the

Persian Gulf and the Somali coast. But last month Johnny had resigned from the navy, and when summer was over he would begin studying at an Orthodox seminary in New York State.

Stephen was also leaving – to retrain as a plumber.

When Johnny asked why I was visiting Mt Athos, I told him that I wanted to learn more about Hesychasm. While hiking across the Balkans, I had visited a few dozen Orthodox churches, but was confused by their dim, dense interiors and their endless chanted services. The more I experienced of Eastern Christianity, I said, the less I understood, until I began to doubt my whole pilgrimage.

Johnny replied that nobody came to Mt Athos by mistake. Then he started discussing the hermits who lived in remote corners of the Holy Mountain, mentioning *theoria*, *Philokalia*, and the uncreated light of the Transfiguration. But, when he realized I wasn't following, he said, 'First lesson any convert needs to learn is: forget everything you know about Christianity.'

'And the second lesson?' I asked.

'Moderation,' said Stephen.

Our path flattened out near Iviron, running between terraced vines and vegetable plots. Bumblebees droned in the flower banks or moved ponderous through the shrubs. Most of the peninsula was untended, but each monastery lay in a cultivated pocket. This one was set back from the sea, surrounded on three sides by hills. Its walls were cliffs of stone crowned by double rows of saffron cells. Through the gates stood a crimson church, the *katholikon*, at the centre of a flagged courtyard. There were more saffron cellblocks bordering the yard, as well as a guest block the size of a manor house and the crumbling remains of a keep.

Before we were shown to our rooms, Johnny took a slim paperback called *The Way of a Pilgrim* from his rucksack. 'Orthodoxy's an eastern religion: you need a guru for the tough stuff,' he said, handing me the book. 'But, if you want to understand Hesychasm, this is the place to start.'

My cell had a wooden desk, a wooden bed and a wooden chair with a wicker seat. A balcony looked down on the allotments, where a pair of monks were putting away their tools and beating the dust from their robes. When they went inside, I could hear nothing but the chattering cicadas and the scuffling sea. Otherwise the evening was calm as the slow movement of clouds.

For the next hour I sat on the balcony, reading Johnny's book. It told the story of a young Russian obsessed by St Paul's instruction to pray without ceasing. He begins living as a *strannik* to learn how this might be done. Soon an elderly mystic teaches him the Jesus Prayer, a contemplative technique whereby the words *Lord Jesus Christ have mercy on me* are repeated so many times they become instinctive. This is the prayer of the heart: the central practice of Hesychasm.

Once the pilgrim perfects the Jesus Prayer he decides to travel to Jerusalem. On the road he meets all sorts of people – some with moving stories to tell, others with religious teaching to share – but his progress is repeatedly interrupted and he never manages to leave Russia. Yet, as the book makes clear, learning the prayer was the true pilgrimage.

I went back inside with the last of the evening light. As the day drew in, the scene began to simplify. Though it looked like every other cell I had stayed in, it was easy to imagine that this room was my own. And I wondered what more I could need in the world, and why I would go anywhere else.

The Way of a Pilgrim might have been the model for Rasputin's memoir. In both texts the narrator is threatened by a wolf, healed by a peasant and comforted by nature. The introduction to Johnny's edition claimed that the book's author was a *strannik* who roamed round Russia in the mid-nineteenth century before ending up on Mt Athos. Here his story was written down by a brother at St Panteleimon, becoming the most popular work of Orthodox spirituality ever published. It also provides a manifesto for Hesychasm, showing how a lowly pilgrim can experience the deepest mysteries of the faith.

I tried to read on, but the words smudged and my attention flagged. After all, I had no idea what these mysteries meant and found little guidance in the book's earnest passages of spiritual instruction. Yet I was charmed by the pilgrim narrator, whose willed innocence seemed familiar to me – at once hopeful and reckless. Like the young Rasputin, he was walking to learn how to live. And later that night, lying in bed, I found a paragraph Johnny had underlined which hinted a way forwards.

> Everything drew me to love and thank God; people, trees, plants, animals. I saw them all as my kinsfolk, I found on all of them the magic of the Name of Jesus. Sometimes I felt as light as though I had no body and was floating happily through the air instead of walking [. . .] And at all such times of happiness, I wished that God would let death come to me quickly, and let me pour out my heart in thankfulness at his feet.

At four in the morning I was woken by a hollow knocking sound: a hammer beating against a wooden beam. It was the *simandron*, calling the monastery to prayer. I put on my clothes, left my cell, and followed the pilgrims into the dark mass of the *katholikon*. There was no light in the nave except for the flicker of candles and a seeping oil lamp, yet from the doorway I noticed Stephen's hulking shape as he circled the icons, kissing some and kneeling in front of others. Johnny went after, repeating each gesture with a sweep of his arm and a flourish of his wrist.

I stayed near these two for much of the service, imitating every time they crossed themselves – thumb, index and middle finger, pinched together and brushed from right to left, once, twice, three times in a row. Otherwise I could see little of the church, apart from a few items bobbing up from the gloom: the silver-screened icons lining the nave and the carved foliage decorating the iconostasis. Monks fluttered back and forth like shreds of black taffeta, sometimes ringing a bell, or shaking a censer, or crowding the choir stalls, or ducking into the sanctuary. And the chanting was endless: it did not cease.

Soon my eyes were heavy from lack of sleep and the air heavy with incense. To keep myself from drifting off, I went outside and walked a lap of the monastery. The courtyard contained a domed fountain, a bell tower with a bare clock face, a strip of tatty cypress trees and a chapel with a wrought-iron awning – all emerging from the night.

For the next hour I sat in the church's narthex, a narrow arcade with banks of leaded windows. As the sun lifted through the sky, the windowpanes cast squares of coloured light over the interior, turning from the frescoed scenes of apocalypse to the fans and foils that jigsawed the floor.

I kept listening to the service, but though I noticed shifts in the plainsong, I could not work out when matins became the hours, or the hours became the Divine Liturgy. When I went back into the church, wisps of silver smoke cobwebbed the chandeliers and from somewhere nearby I heard the shimmer of brass bells. One of the brothers was orbiting the iconostasis in vestments of spun gold, while three more sang from the choir. Yet I wasn't sure if they were reciting the epistle, the Gospel, or the sermon, the Litany of Peace or the Litany of Supplication, the Holy Hymn or the Cherubic.

Some time around seven the room became still. The shuffling stopped, the coughing went quiet, and the monks stood erect. Together they recited the creed, together the Lord's Prayer. Communion. Thanksgiving. Blessing.

Stephen sighed, his face filling with relief. At last the service was done.

Every day on Mt Athos started this way. Each night I stayed at a different monastery and each morning stirred to the hollow knocking of the *simandron*. One morning I slept through the alarm, waking to discover my dormitory empty and a deep tremor rising from outside, *Kyrie eleison, Kyrie eleison, Ky – ri – e – lei – son.*

I planned to spend the services deep in thought, waiting for some sudden revelation. But I was too tired to think, my mind sluggish with boredom. Instead I invented games to pass the time: scoring the monks' beards out of ten, say, with added points for thickness, whiteness, and moustache length. Or guessing the pilgrims' nationalities from their appearance: expensive watches and knock-off trainers, jeans of black denim and jackets of desert-coloured cord. A few times I daydreamed and once stared at a candle for so long that I lost all sense of time: no boredom now, nor any guessing games, nothing but the weeping wax and a buttery light which seemed to last and last and last.

During those mornings, what was knotted within me began to work loose. I had not forgotten that weekend in Thessaloniki, but while on Mt Athos I was glad for the relapse. The thing I feared most had finally happened. My sense of anxious expectation was gone. And the monasteries felt like a refuge, for here I could do myself no harm. Although I had been overwhelmed by the crowds in Rome and intimidated by the churches in Greece, I enjoyed standing anonymous among these pilgrims. I realized it was not faith that made the mornings precious, but the patient practice of a ritual. And I found comfort in the structure of the days, the unchanging routine.

Johnny had explained the monks' schedule to me. As well as rising before dawn to spend four hours in church, the brothers attended afternoon and evening services and passed an hour in private prayer. The rest of the time they cleaned, cooked, mended and farmed. They ate two meals a day, fasted two hundred days a year, and went to bed around nine each night. The monastery clocks ran on Byzantine time – meaning midnight began at sunset – and dates were fixed to the Julian calendar. This routine had not changed for a millennium, Johnny boasted, and it seemed the discipline was part of the draw. 'They're dead to the world,' he told me at one point, eyes wide and blinking.

I meant to ask Johnny if those new to the faith were attracted to its most demanding forms because anything gentler gave too much space for doubt. And if, by leaving the navy to join a seminary, he was exchanging one regimented institution for another. I also wondered whether the severity of the regime was relief from some other anguish, one that went unsaid. Or whether Orthodoxy's unbending traditions gave comfort after long years of uncertainty.

But I never found out, because after Iviron the two friends went south, while I headed north along the coast. However, the following morning I met Fr Constantine, who answered some of my questions.

*

Vatopedi was a grand old monastery the size of a small village. Classical and Byzantine cellblocks framed the central courtyard, along with wooden staircases, metal walkways and galleries of flaking stone. The cobbles in the yard were subsiding, and the ground sagged like the floorboards in an ageing farmhouse.

Fr Constantine's office was in a dilapidated quad in the western corner. The room was dominated by a pair of cabinets, their drawers filled with sheets of marbled paper and lengths of cream and ivory mountboard, while the shelves behind contained rolls of buckram, leather and silk, as well as goatskin parchment and calfskin vellum. Every other surface was covered in books: textblocks with hand-sewn bindings, manuscripts bundled in ribbon, and the shrivelled covers of ancient codices.

Fr Constantine was Vatopedi's bookbinder. He was a large, loafing figure, his white beard woven with grey, like Father Christmas gone to seed. A French convert, before coming to Mt Athos he had worked as a journalist in Paris, an archaeologist in Israel, and the head chef of an Islington restaurant.

'The best French restaurant in London,' he told me, testing a peacock-pattern lining against a page of maroon bookcloth. 'That is what the *Guardian* said.'

'What was it called?'

'It is a play by Noël Coward. I used the name.'

'*Hay Fever*?'

'A decadent one.'

'*Private Lives*?'

'No, I will not say.'

'*Easy Virtue*?' I was running out. '*The Vortex*?'

'*Non*. All gone. Gone since I came to Vatopedi.'

Fr Constantine put down the bookcloth and rootled around on his desk, searching through bundles of needles, spools of thread, a pile of red pressing boards and a plastic case of paper drills. Eventually he found a tin of tea behind a box of scalpels and shears. It was Fortnum & Mason Earl Grey Classic.

'The one thing I keep.'

As the monk filled a teapot, I opened my notebook. There were questions I was planning to ask – about Hesychasm, about the Jesus Prayer – but my host had no interest in answering them. When I mentioned *The Way of a Pilgrim*, he snuffled and snorted. When I outlined my pilgrimage route, he turned back to his work. But when I stopped talking, his face filled with pleasure and he began to tell stories. And what stories they were! As we drank the tea, a decade of anecdotes came bubbling out. We toured round Soho in the early eighties, sharing liquid lunches with the painters at the French and evenings at the Coach with Jeffrey Bernard. We went to the first nights of West End shows, being rude to Alan Bennett – 'You are an odd man, but you make me laugh' – and charming to Maggie Smith – 'I have some letters that Mr Coward wrote your husband, but oh dear they are naughty.' One rambling tale took place in his restaurant on the evening Diane Abbott became the first black woman elected to Parliament. It involved the new MP, two members of the shadow cabinet, a crate of champagne and an argument with a famous actor: 'Too famous, I cannot say . . .'

Every time I recognized one of the names, Fr Constantine would scrunch up his eyes with delight. But when I asked why he gave it all up, he would pour more tea and begin another story. Most of these stories – wine tastings and whisky tastings and road trips in the company of restaurant critics – ended with a mishap in a pub or bar, until I started to guess the answer.

A door on the far side of the office opened onto a balcony. The Aegean lay in the distance, its surface dark as liquorice. I thought of Christos, the sailor who longed for the sea; and Michael, the communist who wanted never to return home; and Fr Constantine, the gourmand retiring into austerity. Perhaps it was chance, my crossing paths with these three, or perhaps some half-conscious instinct drew me towards them. I wasn't sure what linked the men, or whether their experiences shared anything with my own – beyond a vague desire to leave ourselves behind. Yet the deliberate rhythm of life here made this coincidence feel fated, as if there was a lesson for me to learn. And Johnny's voice played over in my thoughts: *Nobody comes to Mt Athos by mistake.*

Did Fr Constantine mourn the life he left behind? Or did the disappointment and regret make it easier to cut ties? Or perhaps he came to Mt Athos with a sense of liberation rather than loss, for despite everything that was missing on the Holy Mountain – most of the brothers managed without computers and phones, televisions and radios – there was freedom in their poverty. During my own stay the simplest things had become pleasures. Metal bowls of boiled vegetables and twice-baked bread, with jugs of spring water so chilled they left me gasping. An afternoon nap in a dormitory of pilgrims – from Bulgaria and Cyprus, Romania and Greece – on a mattress no thicker than my wrist. High ceilings, wide walls, and wooden shutters sifting in the breeze. How little we need to be happy. How little we need to survive.

The tea was finished, Fr Constantine swilling the last sip round his mouth. 'It's true,' he concluded, 'I was not a good little boy. So maybe you see why I had to become a monk.'

'But it sounds like you miss it.'

'France I do not miss. Journalism, restaurants – *non.*' He was searching his desk again, hiding the Fortnum's tin behind boxes of tools and spools of thread. 'But London

I miss. It's true. And the theatre too. And those little sandwiches from Marks & Spencer.'

Before I left Vatopedi, Fr Constantine wrote a name on a piece of paper: *Skiti Agios Andreou*. 'Near Karyes,' he explained. 'If you go there, ask for Fr Philotheos. Oxford philosopher, you know! But now a monk. Any questions, Fr Philotheos will answer.'

I was already planning to visit St Andrew's. Although a minor foundation – the lesser monasteries on the Holy Mountain were known as sketes – it had played a major role in the worst crisis of the republic's recent history. Built in the nineteenth century to accommodate the growing number of Russian monks, it was dominated by an overblown basilica – the largest on Mt Athos. On the eve of the First World War the cellblocks housed some seven hundred brothers, but during the twentieth century the supply from Soviet Russia dwindled and eventually the buildings were abandoned.

However, its decline really began in February 1913, when the entire skete was excommunicated.

First, a little background. In 1907, the year Rasputin published *The Life of an Experienced Pilgrim*, another *strannik*'s memoir was also printed. *In the Mountains of the Caucasus*, by a former brother from St Panteleimon, described a hermit's solitary wanderings in the high region between the Caspian Sea and the Black. It also celebrated the Jesus Prayer, claiming the prayer's miraculous power was contained in the very word *Christ*.

The book was popular among Russians on Mt Athos, who were enchanted by the descriptions of mountain wilderness and impressed by the idea that simply saying God's name might manifest His presence. This seemed to purify Hesychasm, while stamping the practice with its own Slavic identity.

Before long, these supporters formed an unofficial movement known as the *imiaslavie*, or name-glorifiers. Their leader was Fr Antony Bulatovich, a former guards officer and celebrated explorer of Ethiopia, as well as a military aide to its emperor Menelek II. Bulatovich had resigned his commission after killing an enemy soldier and joined the brothers at St Andrew's. On reading *In the Mountains of the Caucasus*, he became convinced that the *imiaslavie* were the true defenders of the Hesychast tradition. However, his critics argued that the book encouraged idolatry and branded its supporters *imiaslavtsy*, or name-worshippers.

By 1912 half the brothers at St Panteleimon were part of the movement, and the majority at St Andrew's. When the skete voted to replace their abbot, he refused to leave, until Bulatovich ousted him and installed an ally. Soon there were reports of monks being denied communion and thrown from windows. Complaints were made to the Russian consul in Thessaloniki, the Russian ambassador in Constantinople, and the Holy Synod in St Petersburg. Next year Mt Athos's governing council excommunicated every member of St Andrew's and ordered a blockade of St Panteleimon, its *imiaslavie* forbidden money, post and food.

In April 1913 the Patriarch of Constantinople accused the movement of heresy, but this only strengthened their conviction. After all, the Hesychasts were heretics once.

Although the Jesus Prayer dated back to the Desert Fathers, its most important revival was on Mt Athos in the first half of the fourteenth century. As brothers began isolating themselves to practise the technique, Byzantine clerics accused them of valuing contemplation over Church sacraments. The Greek *protos*, the Holy

Mountain's most senior monk, was even called – surprise, surprise – a Bogomil. This dispute threatened to split Eastern Christianity, but in 1351 an ecclesiastical council ruled in favour of the Hesychasts. Ever since, monastic mysticism, and in particular the Jesus Prayer, has been embedded in Orthodoxy. The *imiaslavie* took courage from this fact, for even though the Church condemned their beliefs, they knew Hesychasm could raise a pilgrim above a patriarch. They also knew the Gospels teach Christians to expect persecution, even welcome it. This is the courage of the martyr: holding true to your faith in the face of the world. That said, on breaking with the Church they must have felt a rush of reckless purpose, like swimming off the coast until the shoreline slips from sight, or walking without stopping until your life is left behind.

The blockade of St Panteleimon failed, so the Russian synod asked the government to act. Nicholas II had little interest in the affair, but his advisers feared that the empire's regional influence was at risk. As with the Cathars, a political anxiety was projected onto a theological dispute, and the result was persecution.

In June 1913 an Imperial Navy gunboat pulled up off the coast of St Panteleimon. The Bishop of Vologda was sent ashore, making one final attempt to convert the heretics. His sermon was shouted down, however, the monks crying out, '*Imia Bozhie est' Sam Bog!* The name of God is God!'

After him came 118 marines, who set up water cannons and machine guns and ordered the *imiaslavie* to gather in the *katholikon*. The monks refused, barricading themselves in their cells. What happened next is unclear. Official reports claim that Russian forces were attacked, unofficial reports that they opened fire. How many were killed, how many injured – all this is disputed. However, forty brothers ended up in hospital, St Andrew's Skete surrendered without a fight, and by early July eight hundred *imiaslavie* had been shipped to Russia.

In Odessa the Imperial Police interrogated the monks. A small number were put in prison and a small number distributed to local monasteries. The rest had their habits stripped and their beards shaved, and were sent into exile.

'In the Latin Church people need to understand before they can believe,' said Fr Philotheos, when I told him I was finding Orthodoxy much harder to grasp. 'In the Eastern Church they need to believe before they can understand.'

It was Monday morning, my last on Mt Athos. We were sitting in a polished room with marble floors and panelled walls. Outside, men in overalls were putting up scaffolding. The sound of a chisel scraped through the open window and a clock tick-tocked on the mantelpiece, but otherwise the room was still, with the chilly hush of a museum. I perched on the edge of my chair, skin prickled with goosebumps.

In 1992 St Andrew's was repopulated by monks from Vatopedi. It resembled a rundown chateau, with gutted cellblocks and rubble-strewn courtyards. Rooftiles were stacked by the walls, sacks of plaster lined the corridors, and a pair of pilgrims heaved shattered furniture into a skip out front.

Fr Philotheos was tall and slender, his movements delicate and his face fixed without expression. Raised an Anglican, on his third visit to Mt Athos he converted to Orthodoxy and entered a monastery. Now he spoke English with a Greek accent and answered my questions with riddling queries of his own. How did it feel to leave the religion he grew up in? 'How does it feel to be born?' Had he ever found the discipline of monastic life – all those endless hours in church – difficult? 'Is it difficult to spend time with your father?' But he must have found something hard about converting? 'We don't believe there are many paths to God. We believe in Holy Tradition.'

When I mentioned that I was reading *The Way of a Pilgrim*, Fr Philotheos touched his fingertips together. I knew that Orthodoxy drew authority from tradition, but wasn't sure how this fitted with the contemplative life. If a mystic could achieve direct access to the divine, I asked, what need for religious institutions?

'Here everything comes second to prayer,' he replied. 'Scholarship, ritual, charity – they are all in the service of prayer.'

At that point I began to gabble. I said that I used to think of prayer as a pious habit, but on Mt Athos it seemed the foundation of the faith. And that I used to think of monasteries as an escape, but now I wondered if monks quit the world to confront themselves. Regardless of what I said, Fr Philotheos's face remained fixed. It occurred to me that we had less in common than any monk I had met so far. If belief was the path to understanding, these questions were meaningless, for I could not reason my way across a leap of faith. And the longer we spent together, the more defeated I felt, until my voice sounded no louder than a whisper.

Eventually Fr Philotheos spoke. 'Here we are dead to the world,' he said.

That phrase again. That awful phrase. I did not know whether monks came to Mt Athos to extinguish themselves, but if they left this life to escape from suffering, their calling was a substitute suicide.

My companion was silent now. There was no noise except the rasping chisel, the ticking clock, and the chilly hush in the corners of the room. His hands rested on his knees, so brittle he might have been made from glass. When the clock started to chime, I half expected him to crack, but he did not even flinch.

I stood to leave.

'There's no need to go.'

I explained that my pass had run out.

'We can extend your pass. You may stay as long as you wish.'

For a moment I did not answer. When I closed my eyes, another life opened up in front of me. Never finish the pilgrimage or reach Istanbul. Never leave the Holy Mountain, but spend my days binding books in Vatopedi, or tilling allotments in Iviron. All ambition, all desire, all fear for the future – all forgotten, just like that. I felt as if I was floating light through the air instead of walking. As if I was falling through dark clouds without landing. I knew this feeling. It was vertigo.

The clock chimed the hour again, and I opened my eyes. Before Fr Philotheos could make his offer a second time, I thanked him and rushed from the room, from the marble floors and panelled walls and the monk sitting still as a dead man.

An hour later I was on the boat to Ouranoupolis, sailing back up the coast. When we came to St Panteleimon, I looked across at the enormous cellblocks: seven storeys high and forty windows wide, capped with domes and spires and roofs of glistening green. I had hoped that, by working out where Hesychasm shaded into heresy, I might better understand Orthodoxy's mystical tradition. But my interviews left me confused, with a sense that, in their devotion, their self-sacrifice, most heretics resembled the pious. If faith is the echo of our longing, cast against an empty heaven, these men should be called martyrs, but because they strayed from the straight path of dogma, they were exiled from the Church instead.

What was it like to give yourself over to a single cause, only to learn too late that you had followed the wrong course, that your devotion was in fact deviancy? The idea left me with a feeling of stunned sympathy, for I feared it was my own mistake: setting off from home in a mis-guided act of faith. Perhaps this fear was behind my sudden wish to stay on Mt Athos, because here I had found another way to escape this world.

As we passed the monastery, I tried to picture that June morning one hundred years ago. Soldiers in black uniforms fanning through the cellblocks and beating down the doors. *Gospodi pomilui*, Lord have mercy. Monks scattered in the courtyards, their habits drenched, their robes bloodied. *Gospodi pomilui!* Lord have mercy! The air splintering with gunshot, and a prayer echoing off the buildings, louder and louder. *Gospodi, Gospodi, Gospodi!*

Fr Antony was away from Mt Athos during the crisis. He continued to campaign for the *imiaslavie*, but when Russia went to war the next summer he left St Andrew's to become a chaplain on the Eastern Front. After the Revo-lution the movement's status was still unresolved and Bulatovich retired to his family estate, living as a hermit.

In January 1919 he broke all contact with the Holy Synod. By the end of the year he had been murdered – the crime never solved, the culprit never caught.

Nicholas II regretted the raid and urged the Metropol-itan of Moscow to treat the heretics leniently. It is unclear whether anyone was behind this change of heart. We know that his wife, the Empress Alexandra, believed unrepentant *imiaslavie* should be allowed to receive com-munion. And that his sister-in-law, Princess Elisabeth, funded the second and third print-runs of *In the Moun-tains of the Caucasus*. And what about that charismatic *strannik* whose own career was dogged by the charge of heresy, yet whose prayers seemed to heal the tsar's son? According to one biography, Rasputin interceded on behalf of the *imiaslavie*. According to another, he was a member of the movement. I have never been able to confirm these stories, nor the rumour that Rasputin returned to Mt Athos towards the end of his life. However, in 1927 the Abbot of St Panteleimon's secretary described just such a visit to the English travel writer Robert Byron. No biography mentions it, so perhaps the secretary was mistaken, yet it is interesting that he places Rasputin's pilgrimage in the year 1913, a date etched in the memory of every brother at that monastery.

Once I left Mt Athos, the remorse from Thessaloniki returned. Marching up the eastern side of Chalkidiki, I doubted I would make Jerusalem without another mishap. It was the last week of May, and the temperature was rising: twenty-four degrees, twenty-five, twenty-eight. Setting off in midwinter, I had given no thought to hiking in the heat, but now I became listless. Though I walked in T-shirt and swimming trunks, my boots were heavy, my feet hot, and my eyes ached behind sunglasses.

An overexposed light haunted the coast, making the shoreline look stripped, the settlements neglected. The hotel doorways were boarded up and the cafes had newspapered windows. Beach grass grew shaggy on the sand, while the sea was banded like rock strata – layers of cobalt and azure, purple and black. Each afternoon I knelt in the shallows to wash the sweat from my face, or else dived into the dark water and hid from the sun.

At the end of the month I reached Asprovalta and started moving east again – three hundred kilometres to the border. On the plains of Thrace, I wandered down roads with no signs and through hamlets with no names, or entered villages in the noonday still and felt like I was trespassing. No birds sang in the heat, no shadows formed in the light. The men smiled when they did not understand me, the children stared but would not meet my eyes. I saw no women. And I missed the settled rhythm of Mt Athos, for here little seemed lasting.

In early June I arrived at the Nestos Delta, a flat expanse of farmland at the foot of the Rhodope Mountains. Villages floated on the wheat fields – gliding closer towards me, drifting farther away, closer towards me, farther away – and the cornhusks made a burning noise in the breeze, their dry hairs crackling. I kept pushing east, though my knees clicked and my ankles ticked, as if the machinery in my legs were coming loose.

Lagoons punctured the shore beyond the Nestos River, breaking the land into spits and bars, islands and islets. Swarms of midges turned the air opaque, obscuring the rushes and reedbeds. Sunshine floated like soap scum on the water.

That evening I stopped at a campsite. Although a light was on above the gates, the place was abandoned. I tramped round in the gloom, between rows of caravans in black cladding. Their metal shells resembled elephant corpses, the campsite some overgrown graveyard. A few had smashed windows or folded roofs, others were penned in behind plastic fencing, but not one of them was occupied. And yet, despite the darkness, I noticed odd signs of life: a blackened barbecue propped on bricks, or a string of fairy lights with broken bulbs, or a fuse box hanging half-open, its circuits glinting like icons in a dingy grotto.

Pine trees divided the caravans from the beach, their cones sewn together with cobweb. As I pitched my tent beneath the trees, I spotted a bonfire down by the water.

The flames cast quivering shadows over the sand, where six teenagers were sitting in a circle, laughing exhausted laughs. A seventh teenager danced in the waves, making a sound like a siren.

'Sleep anywhere!' one of them shouted. 'We occupy the campsite.'

Another member of the group asked why I was here. I explained that I had been hiking across the Balkans, via Ohrid, Bitola and Thessaloniki. But, when she asked where I was going, I paused. By this point I was certain I should cut short my pilgrimage in Turkey, so I told her I was aiming for Istanbul.

The girl looked troubled. 'Istanbul is fire,' she said, but I did not understand. She began to punch the air, wave an imaginary flag, and then lay on her back as if fainting, but still I did not understand. Eventually a third member of the group showed me his phone. It was playing a clip from the news, the footage cutting between a park covered in tents and a street heaving with demonstrators. Riot police marched through the smoke – but still, still I did not understand.

'Istanbul is fire,' the girl repeated. 'Is fire.'

A dirt road tracked the coastline forty kilometres from the border – a deserted stretch of collapsing cliffs. On Thursday afternoon I discovered a new-built church beside the shore. The work had been abandoned before it was finished, and the renderless walls were corroded by the saltwind off the sea. Inside, marble panels covered the space where the altar should go, but everything else was naked concrete: a great hall of dusty air and stagnant space.

Why build a church in this out-of-the-way place? Why finish two thirds of the work and then leave it to decay? I looked for an answer, picking through the sand-bags and sacks of plaster, but found no clues.

Opening my map, I checked for a village or housing development nearby. All I could see were the suburbs of Alexandroupoli, five hours' walk from here – the last city before the border. Tomorrow morning I would pass a sign on the outskirts of the city decorated with a double-headed eagle: *Constantinopolis 297 km*. The day after, I would reach the border, and then it was a week, eight days, to Istanbul. Something was happening in that city, but I did not know what. There was smoke and chanting, but I did not know . . .

A few icons had been propped on a picnic table in one corner of the church. Underneath I noticed a scrap of paper printed with the words Ἅγιος Εὐγένιος.

Agios Evgénios. St Eugene. Perhaps that was the church's name.

Standing before the empty altar, I made up my mind. When I arrived in Istanbul, I would book a flight home. For five months I had walked in the hope that, if I reached Jerusalem, then I would be well. I had carried this hope the whole way from Canterbury, its burden growing heavier on my back. Too anxious to ask for help, I made a virtue of solitary endurance, mistaking my isolation for something heroic. But what I thought of as courage was in fact a kind of fear. There was no need to keep going and risk another breakdown. Safer to finish the journey while I was still in control.

This was not the first time I had imagined ending my pilgrimage early, but that afternoon it did not feel like a defeat. Instead I felt a surging sense of freedom, as if a rucksack weighing more than all the church had slid from my shoulders and gone tumbling into the sea. So I put away my map, stepped outside, and walked to the end of Europe.

PART FOUR

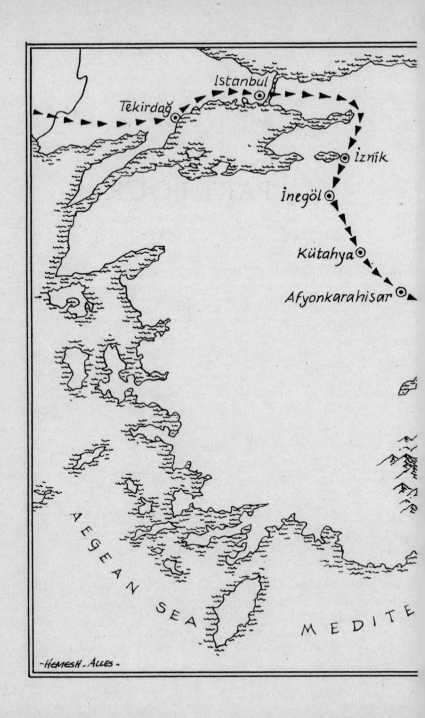

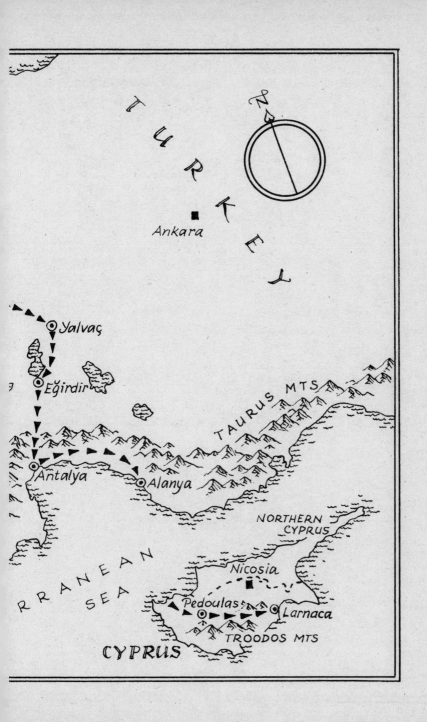

A retired journalist who ran an internet cafe in the border town of İpsala. Who had reported from Russia and Singapore. Who used his twelve-year-old nephew as a translator. Who joked about his nephew's weight ('My uncle says I weigh a hundred kilos . . .'), and then see-sawed off his chair with laughter. Who gave me glass after glass of sugary tea and called the prime minister, Recep Tayyip Erdoğan, a dictator.

I had stopped here to learn more about the unrest in Istanbul. The articles I found online explained how a demonstration against the redevelopment of a park – Gezi Park, near Taksim Square – spread to dozens of Turkish cities when footage of the brutal police response went viral. But, said the retired journalist, Erdoğan was the real reason. People were protesting his rule.

Next morning I hiked along a dual carriageway running the length of eastern Thrace. It was Sunday 9 June; Istanbul was a week's walk away. I was restless to reach the city, but owned no map of the region and had to use traffic signs instead. Although the landscape remained the same – plains of bronze-coloured wheat quaking in the wind – I was more comfortable now with the heat, waking early and walking hard, thirty-seven, thirty-eight, forty-two kilometres a day.

That evening I passed five men sitting by the roadside, drinking Efes beer and smoking Samsun cigarettes. When I mentioned I was heading to Taksim, they began to criticize the prime minister with a few words of English and a series of crude gestures. Erdoğan prayed too much; he liked money too much. He sucked up to the Saudis, or was it Iran? He was a sultan, a pasha. Fuck Tayyip – understand?

One of the men disagreed. While the others spoke, he shook his moustache, repeating, 'Islam good, Erdoğan good.' Then he started to tidy, bagging the empty beer bottles and crushed cigarette packets, muttering, *'Haram, haram.'* Finally he stretched out his arms and cried: *'Allahu Akbar!'*

The other four men were guffawing. The fifth man was laughing too, his chest jolting up and down. When I felt sure that he was making fun of himself, I tried to join in, but managed no more than a smile.

Everyone I met had an opinion about the protests. On Monday afternoon I spoke to a nineteen-year-old boy standing beside a petrol station, who took out his phone to show me photos of his sister, his motorbike, his boyfriend, and the camp occupying Gezi Park. 'Free library, free medicine, free food,' he said. 'Every evening I visit.' Fifteen minutes later two friends turned up in a blotchy blue Renault, the back seat piled with protest gear. 'This mean: Taksim is ours,' the boy explained, pointing at a handmade banner. 'This mean: Gezi is ours,' he added, now pointing at a printed flag. Finally he held up a piece of cardboard painted with the word *İSYANBUL*. 'This mean: rebellion.'

'*İsyan?*' I asked.

He nodded. 'Rebellion.'

The following afternoon the road sank down to the Sea of Marmara. That evening I stopped at Tekirdağ, a coastal town of warped wooden houses and modern hotels. Anxious to know what was happening in Istanbul, I checked into the cheapest and stayed up late watching BBC World.

The correspondent stood on a balcony, the streets behind him clouded with tear gas. This morning police raided the park, he said, this evening the protesters fought back. Then he apologized, because the gas was too thick to say any more.

Two days after that, Thursday evening, I camped on the beach in another coastal town, called Silivri. Thunderheads were massing over the sea, so the owner of a nearby restaurant invited me to shelter on his porch. His wife brought out a plate of almond cake – 'No money! No money!' – and we sat watching lightning fracture the far sky. When they learnt that I was hiking to Istanbul, they shook their heads, told me they were sorry.

The restaurant had a laptop customers could use, so I looked up the news from Taksim, reading about five thousand wounded, three dead, and an opposition politician in hospital. There were photographs of the bruised and bleeding crowds too, and of a man dressed in red playing a piano on the steps of Gezi Park.

That night I lay in my tent and listened to the rain streaming off the sea. I wondered whether the crowds were still demonstrating, the pianist still playing, the tear gas too thick to speak. And I wondered whether the protests would outlast the weekend.

It was raining when I woke next day, but by eleven o'clock the sky had cleared. I folded my tent, shook loose the wet sand, and marched from Silivri.

Istanbul's old city was seventy-five kilometres away. If I walked without resting, I could eat breakfast tomorrow morning in Sultanahmet, the district surrounding Hagia Sophia. In between lay fifteen hours of suburb: I would miss nothing by hiking at night. So I pulled tight the straps of my rucksack and set off for the mother church of Byzantium.

A wide road led out of Silivri, flanked by gated

neighbourhoods. All afternoon I walked beside it, passing fenced apartments and walled bungalows. At teatime the ground dipped towards Lake Büyükçekmece – the first of two lagoons I had to cross. The hillside beyond was stacked with towers of shining glass, like the ramparts of the modern city.

In the early evening, forty-five kilometres from Hagia Sophia, I reached the eastern side of the lagoon and stopped at a roadside cafe. A young man eating rice with his fingers warned that Sultanahmet was too far to walk and offered me a bed on his sofa. I could speak French with his wife, get stoned with his cousin, and hear about the time he hitchhiked across Europe.

I explained that I was travelling through the night.

He grinned, showing grains of rice lodged in his gums. 'I know,' he said. 'You want to join the riots.'

When it was dark I stopped at a second cafe and ordered three cups of coffee. Sitting on the first-floor balcony, I could see strings of traffic tying the hillsides in headlights.

One other person was waiting on the balcony, a hunched figure with a creased forehead. He was drinking alone, eager to talk. 'Turkey?' he said, pinching his shirt and spitting on the floor. I asked what was wrong with Turkey. He tapped his breastbone and beamed. 'Kurdish!' This formula was repeated several times. 'Erdoğan?' He spat. 'Putin?' He spat. 'Obama?' He spat. When I mentioned England, he held his hand flat, tilting the wrist from left to right. 'English OK. But Kurdish –' he tapped his breast again – 'Kurdish number one.'

Later that evening, arriving at the city ramparts, I realized the towers of glass were office blocks with lights left on. They were surrounded by shopping malls and multi-storey car parks, by four-lane roads, eight-arm junctions and overpasses of poured concrete. These ugly stretches of outcity were made strange by the night, like the endless wastes of the ocean floor.

Many of the buildings were under construction. As the darkness spread, they began to resemble ruins, and once the roads had emptied, I was alone among them. At least, I was almost alone.

Passing an unfinished high-rise, I spotted a ladder leading up to a window. The flat was just a shell, but furnished with a sofa, a camp bed and a sleeping bag. Washing lines hung from the walls, pegged with suits of clothing – one each for Mummy, Daddy, and Baby – and a man knelt to pray in the middle of the floor. I could not see his face, only his folded body and the naked soles of his feet.

In the early hours of Saturday, aching and bored, I lay on the pavement with my rucksack as a pillow. On my right were the blinking lights of Atatürk Airport, on my left a steady procession of taxis and rubbish trucks. Half an hour ago I had crossed Lake Küçükçekmece – the second lagoon, the last before the city centre – and water vapour still hung in the air, glistening beneath sodium streetlamps. I imagined wrapping the night round my shoulders and waiting until sunrise, but then I began to shiver, so I put on fresh socks and started walking again. Hagia Sophia was twenty-five kilometres away.

At dawn I heard the muezzin's call from the loud-speakers of a nearby mosque. Then I heard another call, another, and soon the whole city was trembling with the words of the *shahada*: there is no God but God.

I was hiking beside a dual carriageway banked with more glass offices. When I spotted a sign for Fatih, Istanbul's old city, I left the road and hiked between patches of parkland instead. Ten kilometres to go! After a while I reached a gateway of pitted stone, part of the immense fortifications that ringed the Byzantine capital. The streets beyond were lined with flat-roofed, wide-windowed buildings in pale shades of pastel. Eventually these streets became boulevards, plane trees on the pavement and tram tracks on the road. I passed a mosque shaped like a music box, some grandiose institution that I guessed was a university, and the brick cupolas of a covered bazaar.

Finally I arrived in Sultanahmet, a spread of ornate houses stepping down towards the Bosphorus.

The streets were narrow. The streets were steep. The streets were cobbled, or flagged with misshapen stones. On every corner I saw Ottoman-themed restaurants, Ottoman-themed hotels, Ottoman-themed gift shops and stalls selling discount fezzes. I spent an hour wandering the neighbourhood, following signs for the hippodrome. Although I glimpsed Hagia Sophia through the gaps in the buildings, I came no closer, for the signs only sent me in circles. The longer I roamed, the more impatient I became, muttering desperate pleas to the city and begging the streets to straighten. I was near giving up when I entered an open space bounded by lawns, flowerbeds, fountains and obelisks. The hulking basilica lay in the distance, its buttressed walls a tired shade of grey. The minarets were streaked brown and black, turning terracotta where they caught the light. The great dome looked low and heavy and wide. It looked ancient.

I'd done it. I'd reached the New Rome, the second capital of Christianity. Greece was two hundred and fifty kilometres behind me now, a week's walk to the west. Yet I felt no delight, only a weary relief, for my senses were blunted, my mind emptied out. I could hear splashing fountains, clinking trams. Sunlight was everywhere.

The first room of the Mihrimah Sultan restaurant looked like a yacht club. The second room looked like a gastro pub, the third like a beer garden. It was here that I met the Americans. They were sitting outside and sharing a pair of shisha pipes. They worked for IT companies, law firms and the Istanbul branch of the World Bank. They had been watching the protests for the last two weeks. They were excited.

Rob was my host that evening, a large man with a low voice, whose eyes pinched small whenever he emphasized a word.

'Erdoğan was doing a TV interview, and he called the protesters *çapulcu*. It means looters, wasters, whatever. The protesters started using the word to mean anyone who stands up for their rights. Then it became a verb, half-English, half-Turkish: I chapul, you chapul, he/she/it chapuls. Soon you could buy T-shirts that read, *Everyday I'm chapulling*.' He puffed on the shisha, chuckling smoke. 'Gezi went crazy for it, so now you've got a chapul art gallery and a chapul tea shop and signs saying *Welcome to Chapulstan*. Someone even made a book with a cover like a Penguin Classic, *The Art of Chapulling: An Introduction to Turkish Sociology*.'

It was early evening, twelve hours since I had arrived at Hagia Sophia, and my head was tight with tiredness. When Rob asked if I had visited the park, I described crossing Taksim Square earlier that afternoon and skirting round a great swarm of people. I saw the band, the banners, the barricades built from paving slabs – and decided to come back tomorrow. My original plan was to pitch a tent among the protesters, but first give me one good night in a bed.

'I wish you'd been here from the start,' said the woman sitting opposite me. She had dark hair, a wide mouth and a clipped accent. 'The first time protesters took control of the square, people were celebrating. There was fancy dress and dancing in the streets, and it felt like a carnival – but a well-behaved carnival, with everyone tidying up the morning after.'

The woman's name was Alev. Her father was British, her mother from Northern Cyprus. She had grown up in England, but moved to Istanbul in her mid-twenties. Now she was writing a book about her experience, as well as blogging every stage of the demonstrations. I listened to Alev tell stories from the last few weeks: protesters protecting police from a barrage of stones, football hooligans teaching hippies how to immobilize armoured vehicles. They were meant to be funny, but her delivery was weary, and when the stories were finished I asked if she was disappointed.

Alev paused. 'I used to think young Turks were apathetic, until Gezi Park showed me another side of the country. But none of the demonstrators know what they want. They don't have a manifesto, or a political programme, or any demands. It makes me sad to think nothing will come of it.'

At nine o'clock the conversation went quiet. The Americans started checking their phones, texting their friends, paying the bill and standing to leave. Riot police were clearing Gezi Park – that was the rumour. There were images all over Twitter. Digger trucks. Water cannons. Nothing left, not a living soul.

Alev wanted to see for herself, so Rob and I went with her. Our restaurant was fifty metres from İstiklal Caddesi, a pedestrian shopping street running straight to Taksim Square. The square's entrance was blocked, however, and we went via the backstreets instead. Hundreds of protesters were hurrying between the cramped alleyways of the old Christian quarter. We passed a woman in a designer dress, a pair of heels looped through the fingers of her left hand; and a man just out of the office, his tie loose to give space for a gas mask; and students in hard hats and goggles, warpaint smeared on their cheeks, blood types written on their skin; and we passed children, too many children.

Most of the protesters were chanting, their voices bouncing off the buildings. Alev translated for me: '*Tayyip istifa* means, Tayyip resign. *Her yer Taksim, her yer direniş* means, Everywhere is Taksim, everywhere resistance.'

Rob was ahead of us now, moving up an unlit passageway. I guessed it opened onto İstiklal, but wasn't sure, because the figures at the top were hazy. Then I noticed something chemical on my lips, something tainted on my tongue. Not the itch of cigarette smoke, nor the cloy of factory fumes, but something bitter and teasing. I felt it ease into my throat, slip the lids of each eye. I felt coughing, tears, and then I felt choking. But only when I saw Rob rushing back did I realize we had been gassed.

I held my breath, ducked and ran, left and right and left again, wrapping my mouth in my collar, my sleeve, as the streets went blind around me.

When the air was clear, I stood tall once more, gasping with relief. A stranger sprayed a milky liquid into my eyes, which eased the burning. 'Kind of exhilarated,' Rob said, still panting. 'After it's gone you feel kind of exhilarated.'

We were gassed twice more before reaching Taksim. When we arrived at the square's southern entrance, the police would not let us through, until Alev announced that we were guests at the Marmara Taksim – a twenty-storey hotel opposite Gezi Park – and we were escorted to the front door. She marched across the lobby, stepped into a lift and pressed the button for a bar on the top floor.

The bar was darkly lit, with polished furniture and screens of brushed gold. Although the tables lay in bowls of lamplight, everything else was shadowy. Jazz music played from the corners of the room and a few couples whispered at the tables, yet all I could hear was the anxious quiet beneath these sounds.

On the far side of the room a wall of glass looked down on the square. Below was desolation.

Spotlights surrounded the park. The trees were all standing, but nothing else remained, only an empty space bleached white like a hospital ward. Nothing remained of the free library, the free classroom, or the volunteer kitchen giving away free food. Nothing remained of the banners that spelt out *Anti-Capitalista* in silver letters on a red background, or *İstanbul bizim* in black letters on a yellow background, or the signs shouting *GAZI, GAZI, GAZI* in red letters on a blank background. Nothing of the Turkish flags, Kurdish flags, communist and anarchist flags, nor the rainbow flags hanging from every branch. No trace of the pop-up medical centre with baby-blue parasols, or the kidnapped bulldozer painted a garish pink. No chapul art gallery, no chapul tea shop, no chapul tree with leaves made from handwritten wishes, nor any tents, shelters, pavilions, marquees – only the appalling brightness of the light and nine acres of damaged earth. And the dead still where once was so much life.

Rob's flat was a twenty-minute walk from Taksim. To reach it we needed to cross İstiklal, and to cross İstiklal we needed to get away from the square. After waving goodbye to Alev, we dropped into the side streets once more. People were running in the darkness, and the walls were scrawled with slogans. As Rob pushed up another unlit passageway, he said something about civil order coming apart, pointing at a sprayed stencil of a penguin wearing a gas mask.

'The first time the police attacked Gezi, none of the

media covered it. Taksim was a war zone and CNN Türk broadcast a documentary on penguins. That's what the logo means. Biggest protests in decades and people have to use social media to find out what's happening . . .'

Rob kept speaking, but I could not hear him any more. We had stepped into the blaze of İstiklal, and his voice was lost to the din.

Picture the shopping district of any major European city: an avenue of facades, the architecture a mismatch of Neoclassical, Renaissance Revival, mock-Ottoman and Art Nouveau. Buildings three or four storeys high, draped in advertisements or hung with lights – buzzing blue snowflakes suspended above the street. Picture window displays like theatre sets and each shopfront a show of luminous signs. Picture the street at night, and now picture it corrupted. Windows cracked, or covered in cardboard, and the glass disfigured with graffiti. Street-lamps stuttering and monstrous shadows dancing off the walls. Shutters down over every doorway and protesters shaking the slats, until the sound of rattling echoed along İstiklal.

On our right was a temporary barricade made from upturned bins. Some of the rubbish bags had been torn open by street dogs, fouling the air with their smell. Others had been doused in fuel and set alight, creating a sheet of fractured flame. A boy of perhaps ten or eleven stood on one of the bins, his limbs whippet-thin, his teeth wide apart. He was shrieking in high, hysterical shrieks, like a child prophet or an infant king, while ranks of demonstrators marched past him, marching through the night.

At the northern end of the avenue three thousand protesters stood facing Taksim Square. Opposite them, guarding the entrance, were riot police carrying batons and shields, or holding grenade launchers loaded with gas canisters. The armoured trucks parked behind had water cannons mounted on their roofs.

Rob was edging into the crowd, shouting over his shoulder, but I heard only snatches – 'just take a look' – as he moved to the front – 'start a stampede' – and the chanting grew louder – *Her yer Taksim* – and the mob pressed together – 'stay out of trouble' – and there was no noise but chanting –

Tayyip istifa!

 Tayyip istifa!

 Her yer Taksim,

 Taksim!

 TAKSİM!

 her yer direniş,

 Direniş! DİRENİŞ!

her yer Gezi,

 Tak   sim!

 İstifa!

 TAK   SİM!

– and then a pounding as the police fired.

Three thousand people turned to run. Three thousand faces reeled round; three thousand bodies dashed back – an entire protest trying to escape, all channelled in a single direction. Some sprinted with their shoulders bowed, gas gushing towards them. Others raced so fast that they lost their footing, squealing as they fell to the ground. A few broke off from the mob, now ducking into backstreets, now scrambling into doorways, now skidding into the gates of a building site. Where I stood we were jammed in place, shoving and tugging but helpless to get away, until a space opened up before me and I ran with a strange sense of elation, carried along by the madding tide.

After a hundred metres the protesters slowed. A dozen men raised their arms, calling *Yavaş, yavaş* to steady the retreat. Then the crowd reassembled to start the next approach.

All night they played this game.

Eight hours later I was back on İstiklal. The street seemed smaller in the morning light and empty now but for the cleaners wearing fluorescent jackets. I watched a man with a high-pressure hose wash graffiti from the walls, while another swept clear the rubbish, and a third turned upright each tipped bin.

It was still early when I reached Taksim Square. Gezi Park lay behind rows of ambulances, satellite trucks and armoured jeeps – a strip of naked trees and shattered fencing. Banks and travel agents lined the pavement, traffic queued on the ring road, police patrolled the entrances, but nothing remained of the demonstration.

For the next few hours I circled the cafes near Taksim, making notes on last night. After we left the protest, Rob took me to a party, a cheerless affair midway to his flat. One group of guests sat watching the news, the coverage shifting between the Divan Hotel (under siege from the police) and the Bosphorus Bridge (blocked by an army of protesters). A second group read out Twitter rumours from their phones: the Jandarma were raiding student dormitories, the water cannons were laced with chemicals, a woman had miscarried on the steps of the Divan. Meanwhile, our host played YouTube clips on his laptop. Here was Prime Minister Erdoğan praising police restraint. Here was Prime Minister Erdoğan blaming the protests on foreign agitators. Here was the prime minister's spokesman warning that Erdoğan had been the target of a psychic assassination attempt. That's right: telekinetic assassins.

By this point I had been awake forty-three hours.

The following morning, circling Taksim, I noticed ragged-looking protesters assembling in the side streets. From ten o'clock I could hear dispersed chanting. From eleven o'clock I could taste tear gas in the air. By twelve the taxis were turning back on Tarlabaşı and the restaurants locking up in Galata. Yesterday evening I had been too tired to feel afraid, but in the daylight the atmosphere was menacing. Yet I still wandered round in a drowsy state of disbelief, as if caught in the liquid logic of a dream.

That afternoon I found an outdoor cafe some two hundred metres from İstiklal, opposite a street of private galleries and designer boutiques. I sat on a balcony at the rear of the terrace, facing west towards the shining waters of the Golden Horn. Then a hundred things happened at once.

I heard running. Shouting. I heard tables drag, glasses smash.

I looked round and saw fifty, sixty, people rush the terrace. A squad of riot police came after them, firing tear gas under our tables. Smoke burst from the ground and the scene crazed over.

I pushed to the back of the balcony, where the air was still clean. The rest of the cafe did the same, protesters and customers crushing together. Beside me was a middle-aged woman wearing a headscarf and trainers, her eyes startled, her expression embarrassed. Everyone else was screaming and crying; they were terrified.

Police had cordoned the cafe, but there was a gap where the terrace met the balcony. Three teenage boys tried to escape that way, moving with hurried, upright paces. As they came to the street they moved faster, jogging past galleries and boutiques.

I shouldered my rucksack and followed them out, jostling through the gap. But I did not give chase, for though the street looked empty, it seemed safer to keep walking. Sure enough, as I paced down the pavement, an armoured jeep overtook on my right, accelerating towards the boys. By now they were racing along a wall of mixed stone, and when they reached the end of the wall, they turned left to start sprinting downhill. The jeep turned after them, passing from sight, but as I approached the crossroads, I heard shots. Peering round the corner, I saw one boy still sprinting, another stumbling, and a third crying out, his legs buckled beneath him. More police were waiting at the base of the hill, their weapons raised – yet I could see no blood or broken masonry. Then I understood: rubber bullets.

The jeep was maybe fifteen metres away, a vulgar vehicle with outsize tyres and a water cannon propped on top. As the cannon wheeled towards me, I felt a giddy sort of surprise, for I could not believe the thing was solid. It looked so tacky, like a bouncy castle wilting after a day of play.

I waited. Kept waiting. There was nothing between us but space, nothing but absent air. Then the turret squeaked, the gears gulped, and the jeep drove off again.

Letting go of my rucksack, I leant back against the wall. I had forgotten how to breathe, but kept swallowing until my lungs filled with air. Eventually I noticed a polished plaque fixed to the stonework behind me. Reading the plaque, I learnt that I was standing outside the British Consulate.

*

'Last night was the worst yet,' said Alev, as we sat on her roof a few hours later. 'Most of the protests have been violent, but never this bad.'

Alev lived in a top-floor flat two minutes' walk from Taksim Square. Her roof looked out on Kabataş, the buildings capped with cluttered tiles, twisted aerials and miniature chimneys, the balconies dotted with shrubs. Beyond lay the broad sweep of the Bosphorus and the far coast of Asia. The straits were an even grey that evening, the sky smothered in cloud. The distant shoreline was dim. We were waiting for the rain.

Sitting there, I told her what had happened since the Marmara Taksim. I mentioned joining the midnight demonstration on İstiklal and escaping from the police this afternoon. As Alev listened she bit her lip, shook her head. Then she told me about her own adventure.

Yesterday evening, having left Taksim Square, Alev returned to her flat. Before long, friends were texting from another hotel – the Divan – to say that police had forced the doors with water cannons and were filling the lobby with tear gas. She followed the news on social media until, sleepless with worry, she went to look. The hotel was next to Taksim, but the square was on lockdown, and Alev looped round to the far side. On İnönü Caddesi she saw riot squads asleep in police vans, ID numbers blacked out on their helmets and shields. In Maçka Park she saw protesters drifting through the darkness, eyes rimmed white with antacid spray.

It was early morning when she reached the Divan. 'The police were guarding the hotel, so I told them I was a guest again. When I got inside, the whole lobby was flooded, all the furniture and carpets soaked. People were just lying on the floor, holding each other and looking helpless. One of the conference rooms had been turned into an emergency centre – this giant hall with glass chandeliers, full of doctors and patients and crates of medicine. And tear gas everywhere, because none of the ventilation was working. It was the like the aftermath of an earthquake.'

'Nobody knew the reason for the attack,' Alev added. 'Since Gezi Park started the Divan has been feeding protesters and offering them shelter, and when the park was cleared, that's where everybody ran. But the police came after, meaning they were trapped. The hotel belongs to the Koç family. They're billionaires, philanthropists – not the biggest fans of Erdoğan. So maybe it was revenge.'

'Revenge?'

Alev raised her hands in a gesture of surrender. On first moving to Turkey she did not believe all the stories of conspiracy, but living in Istanbul wore down her scepticism. Over the years she had seen building projects begun without consultation and government contracts awarded on a whim, seen regulations ignored and the city becoming spoilt.

'That's what caused the protests: plans to replace Gezi Park with a shopping mall. It wasn't Erdoğan's decision, but he's talked about cleaning up İstiklal, about making the neighbourhood more Islamic. And he wants to build the biggest mosque in Turkey on Çamlıca Hill, where it can be seen from everywhere in the city. I know, it sounds like a joke, like he's pretending to be a sultan.'

When I complained about the endless wastes of concrete that I had passed when walking into the city – kilometre after kilometre of newbuild – Alev explained how the government was using economic growth to justify all this petty despotism, as well as using political tension to make the country more authoritarian. She gave examples of lawyers being arrested, journalists being deported, activists being threatened, and friends becoming paranoid. Then she said: 'Since the protests began it's felt like living in a police state.'

The rain was falling. Although we were close to Taksim, I could hear no chants, no sirens or shouts. Only one noise interrupted the downpour: a wooden spatula knocking against a cast-iron pan. It was coming from the apartment opposite, the spatula beating faster until the whole pan was ringing. This was joined from the flat below by a metal spoon circling an earthenware pot, which made a spiralling sound like poured sand.

Soon half the windows and balconies around us were clanging, clattering – a song of protest joining together the strained voices of the city.

'This happens every evening,' said Alev, running downstairs to collect pans from the kitchen. 'It's how you show support.'

I was a guest at her flat for the rest of my time in Istanbul. Most evenings I would sit on the roof and listen to this improvised orchestra. Sometimes it reminded me of a cheering crowd, sometimes a spitting fire. That night it was the cry of a wounded animal. When Alev came back with a pair of metal pans, we joined the performance, banging their blackened bases until the keening died away and there was no sound but the rain. Rain falling harder, pouring off rooftiles and splashing from gutters. Rain in parks and squares, in alleyways and avenues, on the concrete cages of a thousand building sites. In Karaköy and Kabataş, in Tarlabaşı and Taksim, rain washing clean the exhausted streets.

I stayed a few more days in the city. The demonstrators returned, the tear gas too, but the carnival atmosphere was gone for good. When Taksim Square opened again, a new protest began. People gathered in one corner, facing a poster of Atatürk that hung from a disused cultural centre. There were students and professionals, young families and elderly couples, standing for hours on end. Some held flowers, others taped shut their mouths, and a few listened to music or read books. One or two remained through the night, casting a mood of mourning over the square. This was the march of the defeated.

I stayed a few more days in the city. Much of my time was spent wandering the backways of Beyoğlu and Fatih – old neighbourhoods on either side of the Golden Horn. I found rooftop chapels in Tophane, ruined churches in Cihangir, and the walled compound of the Armenian Cathedral on a quiet road in Yenikapı. The architecture was thrown together in a haphazard fashion, meaning I would turn from a row of stuccoed hotels and stumble into a street of wooden houses, their timber frames misshapen, their clapboard covers coming loose. Often they were deserted, except for a few children ambushing one another with water pistols. But then I would notice a squad of police standing on the pavement, watching the children play.

I stayed a few more days in the city. Each evening I met someone new. A communist activist who smoked and smoked, telling stories about rigged elections and government plots. An Ottoman historian who invited me to dinner and suggested every route I might walk through Turkey. The pianist whose photo I saw when hiking into the city, a lean, loping figure who believed his instrument could bring peace. An ambassador visiting from Ankara, an entrepreneur in town from Beirut, and a foreign correspondent just returned from the Black Sea coast – all with advice on travelling in the region. Some warned me never to mention my destination, others to keep quiet about Gezi Park.

I stayed a few more days in the city. I had the same

conversation dozens of times. It concerned nationalists and separatists, Kemalists and Islamists, AKP and CHP and far-left factions whose acronyms I cannot remember. I was told that the protesters were exhausted. The opposition divided. The military powerless. That the prime minister was loved. The economy booming. The country falling apart. These conversations shared the same tone of hope, of expectation, for the change that must come, surely it must come, after fighting so hard for the future. And shared the same undertow of regret, too, for they knew hope could make nothing happen.

I stayed a few more days in the city. Every morning I told myself I would book a flight home, and every afternoon I delayed. In Greece I had decided to cut short my walk, but something held me in Istanbul. I felt no desire to drink, nor escape the summer crowds. I felt no longing for solitude, either, because the capital made things seem close and urgent. Crossing the Balkans, my pilgrimage had turned into a test of endurance – eyes fixed on the horizon, mind folding in on itself – but reaching Istanbul I forgot about the journey and let the present press in on every side.

Well, I almost forgot. One evening I sat on the roof of Alev's flat, staring towards the Asian shore. As the sun went down on the waterfront neighbourhoods – the parkland scattered with cupolas, domes and the slender spires of a dozen minarets – I saw how far I had come. The Levant was near. The Holy Land was near. Jerusalem was near to me now.

That evening I started to sketch a path through the Middle East. Half the armies of the First Crusade followed the Via Egnatia to Constantinople, arriving in the winter of 1096. Next spring they crossed the Bosphorus and marched into Asia Minor. By autumn they had reached Antioch, and after taking the city they moved down the Mediterranean coast. Civil war in Syria made that route impossible, but I could patch together an alternative. Rather than aiming for Antioch, I would head south to Antalya, hop on a boat, and walk the width of Cyprus. This would make up the distance lost by skipping Syria. A second boat would take me to Lebanon, where I could rejoin the crusader trail.

Although pushing on into Turkey might risk another relapse, I would find no bars in central Anatolia. Besides, if I went home from Istanbul it would not mean I had failed to finish, but given up without ever trying. I no longer believed that the pilgrimage could heal me, but abandoning the journey would fix nothing. And, if I kept going, I might discover a new reason to walk.

So in early July I packed my rucksack and began hiking again.

It was midday when I set off from Hersek, a scrappy village on a headland in the İzmit Gulf. After three weeks at rest my pack felt heavy, my boots tight, my legs not stiff but slow to lift. This was my first time in the Middle East, and though I had learnt a courtesy of Turkish, I was unsure how to explain the pilgrimage, let alone find shelter. My maps of the area were also patchy, and few of the roads had signs, while every attempt to ask directions was met with a baffled grin.

I was climbing through the Yalak Valley, its narrow course leading south towards Lake İznik. Tomato vines strung the riverbank to my right, and on my left rose a series of stunted hills, coarse with tufa and cropped with woodland. The air by the coast was cool, but as I rose higher the sun beat hard against my skin. A breeze carried the muffled cry of traffic up from the coastal road, until I turned a corner and the valley was quiet.

Nine hundred and seventeen years ago, one Wednesday morning in October, this route was choked with dead and dying soldiers. They had been camping near Helenopolis, the Byzantine city that once occupied the Hersek headland, but at daybreak they trooped into the Yalak Valley to take on the forces of the Seljuk sultan.

They did not know that archers were hiding in the woods above the valley. They did not know that they were marching into an ambush.

The soldiers were from Lombardy, northern and eastern France, Rhineland and southern Germany. They had hiked across Europe and were making their way to Jerusalem. Historians would dub them the People's Crusade, but contemporary sources used another name: *peregrini*, or pilgrims.

The inspiration for their pilgrimage can be traced back to 1095, at the Council of Clermont, when three hundred clerics gathered to hear Pope Urban II call for the liberation of the Holy Land. His speech was prompted by a request for help from the Byzantine emperor, Alexios Komnenos, but Urban refashioned this into a cause for conquest.

Although the speech made no mention of pilgrimage, the proposed campaign showed obvious parallels. Before leaving home, a crusader had to settle his debts and seek permission from his priest. While on the road he was meant to visit shrines, venerate relics, and observe the liturgical calendar. And, if he reached Jerusalem, or died in the attempt, he would earn a plenary indulgence, meaning salvation was assured.

By borrowing the template of pilgrimage, the Pope turned an innovative form of holy war into something familiar. Of course, fighting for Christ was nothing new, but during the Middle Ages informal codes of chivalry recast Christian morality in martial terms: courage was a virtue, pacifism a cause for shame. Urban went one further, presenting war as an act of Christian fellowship, a religious duty.

The wandering evangelists who publicized the First Crusade took advantage of this pilgrimage link. Preaching manuals from the period show how they dressed Urban's campaign in the language of penance, calling it a missionary war, or a chance to avenge the death of Christ. A few even claimed that the capture of Jerusalem would spark the Second Coming. The Church did not endorse these arguments, but nor did it prevent their use, because apocalyptic fantasies were a powerful recruiting technique. Yet the majority of crusaders were not waiting for Judgement Day, nor setting off in search of riches and adventure. What sustained them through the journey's hardships – through hunger, sickness and danger – was the belief that they were travelling towards salvation. And, as I climbed onto the Anatolian Plateau, I wondered if this was the only motive that could endure. In Greece I had realized the journey was damaging me, but deep down I still hoped that reaching Jerusalem would solve something. Why else would I keep walking?

The most successful crusade evangelist was Peter the Hermit, an ageing preacher from Picardy. He was not really a hermit, though he dressed in robes and went barefoot or rode a mangy donkey. But he was austere, refusing to eat bread and keeping to a strict diet of fish and wine. During the winter of 1095 Peter toured round Germany, calling for the conquest of the Holy Land. His sermons attracted enormous crowds of carters and bakers, butchers and tanners, surgeons, masons, stewards and cooks, as well as physicians, marshals, chamberlains, constables, notaries, scribes and clerics of every class. These audiences were said to tear the hair from his donkey as if it was a sacred relic.

A story spread that Peter, not Urban, was the true author of the First Crusade. According to legend he visited Jerusalem as a young man and was appalled at the treatment of pilgrims by the city's Muslim rulers, vowing to return with an army.

By the spring of 1096 he had collected almost twenty thousand followers. The generals of the campaign's four largest forces were still deciding whether or not to take part, so Peter set off alone.

From Cologne the People's Crusade marched down the Danube, attracting more pilgrims wherever they stopped. In their wake came a loose band of armies led by a priest named Folkmar and various minor noblemen – Gottschalk, Emich of Flonheim and Walter Sans Avoir.

The journey was a catastrophe. Thanks to propaganda about avenging the death of Christ, Jewish communities were killed all along the route. There were massacres at Speyer and Worms, Mainz and Metz, and forced conversions in Magdeburg and Prague. Local Christians were treated little better. Because the armies left in a hurry, they were not adequately supplied, forcing them to raid the surrounding countryside.

Many of these soldiers never made it beyond Hungary. Folkmar's forces were destroyed at Nitra, and Gottschalk's surrendered at Pannonhalma. The rest ran into trouble in Bulgaria, with Walter Sans Avoir's men routed north of Belgrade and Peter the Hermit's battered near Niš. When the survivors reached Constantinople, they began torching palaces and stealing the lead from local churches, until they were shipped across the Bosphorus and pitched camp outside Helenopolis.

Medieval chroniclers dismissed the People's Crusade as a mob of unruly peasants. However, the image this conveys – of farmhands downing tools to march for Paradise – is misleading. Unlike pilgrimage, crusading was not open to all classes. Despite their ragtag leadership, the social make-up of these armies was little different from the campaign's later forces. Although the chroniclers knew this, they wanted to distance Peter's disastrous mission from the heroic deeds that came after. But the evangelist's shambolic advance party betrayed the ugliness of the entire movement, for underneath the pious guise of pilgrimage this was a vicious war of conquest.

However, pilgrimage was more than an excuse. The pilgrims' belief in the special sanctity of Jerusalem was what turned their campaign into a holy war. After all, the city had little strategic value: faith alone made it precious. A place becomes sacred when people are willing to die for it, the blessing not built in stone but bled into the earth. And my own journey was stained by that same act of sacrifice, because on entering the Levant the history of sacred travel becomes a record of conquest. Though I wanted to make sense of the walk using pilgrim traditions, as I neared Jerusalem those traditions grew ever more ugly.

Enver thought the People's Crusade deserved the horrors waiting for them on the far side of the Bosphorus. This was the prim little man I met in the lakeside town of İznik, who had winking eyes, pointed teeth and a nervous spasm of a smile. He claimed that he was a teacher, a scholar, a student of all the world, and he called the crusaders pirates.

'The West was the third world! The East was the first world! We had the silks, the spices, the sciences. Europe wanted them too.'

We met in a cafe near the lake's edge, where I was plotting my route over the Anatolian Plateau. From here I would hike some seven hundred kilometres south via the Yenişehir Plain, the Domaniç Mountains, the Kütahya Plain and the Taurus Mountains, reaching the Mediterranean coast in a month's time.

When Enver saw my map, he asked where I was going, but I struggled to answer. This was my first conversation for several days, as few villagers on the Anatolian Plateau understood English, and I had been walking in a state of uneasy vigilance: every sentence a test, every stranger a trial. Speaking Turkish, Enver's voice was mumbling, but in English he boomed, interrupting my reply and offering to show me round.

It was Monday morning, ten o'clock. Although I had twenty-five kilometres to hike that day, I could spare an hour or two.

First we went to Hagia Sophia. Like its Istanbul namesake, the church was built in the sixth century by the Emperor Justinian. But this building was modest in comparison, its walls a weathered mix of brick and stone, its base sunk below street level. The plaster was gone, the mortar too, and the stone so worn it was soft to touch.

'You have to feel the history,' said Enver, pressing my fingers against the wall. 'I like to feel my hands on all the history. Most people, they never know history. Why? Because they walk everywhere with their hands in their pockets.'

Inside, the arches and domes were also of brick, rippled with dirt as if lifted from the lakebed. A mihrab dented the room's southern wall, and a dwarf minaret was tacked onto the north-west corner. Below the niche a scowling man in his mid-sixties was laying out a prayer mat on a wooden floor.

I had not appreciated that the building was being used

for worship. When I mentioned this to Enver, he raised his arms in mock innocence. 'Sometimes museum, sometimes mosque. Who can tell?'

At that point the scowling man turned in our direction and shouted a few words of Turkish. My guide raised his arms a second time.

'It's true,' he said. 'I have a loud voice.'

Outside was a garden of palms, cypresses and exposed foundation stones. Enver led me back through the door, still discussing his tactile theory of history. Then his phone rang. The first time he ignored it; the second time he answered. On the other end I heard a woman's voice, high-pitched and pleading. From the way Enver muttered into the cupped mouthpiece, I knew his wife was calling.

He hung up. 'Now where do we see?'

'Perhaps I should go—'

'The tiles!' Enver boomed, so we went to see the tiles.

Many of Turkey's grandest mosques were decorated with İznik tiles. Until the seventeenth century the town's workshops were famous, but as demand for imperial mosques petered out, the industry declined. However, a few workshops remained in a neighbourhood of narrow streets. Their interiors were a confusion of vases, plates, bowls and saucers, with quartz tiles pinned to the walls. Each tile was decorated with a verse from the Qur'an, forming a fragile lattice of Arabic lettering. The colours were complicated: cobalt and turquoise, viridian and coral, or glazed white like a new set of teeth. The shapes were complicated too: tulips and carnations, lotus leaves and saz leaves, spidery strands of ivy and the feathers of a peacock's tail.

As we looked round the workshops, Enver's phone rang a third time. The pleading voice was now accompanied by the sound of splashing water. I wondered if a pipe had burst and his home was flooded, but my guide seemed unconcerned, muttering something else and hanging up again.

By now I was eager to get away, so I asked Enver if he needed to leave. Rather than reply, he started bellowing questions that he answered himself. Did Enver think Tayyip Erdoğan was a good prime minister? Enver did think Tayyip Erdoğan was a good prime minister. Erdoğan was not a conservative; he was not a dictator; he was proud of Turkey's history. Would Enver be fasting for Ramadan? Enver would be fasting for Ramadan. It was duty. It was tradition. Most young people did not fast any more; they were lazy; they watched too many American TV shows. What history did Enver think young people should learn in schools? They should learn Ottoman history. In particular, the reigns of Osman I, Murad I, Mehmed II and Suleiman I. Yes, Suleiman the Magnificent. Remember, the Ottoman Empire lasted six centuries; the Turkish Republic was not even a hundred. We should be proud of the Ottoman Empire. All Turkey should be proud.

By the time Enver finished interviewing himself, we had reached the last workshop. 'Now where do we see?' he asked.

'I really need to get away —'

'The walls!' Enver boomed, so we went to see the walls.

İznik's medieval walls were still standing, as well as its gates and defensive towers. My guide led the way along a road of potholed asphalt, between vans trimmed in mudstain and cars with scuffed snouts. Everything in the town seemed to be coming apart. The timber houses with orange-brick extensions. The concrete apartments painted a dirty pink. The shop stalls crowding the roadside, selling cleaning products and cooking utensils and an extraordinary number of chainsaws. Overhanging the stalls were balconies with rusted banisters and signs displaying half-familiar names – *Durgut Collection*, *Japon Pazarı*, *Marmara Salonu*, *Ziraat Bankası*, *Beymen Business* – but some of their letters were missing, and most of their backlights broken.

The Yenişehir Gate guarded the road south from the city. Its gatehouse was gone, but the tower remained, a rounded brick structure with its top blown off. Nearby stood a pair of stone arches and several shed-sized chunks of masonry.

Enver was describing the scale of the original fortifications – six thousand paces long, forty cubits high etc. – when his phone rang a fourth time. Again the pleading voice, again the splashing water, and a wailing sound that was perhaps a siren. I wondered if his house was on fire, but then Enver muttered the word *turist* and I realized why he could not go home. Whatever the crisis, his duty as host came first.

'Now where do we see?' Enver asked after hanging up.

'I'm off, Enver.'

'Off?'

'I have to go.'

My host would not hear of it, insisting I stay the rest of the day and stay the night too. Tomorrow we would drive to Bursa, first capital of the Ottoman Empire. The day after we would visit Eskişehir, the oldest city in Anatolia. And surely I needed a guide for the Yenişehir Plain?

I shook my head, shook his hand, said thank you, said goodbye.

Enver bowed, his expression a mixture of frustration and relief. The nervous smile twinged his lips, and then he bustled down a side street, running his hand over the medieval walls and booming more questions to himself.

Forty cubits high. Six thousand paces long. Strong enough to keep back a pilgrim army.

Autumn 1096. The People's Crusade were camped outside Helenopolis. Meanwhile, Peter the Hermit was in Constantinople, negotiating with Alexios Komnenos. Although the main forces of the First Crusade had just set off from Western Europe, Peter's advance party refused to wait. In early September they began raiding the Christian villages round İznik – formerly the Greek settlement of Nicaea, now the capital of the Rum sultanate. However, the city was too well defended for the raiders to take unsupported. Instead, six thousand German and Italian soldiers pushed south into Seljuk territory, occupying a deserted castle called Xerigordon. In response, the Sultan of Rum, Kilij Arslan, ordered his army to lay siege to the site.

The sultan's forces surrounded the castle and cut the water. The crusaders stayed put, however, halving their rations once, twice, and one more time. Supplies ran dry, but they still held on. The *Gesta Francorum* records how:

> they bled their horses and asses and drank the blood; others let their girdles and handkerchiefs down into the cistern and squeezed out the water from them into their mouths; some urinated into one another's hollowed hands and drank; and others dug up the moist ground and lay down on their backs and spread the earth over their breasts to relieve the excessive dryness of thirst.

This wretched situation lasted for eight days. Eventually the crusaders surrendered and Turkish soldiers overwhelmed the castle. Anyone who refused to convert was killed.

Confused reports made their way back to the camp at Helenopolis. The first claimed that the German and Italian detachment had captured Nicaea, the second that they had been destroyed. When it was confirmed that the sultan's forces were pushing north, the remaining crusaders marched out to meet them.

At first light on 21 October the entire army – perhaps fifty thousand men – filed into the Yalak Valley. If you want to picture the scene, another campaign might come in handy. The Norman Conquest occurred three decades earlier, and its soldiers were recruited from similar regions. What you need to imagine is the Bayeux Tapestry unrolled over the Turkish countryside. Men moving like puppets, their bodies cut from cloth, their swords and lances embroidered wool. Perhaps they sang as they marched, the words embroidered too in cramped Latin surtitles.

As soon as the army entered the valley, arrows filled the sky. The knights leading the march were worst hit, their hauberks pierced and their horses maimed. The terrain offered little cover from the massed archers, and the Turkish assault was so ferocious that the cavalry were driven back onto the columns of infantry. The infantry, in turn, were scattered. Despite commands to hold firm, the soldiers began to retreat. However, once the entrance to the valley was blocked, they were trapped. Walter Sans Avoir was slain, along with every other nobleman, while anyone who escaped was chased down on the plain or hounded into the sea.

So the tapestry was torn, the bodies shredded, and the river threaded with red.

After the crusader army was destroyed, the Seljuks pressed on towards Helenopolis. It was still morning when they reached the headland. Because the camp's soldiers had joined the dawn march, the place was unguarded. The Turkish troops found women and children sheltering in tents. They killed them. They found the sick and elderly sleeping in beds. They killed them. They found monks, priests and nuns kneeling in prayer. They killed them. They killed anyone they found, except for a few young men and women who were taken as slaves and a handful of soldiers who were rescued by the Byzantine Navy. But of the thousands who joined Peter the Hermit's pilgrimage through Europe – those great crowds hoping to march triumphant into the Holy City – almost none survived.

That was the story of the People's Crusade.

The story does not end there, however, because the army's failure had a profound impact on the crusaders who came after. Conquering Jerusalem was already an unlikely ambition. The utter defeat of the vanguard force made subsequent victories even more surprising.

It's no coincidence that the *Gesta Francorum* opens with an account of this calamity, for it emphasized the miraculous nature of what followed. Later armies were often amazed by their success, and many became convinced that they were acting out divine will.

At the start of my journey I would have found this baffling, but moving south from İznik I began to understand. In Istanbul I had seen crowds running, streets burning and a camp cleared of life. I had experienced the thrill of history happening around me, as events cascaded beyond human control. And that fated feeling – at once exalted and inevitable – of surviving. It would not take much faith to believe that the outcome had already been decided, even directed from above. When you add in three years of starvation, exhaustion, injury and disease, interrupted by the odd bout of horrifying violence, anyone who survived might well assume they were God's chosen.

The landscape also fed such fantasies. As I climbed

onto the Yenişehir Plain, the horizon drew back – mountains and valleys falling away. Though I passed the odd farm building or petrol station, what I noticed most was the vacant space between these places. There was an indifference to the scenery, a vastness; I could walk two hours, four hours, ten, and my surroundings would barely change. And, stepping across that immense stage, it was easy to imagine that I was carrying out some divine command.

This insight encouraged no sympathy, only shame. After all, the crusaders' belief that they were performing God's work helped justify their appalling acts of brutality. By borrowing the rites of pilgrimage and giving their journey a penitential end, they intensified that sense of cosmic support. Perhaps this was why I struggled to explain my pilgrimage to Enver: because he knew the bloody tradition in which the journey shared. And why I felt relieved to be leaving İznik behind. Enough history. Enough religion. Let's forget about God for a while.

I was apprehensive about travelling in Turkey. The Anatolian Plateau was the loneliest stretch of my entire journey, and I felt wary of so much solitude. Alone, any doubts about why I was walking would mount. Also, I did not know if Ramadan would make the journey more difficult, or whether I could cope in the heat. But high on the plateau the air was mild – the skies clear, the breeze cool, and the temperature falling low most nights. Everywhere I was offered bottles of water or bags of fruit, while the cafes brought mimed conversations and glasses of tea too sweet to finish. Having no language in common was a relief, because it freed me from any need to explain. I was reminded of that winter walk in France, when it seemed I could cross an entire continent on charity alone. However, the naive confidence of those early months had been replaced by a cautious resolve, and, hiking south from the Yenişehir Plain, I began laughing for no reason but gladness.

One week on from Istanbul I reached the Domaniç Dağları, a low mountain range marking the northern edge of the Kütahya Plain. My route climbed a thousand metres into forests of chestnut, beech and fir, and then roamed over rolling cropland.

It was harvest time. Families were out in the fields, raking the corn and feeding it into threshing machines. Wheat stalks lay on the ground, along with mounds of chaff and straw, while the air was thick with fines. They poured from the machines in pillar-shaped clouds, flashing whenever they caught the light. I watched them stream across the sky like sparks from a forge, watched the horizon glitter and char.

Where the wheat had been cut, only stubble remained, and the earth showed through in crushed seams of red soil.

Heading south over the plain, my evenings were always the same. The villages were modest places, with houses built from concrete and wood. Some boasted a ruined *kervansaray* or the tomb of a Sufi saint, but otherwise there was little to see. Arriving before sunset, I would find a group of men waiting outside the teahouse, the *kahve*. They might motion me to put down my rucksack, but otherwise remained still, until the *ezan* sounded from the mosque and they hurried off to pray. Returning twenty minutes later, they would sit down with great groans of relief and order glass after glass of tea. Now they were welcoming: unfolding my map, opening my notebooks, testing the weight of my kit and grinning to show sugar-stained teeth.

Soon I would be taken to a sparsely furnished room next door to the mosque. A metal tray would be lying on the floor, covered with bowls of dolma and pilav, *cacık* and *köpoğlu*, goat's cheese, olives and a flatbread the size of a punctured football.

'*Yemek, yemek!*' my hosts repeated. *Eat, eat!*

If there was no teahouse, the men would gather in the office of the village headman, the *muhtar*. Most evenings it was a mixed bunch: an elderly figure with grey hair and grey skin; an overweight chap with sweat showing on his forehead, his cheeks, his chin; a boy aged eleven or twelve who stuttered as he served the tea; and the *muhtar* in a tweed-type jacket, gripping every new arrival by the jaw or clutching the crown of their head.

The men would talk all evening, the room filling with the smell of cigarettes and the tannin taste of tea left brewing too long. They laughed at the Gezi Park protests, laughed at the idea of Turkey joining the EU, and grimaced at the name of Assad. Otherwise I could translate no single word they said, but sat dulled with boredom, gazing at the moths that pattered against the overhead lights, their grey wings trembling like smoke from snuffed candles.

Around midnight the *muhtar* would clear everyone out and insist I sleep on the divan. Alone again, I felt a sudden rush of gratitude. For bottles of water and bags of fruit. For a meal on a metal tray and a bed in an empty office. Thank you.

As I lay on the divan, I would count how many days I had been hiking – was it two hundred since Canterbury? I could still remember the attic dormitory in Orsières and the pilgrim refuge in Radicofani, remember Giulia and Max and the convent of Sveta Bogorodica. What linked these memories was the same sense of gratitude that I felt for the villagers in Turkey. Then, as I drifted into that fluid space before dreaming, I remembered another refuge, one that I visited many years earlier. When the thoughts of suicide were only starting. When I first began to lose my way.

One February afternoon, in my second year at university, a friend took me to a part of town that I had never seen, where each house looked the same, each street like the last. Eventually we stopped at a house where the door was not shut but simply pulled to, the light from inside forming a halo round the doorframe.

My friend went through without knocking, leading me downstairs to a basement with thick carpets and soft-shaded lamps. In one corner of the room there was a box of craft materials, in another corner a plastic kettle, a bowl of clementines and an open tin of Earl Grey tea. The walls were papered with drawings and paintings, the ceiling covered in angels. Their bodies were made from card, their wings from tissue paper and gauze. They had cartoon eyes and smiles wide as clowns, and were tacked up among stars of silver foil – too many to count.

As my friend made tea she explained that this place was a sanctuary. When I asked why we had come, she said that she wanted to heal me.

We had met one another the previous year, when I first arrived at university. At the time she did not believe, but something about faith troubled her, would not leave her be. Then she had an epiphany and afterwards nothing was the same, not the sky, nor the seasons, nor the people she saw in the street. Now her belief was deep, yet impulsive too. Sometimes she fasted, or passed all night in prayer. Sometimes she asked God to make decisions for her and searched Acts to learn His will. But she laughed when she told me these stories, and puzzled over her prophecies when they made no sense.

Everyone who came to the sanctuary had to draw a picture. Soon the floor around us was littered with maps of imaginary landscapes (mine), or verses copied from the Psalms (hers), or a pair of miniature portraits (also mine), or a soppy sketch of a sunrise (whoever was here before us). The whole time I felt uneasy, convinced the house belonged to a cult. I kept expecting someone in a dressing gown and sandals to rush downstairs and barge through the door, babbling about the End of Days. I waited for that moment, but it never came. There was nobody hanging back to speak to me with a photocopied leaflet and a fixed grin. No one asked me to hold hands with them, or pray with them, or offered to baptize me in the bath. I couldn't understand: if this was a cult, why weren't they trying to convert me?

I did not ask my friend because I did not trust her answer. Over the last year, as she grew certain of her belief, my own apathy about religion hardened into contempt. I surrounded myself with the loud voices of atheism – read the books, watched the debates, and became convinced that faith was a child of fear. What I wanted was the bleak landscape of certainty, a disenchanted world which I could control. So I decided that I did not believe, that sin carried no cost, that all things were allowed.

At the same time, my life was coming unmoored. From a distance it was no more chaotic than any other student's, but up close the warnings were there. Night after night I drank until I passed out. When drunk my mind fixated on a single thought: of damaging myself beyond repair. Sometimes I climbed onto the roof of my college and walked unsteady laps of the courtyards – tiles loose beneath me, stars reeling above. I was not unwell, but I wished to be, for the idea of suffering gave depth to empty days.

Where did it come from? This melancholy? This loathing? This hunger for hurt? Was it a flaw buried deep in my childhood, or an adolescent longing after tragedy? For I was too young to understand how fragile this existence, how precious. Instead, when I imagined wrecking my life, it brought a sudden thrill of power. But, as my mind lost balance, that attraction became a compulsion, until I could think of no future except self-destruction.

My friend did not know what was wrong, yet she wanted to help. She took me to the sanctuary because she believed it was a place of healing. In truth, I was put off by the room's snug, smug atmosphere. I never asked who owned the house, or how she learnt about it. I never found out who drew the pictures, or whether she was the one who filled the sky with angels. We left after two hours, and I never returned. But a few weeks later, senseless with drink, I ran the tracks at Baker Street Station as a train screamed in to the platform.

Since then, that afternoon has seemed fated to me – a last chance to change course. However, crossing the Kütahya Plain, my perspective began to alter. Stopping each night at a different refuge, I was reminded of the visit, but it was not the boredom I remembered, nor the sense of unease, nor the crisis gathering outside. Instead, it was the smell of clementines. And a stillness which was not broken by the movements we made, which seemed to belong to the room. And the realization that a sanctuary might be hidden beneath the streets. This was no church or chapel, yet here was charity that gave before anything was asked and gave without hope of return. Charity that was patient, that was kind, that kept no account of wrongs. That bore all things. Believed all things. Hoped all things. Endured all things. That never failed, though prophecies fail, and tongues cease, and knowledge shall vanish away.

Midway through the summer of 1097 the armies of the First Crusade stopped at Antioch in Pisidia. This was the Roman city where the Apostle Paul founded a church in the decades after Christ's death. Then they went east, marching towards the other, more famous, Antioch. My own passage through Turkey did not stay with the crusaders but turned in the direction of Antalya, a Mediterranean port two hundred and fifty kilometres to the south. This would track, in reverse, Paul's missionary journey into Asia Minor.

The saint's itinerary was never recorded, but hikers have waymarked a modern approximation. That route began in Yalvaç, a modern town at the foot of the Sultan Mountains, which I reached in the last week of July. It contained a museum, a mosque, a market and a sun-baked square filled with cafes – all closed in the afternoon heat. The ruins of Antioch in Pisidia occupied its north-east corner: a pitch of yellow earth embedded with paving stones, pillars and eroded foundations.

From Yalvaç I walked fifteen kilometres to a hillside village called Eyüpler, arriving a little before seven. The village was made up of mud-brick houses with stone bases and timber roofs. I was taken to the *oda*, a guestroom off the main street. Inside, the air smelt dank, as if the room were buried below ground. One wall was decorated with maps of Turkey, showing the eastern provinces of Kars and Muş, and the mountain region of Hakkâri. Another wall had posters of Islamic pilgrimage sites: white-robed crowds circling the Kaaba in Mecca, or the green dome of the Prophet's Mosque in Medina.

In the centre of the room was a sofa with clammy cushions and a musty cover. The cover was patterned, as were the cushions, but in the evening light these blended into brown.

A framed picture of Atatürk frowned from above the door.

After dark I left the room and crossed the street to the *kahve*, where a group of teenagers were drinking tea. One of the boys, İsmail, lived eleven months of the year in a Bordeaux suburb. Speaking fluent French, he told me that, although he was marrying a girl from Eyüpler, France was his home now. The jobs were better, the lifestyle too, and dual citizenship meant he could skip national service. This was important because five others in the group – Ahmed, Ozan, Kerim, Samir and one more whose name I did not catch – were about to spend a year in the army. None of them was yet twenty, and none of them had been outside Turkey; however, school was finished and they were restless to start. I presumed they would envy İsmail his escape, but instead they teased him for missing out.

When I asked where they would be posted, İsmail replied that it was a secret. 'Maybe the border. Where the Kurds are. Where NATO are.'

'The Iraqi border?'

His face became tense, the brow folding forwards. 'Iraq. Yes. Samir will keep it safe.'

The friends were puzzled by my journey. A plane, a car, even a bike they could understand, but travelling on foot was too much. My efforts to explain only added to their confusion. While I made halting comparisons with the *hajj* to Mecca, they listed family members who could drive me to the coast, no problem, no problem.

Eyüpler had a tradition. Every year, a few nights before leaving, the new recruits lapped round the village in a farewell procession. Ozan claimed it was to say goodbye to their girlfriends. Ahmed suggested it was in case they died. Whatever the reason, tonight was the night.

At nine o'clock the recruits linked arms and set off. As they walked they chanted – a loud and lurching folk song. İsmail stayed a few paces behind, trying to give me a tour. I could see only the dim outlines of houses, yet he described each building in detail. Here was an Ottoman fountain carved from stone, and there was some Roman masonry lodged into a wall. Here was the primary school, the secondary school, the *muhtar*'s office and the mosque. And look! There was the imam, approaching through the darkness.

Once the imam was gone, Ahmed stamped the ground with a stick – *one, two, three, four* – and the recruits began to march – *bir, iki, üç, dört*. As the stamping grew louder, the rest of the group joined in, until we were all marching. Shoulders back, spine straight, chin up, one, two, *bir, iki,* three, four, *üç, dört*, in, out, swing your arms, turn your head – Salute! – two, three, four – *Selâm verin!* – *iki, üç, dört*. We so resembled a mob that I expected angry shouts from the locals, but I heard only the excited voices of children watching from bedroom windows. Meanwhile, İsmail remained at the back, hands in pockets.

Eventually we stopped at a house, trooping upstairs to the room above the garage. Farm tools hung from the walls and a collapsed television occupied one corner. Everybody sat on the floor, spreading a rug over the carpet and emptying peanuts into the centre. There was no noise now but the splitting of shells and the snapping of husks. Then spitting, gulping, yelling, farting and another burst of song.

The rest of the evening we played a game. A mobile phone was put on speaker and placed in the middle of the room. Each boy took a turn as caller, while the others listened in silence. The number dialled redirected the caller to a second number, this one random, and, whoever answered, the aim was to keep them talking. If the stranger hung up, the group would howl with disappointment, but occasionally they stayed on the line. Sometimes they were baffled, sometimes angry, sometimes bored. Sometimes it was a woman. Sometimes she would play along. İsmail was embarrassed by the game, refusing to take part and getting cross when Kerim suggested I have a go. But I did not mind, because the evening was familiar enough from my own adolescence. Everyone sitting too close and shouting. Shouting lazy jokes and crude stories and their laughter like shouting too. I recognized the bragging, the taunting, the games of knuckles and slaps, the sudden bouts of wrestling. And I recognized the feeling of futility, for there were no girls here to impress or appal, and when the laughter went quiet a look of boredom haunted each face.

After an hour the peanuts were finished. After two hours the conversation was dragging. This whole time we sat cross-legged, until I worried my kneecaps would crack. When I could not face another round of telephone roulette, I asked İsmail the way back to the *oda*.

He offered to take me and once outside he announced: 'They will miss their friends when they leave. The village also – they will miss when they are soldiers.'

'You miss it?' I asked.

'All the time,' he said. 'But I had no choice. I had to go.'

In the darkness I could not tell whether İsmail's face showed shame or pride. Perhaps he wanted to cut loose from his past, but was struggling to leave himself behind. Or perhaps this village haunted his thoughts, no matter how far he travelled.

On reaching the *oda* İsmail cleared the cushions from

the sofa, while I unrolled my sleeping bag. Maybe this reminded him of something, because he started talking about the camp occupying Gezi Park. He explained that he did not support the protesters: he thought they were troublemakers. When I told him I was in Istanbul during the police crackdown, he explained that he did not support Erdoğan either. İsmail wanted balance: 'I know it is not healthy to smoke, but I like cigarettes. So I smoke in the evening, but never during the daytime. Also, I know Islam forbids alcohol, but I like beer. So I drink with my friends, but never with my family. That is how Turkey should be. Not Europe. Not the Gulf.'

The *oda* was lit by a single bulb, the corners of the room lapsing into shadow. I could no longer make out the posters of pilgrims, or the maps of ancient Assyria, and Atatürk's frown was lost to the night.

'Not Europe?' I repeated.

'Europe is Christian. In France I have friends from Morocco, from Algeria, Africa, the Middle East – but the society is Christian. They dress how they like, drink how they like. In winter everywhere is decorated for Christmas. That is history. France cannot pretend there is no history.'

İsmail's brow folded again. His forehead had been knitted the whole evening, which made him look much older than his friends, or troubled by some unspoken loss. 'Turkey is a Muslim country,' he went on. 'When tourists visit Istanbul, when they visit Antalya, it is a secular country, but outside the cities we are not secular. Now it is Ramadan and everyone fasts. That is the culture. I love Turkey, it's true, but we are not Europe.'

Though İsmail's lips were still moving, no sound came out. It seemed there was something else he wanted to tell me, but he could not find the words. Perhaps he wanted to say that he knew how it felt to be a stranger. That he was a stranger too.

Five hundred kilometres from Istanbul lay Göller Yöresi, a region of inland lakes formed in the high valleys of the Taurus Mountains. The largest, Lake Eğirdir, stretched fifty kilometres north to south. Its western side was covered in orchards, apple and peach trees blushing with fruit. Its eastern side was flanked by limestone cliffs.

I spent the last weekend of July pacing round the lake. On Saturday morning the air was hazy and the water looked papery, while the cliffs were crumpled pieces of card. Approaching midday the air cleared and the water became a jewelled green. By teatime it was a fat blue, glinting as if smeared with grease, but in the late afternoon it changed again, filling with sunlight and turning bright white. Then the coastal road lifted and I could see the full length of the lake: folded spurs of land closing like curtains on a shining stage of water. I watched without tiredness, without delight, but with a steady sort of calm. Istanbul was far from here, Jerusalem too. Thessaloniki, Rome, they were far away now.

That evening the road dropped back to the shore and the brightness gave way to a polished grey. Fishing boats left tracks on the laketop like scratches on stone. Then the sun went down and the waves were still.

It was eight o'clock when I pitched my tent on a pebble beach by the lake's edge. After dark I stripped and waded into the water, scrubbing the sweat from my arms and face. The shore was webbed with reedbeds, but I kept swimming until I could see the sky. Stars filled the night like metal filings: nickel and iron, platinum and zinc, tin and chrome and copper and gold – red gold, yellow gold, white gold too, flakes and flecks and specks of golden dust.

When I ducked below the water, I could still see the stars. They were closer now, floating on the surface of the lake. I breathed out, sank down, and watched the metal dissolve. Water sluiced cool through my fingers, the taste of reeds becoming the mineral flavour of mountains, blue and black and plunging deep. I felt as if I were leaving my body, or falling into the night.

From here my route lifted towards the southern slopes of the Taurus Range. I spent the first week of August crossing the mountains: five days of shaded pathways, overgrown lanes and villages hidden in valleys; five days of lakes and streams, of gorges and waterfalls, of rocky riverbeds strewn like carnage.

On Wednesday afternoon I reached the Yazılı Canyon, which guarded the entrance to Lake Karacaören.

It was already late when I approached the canyon's upper rim – the sun low and the shadows long. Footpaths rose over steep pastures and sloping terraces before disappearing among banks of trees. I walked hard, hoping to make up time, but the paths were confused and I kept having to double back on myself.

Finally I joined a cobbled track leading to a hamlet of rough-built houses with animal pens outside. I expected the houses to be occupied in the summer months, but they were empty that evening. The pens were empty too, the dead earth littered with the droppings of absent animals. A few weather-worn clothes hung on a washing line, and a stale smell edged the air, mixed from crumbling stone, flaking paint, scattered cinders and fouled water. Otherwise there was no sign of life.

I left the hamlet at seven, climbing fast through thickets of pine. Boulders shaped like ruined fortifications blocked my path, but eventually I reached the edge of the canyon. Then the trees parted and the landscape was revealed.

Lake Karacaören lay seven hundred metres below. On my map it resembled a child's drawing of a dragon, with three legs, a coiled tail, and an armoured head nosing north. Seen from this height, however, it resembled the body of an angel: wings splitting the valleys, limbs dividing the forests, and robes splayed out as if fallen from the sky. West of the lake the sun had snagged on a ridgeline, meaning the valley was in shadow.

I needed to get off the canyon before dusk and guessed there was an hour of light left at most, but I wasn't sure how long it would take to reach the campsite on the valley floor. Two hours? More? To my right a series of limestone shelves slumped towards a wall of pine, trails scrambling over the rock and zigzagging into the trees. I began edging across the loose scree and shattered cliffs, licking my lips and chewing my cheeks and urging myself onwards. Yet when I tried to go faster I lost my balance. Three times I tripped, three times scraped the skin from my palms. On the final occasion I sprawled towards a precipice, seventeen storeys of empty air opening out in front of me.

When I entered the woods, the sun was setting and darkness poured into the valley. The pine bark went orange, the pinecones too, while the air was dim and drowsy. Jogging along the path, I set off snickering streams of needles.

The deeper I went, the more frantic the noise of cicadas. First it was a brittle lisp, then a dry hissing, and soon every branch was shaking with the sound. I listened to them rattling round my head, louder and louder, as if armies of insects were scouring the forest with sand. As if the air itself were seething.

By the time I stepped onto the valley floor, dusk was

here. The mountains closed in, forming a corridor of stone cliffs, with a torrent leading to Lake Karacaören. Now I could hear nothing except the thrashing of water.

It was past nine when I arrived at the campsite. Shallow streams enclosed the space, each one bridged by a wooden deck. More decking hung from the trees, with tents pitched on top as if suspended from the ground. Children crawled along the raised walkways, under hanging branches rigged with lights. I watched them in a dizzy state of disbelief, for I felt like I had stepped into a fairy kingdom, or drifted off to Neverland.

Then I pitched my tent, fell to sleep, and dreamed I was a boy again.

Something had shifted in the last month. More and more I was grateful for what went wrong in the Balkans, because it made me appreciate the kindness I was shown in Turkey. Although I knew that I was vulnerable here, there was freedom in this knowledge, because rather than closing in on myself, I had no choice but to ask for help. And, passing each evening with strangers, my confidence began to build. Meanwhile the scale of the country meant that I walked with little thought for the future, learning to be patient again. I felt smaller now, but safer too, and though I had found no reason to continue my journey, I could forget about the question by simply hiking one day at a time.

As I descended from the plateau, I wondered about the cause of all this kindness. Perhaps it was the remoteness of my route – some of the villages had shops, but never restaurants or hotels. Perhaps it was the Islamic emphasis on hospitality, or the Turkish fondness for strangers. Or perhaps Ramadan was the reason. Many of those I met were fasting – hungry and thirsty from sunrise to sunset – and the curiosity in their expressions was mixed with concern. Their religion was not ritual or prayer, but the practice of sympathy performed day after day. And their faith was something felt as much as thought, a habit inscribed in the heart.

On Friday morning, my last in the Taurus, I tramped between a series of high hamlets. Men with carved features sat in the doorways, and when I asked for directions to Antalya, they pointed me south without saying a word. Except for Mustafa, a fruit farmer with a beautiful moustache, who beamed and motioned me to follow.

He led the way out of the hamlet, chattering over his shoulder. Somehow I could understand every word he said. I had been in Turkey almost two months and perhaps absorbed a little of the language. Or perhaps I was sunsick, confused, more tired than I knew, and our conversation was nothing but nonsense.

Mustafa's farm lay in the lee of a ridgeline, the hillsides draped with orchards and vines. Passing the gate, he offered to show me round. Then we circled the site, plucking down fruit and taking bites to test for ripeness. As my guide worked he made a growling noise that I guessed was a laugh. The air smelt new here, the shadows damp. Summer had been cool, Mustafa explained, and the crop was two weeks behind schedule. The apples were not ready yet, nor the grapes, but the plums were ripe enough to fill a pair of plastic buckets.

Footpaths rose into the woods sheltering the farm. After the tour, we carried on hiking, Mustafa splashing through the yellow-green foliage, while I struggled to keep up. He was sixty-four, yet his legs were strong and his stride relentless. He showed no sign of tiring, either, though he walked in silence and dabbed his forehead with a spotted handkerchief.

Forty-five minutes later the path levelled and we came

to a clearing on the crest of the ridgeline. Mustafa pointed ahead, to where the ground fell away.

'Antalya!' he said.

I could see no city. But I could see the mountains collapsing towards the coast and the jagged peaks becoming level plains. See the slopes becoming flats, the grass becoming scrub, and the pinewoods thinning to copses of carob and bay. Fruit farms hemmed the base of the range, a pleated canopy like the spread of a skirt. Beyond lay the sweated skin of the Mediterranean, twitching in the heat.

This was it. After seven hundred kilometres I had reached the end of Turkey. My calves were clenched, my thighs burning, but I did not notice, because the rest of my body felt slack with relief.

'Antalya,' Mustafa repeated.

'*Evet*,' I said. Yes.

Beyond the clearing stood a two-room hut with hardboard walls and a roof of corrugated iron. There was no electricity or running water, though a stream flowed past the front door. Mustafa told me he built the place twenty years ago, claiming it had withstood snow and storms and the wild winds off the sea.

Rugs were laid on the floor inside, with more rugs hanging from the sideboards. A blue water butt balanced on one worktop, alongside tins of food and jars of olive oil. Bags of grain bulged on another worktop, and bungee cords belted the jerry cans into the corners. Mustafa's wife stood in the middle of the room, small and stout and shaped like a spinning top. Motioning me to sit, she brought out plates of pilav, pide, stuffed vegetables, raw salads and homemade *ayran* mixed from water, yoghurt, ice and salt – so cold it stung behind each eye. After that came more fruit, as well as wafers, tea, and cigarettes with a peppery taste.

When the meal was over, my host leant back against

the wall, burping and breathing smoke through his nose. With each exhalation his moustache seemed to plume. He told me that, when he was a young man, he walked from here to Antalya in a single day. That's right. Fifty kilometres: one day. The mountains made his legs strong, his lungs strong. Even now, said Mustafa, holding his chest and ballooning his ribcage, even now he had the lungs of a young man. Then he gripped his breasts and puffed out hard, smoke streaming from his moustache. It was the mountain air, he went on, the mountain air kept him young.

I nodded, my eyes pinching from the cigarettes.

'Fifty kilometres. One day. You understand?'

I smiled. Mustafa's wife smiled. Everyone was smiling.

'*Elli kilometre*,' he said again. 'You understand me?'

I laughed. We all laughed. I never wanted to leave.

'*Bir gün*,' Mustafa repeated. '*Anlıyorsun değil mi?*'

'*Evet*,' I said. '*Anlıyorum.*'

When I arrived in Cyprus it was too hot to walk on the plain. Instead I climbed into the mountains and crossed the country at a thousand metres. The temperature was not my only reason for staying up high: since Thessaloniki I had been anxious about bars and clubs and restless summer crowds, and this way I avoided the holiday resorts along the coast.

The Troodos Mountains run the width of Cyprus's southern half, from the Chrysochou Bay in the west to the Bay of Larnaca in the east. I began walking in the second week of August, rising from the island's western shore between valleys of cedar and hillsides of black pine. As I neared the summit of Mt Olympus, I passed Kykkos

Monastery (a palace of polished stone founded by our old friend Alexios Komnenos) and Throni Hill (where Archbishop Makarios, first president of Cyprus, lay buried in a hilltop tomb). On Saturday afternoon I reached Pedoulas, a sloping village crowded with churches and chapels, including the Church of the Holy Cross, the Church of the Fithkia Cross, the churches of St Marina and St George, the chapels of St Paraskevi, St Panayiotis and St Raphael, the Virgin Mary of Vorini Chapel and the Church of the Archangel Michael.

This last was the one that I wanted.

The church was built from rough-cut stone, the timber roof angled down to one side. It resembled a stables or barn, with a wooden door at the front and a hanging bell round the back. Inside, the air was baked.

Stepping through the door was like walking into a tapestry. Murals covered the interior with pictures of saints and scenes from the Gospels. There were ranks of apostles in robes of red and gold, gold and red. There were twin portraits of Constantine the Great and the Empress Helena, their haloes large as moons against a backdrop of midnight blue. And there was an archangel in Byzantine armour, its bronze wings filling the wall with feathered metal. At the front, the wooden templon was inked with patterns and the wooden altar wrapped in rich damask.

Standing opposite the altar, I thought back to that other Mt Olympus, in Greece. Three months ago, hiking in the foothills of the range, I met a Cypriot shepherd named George. He was small and slight and alive with worry, and he urged me to visit the Troodos churches. But, when I explained that I was heading to Jerusalem, his face became sour. Surely I knew that Israel was home to the Zionist plot that had crippled Cyprus's economy?

I asked whether the financial crisis was also to blame, but George slapped his forehead. 'Kabbalah,' he said.

'Black magic.' Then he added: 'The Kingdom of Satan.' Then: 'The son-of-a-bitch USA.'

I had a similar experience on my last afternoon in Mt Athos. Approaching St Andrew's Skete I met three Romanians in canvas fishing vests. They were chubby and cheerful, nodding their bald heads in harmony.

The chubbiest of the three spoke English. He asked where I was from and then told me he was travelling to Britain in autumn. A holiday? No. A work trip? Not quite. Raising a hand to his neck, he opened the collar to reveal a metal cross hanging off a chain. Its arms flared out from the centre, the shape vaguely familiar.

'International conference of Templar knights,' said the man.

Was he a Templar knight? He was! His friends too? They were!

The knight showed me a photo on his phone. It featured seven adults standing in a cellar, each one wearing a white mantle quartered by a red cross. 'Romanian Order of the Temple,' he explained, grimacing with pride. 'Bucharest Chapter.' He pointed at the woman in the middle of the group, who held a sword so long it grazed the cellar ceiling. 'My wife,' he added. 'Chapter officer.'

The second-chubbiest Romanian began to speak. He told me the order was meeting in Edinburgh to discuss the crisis facing Europe. When I asked what crisis, he announced, 'Europe has too many Muslims. Muslims has too many babies. Britain, Germany, Romania – soon we has no Christians.'

'The Christians are tolerant,' the chubbiest man added. 'The Muslims are not tolerant. In Saudi Arabia, the capital of Islam, women cannot drive. Twenty-first century and still they cannot drive.'

'Muslim values are not modern values,' the third man,

the least chubby, chipped in. 'The Templars must quit Europe of the Muslims.'

I wondered out loud whether they would liberate the Holy Land as well.

The chubbiest Romanian moved nearer. 'We are Templars,' he said, his breath hot in my ear. 'We must quit Europe of the Muslims. But our brother knights, the Hospitallers, they will conquer Jerusalem.'

That afternoon I found the encounter funny. Now, standing in the Church of the Archangel Michael, I felt a tug of pity. For those who feel helpless before history, conspiracy theories are a perverse kind of empowerment.

It was warm in the church. I could smell warm wood, warm dust, and the grainy odour of ancient paint. Looking at the huddle of haloed faces, I remembered that this was Templar ground once. In 1192 all Cyprus belonged to the order. They had bought it off Richard the Lionheart, who accidentally conquered the place en route to the Third Crusade. But why did they decide to settle here? And what reckless ambition led them to found a kingdom? And how did an order of knights devoted to poverty – the Poor Fellow-Soldiers of Christ and of the Temple of Solomon, no less – end up purchasing an island?

The first Templars lived off charity. William of Tyre, a crusader bishop, gives the standard account of their founding. His *Historia Hierosolymitana* records how nine knights remained in the Holy Land after the First Crusade, taking monastic vows and committing themselves to the defence of pilgrims. In return, Baldwin II lent them a corner of the rocky hilltop in the centre of Jerusalem known as Solomon's Temple. Here they established their headquarters.

Within a decade the Templars had been endorsed by the Catholic Church. At the same time their Grand Master Hugues de Payens toured round France raising money and recruiting brothers.

The order grew quickly, like that other austere twelfth-century institution: the Cistercians. Hardly surprising, given that Bernard of Clairvaux – a nephew to one of the nine original knights – helped write the Templar Rule. Thanks to Bernard there was no drinking, swearing or gambling. Members were forbidden fur on their clothes, silver on their spurs, and gold on their horses' bridles. Shoes and shoelaces were also banned, 'for it is well known that these abominable things belong to pagans'. Hunting animals was likewise prohibited, whether with hawks or hounds (although hunting lions was still allowed), and members of the opposite sex were definitely off limits. 'Avoid at all costs the embraces of women,' Bernard wrote, 'by which men have perished many times.'

There was a point to all this privation. The Templar Rule was meant to flatten social hierarchies, while voluntary poverty strengthened their communal ethic. That was the idea behind the order's seal: two knights riding a single horse.

As with the Cistercians, the strictness of the regime made it popular among the nobility. This was a new generation of knights, eager to share in the triumphs of their crusading ancestors. It's easy to imagine what drew them to the defence of the Holy Land, but the appeal of Templar piety is harder to pin down. At the time, however, parallels between military and monastic experience were commonplace.

The chroniclers of the First Crusade compared the army setting off for Jerusalem with a monastery on the move. By renouncing earthly possessions to endure exile and hardship, its knights resembled their brothers in the cloister, exchanging everyday pleasures for a life of denial and a death with meaning. As well as the regime of poverty, chastity and obedience, they shared a longing to submit, to suffer. This longing was familiar from the early stages of my walk, when I tried to make sense of belief through the tragic lives of pilgrim saints. Its consequences were familiar too, for many of these monks became martyrs.

Admittedly, the chronicles were written by clergy. It's not clear how many crusaders actually held their goods in common or marched willingly towards martyrdom. However, during this period the devotional practices of lay and religious increasingly overlapped. In the same way that pilgrimage popularized the apostolic life, crusading gave ordinary soldiers a chance for saint-like feats of sacrifice.

Orders of knights were the next step. By directing the aggressive ambitions of the nobility to the service of the Church, they sanctified the status of the warrior. Some knights even joined the Templars to atone for their sins, turning military service into perpetual penance.

This fusing of martial and spiritual glory helped justify the order's protected status. Its brothers were afforded similar rights to clergy: excused various tithes and taxes, and accountable only to the pope. They exploited this status for commercial gain, acquiring a vast property empire – nine thousand estates, according to one estimate – with interests in farming, manufacturing and ship-building. Having developed an early form of traveller's cheque to spare pilgrims the risk of carrying cash, they also provided banking services to a number of European monarchs.

Money, manpower, military resources – now all they needed was a kingdom.

Cyprus was the key stopping point for pilgrim traffic

to the Holy Land, and Richard the Lionheart's accidental occupation gave them the perfect opportunity to claim it. However, the Third Crusade was under way and the order was stretched. Despite raising local taxes to pay for their purchase, they failed to garrison the place properly. Riots broke out, knights were attacked, and by the end of the year Cyprus had been handed on to Guy of Lusignan, deposed King of Jerusalem.

The Templar presence on Cyprus remained, with castles and convents in Nicosia, Limassol, Gastria and Templos. And, as I learnt while crossing the island, it played a key role in the order's downfall. Something of this history seemed to linger in the stale air, the worn light, in the dust that brushed the back of my throat. Looking round the Church of the Archangel Michael, the past felt close, as if I could dig my nails into the earth and scratch away centuries of suffering.

Circle round Mt Olympus, onto the southern side of the Troodos Range, and you will notice signs for the Mesa Potamos waterfall. Near the waterfall lies a monastery dedicated to St John the Baptist. Its guest master, Fr Prodromos, was in his mid-thirties, but seemed younger, his eyes wide and blinking, his mouth never quite closing shut. His movements were wide open too, limbs sewn loose to his body.

We took a tour of the monastery, but there was little to see. The chapel was made from the same rough-cut stone as the Church of the Archangel Michael, while every other building had cream-coloured walls and timber verandas. Some had been recently renovated, and one of the cellblocks was fenced in behind scaffolding. The interiors had been renovated too, their polished surfaces shining.

After vespers the guest master escorted me to the refectory, bringing out plates of seasoned rice and a tray of pumpkin-stuffed pastries. He ate nothing himself, only picked at a bowl of fruit and talked about the two years he spent living in London, studying music and singing in bands. Aged twenty-one he left the city, moving to Thessaloniki to study theology. Then he felt his calling: 'To begin with I wanted to join the monks on Mt Athos, yet when I visited it was not right. Instead I came to Machairas, here in the Troodos, where I learnt that a few brothers were repopulating the Monastery of St John the Baptist. Then I felt sure that God was guiding me, because I knew the monastery! When I was a boy, my priest organized camping trips to Mesa Potamos. Even though the buildings were abandoned, we would hear vespers in the chapel and sleep in the courtyard. Some of the children thought there were ghosts, but for me it was a magic place.'

I mentioned that, on my own visit to Mt Athos, I learnt of monasteries being restored and sketes being revived. Fr Prodromos nodded, his expression blissful, grateful, vacant.

Then he started talking about a bishop called Fr Athanasios: 'The bishop grew up in Cyprus, but left to become a monk at Vatopedi. After sixteen years the Patriarch asked him to return home. Fr Athanasios was a humble man. He wanted to spend his days in prayer, but instead he was made Bishop of Limassol and Abbot of Machairas. Now our services are full of families. Now young men stay in our monasteries every week. And do you know who founded the community here at Mesa Potamos? Yes, it was Fr Athanasios.'

'What's his secret?' I asked.

'The bishop has reminded us that religion is more than just the habits of faith. It is a spiritual exercise. He has reminded us all, not only the monks: the whole Church.'

When I finished eating, the guest master led me into the rear courtyard. A pavilion occupied the centre of the yard – a ring of benches with a tiled roof. We sat facing one another, the evening air becoming cool between us. In the refectory his gestures were restless, but now Fr Prodromos sat without moving, leaning back against the pavilion's wooden frame.

I said that I was surprised monastic spirituality could make the church more popular. I would never have the courage, the conviction, to enter a monastery—

'We're not here because we're strong,' the guest master replied. 'We're here because we're weak. If my faith was stronger, I could have stayed in the world.'

I tried to imagine the anxious student, the failed musician, giving up his life for God. Since Mt Athos I understood how belief might be built from practice, yet was unsure what sustained this discipline. Does a calling last a lifetime, or does faith fade – like ambition, like desire? If so, how does a monk keep to his solitary course? I was hoping Fr Prodromos's answer would give me a reason to keep walking, for though I knew pilgrimage was more than a distance covered, I had no language for what lay beyond the ritual. 'But you must feel doubt at times,' I said. 'You must feel lonely, or wonder if you made the right decision.'

Fr Prodromos did not answer. Evening was coming on, the cellblocks sliding into shadow. 'A monk is very lucky,' he said after a while. 'The monastery lets him devote his whole life to God, without any distractions. In the rest of the world people have responsibilities – to family, to work – and they can't ignore those responsibilities, they can't, it's impossible. But here even our daily duties help us to become a better monk.'

I asked for an example.

'Anything I want to do I have to receive the abbot's permission. We call it blessing, the abbot's blessing. Sometimes he gives me a job I do not want, or the same job every single day. He is not trying to punish me, but to teach me. If I feel – not anger, that's too strong, but negative feelings – then I know there is still pride in my heart.'

Once more, the emptying of self. Once more, the substitute suicide. Yet it seemed this was less freedom from emption than a willed return to innocence. 'Like being a child again,' I said.

Darkness was pouring down from the sky, the courtyard growing dim, the guest master dissolving. 'Everything in the monastery is teaching us humility.' His body was gone, the black habit extinguished. 'When Christ died he was the lowest of the low, a criminal on the cross – yet he was the Lord of Creation.' His eyes were shining, the cheekbones wet with tears. 'Today there's nobody to crucify us. Today we have to crucify ourselves.'

I left Mesa Potamos on Monday morning and spent two days crossing Pitsilia, the highlands to the east of Olympus. In places the landscape was rugged; in places it was barren. Although this scenery was familiar from Greece, I no longer marched along with my head bowed, impatient to reach the next village. Since Turkey I felt little sense of urgency, but paced slow through the blunt heat, the bare light. My route took in more painted churches – in Pelendri and Palaichori – as well as the grand old monastery of Machairas. Otherwise I travelled alone on mountain roads, stopping at half the hilltop chapels and roadside shrines.

Come the end of the week I would approach the island's eastern shore and face the holiday crowds in Larnaca, but up here the only people I met were locals. When I explained that I was walking the Troodos Range, they urged me to change course. I must visit the Byzantine catacombs at Kyrenia, and the Ayia Thekla chapel near the Cape Greco peninsula. And the House of Eustolios, and the Soli Basilica, and the ruined abbey of Bellapais. Then there was the hermitage of St Neophytos outside Paphos and the cave of the forty saints outside Famagusta – certainly I must go there.

I noted the suggestions down and promised to try my best.

Others told stories about their favourite saints. Did I know that St Paul travelled to Cyprus twelve years after the death of Christ, where he was taken to a synagogue, bound to a pillar, and whipped? And that St Barnabas was martyred in Salamis: stoned, suffocated, or perhaps set alight? And that the Empress Helena stopped off here on her way home from Palestine, bringing a fragment of the True Cross and an army of cats, for the island was plagued by snakes? I was also told about the Persian Conquest of 526 BC, the Jewish uprising of AD 117, the seventh-century Arab invasion and Isaac Komnenos's 1185 rebellion. And surely I knew that Cyprus was the true scene of the Templars' downfall?

In the year 1291 the city of Acre was conquered by the Mamluk sultan Al-Ashraf Khalil. This was the Kingdom of Jerusalem's final stronghold; once lost, the Templars forfeited their status as guardians of the Holy Land.

A number of contemporary chroniclers held the knights responsible for the defeat. Some blamed their military strategy, some their corrupt practices – for they were widely suspected of performing pagan rites. In 1306 a Venetian geographer called Marino Sanuto started to write a history of the crusader states containing many of the more lurid rumours about the order. He claimed that, when a knight died in battle, the body was cremated, his brother knights drinking the dissolved ashes. The babies born of Templar orgies were also cremated, the infants' roasted fat smeared onto the golden idol that they worshipped.

Next year the French king, Philip IV, used similar rumours to justify his suppression of the order. Which brings us to that infamous date: Friday 13 October.

The story of the Templars' suppression has been told many times. The raid on every chapter house in France, the arrest of each member, the mass trials, the torture, the confessions, the bonfires of knights and the burning of the Grand Master Jacques de Molay – this is the dramatic material behind a hundred conspiracy theories. But the role Cyprus played in the story is less well known.

After the fall of Acre, the Templars moved their head-quarters to the island. Inspired by the Teutonic Knights, who were establishing a crusader state in Prussia, they began taking a hand in local politics. In April 1306 they supported an attempt to seize control by Amaury, Lord of Tyre and brother of the Cypriot king, Henry II.

As soon as the order's future in the Mediterranean was secure, its European operation came under attack. Philip IV was in debt to the knights, which may account for his behaviour. Or, given that the Templars owned estates in southern and eastern France, had the freedom to march their armies across European borders, and were backing coups in vulnerable Frankish kingdoms, perhaps the per-ceived threat was less financial than military.

In November 1307 Pope Clement V endorsed the order's suppression. Amaury had no choice but to arrest the island's Templars. In the riots that followed he was murdered by one of his noblemen and Henry II was restored to the throne.

Henry II immediately destroyed the Templar head-quarters on Cyprus, handing the rest of their property to the Knights Hospitaller. Without a base of operations the order could not survive.

While on trial, the brothers were accused of denying Christ, spitting on the cross, irreligious kissing and homosexuality – the standard charges against heretics. As with the Bogomils, paranoia was disguised as piety, and prejudice became an excuse for persecution. But another, more vivid, accusation was also made: that they wor-shipped the idol of a bearded prophet called Baphomet. This may have been a recovered relic from the martyred St Euphemia, or a recycled rumour about witchcraft. Whatever the truth, it gave a pagan flavour to the order's reputation that lasted beyond the Middle Ages.

In *De Occulta Philosophia*, published in 1531, the Ger-man polymath Heinrich Cornelius Agrippa compared these profane practices to the 'disgusting and foul abom-inations' of the Gnostic magicians. According to the Byzantine author Psellus – Agrippa's source on the subject – eleventh-century heretics also burnt their un-wanted babies, baking the ashes into a special sort of bread. Gnostics, orgies, baby-seasoned bread – if this sounds familiar it's because the magicians Psellus had in mind were otherwise known as Bogomils.

De Occulta Philosophia was one of the most influential works of sixteenth-century scholarship. References to medieval historians and classical rites helped secure its reputation among Renaissance humanists, and thanks to authors like Agrippa, the Templars' rumoured links with Bogomilism, Gnosticism and pagan mischief endure to this day.

Cyprus would have suited them. The country seemed older than anywhere else I had visited. Crossing Pitsilia, the landscape looked exhausted: eroded terraces and broken paths; twisted orchards and tangled vines; scabbed earth, muddy shade, and mountainsides ribbed like the lining of an opencast mine. Yet this only deepened the sense of what endured, like an ancient face made stronger by every wrinkle etched into its features.

Although I remained on the high ground for much of the week, the heat was fierce. As I travelled east towards the Machairas Forest, the sun scorched a hole in the sky. I told myself that I was nearing the end of August and counted down the days until autumn, but my progress had slowed into a sunsick stupor.

Soon my senses confused and the days began to daze.

I remember climbing past a dam on a winding tarmac road, its black surface bubbling in the heat. The dam's reservoir was a flawless blue, the water spangled with light. When a breeze brushed the water, the light scattered, and I turned away with eyes scalded . . . I remember a valley shaped like a bowl, the air blossoming with butterflies. Nearing the valley floor, I almost stepped on a snake, a blunt-nosed viper lying fat across the track. Its body was as long as a man's, its scales the same shade as the grey-green thornscrub, becoming black at its knuckled head. Then the thorns snapped, the gravel shifted, and when I looked again the snake was gone . . . I remember a village of walled gardens and steep streets, where I listened to a quivering sound that was not birdsong, nor bellchime, nor the chatter of an overheard radio. Eventually I realized it was panpipes, playing from one of the houses, enchanting the whole village . . . Panpipes, butterflies, jewelled water and scaled skin: the place was pagan haunted. Here was Hermes, here Pan, here the footprints of Dionysus. Here the maenads and satyrs and nymphs. Here the mysteries.

My last monastery was perched on a spire of stone at the eastern edge of the Troodos. Stavrovouni was its name: the Mountain of the Cross. I arrived late on Wednesday, having spent all afternoon sinking into the Machairas Forest – a slope of Turkish pine above the arid farmland of the Mesaoria Plain. It was almost six when I started climbing. The monastery at the top shut its gates at seven.

Military camps surrounded the base, giving way to steep rises of stony ground. A footpath scratched up one side, running over stone-cut steps. Some were tilted with age, others worn flat from use. Then the path became an animal track and pebbles trickled beneath my boots, the low growth cutting at my shins, my shorts.

The evening was warm, the going slow. Midway up the mountain my hair was wet, my clothes wet, my socks soaked and my back burning beneath the rucksack. Sweat dripped off my elbows, splashing onto the powdered earth. It dripped off my face too, slick on my forehead, my cheeks, in the socket of each eye. Salt stung the tender flesh at the corners of the lids and my sight began to blur. Yet I pressed on, higher and higher. Five hundred metres and ten thousand paces and still I was climbing.

After an hour I paused to catch my breath. When I turned round, the landscape swept out in every direction. The sun had dipped and shadows lay on the earth: the thin greens of the Mesaoria Plain made deep by blue shadow, the broken greys of the Troodos made black. How small the country was, how tiny! All those centuries of history, all those empires and kingdoms – just eight days' walk from end to end.

The slopes heaved. The shale poured. The air was hot in my mouth. Then I hauled myself up the cracked lip of a cliff and the ground was level again.

Stavrovouni Monastery occupied the mountain summit, built low and dense as a fortress. The guard waiting at the gate turned me away, explaining that the monastery was closed, but when I refused to leave he became curious. Where was my car? Where was my bike? How would I get down before nightfall?

Eventually I was directed up another stone-cut staircase to the main entrance. Here I met a second guard, a monk name Fr Panaiotis. He wanted to know if I was Orthodox, if I was married, if I had ever visited the Holy Mountain.

'We live like the monks of Mt Athos,' he explained, his face stern, his features spare. 'We live outside the world.'

Inside it did remind me of Mt Athos. There was an entrance hall with parquet flooring and a clouded smell of polish. And there was a guest dormitory with iron-framed beds, the mattresses thin as paperbacks. The evening meal was familiar too: boiled beans mixed with parsley and oil, served cold in metal bowls. We ate in the refectory, while a novice read from the Church Fathers. The walls were slung with shadows, but then the sun pierced through the western window, giving the bowed head of each monk a backlit halo.

When the meal was done, Fr Panaiotis invited me onto the balcony. As we watched the sun ducking behind the Troodos, he explained how the Empress Helena founded the original church on this mountain, endowing it with a piece of the True Cross. By the Middle Ages the church was a monastery, popular with pilgrims travelling to the Holy Land. Since then it had been emptied by Franks, destroyed by Ottomans, flattened by an earthquake and gutted by fire. Yet on every occasion the fragment of the cross survived.

I grew bored listening to Fr Panaiotis list the miracles associated with the relic, so I asked if he missed his family. He told me that he felt close to them whenever he prayed. I asked whether his family missed him. He told me that three times a year – on Christmas, Easter and the Feast of the Assumption – he left Stavrovouni to spend a day with his parents. 'Some families cannot understand our vocation. They think it is an unnatural way to live. They think their child has been taken from them. A few times parents have come here and refused to leave. They shout at the gates until the novice has to be moved elsewhere—' He interrupted himself: 'But my family was not this way. Even though my father had his doubts, on the day I entered the monastery he drove me right to the door.'

I tried to picture the scene. The monk like a schoolboy on his first day of term. The father's expression fixed, giving no hint of the regret he felt. And a moment of devotion, of sacrifice, as they said goodbye to one another.

'It's very rare that a parent will do this for their child,' Fr Panaiotis added.

I tried to work out whether he ever felt guilty. If the monastic calling was a sacrifice, the monk did not bear this burden alone. Like a young man going to fight, or a young martyr going to die, his family waited at home for the child who would never return. And I realized that this model of religious life – as some grand act of abandonment – could no longer justify my own journey. Maybe I left Canterbury looking to forsake the world, yet I needed a better reason to reach Jerusalem.

At twilight we assembled in Stavrovouni's main courtyard. Thirty brothers crowded round the abbot as he sat reciting prayers. By this point I could recognize the different stages of the liturgy – the creed, the psalms, and the

Kyrie eleison repeated forty, eighty, one hundred and twenty times – yet I could not tell how long the service would last. After three quarters of an hour my legs were numb and the minutes had slipped from my mind. But, when I looked up, I felt a sudden shock of wonder, for we were high above the ground here and the sky was foiled with stars.

It was dark when the monks shuffled into the church. A silver cross stood in one of the alcoves, framed by an arch of gilded scrollwork. The surface was embossed with the final scenes of the Passion, lamplight twinkling off the metal like a casino slot machine. The piece of the True Cross was sealed inside.

I watched the brothers queuing at the alcove. Thirty heads bowed to kiss the shrine. Thirty bodies knelt for the abbot's blessing. Then they stepped out into the still-warm air.

When I returned to my dormitory the lights were off. Through an open window I could see the dark pool of the Mesaoria Plain sprinkled with headlights. Nicosia glimmered in the distance, its buildings outlined against the night. It seemed so unlikely that, less than forty kilometres away, the city was alive with people, while I had spent the evening gathered round a splinter of wood. Maybe there was something miraculous about this: not the sacred relic, but the ritual itself. Although it was a fragile thing – just a few words and gestures – it had outlasted centuries of conquest. I still thought of monastic life as a substitute suicide, yet here was a pattern much older than Stavrovouni; and one which does not decay, though buildings decay, and churches empty, and nations crumble into dust. Perhaps the monks' calling was not a willed sacrifice, but a way of outlasting death – a single life given up to a shared ritual. And perhaps pilgrimage was not an escape from this world, but a surrender to something larger than ourselves.

On the floor beside the bed was a lamp. I switched it on and knelt to darn my shorts. When I looked up again the view from the window was fading, made faint by the brightness within.

Next day I walked to the sea. As I approached the coast, the land became blistered. Olive trees crawled over the hillsides and the fields were sown with stones. The parched terraces resembled ivory piano keys, their edges shrunken with age. In each village the streets were empty, the houses still. Dogs lay in the shade like dead things; otherwise I saw nobody, not a living soul. I hitched my T-shirt to my rucksack and hiked topless down the road, skin greasy with suncream and shoulders rubbing beneath each strap. Sometimes a breeze crept in off the shore, but whenever it flagged I could feel the thickness of the air, the weight of the heat, and smell the rubbish bags cooking in roadside bins.

Early that afternoon my route lifted onto a low hill. From the crest of the hill I saw the broad arc of a bay and the blazing Mediterranean beyond. Larnaca lazed along the shore, built from sheet metal, plate glass, and apartment blocks fifteen storeys high.

South of the city the sky looked creased. At first I thought the clouds were hanging flat above the horizon, but then I realized it was not cloud. It was not sea, nor sky, nor folded plates of empty air. Instead it was the mountains of Lebanon rising up two hundred kilometres away.

Or maybe I was imagining things in the stunning afternoon heat.

Four hours later I stopped in the centre of Larnaca.

Earlier that week I had been given the address of a cafe owner with a bed for pilgrims, but I could not find the place. Although I wanted to avoid the tourist strip on the waterfront, soon I was marching down the esplanade, wondering what to do. Hotels were piled up on one side, their walls pulsing with colour, while restaurants and bars filled the spaces beneath. Some were lit a searing white, the rest a screaming neon. Holiday crowds horded the tables, shouting at one another in a dozen languages, and the warmth of the day hummed off the buildings.

I waited for the panic to begin, but all I experienced was weariness. For two months I had walked in the summer heat, anxious about the crowds on the coast and anxious about another collapse. Now those crowds were passing through me without leaving any mark. Now summer was ending and the walk was entering its final stage. But, unlike the thoughtless optimism that carried me over the Alps, this fear seemed honest – an admission of my own vulnerability. And that honesty made me hopeful about finishing the journey without another crisis. Tripoli and Beirut. Haifa and Tel Aviv. Nine hundred kilometres to go.

After dark I came to a square at the southern end of the esplanade. The Church of St Lazarus occupied its centre, a Byzantine shell with a Romanesque bell tower.

An overweight man sat on the bench opposite, his breathing slow, his eyes barely open. The man's hands and beard were stained with paint. His name was Mitch.

Mitch was an American sculptor spending the summer at an art school in Larnaca. When I asked about his work, he did not answer, but launched into a confused history of the city, claiming that Plato was born here, Othello was its governor, and a mosque in the suburbs was among the holiest sites in Islam. Almost everything he said ended with the phrase, *it is what it is*, as if no matter how improbable the story, he could not be blamed for telling it. As we sat on the bench together, he skipped between subjects at random. The fact that he left all his artwork unfinished – it is what it is – or that his wallet was stolen twice in one week – it was what it was – and gun crime and global warming and the industrial medication of American toddlers – they were what they were, I am what I am, it is what it is.

Mitch found the pilgrimage hard to believe, however. When I talked about walking the Troodos, he made faces and stuck out his tongue. When I described the monasteries of Kykkos and Machairas, of Mesa Potamos and Stavrovouni, he gave a frightened laugh. And, when I mentioned that I left Canterbury almost thirty-three weeks ago, he peered at his trainers to avoid my eye.

Then, for no reason, he asked: 'How much you know about the Templars?'

The Templar connection with Cyprus ended in 1571, when the island was seized by the Ottoman Empire and the order's archives were destroyed. This preserved their unsavoury reputation better than any rumour, because it made allegations against the knights much harder to disprove. To a suspicious mind absence is a form of evidence.

However, it was not until the eighteenth century that Templar legends were reworked into contemporary conspiracies.

During the Enlightenment the number of members' clubs, professional guilds and scholarly societies grew rapidly. A few of these organizations operated in secret, most notably the Masonic lodges founded across Britain, America and continental Europe. In German-speaking countries the lodges were popular with the nobility, who expanded the ritual element of their meetings with ceremonies based on Templar traditions. The more eccentric even claimed an unbroken lineage with the order's better-known knights.

Other fraternities started to imitate this chivalric play-acting. For example, the Bavarian Illuminati borrowed elements of Freemasonry's ritual flummery, but recruited from the professional classes. When the Bavarian government tried to shut the organization down in 1784, and again in 1785, its membership of judges, politicians and civil servants caused a scandal. The magicians had infiltrated the establishment.

You might expect Enlightenment thinkers to pardon medieval heretics. Voltaire called the trial of the Templars one of many 'conspiracies against the people' performed by persecuting governments, comparing it to Innocent III's Albigensian Crusade. Unfortunately this sceptical response lost out to popular superstition. And, when Europe's political order began breaking apart, the idea that the knights had survived in secret became a subject of public fascination. Dead Templars merged with living Masons in the popular imagination, and before long a number of extravagantly named occultists were coming up with the evidence.

The first was an Italian alchemist known as Count Cagliostro. In 1789 Cagliostro was imprisoned in Rome for his membership of the Masons. Under interrogation he confessed that the organization was working to destroy the Catholic Church and the royal houses of Europe. Why? To avenge the death of the Templar Grand Master Jacques de Molay. Unlikely though this sounds, the French Revolution was under way and Roman authorities were easily convinced. Next was Charles-Louis Cadet de Gassicourt, a lawyer, essayist, chemist and – according to some sources – the illegitimate son of the French king. In 1796 he published *The Tomb of Jacques de Molay*, which argued that Templar knights were the founders of

Freemasonry and still commanded a network of secret societies responsible for the execution of Louis XVI and the Reign of Terror. Finally, in the year 1818, the Austrian orientalist Joseph von Hammer-Purgstall wrote *The Mystery of Baphomet Revealed*. The book not only connected Templar practices with the pagan religions of Antiquity – that bearded head was in fact a Gnostic idol – but also linked the order to medieval sects like the Cathars and Assassins, as well as modern fraternities like the Masons and the Illuminati. And it wove them all together into a web of anarchist plotters responsible for Europe's recent unrest.

Here, then, was the blueprint for the modern conspiracy theory.

The book's evidence was pretty flimsy. Joseph von Hammer-Purgstall attempted to involve the Templars with the quest for the Holy Grail – another Gnostic idol – yet his case relied on little more than coincidence. He noted that King Arthur's round table contained the 'Templar number' of twelve knights and that the thirteenth-century Arthurian romance *Parzival* featured grail guardians known as *Templeisen*. What gave the book weight, however, was its use of coins, medals and measurements as archaeological evidence. It was even written in Latin for added authority.

This sham methodology, combined with the Hammer Horror title, influenced an entire industry of pseudo-history. Since its publication *The Mystery of Baphomet Revealed* has been imitated by bestselling novelists, far-right fantasists and the fretful ranks of online conspiracists.

Mitch collected these theories. While we sat opposite the church that evening, he listed his favourites. What if refugee knights rescued Robert the Bruce at the Battle of Bannockburn? Or what if Templar builders helped carve the rock churches of Lalibela? And what about the order's missing fleet? Perhaps soldier-sailors fled across the Atlantic and constructed a lighthouse on Rhode Island. Sounds unlikely? Hey, it is what it is.

'Or maybe they escaped through the Alps and helped found Switzerland.' Mitch chortled. 'Take a look at the Swiss flag – not much of a disguise.' He chuckled. 'And who else you think set up those banks?' He giggled and gaped. 'I'm telling you, it was the Templars.'

I left the bench to hysterics.

Bunting surrounded the Church of St Lazarus, miniature flags of Cyprus and Greece netting the night sky. A full-sized flag of Byzantium hung limp in one corner, its folded fabric a sallow shade of gold. The church was lit the same colour, each limestone block a sickly yellow.

By now it was past eight, but the door was wide open, with steps leading into clotted darkness. Standing by the door I could make out the Classical gallery at the back of the church and the Baroque iconostasis at the front. A chandelier hung heavy from the roof, its lamps casting no colour. Signs for the tomb of St Lazarus pointed me downstairs.

I was expecting a Gothic catacomb, but instead found a cramped little cellar. Strip lights made everything look ugly: the polystyrene tiles on the ceiling, the cement slabs on the floor, the marble coffins in the centre of the room and the bottles of bleach by the wall. The lid on one coffin was cracked three quarters of the way up, its contents on show.

Lazarus came to Cyprus after being raised by Christ. He spent thirty years preaching the Gospel here, and according to legend he smiled only once in that entire time. I briefly hoped to see a frowning skull inside the coffin, but it was empty, of course. The saint's remains were taken to Constantinople at the end of the ninth century, moved to France at the beginning of the thirteenth century, and then lost to history. Or perhaps they were taken to Russia in the sixteenth century and hidden in a monastery on the Estonian border. Or perhaps buried under the church all along and finally unearthed in the year 1972. Unless, that is, Lazarus never visited Cyprus, but travelled to Marseille on a ship with no sails and ended up beneath the altar of Autun Cathedral. To a suspicious mind absence is a form of evidence.

Conspiracy theories turn disorder into pattern. After the French Revolution the possibility of a secret society directing events proved reassuring to some. It meant an aristocratic elite with clear – if melodramatic – aims was still in control. Brute chaos is what truly terrifies, which is why we prefer a gloved hand to pull the strings of history than admit we are playthings of the storm. Maybe faith is born from a similar fear – of a world made meaningless by chance. And maybe I was walking to print my life with a pattern of its own.

Joseph von Hammer-Purgstall was once a respected poet whose translation of Hafez inspired Goethe's collection of lyric poems, *West-östlicher Divan.* By seeking signs of primitive religious practices in Christian worship, he anticipated the work of writers such as James Frazer, Northrop Frye and Claude Lévi-Strauss. To him the dead were not lost but simply waiting to be raised, and this was easier for me to understand now, because since coming to Cyprus I had seen landscapes haunted with gods and rituals make ghosts of men.

The religion I encountered on Cyprus had seemed ancient too – deep and lasting like the landscape. Hiking between the Troodos monasteries it felt as if I was outside time, and in the Church of St Lazarus I began to wonder if faith could free us from history, bearing its burden, consoling its losses. In the same way that religion rewrites a life, teaching that death is never the end, the pilgrimage had restored my past, suggesting that these memories need not tend towards tragedy, that this history might yet be redeemed.

The marble coffin was cold to touch. There was nothing inside except for a grainy residue and the chemical stink of cleaning products. *Where have ye laid him?* Standing in the crypt, I thought back to a February afternoon and a sanctuary beneath the street. *This sickness is not unto death.* I remembered a bowl of clementines, an open tin of tea, and a ceiling made silver with angels. *He that was dead came forth.* And I longed to turn the broken pieces of the past into a story.

PART FIVE

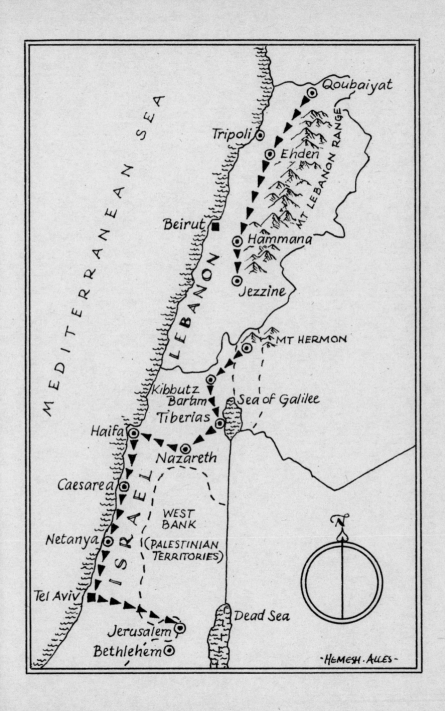

From Cyprus I took a boat back to Turkey and another boat to Lebanon. The second boat was delayed by a day with no reason given. However, on the night we were meant to sail a Damascus suburb called Ghouta was hit by government airstrikes. The attack used sarin gas, killing some fifteen hundred people. Chemical weapons were one of President Obama's red lines, and soon the whole region was waiting to see if America would intervene. Although our boat was cancelled hours before the attack, every passenger blamed Assad for the delay. And the threat of war shadowed my time in Lebanon.

The following evening we were away. Next morning I woke as the ferry washed into Tripoli Harbour, passing metal cranes, concrete wharves and coloured storage tanks stacked like Lego bricks. The taxi drivers at the ferry port warned me about travelling on foot, miming slit throats and sudden explosions. As did the bus drivers in Al-Tell Square, who claimed that northern Lebanon was too dangerous for hiking. Otherwise I met nobody, but wandered anxious round the glossy glass offices of El Mina and the narrow alleyways of the Old City. The apartments by the riverbank were hung with black flags, and the stall owners in the souk – a cramped complex of granite columns and vaulted roofs – avoided my eyes.

I pushed on, into the hills, and two hours later I was knocking at the door of Balamand Monastery.

The monastery stood on a shelf of rock three hundred

metres above Tripoli. It was white on the outside, white on the inside, with walls of dressed limestone and bare plaster. Founded by crusaders, built by Cistercians, since the seventeenth century it had belonged to the Antiochian Orthodox Church.

Fr Paul was there to welcome me. He was in his seventies, grey-haired and spare. Each time he spoke his chin twitched, his knees dipped, and his arms jogged in circles. As I described my journey so far – making apologies for the patchwork route I had followed across the region – he slapped his cheeks with surprise.

Before coming to Balamand Fr Paul had spent time at St Andrew's Skete on Mt Athos and Stavrovouni Monastery in the Troodos Mountains. When I asked how he ended up in Lebanon, he said, 'Monks are the nerves of the Church. If a body has no nerves, it's paralysed.'

Fr Paul led me into the main courtyard. The cloistered square looked familiar from dozens of monasteries, yet what struck me most was the sense of sanctuary, for we were high above the city here, and fortified from the world outside. A terrace bordered the upper storey, with a row of cells on the left. They had narrow doors, narrow beds, and windows no bigger than cat flaps. There were eight in total, and all except one were occupied, their floors a mess of branded sports bags with plastic logos peeling loose.

'The Syrians are here to stay,' said Fr Paul. 'So no room for guests. Understand?'

I did not understand. But that evening I met the bishop and realized who I was sharing with.

Archimandrite Jack Khalil was tall and lean, and he moved with the delicate grace of a mantis. After leading vespers in the monastery church, he stood by the door, bowing his head as people filed outside.

The bishop had recently returned from Syria. When

I asked about the trip, he began listing churches lying empty in Aleppo and Homs, in Hama and Mahardah. 'The Christians do not want to choose sides. But both sides – the government, the rebels – tell them that if you are not my ally, then you are my enemy. So they have no choice. They have to leave.'

Once the service was over, I walked a lap of the courtyard with Fr Paul. It was evening now and the walls had turned a chilly blue. 'The bishop has to keep out of the fighting,' my host explained. 'In the Middle East people assume a religious leader speaks for his whole congregation. If he criticizes one side, the other – it's not safe.' As Fr Paul spoke, a group of men entered the yard, climbed the staircase and hurried into the cells surrounding mine. 'But he lets seven Syrian Christians hide in his monastery, so maybe you can guess which side he supports.'

When I returned to my cell, one of the men was waiting for me. He asked if I would keep watch while he smoked, because cigarettes were forbidden in the monastery. Then we sat above the gatehouse, my companion cupping his cigarette while I stared into the dusk. Downstairs I heard clanging as Fr Paul locked the gates, but otherwise we were alone.

The smoker's name was Ibrahim. He was about my age, but his face was drained, his shoulders stooped, and a band of elastic showed through the worn collar of his T-shirt. As he smoked he explained that the other Syrians at Balamand had fled the country rather than fight for Assad. Dodging the draft meant they could not return home, so instead they lived here in secret, working for local businesses during the day and slipping back into the monastery each evening. Meanwhile their families remained in Syria, waiting out the war – though Ibrahim feared the fighting would last until there was nothing left of his country.

Was that the reason he came here?

He shook his head. In 2011, at the start of the revolution, Ibrahim was finishing national service. This made it dangerous for him to take part in the protests, so instead he helped them organize online. At one demonstration his brother was shot in the leg, and later that day the *mukhabarat*, the secret police, raided his family home. The injured brother hid on the roof, but Ibrahim was arrested. Then he was held without charge until his parents paid for his release. 'I was not tortured, no. I was taken to a room, my eyes tied, my hands tied, hanging by my arms. Sometimes I hear bullets loaded into a gun. Sometimes I feel a man standing behind me, breathing on my neck. I wait and wait, never knowing when it will end, never knowing if I will die.'

He began telling me about the Christians he knew who had left the country, and the Muslims who had turned against the government, and the many victims of the *mukhabarat*. One friend was beaten on the soles of his feet until he could no longer walk. Another friend's wife was raped by a squad of secret police, the husband forced to watch. Both men ended up joining the rebels.

'The worst part is not the pain. The worst part is the humiliation. That is why there cannot be peace. That is why Assad will fight to the death. He knows it is too late to forgive.'

Night had fallen. Ibrahim pinched out his cigarette and eased the stub into the pocket of his jeans. I wanted to offer some comfort, or tell him some hopeful story, but there was nothing I could say. I could only watch him brush the tobacco from his palms and blow the ash from his fingers. Then he said goodnight and returned to his cell.

*

I left Balamand next morning and hiked back to Tripoli. It was Friday 23 August. Yesterday I had passed roadside checkpoints made from oil drums – striped red and white, strung with barbed wire – but none of them were manned. Like the dingy alleyways of the Old City or the cramped corridors of the souk, they had a forgotten, leftover feel. Today soldiers stood at the checkpoints, police patrolled the streets, and armoured cars were parked on the pavement – brutish vehicles painted muddy shades of brown.

I roamed round in the dense sunshine, looking to buy a map. Eventually I found one in a bookshop near Al-Tell Square. The owner spoke to me in nervous French, repeating the words, *s'il vous plaît, s'il vous plaît*.

An Ottoman clock tower stood in the corner of the square, five storeys of stacked stone with a tiled pyramid at its peak. Opposite the clock tower was a disused building from the colonial period. Dust fogged the marble floors and the windows were foxed with dirt. A coffee stall squatted in the entrance hall, among mismatched tables and chairs – wrought metal, striped cane and red plastic with Coca-Cola branding.

I sat at one of the tables and unfolded the map. My plan was to start walking in Al-Qoubaiyat, a town two hours' hike from the Syrian border, and spend three weeks travelling south along Lebanon's mountain spine. However, Al-Qoubaiyat was fifty kilometres from Tripoli and I was unsure how to reach it.

A pair of men played backgammon at the table behind mine, slapping wooden counters onto a wooden board. At another table a man wearing rings on every finger joked with one of the waiters. I could hear music murmuring from the radio, while from the streets came snatched conversations and coughing cars. And from far off came a noise I could not name, like a low thunderclap or distant firework. Like the crust of the earth had cracked.

The backgammon stopped. The laughter too. The conversation went quiet as the waiters stared into the square. I tried to guess what was happening from the faces around me, but found no answer in the startled eyes, the jutting jaws, the gulping motion at each throat.

The second noise was closer, a deep beat followed by a smothered echo. It was the sound of concrete walls coming apart. This time there was no doubt: a bomb, two bombs, detonating somewhere in the city.

The waiters shut the windows and the backgammon players tidied their game. Everyone was standing now, so I folded my map and shouldered my rucksack, but midway to the door I remembered that I had nowhere to go. When the man with too many rings asked the name of my hotel, I struggled to answer. He told me to cross the square, find a taxi, and stay seated until Beirut. 'You will not be safe in Tripoli,' he warned, taking my arm in his glinting fingers and walking me out into the bright tumult of the city.

Leaving the cafe, I passed a cluster of women wearing loose clothes and coloured headscarves, some carrying bags of food, others holding the hands of children, rushing in a dozen directions, as groups of men jogged into the traffic, a few darting between the cars that were jammed in place, their horns blaring, their drivers shouting, hundreds of vehicles jostling onto the road south, one or two even mounting the pavement to get away, causing engines to grind and breaks to scream, these noises growing louder until they were drowned by the sound of sirens, coming first from police motorbikes, and then from ambulances and armoured jeeps, racing through the square on the road north, their lights bouncing blue and red off the buildings, while on the pavements below, every cafe and shop was shutting up for the day, clearing their stalls and locking their doors, meaning that by the time I had crossed the square and reached the Ottoman clock tower it was obvious that I would find nowhere to shelter in the city, obvious that I must get out as soon as possible, not south in the direction of Beirut but north towards Al-Qoubaiyat, Al-Qoubaiyat, Al-Qoubaiyat, a name I had to repeat to the crowds mobbing the mini-buses, even though none of them was going north because that was the direction of the first explosion – or so I was told by a young man who spoke to me with stifled impatience, marching between the buses and asking each driver if they were heading to Al-Qoubaiyat, and then chewing his lips as one after another they told him no, no chance, not today, until at last he found a bus driving two thirds of the way and insisted I get on board, despite the fact that its twelve seats were packed with eighteen passengers and its footwell filled with luggage, because sure enough there was space for me on the edge of the footwell, one arm hugging my rucksack, the other arm clinging to the doorframe, my body half hanging from the door as the driver turned onto the road north and accelerated along an avenue of office blocks, while a procession of cars came in the opposite direction, most of them ageing Mercedes with faded coats of terracotta and cream – the same colour as the low-rise flats and high-rise hotels bordering the street, as well as the garages with gaping signs and the shops with smashed windows, glass glittering on their displays of furniture and clothes – the first evidence that we were nearing the blast zone, but soon joined by four-wheel drives with cracked black bodywork and shattered black windscreens, and by sheets of smoke drifting between the traffic, the air becoming bitter, the sirens howling louder, the stench of asphalt rising from the road, yet dead silence inside the minibus as people peered into the streets, hoping for a view of the bombsite and seeing nothing but smoke, nothing but a wall of smoke rising towards the sky, until our driver realized that the road north was impassable – barricaded by ambulances and blast wreckage – and the bus began turning, meaning I had to grip my bag again, grip the doorframe again, and glimpsed for a moment the scene of the attack, or rather glimpsed several stray pieces of pavement and a car with fire pouring from its windows, as well as three survivors standing by the roadside: a man whose T-shirt was torn from his chest, a woman whose arms were black up to the elbows, and another man whose face was damaged, no face at all but a mask of blood, blood wet in his hair and leaking from his nose, blood shining on his forehead and spilling from his mouth, blood clotting his eyes and eating his cheeks and no skin no skull no body but blood – and then we pushed back onto the road, this time speeding south, past shops with smashed windows and garages with gaping signs, past low-rise flats and high-rise hotels, the smell of burning fainter, the sound of sirens waning, our minibus turning onto a tree-lined street and climbing into a hillside suburb, where the terrified silence gave way to stuttered conversations as the passengers tried to phone home, their voices nervous at first, but the words flowing out between sobs and sighs when a friend or family member answered, so that, by the time we had reached the ring road above Tripoli and were heading north again, our minibus was breathless with relief, some of the passengers gossiping, others gabbling, a few reciting elated monologues, and one or two asking me questions, wanting to know where I was from, where I was going, how long I had been in the country, and laughing when I answered yesterday, I came here yesterday, just twenty-four hours in Tripoli. 'Ah!'

they said. 'My God!' they said. 'Welcome, welcome to Lebanon.'

Hiking south from Al-Qoubaiyat, I met others who had been caught in the attack – one man whose car was destroyed, a second whose brother ended up in hospital – and from them I pieced together what happened that morning. Two bombs: the first outside Al-Taqwa Mosque in the north of Tripoli, the second outside Al-Salam Mosque in the east. Both were aimed at the crowds leaving Friday prayers, but both detonated while everyone was inside. All the same, forty-seven people were killed and maybe eight hundred injured. The worst bombing since the civil war. Nobody had claimed responsibility, but the mosques were associated with fierce Salafi preachers and the attack took place eight days after a car bomb in southern Beirut. So maybe it was revenge, the men said, shaking their heads with worry.

Though I tried to fit together these accounts, I soon became overwhelmed. I could give no shape to the rush of sensations, nor any perspective to the vast movements of people. Instead, rising into the foothills of the Mt Lebanon Range, I was aware only of my helplessness before history.

All weekend I climbed through the range, and on Monday afternoon I reached Sir El Danniyeh, a holiday town on the lower slopes of Lebanon's highest peak, Qornet es Saouda. It was once a popular summer spot for Tripoli's grander families, containing guesthouses, holiday homes and a pink mansion called the Hôtel Jazzar Raad. White balconies hung from the hotel facade, and harlequin tiles patterned the lobby. The windows were inlaid with tinted panes – red and green and gold – but otherwise the interior was dim.

A man with an appalling smile stood by the door. When I entered, he launched into a lisping history of the hotel. I heard only a few phrases – 'Alpine surroundings . . . Art Deco design . . . 1937, sir . . .' – but guessed that he was the manager.

A fountain shaped like a wedding cake sat in the centre of the terrace. Wooden trellises bordered each side, screening the valley below. My table looked down on the Abou Ali River as it cut a violent course towards Tripoli. The scenery was spectacular, but polluted too, with bin bags padding the roadside, drinks cans flashing in the gullies, and plastic wrappers clinging to the scrub. Tin-roofed houses cluttered the slopes, as well as a concrete mock-up of an Ottoman villa and a mosque with a neon-wrapped minaret.

The manager brought coffee and asked about my walk. It seemed there were no other staff at the hotel, nor any guests, but minutes later he returned with a squat man in a boxy black shirt. The man's name was Colonel Masor. The colonel just happened to be visiting the hotel and hoped to ask a few questions. He simply wanted to know my name, my age, my occupation, my nationality, how I entered Lebanon, who I had stayed with, every stage of my walk so far and each stop on the journey south.

I unfolded my map and outlined the route. From Sir El Danniyeh I would track the western slopes of the Mt Lebanon Range for three hundred kilometres, before dropping into the Beqaa Valley and approaching the Israeli border. I listed the towns along the way – Ehden, Bcharre, Hammana, Jezzine – while the colonel noted them down. Then he marched off to make some phone calls.

Once he was gone, the manager gave another ghastly smile.

'Colonel Masor is from the secret police,' he explained. 'Like Scotland Yard. He wants to make you safe.'

When the colonel returned he was grinning. Then laughter, handshakes, a second round of coffee, and an invitation to spend the night – which I immediately refused. I had seen enough of the Hôtel Jazzar Raad.

The following morning I was questioned twice more – by a soldier at a checkpoint and by a pair of hikers using golf clubs as walking sticks. They hinted that there was no route over Mt Saouda, but the map showed a frail footpath circling the summit, so I pushed on, masking my doubts with a brisk determination. The road became a track, the track became a path, and soon I was scrambling up the rocky course of a riverbed.

By midday I had topped two thousand metres and was balanced on the brim of the mountain. This area was under snow for much of the year, but in summer the snow melted to reveal waves of boulder and scree. There were no landmarks now, only a sky of relentless blue and a carpet of cloud at my feet. I followed a bearing and hoped for the best, edging round the summit for the next two hours, over a moonscape of split shale and loose maquis. At that height I could hear nothing but the heaving wind – my ears popping, my eyes watering, and my rucksack vibrating with each burst of air.

Eventually I came to another track, this one dipping under the cloudline on the southern side of Saouda. Layers of stratus drew back to reveal a forest of cedar and oak, fanning over the slopes or sinking into the valleys.

It was almost seven when I reached the road. To my right, a ring of hilltop villages formed a crown of slender belfries. Ahead I could make out the tiled roofs of Ehden – a muddle of convents and churches. Approaching the town, I heard bellchime tumble through the evening air and felt a sheltered sense of safety. This was the start of Qadisha, the Holy Valley, Lebanon's Christian heartland.

The presbytery in Ehden contained a crumpled priest with an angry expression. He complained that he could not help me – he was old, he was sick, there was nowhere to stay – but minutes later a younger priest turned up, dressed in a Lazio football strip. His name was Fr Joseph.

'The most beautiful thing in life is choice,' said Fr Joseph. 'Will I go to heaven, or will I go to hell? Will I live in sin, or will I pray to God?'

Today I had two choices. First: the guestroom upstairs or the apartment downstairs. Second: a meal in a restaurant or an invitation to a dinner party.

I chose the latter both times.

The dinner party was taking place on the far side of town. Fr Joseph led the way down a crowded street of cafes, their tables tied with orange lights. He greeted every person we passed, shouting and waving and poking his tongue between his teeth.

We arrived at the flat after nine. The whole place was furnished with metal. There were aluminium-framed mirrors covering the walls and chrome-coated cupboards lining the kitchen. Copper lamps hung off the ceiling, and brass bowls shone from the table. Our host's name was Rami, a childhood friend of Fr Joseph. He looked much older, however, with a shaved scalp and a pointed skull. Rami's wife, Marie-Rose, had pink lips and bleached hair, and she greeted us with short, excited screams. Then she brought out plates of hummus and labne, tabbouleh and fatoush, stuffed aubergine, stuffed pastry and half a dozen salads. Three more guests waited at the table, with twice that number of vodka bottles piled in buckets of ice.

Fr Joseph never touched the food, sitting at the head

of the table and talking the whole time. Sometimes he sounded cheerful, sometimes exasperated. The other guests nodded along, crossing themselves and mouthing the words: *Amen, Bravo, Amen, Bravo*. Occasionally they repeated a sentence in English, but otherwise I had to guess Fr Joseph's meaning. From what I could gather, the priest had recently been in trouble because he asked his congregation to pray for the victims of the Tripoli bombings. Another priest, more senior, warned him about taking sides, about appearing too political. 'I was praying for peace,' said Fr Joseph. 'I was praying for all the victims of violence. Sunni and Shia, Muslim and Christian – God created every one of us. Why should I tell people not to pray?'

The table nodded. 'Amen,' they said. 'Bravo.'

As the priest spoke, Rami slurred in my ear. First he tried to translate the speech; next he attempted a commentary. He mentioned the million Syrian refugees that had *crushed* Lebanon. He claimed the Muslim population was *eating* the Christian one. He said if I saw a church I should walk towards it, but if I saw a mosque I must *fly away*.

At the same time he emptied glass after glass of vodka. When he offered me some, I turned him down. Then he explained: 'I was seven years in Russia. In Ukraine. I went for work. So now I drink vodka.'

'What work was that?'

'Vodka,' Rami repeated, 'every day. And women,' he added, 'every day. Every day for seven years.' He stared at his glass. 'I swear to you I fucked a thousand women. Too many.' Fr Joseph's words played in my thoughts: *The most beautiful thing in life is choice*. 'So now I am married,' Rami went on. 'It's better that way.' *Will I go to heaven, or will I go to hell? Will I live in sin, or will I pray to God?* 'Now I have come home. Ehden is my home.'

More plates of food, more bottles of vodka, coffee and chocolate and a pudding made from pastry, pistachios and cream. Fr Joseph talked and Rami slurred and Marie-Rose urged me to have one last helping. Candlelight flickered off the copper fittings and one of the guests was always laughing, yet the whole meal had a delinquent energy that was neither drink nor delight, but something closer to desperation. I began to share in the frantic mood, as if this evening was our last together, and we feared the moment when the party would end.

Then it was midnight. Fr Joseph stood to leave.

As we walked back to the presbytery, he announced that he was moving to Rome in January. When I asked why, he said: 'America, Europe – they do not care about the Middle East. Sometimes I swear they do not even like us. In Syria the Christians are being slaughtered – slaughtered, do you know what that means? The worst kind of death. Muslims help other Muslims, but Christian countries do nothing.'

I was curious how long he would stay in Italy, but Fr Joseph did not know. Perhaps one year, perhaps five, perhaps he would never return.

We went the rest of the way in silence. The cafes on the high street were empty now, their tables cleared, their lights burnt out. When we reached the presbytery, the priest placed his hands on my shoulders, resting his weight against me. I wondered if he was holding back tears, or trying to smother his anger, but then he wished me luck and turned away.

The apartment below the presbytery contained a bedroom, a bathroom, a dining room and a kitchen. Inside, the air was damp and the curtains drawn. I spent all night on the bathroom floor, knees on the tiles, knuckles on the toilet bowl, throwing up every mouthful of the dinner party. Then, as the curtains fattened with dawn light, I lay on the bedroom carpet, stomach aching and empty, astonished at how sick I had been.

I left Ehden around midday. A road ran west out of town, spiralling down the side of a mountain. After twelve kilometres it slipped between twin flanks of eroded sandstone and entered a narrow valley. Orchards layered the ground below, and the slopes were shuttered with pine. A monastery was propped above the orchards: an Italianate cellblock with an ornate church set into the cliffs and storehouses notching the hillsides.

This was Mar Antonios, the richest of Lebanon's religious houses.

A few visitors had gathered near the gatehouse. One of them explained how the monastery used to be a pilgrim shrine for the country's lunatics, who would spend nights chained up in the grotto of St Antony.

As the afternoon light became dense, the monastery buildings blushed. At five o'clock a line of monks filed into the church for evening prayers. The outer wall was striped like a duomo facade, with a triple bell tower propped on top, hewn from a single monolith of stone. The cave behind formed the church nave, its piers made from loose-packed stone, its apse from mortared rubble. A barrel vault supported the front half of the ceiling, but the rear half was bare rock.

I sat at the back, struggling to stay awake. Some parts of the service resembled Orthodox vespers, other parts reminded me of Catholic liturgy, but the prayers were all in Syriac – an Aramaic dialect close to the language used by Christ. They were softer than the prayers at Balamand, delicate and dragging, like the hither and thither of waves, or the cymbal hiss of the surf. Beneath these sounds I could hear a silence louder than anything else in the valley – silence that was presence, that was purpose. It seemed to fill the monastery, deadening the air with a heavy hush. At that point, the unease I had felt since Tripoli became a settled calm.

When the service was done I was shown to a bedroom above the gatehouse. Although laity were not allowed in the main cellblock, the monks made an exception and invited me to dinner. Their refectory was a kind of burrow, with a curved ceiling and windowless walls. I mentioned that I had been unwell, but they laid out metal bowls of soup and bread, noodles and beans. So I ate what I could, listening to a potted history of the Maronite Church.

The Church was founded in the fourth century by a Syrian hermit called St Maron and brought to Lebanon by his disciple, Abraham of Cyrrhus. Its first members settled in the Holy Valley, which kept them safe during the Arab conquest of the region. Then, in the crusader era, Maronite bishops affirmed their loyalty to Rome and joined the Catholic family. 'Solitaries were the heart of our Church, right from the beginning,' said Peter, the novice sitting on my right. 'Search the Holy Valley and you won't find a single cave that wasn't a hermitage. You might even find a few hermits.'

Although born in Beirut, Peter had grown up in Sydney. He had none of the mild, earnest manner I associated with young monks, but an easy smile and a slack sort of charm. I presumed this last comment was a joke, yet my companion kept talking, describing three members of the monastery who lived in remote corners of the valley. 'No electricity, no technology, no food except what they grow themselves. And only one meal a day – plus five hours' sleep, two hours' study and three hours' work. The rest of the time they pray.'

'Fourteen hours?'

'No holidays either, unless they get sick.'

Peter's face looked dazed with delight, as if he could not believe what he was telling me. I asked whether he wanted to become a hermit too.

He paused. 'It's not my decision.'

'You do!'

He gave an embarrassed grin. 'The hermits who live in Qadisha are wise men, scholars. Often our bishops visit them for advice. The rest of the Church – the monks, the priests – we're inspired by their example. When they die, many of the brothers at Mar Antonios hope to be chosen next.'

There was something familiar about this: not the hermit's quiet devotion, but Peter's awed description, as if the solitude were somehow reckless, even heroic. The nearest thing to martyrdom. It was the same model of surrender that had shaped my own understanding of the religious life, until I realized that sacrifice alone could not sustain a faith. But, I asked, wasn't living in community one of the principles of monasticism? How could you practise virtue when living alone? And didn't Jesus leave the desert after forty days?

'We don't enter the monastery to escape the world,' Peter replied. 'We enter the monastery because of our love for God. A hermit's heart is filled with love. He lives alone to spend all his time in God's presence.' The grin faltered for a moment. 'But that calling is a gift. I cannot choose for myself.'

Next morning I decided to visit one of the hermits. When mass was finished I left Mar Antonios and climbed onto the spur of rock dividing the monastery from the Holy Valley. A sign mapped the medieval foundations along the valley floor, as well as the ruined sanctuaries let into its sides. Below the sign an arrow pointed towards a narrow staircase, tripping off the spur and through the clouds.

From the top of the staircase I could see Qadisha stretching away to the east – a ten-kilometre rift cut into the Mt Lebanon Range. It looked tropical, with soaring slopes, frothing woodland, and a veil of clouded vapour between.

Although I had copied the map into my notebook, I could not make sense of the scenery below. I could not guess the location of Notre Dame de Qannoubine, the oldest of the valley monasteries, housing the tombs of eighteen Maronite patriarchs; nor the monastery of Mar Lichaa, a fourteenth-century sanctuary with cavern chambers and halls of carved sandstone; nor the mountaintop refuge of Mar Sarkis, perched at fifteen hundred metres; nor the abandoned foundations of Mar Assia and Mar Aboun, of Mar Girgis and Mar Yuhanna; nor the ruined refuges of Mar Mora and Deir Es-Salib. All I could see was the cloud thrown up like seaspray from the crashing cliffs.

Midway down, the staircase divided. One half turned left towards the monasteries, the other half went right onto a footpath. Turning right, I glimpsed a decayed hive of hermit caves on the slopes opposite and heard the rasping of the river below.

After a while the path became a paved walkway with metal railings hanging from mortared cairns. It skirted a narrow allotment and entered a tiny courtyard. Three cells occupied one side of the yard, embedded into a wall of sheer sandstone. Wooden benches ringed the remaining sides, with more metal railings guarding against the fall.

One of the cells contained a cave chapel the size of a cupboard, its walls wrinkled like peachstone. Each ledge was adorned with a painted plaster statue, and votive candles threw creased shadows round the room.

A man little bigger than a child bent over at one of the pews. Yesterday evening Peter told me about him. I remembered that he was born in Colombia to a wealthy family, but now owned nothing except his cassock. And that, before coming to Qadisha, he had been a doctor of psychology and a professor of theology. That he was in his late seventies, that he spoke six languages, and that his name was Fr Dario Escobar. Peter also told me about the pilgrims who visited Fr Dario, asking when they would get married and who would win the presidential election – mistaking the hermit for a soothsayer. And how he woke before dawn each morning, watched the sun breaking open the valley, heard birdsong rising from the forest below, and knew – not hoped, not believed, but knew – this place was paradise.

The little figure went on kneeling, head bowed, shoulders hunched. Fourteen hours a day! I was hoping to speak with him – to tell him the stories of exile that I heard in Balamand, or describe the scenes of wreckage that I witnessed in Tripoli. I wanted to explain how my understanding of monastic life had changed when I learnt that it was not an escape from the world, but a confrontation with the self. Alone there was no hiding from your failings, meaning you dropped deep into the past like diving down to touch the cold sea floor. However, I did not wish to interrupt his prayers, so I sat by the door and listened. I listened to the wax stuttering off the candles and the creaking of the hermit's breath. In that moment the chapel did not seem a lonely place, but a theatre of living voices. As if we spoke without words. As if you heard me in the silence.

When I stepped outside, the cloud was burning off and sunlight filled the valley.

I left Qadisha in the last days of August, hiking the high road south. The temperature stayed the same, but the light was piercing, and the afternoon's walk left me sunblind. Ahead, the landscape was craggy and the settlements sparse. Cedars freckled the ridgelines and boulders sat stranded on the slopes. Every hour I passed another army checkpoint – more red-and-white oil drums, more spools of rusting wire, but each one unmanned. The safety I had felt in the Holy Valley became a nagging fear.

That evening I was offered a bed in a roadside cafe. The owner woke me next morning with *markouk* bread and apple jam. Over breakfast he asked about my route, but when I opened my map he shook his head. 'Aaqora is Christian,' he said, pointing at a village five kilometres down the road. 'Afqa is Muslim,' he added, sliding his finger another five kilometres. Then he tugged my arm. 'Shia. Hezbollah.' Finally he pointed at Kesrouane, five kilometres after that. 'In Aaqora you must ask for a taxi to drive you to Kesrouane. Understand?'

I wasn't sure how to respond. In the past I had ignored such warnings, but that was no longer possible, for since Tripoli I was aware of the risks that I faced. However, I would not skip ten kilometres on the basis of a stranger's prejudice, so I thanked my host and hiked off.

The road ran towards a crescent of cliffs at the head of the Abraham Valley – a limestone sail billowing towards the coast. Morning light coloured the stone like a Rothko canvas, bleeding slabs of orange and pink. Villages hung from the base of each cliff, and litter glistened in the streambeds below.

Approaching Afqa, I noticed a gutted chapel beside the road. The niche above the door was blackened, and the smell of wet bark lingered in the doorway. A faceless statue of the Virgin Mary stood half-hidden in the shadows.

Banners were draped over the village entrance, with images of injured soldiers printed on the fabric, their bodies broken, eyes closed. The houses were also decorated, each flag bearing the same design: green lettering circled by a globe, a book and an assault rifle. I could not read the letters, but I recognized the emblem. Hezbollah, the Party of God.

A pair of elderly men with clipped beards and careworn faces sat outside the cafe. I called out to them – *Salaam Alaikum!* – but received no reply. There was no other sound except the scrunch of my boots on the gravel and the mutter of flags in the breeze.

As I neared the far side of the village, a sputtering engine interrupted the quiet. A motorbike slowed at my shoulder, the driver urging me onto the back. His teeth were cracked and his fingers purple-scabbed, yet I could not tell if his voice was friendly or frightened.

He spoke to me a second time, a third, making haggling gestures with his left hand. I shook my head, legs straining to keep the pace.

Eventually his mouth snapped shut and he sputtered off.

The next two villages were the same: tatty houses garlanded with propaganda. Posters lined the roads between, stapled onto boards and staked into the ground. More portraits of soldiers, their lips pink, cheeks pale, beards a feathery black – yet the ink was blurred, the images pixelated.

By the third village I was marching hard, my lungs clamped, my legs burning. On the northern side of the valley Maronite churches were pinned to the hills, but on this side I saw nothing except flags, banners and the parade of martyrs' faces. I stared at the ground, trying to calculate the distance I had covered. Seven kilometres? Eight? Not enough – but if I started running I knew the panic would overwhelm me. Instead I kept my eyes down, until the posters petered out and all I could see was banked earth and scorched brush. Then I spotted the striped drums of a checkpoint up ahead. When I noticed that this one was manned, I felt a sudden surge of relief. Beyond the checkpoint, a street of scrappy buildings marked the outskirts of Kesrouane.

I hoped my sickness in Ehden was a one-off. However, as I approached the country's midway point, I became dizzy and flushed. The mountain summits swayed above me, and the limestone tableland was unsteady at my feet. Sometimes I shivered for no reason; sometimes my insides felt tender, melting. Skirting the eastern edge of Mt Sannine, I kept having to run from the road and squat among the umbrella pines. I tried not to eat, but that made me weak, so I ate and the diarrhoea dehydrated me. My pace slowed to a shuffle, and, no matter how many times I spat, my mouth was gummed with saliva.

In early September I passed a series of Christian towns built on shallow hills. Hammana was one of them. It had a convent, a monastery, a school and three churches, but the only spare bed was at the fire station. So I spent Monday evening bunking down with the civil defence team – three volunteers in their early twenties. There was Louis, the team leader, who had chubby hands and chubby cheeks, and who counted using fingers and thumbs. There was Jules, the deputy, who spent the whole evening sipping bottles of Almaza beer. And there was Osama, who had a swollen stomach and a helpless smile, and who claimed to be a captain in the Lebanese Army. They welcomed me with a flurry of hospitality – cups of coffee, cans of Coke and three different brands of cigarette – as if they had been waiting all week for this chance.

Jules was interested in my journey – not the route of the walk, but the transit between each country. He asked complicated questions about passport restrictions and travel times, and kept reminding me that the Lebanon–Israel border was closed. He smirked when I mentioned the ferry to Tripoli, scowled when I discussed the cost of a Turkish visa and, when I explained how I would detour round the border (a bus to Beirut, a plane to Amman, and a coach to northern Israel), he shook his head sadly.

The office contained a television, two sofas and an antique fridge. Insect nets peeled from the windows, and the ceiling fan squeaked as it stirred the warm air. My hosts sat on the sofas, smoking and squabbling over the remote.

At nine o'clock Louis left the office, returning with two roast chickens, four bags of chips and six servings of mezze in styrofoam pots. Osama loaded my plate with fistfuls of food, and then everyone ate at a furious pace. Eight minutes later they leant back on the sofas, fingers splayed across their bellies. Soon Louis and Jules were bickering again. A few days ago the British Parliament voted against airstrikes in Syria, but America and France were still debating the possibility, and the two friends disagreed about what would happen next. Their argument was held in English for my benefit, which meant swear words translated using online dictionaries and obscene jokes acted out with office equipment: rulers, staplers, fire extinguishers etc.

By this point the room was shrouded in cigarette smoke. And, when Osama joined in, the conversation splintered:

'– waiting to know what America will do. If Obama drops bombs on Assad, then Hezbollah fires rockets on Israel, then Israel sends soldiers into Beirut, then we have war –'

'– we go hiking in the Beqaa Valley. In Syria! Why not –'

'– already the Americans are sending their diplomats home. My cousin, he works in the embassy, he knows the day –'

'– until the hair grows over my whole face. My friends say I look like an imam, but I tell them I cannot cut my beard because I am becoming a monk. So they arrange a party, big party, dancing, drinking, the whole night –'

'– will teach you how to speak Arabic. Egyptian, Saudi, all kinds of Arabic –'

'– afterwards they ask me: you want to be monk? So I tell them: before I was joking, but now I have no choice –'

'– say you stayed with nuns. Otherwise we will be in too much trouble –'

'– impossible to walk past Jezzine. The army will not allow it. Even if you have a pass, they will tell you –'

'– like we are living on the edge of destruction. Syria is not the reason. Israel is the reason. Wherever you go in Lebanon you see buildings destroyed, bridges destroyed, and you think the civil war is to blame. But Israel is to blame –'

After an hour the conversation lapsed. There was no light in the room now except for the blue pulse of the television screen. An episode of *Arab Idol* was playing with the sound turned down, and I could hear Osama dragging on a cigarette, hear Jules scraping the wrapper from a beer bottle, hear Louis licking the grease off his fingers. Hear the fridge thrumming, the fan squeaking, and the mosquitoes squealing too close to my face. Beneath this restless chorus, one of the men was still speaking, but I could not understand him, and he could not help me.

*

Though I had taken antibiotics, the sickness was getting worse, and next morning my stomach felt damaged. Walking away from Hammana, my thoughts became feverish. A narrow ridgeline formed the last fifty kilometres of the Mt Lebanon Range, sagging with copses of cedar, oak and pine. After that my route tipped into the Beqaa Valley. Last night Louis warned that I would not be allowed into the valley without a pass and Jules claimed that no pass would be given. Meanwhile Osama listed all the dreadful things that would happen if I were kidnapped. My hosts' paranoia was easy to explain – there were few Christian settlements in southern Lebanon – yet their predictions stayed with me, sticking in my thoughts, my throat.

At teatime I came to a village called Barouk. The streets were filled with signs for a cedar park midway up the mountain. Scanning my map, it seemed possible to hike through the park and make Maasser El Chouf – my next destination – before nightfall.

I followed the signs out of the village and began climbing. My plan, however, was hopeless. As the road rose higher it swept back and forth between chopped-up chunks of rock, doubling and redoubling the distance. It took two hours to reach the fir trees on the rim of the park, and when I arrived at the entrance, the gates were closed. A ranger in a nearby cabin explained that the reserve shut at six each evening. Although I tried to protest – it was just five thirty – he told me there was no route to Maasser El Chouf anyway.

So, back the way I had come.

As I retreated from the gates, my insides seemed to spill. Hips clenched, I ran from the road, yet the mountainside offered no cover. Instead I had to climb to the boundary of the reserve and rush between the fir trees, slipping the rucksack from my shoulders, plucking the tissues from my pockets, and then bowing to the ground with left arm propped behind me, right hand in front, heels kicked, knees wide, shorts rucked round my ankles – but it was too late and there was shit on my shorts, on my socks, on my boots. Shit on my hand – I could smell it, the stink of it. Sweat on my skin and dust in my eyes, and tears too because now I was crying. Crying at the shame and crying at the pain and crying at the fear as well. All this time I had been afraid. Afraid of crowded cities and lonely villages. Afraid of posters and flags, of checkpoints and police, of blood eating a man's features from his face. I wanted it over, oh when would it be over, how much longer must I walk this way—

Cedars. A hundred metres above.

Three, four cedars, their branches splayed out like a hand.

Four cedars of Lebanon, with boughs waving gently towards me.

When I had cleaned myself, I moved up to the nearest tree. The air was warm here, sheltered from the wind, but the ground was cool beneath matted shadows. Grass grew at the foot of the tree, and the fallen needles were soft as down. I could smell dry bark, damp earth and the rich green reek of the forest.

Lying among the roots, tears still blotted my sight. It was not the accident that upset me, but those spoilt years before the walk. I worried that I was walking simply to punish myself, to purge the guilt of the suicide attempt. Yet, as I lay under the trees, I began to picture a little boy far from home, wandering lost through the world – and my fierce humiliation faded, giving way to a gentle sympathy.

I looked up at the ancient cedar skin. The undersides of each bough were silvery, and through the branches an afternoon moon chipped the sky. There was little chance I would make Maasser El Chouf tonight, but no matter.

I did not feel ashamed any more; instead, I felt very small beneath the cedars. Somewhere in this reserve were trees two thousand years old, offspring of the trees used to build King Solomon's Temple. The timber felled to frame a house for God.

Over the next few evenings I stayed at a Maronite monastery, a Melkite seminary, and a presbytery in the town of Jezzine. Then I descended into a wide valley, its base flat like the mirrored surface of a lake, and approached the Litani River.

The bridge over the river was guarded by a checkpoint, the checkpoint guarded by a soldier. He refused to let me through, so I sat by the roadside and waited for his officer. But the officer simply confirmed that, even though the checkpoint was forty kilometres from the border, I could hike no farther without a pass. He mentioned an address in Sidon and an interview with military intelligence. He discussed passport copies, hotel bookings, letters of recommendation and week-long delays. Then he said it was unlikely I would be given permission anyway.

I wanted to argue, or else try a different route, but after walking sick for ten days straight my strength was gone. I told myself it was an achievement to get this far, given the spoilt landscape, the warnings and threats, and the mayhem of that first Friday in Tripoli. I told myself the plan was unchanged – I would still fly to Israel, still hike to Jerusalem – yet trudging back to Jezzine all I felt was defeat. But then I reached the town and realized that, despite the obstacles I faced in Lebanon, I had never once tried to abandon the walk. Also, when it seemed I might fall apart, I found consolation in the landscape. In Istanbul the risks had seemed thrilling, for the smoke was only tear gas and the bullets only rubber, but in Lebanon the danger was real. However, the recklessness I remembered from Taksim Square had been replaced by a courage that understood the hazards it faced. I had tested myself. I had overcome the test. It did not mean that a cure was waiting for me in Jerusalem, but it meant I could keep walking without fear of collapse. And maybe that was recovery enough.

Before leaving Lebanon I spent a week in Beirut. Two days after I arrived, the US secretary of state held a press conference in London. During questions he made an off-hand comment about Assad's chemical weapons. If the president gave up his entire stockpile, John Kerry suggested, airstrikes could be avoided. Although unplanned, Russia welcomed the suggestion, convincing the Syrian government to accept. Just like that, the conflict was avoided.

At the end of the week I caught a plane to Amman.

One flight, two coach journeys and three bus rides later, I reached the Golan Heights – the rugged plateau that corners Israel, Lebanon and Syria. From here I joined a chain of footpaths called the Israel National Trail, which would lead me south through Galilee, west towards the coast, south again to Tel Aviv, and inland as far as Jerusalem. Five hundred and sixty-eight kilometres to go.

The trail began in the Hula Valley, an expanse of cultivated plain that bordered the Upper Jordan. Here the yellow hills of southern Lebanon became planted fields netted with irrigation channels. The river ran to the Sea of Galilee, but I did not follow its course, climbing instead into the Naftali Mountains and travelling along the valley's western flank.

On Monday morning I met three men in their mid-twenties. They were hiking to the Sea of Galilee and asked me to join them. At first I was reluctant – embarrassed by my torn shorts, my collapsing rucksack – but they grinned and laughed and urged me along.

Or, Tal and Eldad had become friends while on national service. When I asked about their time in the army, Tal, the heftiest and moodiest of the three, said: 'We were rangers. You know rangers?' I did not. 'We dress like trees, carry hundred-pound radios, stand in the woods for a week.' I told him it sounded like Special Forces. 'Like Special Forces, yes, but they spend too much time in the gym, we spend too much time like trees.' And did he enjoy serving in the army? 'Never. But we have no choice. We have to fight.'

That afternoon I walked with Or. He had fair hair, large teeth and a voice made up of impersonations. As we talked he would shuffle between accents: a cockney, a Scouser, the Queen. And he cooed at my own accent, mimicking each turn of phrase – *cheers, course, fine by me*. Otherwise he spoke English with a New Jersey twang picked up during a summer in the States, when he sold Dead Sea skincare products door-to-door. America and Israel were the same, he told me, young countries where exiles were welcome. Here you could start your life again.

Every two hours we stopped so that Tal could make coffee on a portable stove. If there was a pomegranate farm nearby, Or would scale the fence to steal some food. But the fruit was too ripe, their skins a sunburnt pink and their flesh beginning to ferment.

After lunch we stopped for longer, Or and Tal napping while Eldad removed a prayer shawl from his rucksack, placed the shawl on his shoulders, and started reading from a pocket copy of the Torah. When the others joked that he would soon become a scholar, he laughed in a vague fashion which suggested it might be true. He also asked questions about my journey, wanting to know how long I had been walking (roughly nine and a half months), what distance I had covered (roughly five thousand kilometres) and what lessons I had learnt along the way. My answers he referred to the Hebrew Bible. The hospitality I had been shown by strangers – yes, I would find this in Scripture – or the realization that faith was something felt as much as thought – this too I would find in Scripture – or the freedom that comes from owning only what you can carry – certainly this could be found in Scripture.

The three friends hiked at a steady pace, telling jokes and teaching me Hebrew. They were easy company, as if we had already crossed mountains and deserts together. Whenever the conversation flagged, Or would perform another impersonation, mimicking farm animals and TV adverts and the cast of an Israeli sitcom.

Our path skirted the crests of hills, occasionally diving into narrow gullies where the air was damp and the oak trees sprawled like something prehistoric. It was late September, yet I saw little trace of autumn, except for the misted mornings and the sudden chill each evening. But the sun was losing its strength, and though the midday heat still blazed, by early evening the light flopped lazy over the floor.

The villages along our route were enclosed by metal fences. Their houses were tidy, their gardens tidy, with pristine lawns of electric green and flowerbeds shining and clean. Otherwise the streets were empty, with the suffocated atmosphere of a new-built suburb. One or two villages contained spare rooms where trail hikers could spend the night: a hall with wooden floors and foam mats, or a classroom with tiny chairs and knee-high tables, the walls decorated in the twenty-two consonants of the Hebrew alphabet and an illustrated map labelling the fifty states of America.

On Wednesday afternoon we came to a hilltop village

called Kibbutz Bar'am. The trail stop was an apartment smarter than anywhere else we had stayed, containing two bedrooms, two bathrooms, a dining room and a kitchen. Handwritten rules were stuck to the walls, and the corridors smelt of paint.

That evening we were celebrating Sukkot. 'For the end of harvest,' Eldad explained. 'Also, in the time of the Temple, for making pilgrimage to Jerusalem. Also for the Exodus, when the Jews were in the desert. When we were lost.'

Soon after we arrived, Tal's parents and two sisters showed up. They did not live in the village, but had driven here with a car full of food. Or's father came too, bringing a bottle of sparkling wine and three boxes of baklava. We spent an hour cooking and cleaning, and then laid the table with plastic plates. Then we tucked into a spread of stuffed vegetables, stuffed dumplings, flatbread, sweetbread and cheesecake. A sense of celebration filled the room – not the aggressive hospitality I had been shown in Hammana, but something quieter and more sincere. I was neither an honoured guest nor an object of curiosity. Instead, I was a stranger welcomed at a feast.

Finally, the excited unease of Lebanon gave way to a submerged relief.

I sat next to Or's father, a streamlined version of his son – mouth sharper, teeth larger, head shaved clean of hair. He told a long story about a friend who was captured during the 1973 war. It wasn't clear where the story was going, until he said: 'Two days ago I am listening to the radio when I hear his voice. All the radio shows are remembering the war – forty years anniversary – and he is describing the time he was a prisoner. He is telling how he was put in a room with no light, no space, no air. All alone. He is so afraid he begins to pray, and the more he prays, the more his fear goes away.' Or's father grinned, flashing each one of his thirty-two teeth. 'Before the war, he says, I did not believe, but when I needed God, He was waiting for me.'

Midway through the meal Eldad recited a prayer. As he spoke, Tal held a napkin over his head, while Or repeated the words *Amen, Amen*. For much of the evening they had been laughing, but now their voices were solemn. The mood in the room grew sombre, as if our journey together were an act of commemoration or a show of solidarity.

Afterwards, Or's father filled a Kiddush cup and passed it round the table. He talked about the fellowship of Jews and the hospitality of exiles. He said that living in Israel was a miracle, every day another miracle. Finally he wrote down a verse from Isaiah and urged me to learn it off by heart. The words were in Hebrew, so I could not guess their meaning, but later that night I looked up the line. It said: 'They that wait on God shall renew their strength; they shall put forth new feathers like eagles; they shall run and not be weary; they shall walk and not hunger.'

On Friday morning the three friends left me. That afternoon I reached the Sea of Galilee, a twenty-kilometre strip of water enclosed by low hills. Their southern slopes were bright with vegetation, their northern slopes khaki-coloured – a grainy texture like the husk of an older landscape. Banana plantations lined the western shore, each drooping leaf cobwebbed with yellow cloth. But the water looked shallow and silty – no place for miracles.

On Saturday morning I visited the lake's pilgrim shrines. My first stop was the Church of the Primacy of

St Peter, which was built from black basalt and white mortar and set above a pebble beach. A dozen Chinese pilgrims knelt near the water, collecting tidewashed pebbles in ziplock bags.

A man wearing robes stood next to the church, holding a microphone in one hand and a speaker in the other. I could not tell if he was a tour guide or a priest. The man addressed the pilgrims in English, his voice thin and pleading. He explained that this was the spot where Christ appeared to the disciples after his death, filling their nets with 153 fish. 'The church is an antique,' he said. 'From the Franciscan period. But the most important church is the one on the inside.'

He went on: 'Many of the churches in Israel are new because the old ones have fallen down in earthquakes or been destroyed by fighting. Buildings fall down when the earth shakes, but the church in your soul can never die.'

Finally he said: 'Walk along the shore. Have a moment of self-meditation. Imagine Jesus standing beside you. Imagine him stepping onto the water. Do you have the courage to follow?'

I bumped into the pilgrims again at the Church of the Multiplication ('You may not be rich, but the love of Jesus can feed five thousand people.') And again at the Capernaum archaeological park, in a glass-bottomed church over the exposed foundations of the House of Peter. ('Jesus tells the disciples to leave their lives behind. Could you give up your home? Could you say goodbye to your family?') As the day wore on, the sun glared and the pilgrims' expressions blanked.

In the afternoon I climbed onto a hill set back from the lakeshore. The track ascended through fields of clodded earth and bony groves of olive. My rucksack's metal frame was bent and it weighed unsteady on my shoulders, meaning that I staggered with every step.

A religious complex occupied the hilltop, centring on a Neo-Byzantine extravaganza called the Church of the Beatitudes. More walls of black basalt, with a dome of dark copper and slender pillars skirting the sides. Pristine buildings surrounded the church, and eight plaques were buried in the grass, engraved with verses from the famous sermon: blessed are the meek, blessed are the peacemakers etc. But the only people I saw were the tour groups patrolling the lawn.

My eyes were tired from too much sun, so I crossed the lawn and sat beneath a palm tree. Moments later I noticed the same group of Chinese pilgrims gathering gravel from the paths, and soon I heard a familiar voice: 'Are you pure in heart? Are you poor in spirit? Do you hunger and thirst for righteousness? Well, friend, yours is the kingdom of heaven.'

On Sunday morning I reached Yardenit, a narrow passage of water where the River Jordan flowed from the Sea of Galilee. Almost all the archaeological evidence suggests that Christ was baptized a hundred kilometres south of here, on the eastern side of the river, but when visitors arrive at the site they see eighty-five stone slates repeating the lines from Mark's Gospel in eighty-five different languages: a voice from heaven ... the spirit descending ... *Thou art my beloved son.*

Eucalyptus trees floundered on the far bank, laying green and grey shadows like camouflage over the water. On the near bank 111 men from the Indonesian Church of Jesus were queuing to be baptized. Their voices were hushed, their smiles squashed, and they seemed insane with happiness.

A priest stood in the river, dunking pilgrims in rapid succession. Every time someone plunged beneath the water, silver ripples stirred the surface. Then the pilgrims splashed up again, their faces shining, their clothes collapsed.

Meanwhile 111 wives watched from the shore, applauding as each one went under.

A gift shop the size of a small hangar opened out near the entrance. Inside I found a remarkable selection of souvenirs. There were bottles of eau de toilette with Biblical names – King David, King Solomon, and the Lion of Judah – on sale for $45. And there were bottles of pomegranate wine – dry, sparkling, and premium port, this last for $85. And olivewood bookrests shaped like praying hands, on sale for $76.50. And a Cana Wine Holy Communion set, on sale for $55. A Dead Sea gourmet salt set for $39.50. A Jerusalem tote bag with black, white, yellow and gold lettering for $29.50. A sterling silver Code of Moses amulet for $136.30. A glow-in-the-dark rosary wall hanging for $15.30. A glass cross filled with Jordan River water and adorned with crystals for $47.60. And a book promising to teach the reader Hebrew in just ten minutes a day, originally priced at $42, but now discounted to $37.50.

Photographs covered the entrance hall with smiles from the many, many celebrities who had visited Yardenit. Alas, I forgot to note down their names.

By this point I was sick of pilgrim shrines, but there was one more site to see. So I hiked west from the River Jordan in the direction of Nazareth, and after a day and a half I reached the lonely summit of Mt Tabor. A walled monastery occupied the heights, with medieval fortifications embedded into the hillsides. I spent an hour circling the ramparts, eventually arriving at a grand set of gates. Beyond the gates an avenue of cypresses led to the Church of the Transfiguration. Although built in 1924, it was styled like something older, with triangular gables, rectangular windows, and a stocky arch framing the entrance – robust as a Romanesque basilica. But, coming closer, I noticed delicate patterns chiselled into the capitals, cornices, pediments and eaves.

Inside, twin arches separated the aisles from the nave, while the nave was also divided, the front half leading to the crypt chapel and the sanctuary elevated above. Above that was a domed apse decorated with a mosaic of Christ in blinding robes, floating on a flat gold sky. Moses hung to his right, Elijah to his left, watching the scene from a polite pair of clouds.

A group of American priests were gathering near the crypt. Their guide explained that, although the Bible never names the site where Christ met the Old Testament prophets, tradition places the event on Mt Tabor. Surrounded by the level farmland of the Jezreel Valley, its peak could be seen from all over Galilee. According to one medieval source, the Empress Helena founded the first chapel on Mt Tabor when touring the Holy Land in the fourth century. No other record of that chapel exists, but towards the end of the century St Jerome wrote of visiting the tabernacle here. By the year 570, according to the anonymous Piacenza pilgrim, three churches occupied the site, and a century later the German bishop Arculf recorded a monastery and several cells.

St Helena, St Jerome, Bishop Arculf and the Piacenza pilgrim – these were some of the earliest Christian travellers in the region. The accounts of their journeys give the impression that, even in Antiquity, the basic pilgrim infrastructure was in place: monasteries, guesthouses and guided tours. But it was not until the Middle Ages that travel to holy sites was widely encouraged as a path to salvation.

To understand why, we need to meet another pilgrim

from this period. He did not set out for Galilee or Jerusalem, but to find the Garden of Eden.

His name was Brendan the Bold.

Brendan was born on the west coast of Ireland in the last decades of the fifth century. As a young man he established monasteries in Wales, Brittany and Scotland. Then, aged seventy, he left Ireland with seventeen monks to sail in search of Paradise.

The pilgrims spent the next seven years drifting between improbable islands on a boat made from leather. During this time they exorcized an Ethiopian devil, dined on a sea monster and met an elderly hermit who ate nothing but fish, fed to him by a friendly otter. Landing on one island, the crew lit a fire, causing the ground to shake – too late they noticed that they were parked on the shoulder of a whale. Passing another island, this one a stub of rock, they spotted a figure crouching on top while the waves flayed the flesh from his body. It turned out to be Judas, on holiday from hell.

Eventually the boat reached an island where the sun never set. A glowing young man greeted the monks and explained the true purpose of their pilgrimage: not to find Paradise, but to discover the secrets of the ocean. Then he sent Brendan home again, for soon the abbot would die.

Brendan's journey entered Irish folklore. During the ninth century these legends were collected in a manuscript called the *Navigatio Sancti Brendani Abbatis*. The story was so popular it was still being read during the Age of Exploration, when scholars assumed that Brendan had made it across the ocean. Unlikely though it sounds, the islands visited by the saint correspond loosely with those that crown the North Atlantic. On one island the rivers flowed with molten gold, rather like an Icelandic volcano.

Another was called the Isle of Sheep, which is the meaning of the word *faroe*. We know that Irish hermits travelled at least this far because Norse settlers in Iceland and the Faroe Islands found the bells and crosiers they left behind. Keep sailing north and the 'crystal pillars' described in the *Navigatio* look a lot like icebergs, while the veil of cloud concealing the final island might be the fog zone off the Grand Banks of Newfoundland.

Whether or not Brendan made it to America, his journey was only one of many long-distance pilgrimages performed by Celtic clerics in the Early Middle Ages. As the saint was sailing west, Irish bishops were travelling south in the direction of Rome – the first pilgrims on the Via Francigena. By the seventh century a monk named Cathaldus had arrived in Jerusalem.

At the time Ireland, not Italy, was the continent's Christian heartland.

Chart the first five hundred years of Christianity on a map and the religion will begin in Palestine, disperse across the Levant, establish a colony in Rome, migrate through the Roman Empire, and eventually reach its far Celtic fringe. But in Late Antiquity that map was turned inside out. Rome was sacked twice in the fifth century, and then fought over by Germanic tribes. Jerusalem was lost to both Sassanid and Arab armies. Once the Roman legions retreated from their northern provinces, only Ireland – which had never been under imperial rule – remained Christian.

Ireland's monastic communities were modelled on Egypt's Desert Fathers. However, Irish monks sought their deserts overseas, establishing hermit cells on the islands and edgelands of the Anglo-Celtic archipelago. From the mid-sixth century they also discovered a wilderness in the ruins of the Roman Empire.

The most famous was St Columbanus, who sailed

from County Down in the last years of the sixth century to evangelize the Merovingian Empire. Columbanus founded monasteries in the Frankish and Lombard kingdoms that have survived to the present day, while his companions took Celtic Christianity from Sweden to southern Italy, a handful even making it to Kiev. They were known as *peregrini pro Christo*, exiles for Christ. The term was derived from the Roman word for foreigner – *peregrinus* – and our modern word pilgrim preserves this sense of being a visitor in a distant land. Although the New Testament contains no teaching on pilgrimage, the word *peregrini* was used in St Jerome's Vulgate Bible to describe the holy men and women who lived before Jesus: strangers and pilgrims on this earth. In other words, they were exiles in a fallen world, their true home in the company of Christ.

But, to get a sense of what moved St Brendan, St Columbanus and the armies of *peregrini*, it's best to look at the Cambrai Homily – the first example of extended prose in Old Irish. The homily describes three states of martyrdom. A red martyr is one who has been killed for his faith. A white martyr is one who gives up his life for God, perhaps leaving his family to withdraw from the world. A green martyr is one who experiences death without dying, spending the night on a bed of nettles, say, or sleeping next to a corpse.

Unlike the first Christians, who were persecuted for their beliefs, the Irish Church had no blood martyrs. Yet, the homily argued, inner martyrdom was possible through pilgrimage and penitent works. Departing your monastery to explore pagan Europe was a sacrifice of the self.

In eighth-century Ireland this argument became canon law. Pilgrimage was given as penance for the most grievous sins: incest, bestiality and sacrilege. Cain – the first born, the first to kill – was banished by God to live always in exile, and thus St Columbanus's penitential handbook condemned a murderer to be 'like Cain a wanderer and fugitive on the face of the earth.'

If you killed a stranger, you were forbidden any fixed abode for seven years. Kill a family member and the punishment was everlasting exile.

So the idea that each sin carried a specific tariff of penance and that sacred travel could atone for the worst sins – this was a creation of Celtic Christianity. Even though wandering is threaded through the Bible – the Exodus from Egypt and the long march to the Promised Land; Christ roaming round Judea and his apostles crisscrossing the Roman Empire – it was the *peregrini* who turned it into a penitential practice. They were the ones who saw sin as suffering and pilgrimage as a path to salvation, providing the foundation for the whole edifice of sacred travel, from networks of monasteries to flagellant armies, from crusader campaigns to Roman Jubilees. Nearing the end of my journey, I felt close to those exiles, walking alone through an unknown world. And I was not surprised to learn that, when the first English pilgrim travelled to Jerusalem – St Willibald, who left Wessex in the year 722 – it was in imitation of the Irish monks. On reaching the Holy Land, Willibald visited Bethlehem, Nazareth and Galilee, even stopping for a night at the monastery on Mt Tabor.

September became October. I stayed a day in Nazareth and then crossed the Mt Carmel Range, the ridgeline dividing Galilee from the Mediterranean coast. By now the rucksack's frame had snapped, its broken edge jabbing at the base of my spine. Meanwhile the sun lowered and the light thinned – autumn almost here. As I walked I counted down the stops until Jerusalem: Netanya, Tel Aviv, and then the slow climb into the Judean Hills. Although I was confident about reaching the city, I was unsure if finishing the journey would make anything better. Yet I took comfort in the idea that there was no distance which patience could not endure, and sometimes thought of extending my route – south to Eilat, east into Egypt, and south once more to Mt Sinai. At other times I thought of England, and the misted colours that mark the turning season. But most of the time my mind was empty.

On Saturday I was back by the sea, and for the next three days I tramped on the beach, all the way to Tel Aviv. That afternoon the wind was up and the horizon tainted with storms. I shuffled over the loose sand, past shacks made from weather-worn boards. One contained a rack of plastic canoes, another was cluttered with holiday tat – buckets, spades, and towels blown loose from their hangings. Two fishermen sat in the last shack, their faces ancient, their hands too, their limbs like knotted twine. After that came beachside apartments with salt-chapped skin and sandy hillocks topped with bleached tufts of grass. Rubbish lay stranded on the foreshore – mostly picnic castoffs and punctured pieces of netting. Out at sea a truck tyre wheeled in the current and two kite surfers wrestled with the clouds.

At teatime I heard thudding up ahead. To begin with I could not tell if it was an orbiting helicopter or some industrial machinery, but then I realized it was bass being pumped from a speaker. As I rounded a crag in the coast-line, I found a hundred people in a huddle of bluffs. There were children splashing on the shore, teenagers drinking on the heights, and a large group in their late twenties, early thirties, dancing on the sand. Most wore swimming costumes with rainbow scarves tied to their necks and luminous handprints slapped on their skin. They were tanned and fit and shining with sweat.

A woman stood at the edge, smelling of suncream and spirits. When I asked what was happening, she told me it was a birthday party, a secret party.

Then she said: 'I lived in New York, Berlin, San Francisco, but I never found parties like this.'

Then she danced off into the sea.

On the far side of the crowd, beyond the makeshift bar and the portable decks, a pair of Ethiopian men sat on the back of a horse, wearing pink shorts and matching pink polo shirts. A ruined aqueduct rose from the sand behind them, running down the beach for a kilometre or so. Three more men – these ones dressed in pirate outfits – were leaning against its base, peeing on the pitted yellow stone.

The following afternoon I reached Netanya, and that evening stayed in a village on the outskirts of the city, in a bungalow with timber walls and lino floors. My host was from South Africa originally, but emigrated to Israel in her twenties. She had a round face and round eyes, with a lingering look of bemusement. Her name was Channi.

We sat in the kitchen drinking milky cups of coffee. The room was clean, but as Channi spoke she wiped invisible stains from the sideboard and rearranged the uncluttered shelves. At first she seemed timid, until I mentioned this afternoon's beach party and she began to beam, telling me about the hippies who used to live at the bottom of her garden. They were part of a collective she met in the Negev Desert and invited to camp in the field beside the bungalow. Channi hoped they would farm the land, but instead they sat in their tents getting stoned. 'One time there were twenty-six people here – Buddhists and spiritualists and crystal healers. Every day I came home from work I would find another person doing walking meditation or silent retreat. Some of them stayed for years.'

I wondered why Channi had left South Africa, but when I asked the reason she started talking about her husband. Bernard ran the veterinary clinic next door, she explained, and if the garden wasn't draped in hippies, it housed a menagerie of animals instead.

'Every animal you can think of – even alligators. There was an alligator farm near here and we helped look after the babies. A few years ago Bernie had to perform surgery on one of the males, until halfway through the operation it stopped breathing. So then he gave it mouth-to-mouth with a straw.' She looked up, her expression flushed with pride. 'It was on the news – in all the newspapers – *Man gives kiss of life to a croc.*'

At nine o'clock Bernard came in from the clinic. He was very short, very wide, with stubby fingers and a stringy beard. When he moved, his shoulders swayed from side to side, as if warming up for a fight.

Channi prepared three plates of avocado, toast and cottage cheese, and then we ate together in the kitchen. During the meal Bernard discussed the kibbutz reunion he had attended last weekend, for those like him who moved to Israel in the 1960s. Since then the group had scattered, the majority emigrating to Britain, America and Canada. They either grew disillusioned with community life, or else felt betrayed by Israel's treatment of the Palestinians. Bernard called this *the dilemma*.

'During the dinner I made a joke. It was about religious fundamentalists – Orthodox, *haredi*, the hats, the wigs – I don't remember what it was about. But I remember the response. People were shocked. They were offended. Nobody laughed. Nobody found it funny. One person told me to apologize. Apologize! For a joke! It has been a terrible lesson. A terrible lesson. Other people have lived their lives. I can't know what they think. I can't know what they've experienced. I can never know what they will find offensive. I have learnt a terrible lesson.'

The more he spoke, the louder his voice. He never shouted; it simply swelled from inside his chest.

On the last day of the reunion Bernard went round each guest asking why they left Israel. Most people mentioned *the dilemma*. 'I told them: you've lost sight! You've lost sight of the bigger picture! For thousands of years the Jews have been persecuted. For thousands of years we were treated like dirt, massacred at the slightest excuse. Not just the twentieth century – right through the Middle Ages. When the crusaders marched to Jerusalem, they massacred every Jew they could get their hands on. Every one! And all that time, all those thousands of years, the Jews waited. They waited and prayed: won't it be great when we have a state of our own. When we can live in safety. When we can worship how we like. Thousands of years! I was born in 1948. I was given the best birthday present ever. I was born in that tiny window of time when the Jews had a homeland. There was never any doubt in my mind where I would live. Never any question. Thousands of years of suffering and finally we have a state where we're the majority. Finally we have a home. We're not going to give that up. Sometimes the EU, the UN, they can't understand. Sometimes they criticize us. That's the dilemma we have to live with every day. Sure it's hard. Sure you get let down. But I feel sorry for those people who left, because they don't know the joy of living here. They don't know the joy of living in this miracle of history.'

Bernard kept talking. He talked about the 1967 war and the 1973 war, about the Golan Heights and the Sinai Peninsula. While he spoke, Channi circled the room with impatient movements, now cleaning the sideboard, now restacking the shelves. Then she washed the food from our plates and announced that she was off to bed. But her husband paid no attention, going on and on about Obama and Netanyahu, about Saudi Arabia and Iran.

By the end of the evening his face was purple, his lips flecked with spit.

'Everyone has tried to conquer this land. The Persians, the Romans, the Arabs, the Ottomans, the French, the British – every empire wants Jerusalem for its own. But we will never give up the State of Israel. We will destroy Iran if we have to. If we have to, we will be the only country to stand up for freedom, for democracy, the only country to stand up against terrorism. Because they want one thing: to drive us into the sea. They will stop at nothing until they have driven us into the sea.' He was heaving now like a boxer midway through a bout. 'We will destroy the world before we give up the State of Israel, understand? We will destroy the world before we give up our home.'

Perhaps my host talked himself tired that night, because at breakfast next morning he was subdued. We sat in the kitchen again, Bernard wearing striped pyjama trousers and a stained vest, sipping his coffee in silence. Then the telephone rang, an anxious voice at the other end. A friend's dogs had just eaten a packet of rat poison.

In an instant Bernard was bellowing. 'Bring them here! Bring them right here!'

He charged off to get changed. 'You're about to see a whole load of dogs being sick.'

Minutes later a jeep pulled up outside the bungalow, carrying three Alsatians and a young man with a fretful expression. Bernard, now dressed in dungarees, herded the dogs into the garden, fed each one an emetic, and stood around with arms crossed, waiting for them to throw up. Occasionally a dog would whimper, but none of them retched.

I went inside to pack, yet I could still hear my host's voice in the garden, interrogating his friend and shouting at the Alsatians: 'I don't want anyone eating anyone else's vomit . . . No vomit? Nobody's been sick? . . . You're definitely having your stomachs pumped.'

When I went outside again, the dogs were being ushered towards the clinic.

'Leaving?' Bernard asked. 'I thought you were staying for weeks.'

I explained that I still had 130 kilometres to walk.

'But we haven't finished your Zionist education!'

I said that I was sorry.

'Don't forget what I taught you. Don't ever forget what I taught you.'

I promised to remember.

'Now shake my hand.'

We shook hands. Then he hurried inside to rescue the dying dogs.

The rest of the day I walked barefoot along the beach. At first the air was clear, and twenty-five kilometres away I could see the shining towers of Tel Aviv. Later the air hazed and the neat geometry of the scene – sea and sand, earth and sky – lost all focus. I hiked one hour, two hours, three, my surroundings changing so slowly that I seemed barely to be moving. I was hoping to walk without hurry, patient as a saint after ten months on foot, but tramping over the cushioned ground, I soon became bored. My back was blistered from where the rucksack rubbed, the skin beginning to peel. Sunlight shone off the burning sand, and the waves shuddered beside me.

That afternoon I came to a nudist beach. There was no

notice, only a dozen naked bathers arranged on the sand. Middle-aged men strutted on the shore, and a couple eased into the water with gasps of laughter. Farther on, an old man slept in the shade, his body wire-thin but for the pot belly he cradled in his arms.

Afterwards the beach disappeared, the coast collapsing to form a cliff of rock and a causeway of broken boulders. A sign sent hikers off the sand on a four-kilometre detour, but I was barely halfway to Tel Aviv, so I clambered onto the boulders and kept hiking.

Sometimes the causeway was level, creating a path of even-packed rubble. Sometimes it was jagged and I had to edge forwards with arms open wide, as if balancing on a tightrope. Sometimes the water gurgled between my feet and I imagined the tide coming in, lifting me off the tightrope, out into endless space. To my left the cliffs rose sheer; to my right the sea stretched away without seeming to touch the sky. Ahead the shoreline was crooked, making it impossible to see how far the landfall lasted. Yet I kept peering forwards, eyes stinging in the spray thrown up from the waves. I passed boulders black with water. Pebbles glinting with salt. Shells like sharded porcelain and gravel gritting the sand. Sheets of sunlight tremored over the water, as the afternoon sun bleared.

An hour later I was back on the sand, hiking into the marina town of Herzliya. It was six o'clock. Tel Aviv was ten kilometres away. My ankles felt feeble, my knees collapsed, but I could glimpse the dim mass of mixed industry on the city's rim, as well as the distant high-rises like blinking ladders of light.

As I walked the final length of beach, tragic colours filled the sky. People were out jogging and surfing, but nobody noticed the quiet apocalypse going on above. To the west burnt pieces of evening hung over the horizon – yellow and orange, ember and flame – while the clouds to the east were smothered in purple smoke. In front of me the blue sand was ribbed with shadows. When the wind dragged across the beach, it caused dustings of sand to shift from one rib to another, creating a web of white powder that quivered at my feet, as though the surf had drifted in off the sea and floated onto the foreshore.

When I reached Tel Aviv, night was burying the city. A park ran parallel to the beach, leading into the harbour. Playground rides were propped on the sand, the wind shaking the swings and twisting the merry-go-round.

An Orthodox family had gathered in one corner of the playground. The father's head was bowed, one hand clamping down his black fedora, the other hand holding his frock coat together. When the coat-tails flapped out behind him, his figure was exposed, slight as a charcoal sketch. The mother wore a long skirt and a woollen jacket, hair blown hectic over her face. She was kneeling to play with her daughter, yet when the child ran away she did not give chase, her eyes turned towards the sea. Meanwhile the daughter ran forwards with flailing arms, willing the wind to lift her. But no matter how high she jumped, she could not quit this earth.

What was the verse from Isaiah that Or's father urged me to remember? *They that wait on God shall renew their strength; they shall put forth new feathers like eagles; they shall run and not be weary; they shall walk and not hunger.* And then there was Bernard's warning from last night: *We will destroy the world before we give up our home.* Was it fear that made them talk this way? Or the belief that Israel must hold onto Jerusalem until the end of time? According to the Book of Isaiah, before the world ends the Messiah will lead the Jewish people into an age of peace and justice. As they assemble in the Promised Land, the Temple will be rebuilt and all nations recognize the God of Israel. This is why, when the crusaders set off from Europe, they hoped to restore the Temple and so cause Christ's return. And why, when Christopher Columbus journeyed across the Atlantic four centuries later, he was not planning to discover a continent, but to spark the Second Coming.

Although Columbus's first voyage has traditionally been explained in terms of trade – accessing the valuable spice markets in the East by establishing a new route to Cathay – that was not how the explorer understood his journey. For him, Jerusalem was the true target.

When raising funds for his voyage, Columbus argued that a western route to Asia would allow European armies to outflank the Caliphate, and that the riches of the Indies could fund future campaigns in the Holy Land. True, he was playing on the imperial fantasies of his patrons, but only because they coincided with his own pious sense of purpose.

The logbook from Columbus's first voyage shows how he fitted his journey into the crusader tradition. In the prologue to the published version – a rough copy of the original made by Bartolomé de las Casas and nicknamed the *Diario* – Columbus presents himself as a missionary, travelling to the Indies to convert the native population. While at sea he more closely resembles a monk, keeping the canonical hours and celebrating mass each Sunday. During times of danger the whole crew become pilgrims, vowing to visit Europe's major shrines if they survive the journey. They even stop midway across the ocean to look for the phantom isles visited by Brendan the Bold, whose *Navigatio* Columbus consulted before leaving.

Once the crew make it over the Atlantic, more and more of the *Diario* is devoted to the search for gold. A sort of prophetic geography was at work here. Solomon built his temple using treasure from Ophir, a lost region that Biblical scholars placed in India. According to one alchemical theory, the heat of the tropics intensified the process through which base metals matured into precious. Columbus was confident that, if he could locate the treasures of Ophir, he could finance the retaking of Jerusalem. As he claimed in a letter to Ferdinand and Isabella, written shortly before his return to Spain: 'In seven years from today I will be able to pay Your Highnesses for five thousand cavalry and fifty thousand foot soldiers for the war and conquest of Jerusalem, for which purpose this enterprise was undertaken.'

But Columbus's journey was more than just an ambitious scheme to fund a final crusade. It was also a necessary step to bring about Judgement Day.

In order for Christ to return, the whole world had to be converted. This meant the globe must be mapped and every civilization taught the Gospels. And time was running out, because Columbus believed the world would end in 1656.

This argument was put forward in *El Libro de las Profecías*, a commonplace book that he assembled between the third and fourth voyages to the New World. It provides a commentary on various quotations culled from the Bible and the Church Fathers, as well as a range of classical and medieval authors. The opening pages summarize its purpose: 'Here begins the book, or handbook, of sources, statements, opinions and prophecies on the subject of the recovery of God's Holy City and Mount Zion, and on the discovery and evangelization of the Indies and of all other peoples and nations.'

The book's apocalyptic timetable drew on three sources. First, St Augustine, who claimed Creation would last for seven millennia. Second, Joachim of Fiore, the twelfth-century theologian who argued that history would enter its third and final stage some time around 1260. Third, Cardinal Pierre d'Ailly, a fourteenth-century astrologer who totted up the years between Adam and Christ, subtracted the total from seven thousand, and concluded the apocalypse was due in 1656.

Columbus also believed the discovery of the West Indies was one of the events preceding the Second Coming. Several passages in the *Libro* suggest that finding new islands was a prophetic sign. Taken together, they imply that the Americas were revealed as the final step in a cosmic plan. It was not some happy accident, but a moment of providential history. Like those crusader knights who sought God's hand in every stage of their campaign, Columbus became convinced that heaven was on his side.

The explorer often referred to his discoveries in Biblical terms. Soon after his death, the Spanish historian Francisco López de Gómara did the same, calling them 'The greatest event since the creation of the world, excluding only the incarnation of Him that created it'. This was the kind of exalted rhetoric that accompanied the conquest of Jerusalem. Its target had shifted from east to west, but the sense of divine endorsement remained the same.

Such language helped turn the Age of Exploration into an Age of Empire, justifying both commercial exploitation and military conquest. The natural resources uncovered in the Americas were seen as heavenly rewards, while the new civilizations were vast invitations to evangelize. And the campaigns fought against native populations became holy wars.

Before long, the ranks of sailors, traders and missionaries filled with ambitious young men united by a sense that they were performing God's work – the same young men who once filled the ranks of crusader armies.

For all I had learnt about the crusades, I still struggled to understand that righteous blindness – reading divine intention into the turmoil of history. However, the following evening I visited the Baptists' Village and met one of its modern manifestations.

I reached the village at dusk. All afternoon I had hiked east from Tel Aviv, by the banks of the Yarkon River, and after twenty kilometres came to a spread of bungalows bordered by a chain-link fence. A young man called David said I could camp in the orchard at the centre of the village. Its orange trees were flooded with light from a nearby baseball field, where a game was being played between two teams of teenage boys. As I pitched my tent, I heard the umpire calling strikes.

David came back a few minutes later, carrying a tray of sandwiches. He was tall, slim, soft-spoken and smiling, like those gentle figures I had met in dozens of monasteries.

We sat at a picnic table together, my host asking questions: how long since I left, how far I had come, and how it felt to be a few days from finishing. This last question I failed to answer, because I did not know if I would be glad to reach Jerusalem, or whether anything was healed by walking all this way. So I said that perhaps I would keep going; perhaps the pilgrimage would never end.

David began talking about himself. He explained that he came to Israel a decade ago, after his family emigrated from Georgia. When I asked how he ended up here, he told me that the village was once owned by an American branch of the Baptist Church, but was now an informal headquarters for Israel's Messianic Jews.

'Messianic Jews?'

'Jews who believe Jesus was the Messiah.'

'Like Christians?'

'We believe in the Old Testament and the New Testament. Both the same.'

'I see,' I said, but I did not see.

'When the Jews were offered the Messiah, they turned him down. Christianity became the religion of the Gentiles and the Chosen People suffered many years of hardship. But, when the Jews accept Jesus, it will bring a thousand years of peace to Israel.'

After I finished eating, David showed me the village office. Inside there were racks of leaflets printed with a cross at the centre of a six-point star. As David made tea he explained that missionary work was forbidden in Israel and that many Israelis were suspicious of Christianity – the reason none of the village buildings looked like churches. However, people visited to use the sports facilities and conference facilities, or sent their children to the summer camp. And, if they wanted to find out about Jesus, there were classes and study groups every day.

'Does the Baptist Church pay for all this?' I asked.

David looked embarrassed. 'Some people think Jesus will not come again until the Holy Land is in Christian hands. But, if the Jews are taught that Jesus was the Messiah, maybe—'

'Maybe the world will end?'

My host sniffed, smiled, said nothing more. Moments later he hurried outside, claiming that there was somebody who wanted to meet me.

Once David was gone, I flicked through the leaflets. One or two were in English, containing a mix of Old Testament prophecies, Gospel parables and the odd verse from the Book of Revelation. What a curious place! A tiny slice of the Bible Belt transplanted to Tel Aviv. Then

David was back, accompanied by a scruffy man in green overalls, his white hair wisping loose from under a red cap. Before greeting me or introducing himself, the man asked: 'When were you saved?'

I did not understand the question.

He tried again: 'When did you accept Jesus as your personal saviour?'

I was not sure that I had.

He looked alarmed. 'Listen, you can walk from here to China, walk the whole world round, but if you haven't accepted Jesus, it won't matter one bit.'

The stranger's name was Stan. He was an American, but had lived in Israel for decades, working as the village handyman.

Standing in the doorway, Stan lectured me on the path to salvation. 'You could be a good friend, good husband, good son. You could work hard at your job and volunteer all your free time. You could be the best dad ever, but if you haven't accepted Jesus, you're down here—' He motioned towards his shin. 'I'm no saint, but no matter how many times I mess up, I've let Jesus into my life, so I'm up here—' He gestured at the ceiling. 'I know I'm going to be saved.'

When I asked Stan why he wasn't troubled by divine justice – all those hard-working husbands condemned to hell – he repeated the line: *No one comes to the Father except through me.* Then he started talking about the afterlife. 'Imagine your hand strapped above a candle. Imagine the skin turning pink, turning red. Imagine it blistering, going black, your whole arm shaking. But the skin grows back every time it burns away, so no matter what you do, the pain will never die.'

Next he talked about heaven. It sounded even worse. 'I'll be there. David'll be there. We'll be laughing and high-fiving and praising Jesus all day long. And if we see you there we'll jump around like crazy, because we'll know you accepted him too. You accepted Jesus as your personal saviour.'

David stared at the ground, nodding his head without saying a word.

I asked Stan if he ever had doubts. Never, he said. He remembered when he was a boy, just seven years old, sleeping in a bunk bed that he shared with his brother. Even though the mattress was small, he would press up on one side to make space for Jesus. It was an innocent love, he explained. An innocent, childlike love. He had never lost it. Never once in his life had he doubted his love for Jesus. 'Tomorrow you might be run down on the road, killed dead by a truck. Tomorrow you could see angels stepping out of the sky and every one of us raptured. Eternity with the flames in hell, or eternity with the Saviour in heaven – for me it's a no-brainer.'

Listening to Stan speak, I felt exposed, as though my pilgrimage was just playing at faith. But I also felt disappointed, because if this was conviction, I wanted no share in it. Yet the more he talked – 'You coming here wasn't an accident. You meeting us, you learning about Jesus: that wasn't a coincidence!' – the more I wondered if his certainty was something different from faith, was in fact its opposite.

It was getting late. While David switched off the lights, Stan gripped my shoulder, saying: 'Two days', three days' time, when you're done walking, just remember you haven't reached the real Jerusalem yet. That journey hasn't even started.'

David escorted me back to my tent. The air was cool, and he rubbed his hands to keep warm. As we crossed the village, I asked whether he had always been a Messianic Jew. He replied that, even though his family were Jewish, his childhood was secular, and when he applied for *aliyah* he unthinkingly gave Christianity as his religion. The embassy corrected the mistake; the application was successful; he moved to Israel and was promptly converted.

'I was a normal teenager. I wasn't interested in religion. I didn't know anything about the Messiah, until one day I read the Gospels and learnt that Jesus was tortured for me, that he died for me. Afterwards my whole life changed.'

'How?'

'Do you know *The Pilgrim's Progress*?'

'Of course!'

'At the beginning, the pilgrim has a burden on his back. The burden is so heavy he has to leave his home, his family, just to be free. But only when he finds the true way – then his burden falls off. No more sin. No more death. That's how it was for me.'

The village was dark now, the grass in the orchard damp. Even though the baseball game had ended, the field was awash with light, glossing the dew on the door to my tent. As I shook hands with David, I could smell woodsmoke and leafmould at the edges of the night, and see a misted moon rising above the branches. Then I ducked inside, dug through my rucksack, and took out a copy of *The Pilgrim's Progress*. I had carried the book from Canterbury and tried several times to read it. Though I sympathized with the hapless protagonist, I was put off by the self-righteous narrator. But David's description moved me, because I understood his desperate desire to walk free from the past, carrying his sins like a burden on his back. So I slipped into my sleeping bag and began reading again.

The Pilgrim's Progress was published in 1678 and provides a coda of sorts to the story of medieval pilgrimage. Although the Reformation should have ended pilgrimage in Protestant countries – along with relics, indulgences and belief in Purgatory – Puritan preachers still relied on the metaphor of sacred travel. Bunyan's book is the best-known example, using the journey to the Celestial City as an allegory for the Christian's passage through this life. I was surprised that David mentioned the text, but I knew that it was popular in America. At the end of the seventeenth century, while Puritan colonies spread through the country, two books could be found in every household: the Bible, of course, and a copy of *The Pilgrim's Progress*.

During this period Bunyan's severe, self-reliant faith was married to something more hysterical.

After the Reformation, the increased attention paid to Scripture, and the literal reading of Biblical passages, renewed popular interest in eschatology. There was a growing sense among Protestant sects that the end times were not some distant allegory, but an imminent reality. The Pilgrim Fathers carried this conviction to America.

In 'A Model of Christian Charity' – John Winthrop's famous 'City upon a Hill' sermon from 1630 – the future governor of the Massachusetts Bay Colony compared his fellow emigrants to Israelites, escaping bondage in Egypt to cross the desert in search of freedom. By eliding the New World and the Promised Land, Winthrop not only looked back to Exodus, but looked forward to Revelation.

Millenarian theology makes a mirror of history. What started with Creation will end with Apocalypse. Thus, if contemporary events echo the Old Testament, the end times must be near. This was why Winthrop's contemporary, John Cotton, argued that the Puritan migration to New England was a necessary step before Judgement Day. The next step, according to his close friend and fellow minister, Increase Mather, was for the Jewish people to gather in Israel and convert to Christianity. In this way, the apocalyptic fantasies of those Renaissance explorers survived into the modern era.

Winthrop, Cotton, Mather – these were the founding intellects behind the Puritan project in America. Although the sect's influence waned in England, it remained an important presence in religious life across the Atlantic, and vital to the idea of American exceptionalism. For some historians the national myth began in that dizzying moment when a few exiles on the edge of an immense landmass bound their fate with Israel's.

To a modern audience these eschatological theories seem at once paranoid and preposterous. Perhaps, however, the longing for apocalypse is something hopeful, because when the end draws near what we love becomes more precious. Or perhaps it is an epic form of that more basic religious impulse: to stamp the everyday with lasting consequence. According to one apocalyptic tradition, as history comes to a close we shall return to the Garden of Eden – and maybe Stan was waiting for that promised moment when Creation is finally perfected. Of course, once the truth of prophecy is plain to see, once heaven burns bright upon the earth, there will be no need for belief. So the Second Coming means the end of religion too. Yet, lying in my tent that night, what I felt was not hope, not fear, but pity. Stan was a long way from home, exiled on the edge of an immense landmass, and desperate to see Paradise before he died.

On Friday morning I entered the Judean Hills. That evening I reached a monastery on the outskirts of Jerusalem called St John in the Desert. I was hoping to spend the night, but when I arrived one of the sisters explained that no men were allowed inside. Instead she gave me a bag of food – apples, pitta bread, tinned sardines – and told me about the time she walked from Marseille to Rome. When her pilgrimage ended, she decided to become a nun.

St John in the Desert was built on the side of a hill, below a village named Even Sapir. From the village's highest point I could see Jerusalem extending to the east. As the sun went down, streetlamps pierced the darkness and headlights poured liquid along the roads. The Old City was twelve kilometres away, but I did not wish to end my journey at night, so I ducked into a gully and found a quiet spot to camp.

Next morning, a little after four, I was off.

For the first hour I followed untidy footpaths onto the Mt Herzl ridgeline. The landscape looked ancient in the dim dawn: terraced hillsides, sloping orchards and villages of piled stone. By five o'clock the stars were smudged and the night was washed with grey.

A wide road topped the ridgeline, two lanes one way and three lanes the other, with twin tram tracks running down the middle. This was the Herzl Boulevard, which formed the western border of Jerusalem. Office blocks and apartment buildings lined the road, all built from the same pallid stone – sometimes pinkish, sometimes yellow, and sometimes an off-white shade like linen. The air was clear, dawn stripping the dead skin of the night and sharpening the city's outlines. When a band of daylight lifted the horizon, it caused the walls to shimmer, the windows to shine. Then the daylight raised the rest of the sky, solar panels flashing and satellite dishes blinking. I kept repeating the same phrase to myself – *the Celestial City, the Celestial City* – until the sun came up and I lost my way.

From Mt Herzel the route dropped towards a motorway and climbed into a neighbourhood of public buildings shaped like monumental rubble. I was walking fast, but there was still no sign of the Old City. I turned left, turned right, circling fenced compounds and walled campuses, or marching up avenues of government offices. I doubled back on myself once, twice, one more time, until eventually I arrived at the Knesset – the Israeli parliament – a flat-roofed slab of tawny stone with pillared sides. It sat on a rocky hill sprinkled with shrubs and was empty that morning except for the police standing guard at the gate. When I asked directions, they could not understand me, and though I repeated the question until I was panting with frustration, they simply patted my shoulder and pointed me back.

Another hill rose up beyond the parliament, its base banked with apartments, its slopes stacked with towers. These neighbourhoods were set tight together, the streets between either steep or winding. The buildings at the top were wider spaced, each one tagged with a sign – the Van Leer Institute, the Shalom Hartman Institute, and the president's official residence. Next to them were rows of stone villas, their gardens bursting with palms, their balconies strung with bougainvillea.

The place was awake now – traffic in the roads, joggers on the pavement – and from open windows I heard the babble of televisions and the shrieking of children. By this point my rucksack hung off my shoulders, the padding fallen away from the broken frame and the skin on my back beginning to sore. Though I traipsed down avenues of offices, down avenues of apartments, the Old City seemed no closer.

Some time after seven I joined King David Street, which lifted through playgrounds and parkland towards the stepped shell of a modernist hotel. On the right of the road was a stubby column of stone with shuttered blades pinned to the cupola. It was a windmill, a tiny Kentish windmill.

The windmill looked out on one last hill: Mt Zion. An abbey occupied the summit, four towers buttressing the church and a fifth tower rising from the cellblock. Its walls were striped with blue stone, its dome a cone of blue metal.

The Valley of Hinnom fell away to the south, desert-coloured buildings tumbling from its sides. To the north ran the walls of the Old City, a shelf of rock three or four storeys high, divided by watchtowers and crested with battlements. Behind the battlements I could see clustered spires and minarets.

Fifteen minutes later I was standing beneath the walls. In places the stone was enamel-smooth, in places textured like porridge. A paved walkway ringed the site, which I followed as far as the Jaffa Gate.

When I reached the gate, I knelt to take off my boots. The paving was still cool from the night, its surface weathered soft by fifty centuries of footfall.

Lacing the boots around my neck, I stepped barefoot into the Old City.

The Tower of David reared up on my right, great banks of masonry securing the citadel. Hotels and gift shops filled the square beyond, where a tour group dressed in floppy hats were gathering. I imagined striding up to shake their hands, crying out that it was over, it was finally over. But I was too stunned to speak, so instead I slipped my rucksack from my shoulders and lay on the floor. When I looked up, the dawn sky had given way to bright blue. The sun was bright, the air bright, the buildings gauzy with light.

Glance at a map of Jerusalem's Old City and you will see a lopsided square split into four uneven quarters. Top left is the Christian Quarter, top right the Muslim Quarter, bottom left the Armenian Quarter, and bottom right the Jewish Quarter. Temple Mount straddles the eastern half, while the Church of the Holy Sepulchre floats somewhere off-centre.

I spent my first days in Jerusalem wandering the warren streets of this square, between churches and chapels, monasteries and convents, synagogues, mosques, museums and tombs. As I roamed round I felt a growing sense of disappointment. I knew that thousands of pilgrims arrived in Jerusalem each week, yet I was hoping for some kind of welcome. My imagination had conjured up trumpets, banners, fireworks and parades, but the real city was too preoccupied to take notice, its focus fixed on the competing rounds of worship. Alone I could pretend my journey mattered. Here I was just another pilgrim.

Every building was the same colour – a mixture of milk-white and honey-yellow stone – which made it easy to get lost. Yet I could always guess my position from the people around me, because each quarter drew its own pilgrims: either shouldering wooden crosses and processing towards the Holy Sepulchre, or bowing capped heads while they approached the Western Wall, or queuing outside the Dome of the Rock at one and four and six o'clock. Standing among these pilgrims, I was reminded of Easter in Rome: any devotion overwhelmed by the drama and display.

In the Christian Quarter I often noticed a man in a cotton tunic and woollen stole pacing behind the processions. He had long brown hair and a brown beard brushed with grey. His face was chubby, his feet bare, and his belly tied with rope. He looked like Jesus, like an overweight Jesus.

The man's name was James. This is his story:

James was born in Detroit in the early 1960s. Growing

up, he felt drawn to saints such as Francis of Assisi – saints who gave up everything for faith. Aged twelve he converted to Catholicism, but during his teenage years he forgot about the Church, growing interested in New Age spirituality instead. However, as a young man he became depressed, and his depression did not lift until he realized that only the love of Jesus could save him.

Then he heard about the Miracle of the Sun. 'It was in Fatima, in Portugal, during World War One. Three kids kept having visions of Our Lady, but they were just shepherds, and nobody believed them. One day they asked the Virgin for help, so she told them to gather a big crowd together. Thousands of people came – thirty, forty thousand – believers and non-believers, all hoping for proof. And they all saw the same thing. Midday the sun drops out of the sky and falls towards the earth. Then it sits on the horizon, getting bigger and bigger, spinning round and changing colour. And all the scientists and journalists – they all saw it too. So now they had to believe.'

In his twenties James joined a Catholic movement devoted to teaching people about the Virgin Mary. But the whole time he felt dissatisfied, as if God was calling him to something more.

Aged thirty-one he gave up his possessions and began living like a pilgrim.

'At the start I had normal clothes and a backpack with some essentials, but pretty soon it got stolen. I took it as a sign. Jesus lived off charity, so why couldn't I?'

Since then he had gone without money, a sleeping bag, or even any shoes. And it worked: 'I've been to Ireland, England, Belgium, Holland, France, Italy, Greece, Egypt, Spain, Germany, India, Canada, the whole United States minus Alaska and Hawaii, and all through Mexico. Twenty-two years a pilgrim. Mostly I travel on foot, sometimes preaching, oftentimes just worshipping. The last few summers I've spent in Jerusalem, right here in the Old City. I've got a deal with an airline that lets me fly for free. Plus I've got a friend who lends me clothes for the flight. And I get invitations to visit places and preach – but never for money. People ask me to eat with them, ask me into their homes.'

Three days was the longest he had ever gone hungry. How he stayed so plump, I never found out.

I met James on Sunday afternoon and several times more that week. Each time he asked how things were going, and I would tell him that I was still getting used to Jerusalem, to the cramped lanes and sunken passages, to the hordes of tourists and mobs of pilgrims and the shrines grown hectic with half the world's believers.

'But how's it going *spiritually*?' he would ask.

What could I say? Even though Jerusalem was built from ancient stone and set upon ancient ground – even though time was heavy here – I noticed only the city's shining surfaces: the busy streets and jumbled buildings. Yet I encountered little sense of the sacred – that threadbare hint of something big beyond human spectacle – and doubted that my life had been transformed by reaching the city. So I replied with a hopeful phrase or two – 'Still searching!' – while James repeated the words, 'Praise be, praise be.' Then he started discussing himself again.

One afternoon James listed his recent media appearances. A few months ago he was interviewed by the BBC. Before that he had featured in *Time* magazine, appeared on *Good Morning America* and been profiled by several newspapers in the States. He even starred in a documentary called *The Jesus Guy*. 'You know, people see me walking round, they say: Hey, d'you see the Jesus guy? But I don't think I'm some kind of Messiah.

I'm just trying to stick to the example the Good Lord gave us.'

Another afternoon he told me about the city's secret places. About a ledge halfway up the Mount of Olives, where you could spend the whole night hiding. And a balcony above King David's Tomb, where you could pray all day without being disturbed. And the graveyard behind the Western Wall, where you could shelter for hours among the open tombs. And the crypt below the Chapel of the Holy Face, where you could sit in the shadows without ever being seen. As James listed these places, he sounded like a fugitive, and it was easy to imagine him shuffling between sanctuaries under cover of darkness.

'But my favourite has to be Deir Es-Sultan,' he concluded.

'Where's that?'

'The Ethiopian Monastery. Right on top of the Holy Sepulchre.'

'Show me.'

So James took me to Chabad Street, a souk running south from the Damascus Gate, dense with stalls and teeming with people. I followed my guide past ranks of leather belts with metal buckles, screens of plastic sunglasses on wire grids, pyramids of baklava with dustings of powdered pistachio, and rubber armbands fastened to rusted girders. In places we crossed through vaulted chambers containing windowless restaurants, lightless cafes, dingy barber shops and shabby hotels, as well as toyshops, shoe shops and shops selling nothing but baby clothes. Elsewhere the street was covered with corrugated roofing, making the passages dim, the voices loud, and the air rich with the smell of spices.

Midway along there was a break in the stalls and a staircase leading up to a green gateway. The gates opened onto a flat rooftop, a Coptic chapel on the right, its interior gaudy with icons, and a courtyard of cells on the left, their lumpen walls built from adobe and mortar. I followed James into the yard, stepping over clipped lengths of cable and folded metal chairs. Though the cell doors were padlocked, I noticed a crumbling sink behind a plastic shower curtain and a makeshift kitchen behind a smoke-stained blind.

James's woollen stole was hanging in one corner. 'The Ethiopians are friends,' he told me, pulling down the fabric and draping it over his shoulder. 'The other churches won't let them inside the basilica. That's why they live on the roof.'

He went on: 'Of all the places I've visited, Jerusalem must be the least kind. It's proof of the world's sickness when our holiest city shows so little Christian compassion.'

As we sat near the compound entrance, a pair of monks passed by. They were very tall, very thin, wearing strappy leather sandals and habits of grey serge.

James greeted them, but they made no reply. Once they were gone, he said: 'You know why the Franciscans are custodians of the Holy Land? At the end of his life St Francis visited the Sultan of Egypt, who was ruling over Jerusalem at the time. The sultan was so impressed by the saint's poverty, he gave the brothers control of all the Christian shrines in his kingdom.' James fingered the tied rope round his waist, framing the next sentence with care. 'Although, to tell the truth, I don't see much of St Francis in the Old City any more.'

I asked him to explain.

'One of my favourite places to pray is the third station of the Via Crucis – the crypt chapel with the Blessed Sacrament on show. But this year I was told I couldn't worship there.'

'You were banned?'

'Well, like a lot of saints – like Francis of Assisi, like Thérèse of Lisieux – when I pray, I repose. So I went to the crypt to worship because, you know, I don't have a bed or anything. Just because I've got my eyes closed doesn't mean I'm not praying – a lot. But someone complained – said it was disrespectful to the host – told me I couldn't come back.'

I wondered about James's time in Jerusalem and the confusion he must have faced here. I wondered whether the city's indifference had punctured his sense of purpose, or encouraged his lonely mission. However, when I asked what was hardest about his life, he told me it was travelling in America.

'Surely America's much more religious than Europe?'

'Ordinary folks, maybe, but the media treat religion like it's dangerous. Not just the Muslims – Christians too. Either they make fun of you, else they think you want money, else they think you're crazy. There was one city I spent time in – lot of unemployment – lot of crime – where I made a big impact. But the media just wanted to know about my family, my childhood. They just want to make religion look bad.'

'If you dressed in jeans, nobody would notice,' I said. 'If you were a parish priest, nobody would care.'

James paused, plucking his cheeks into a joyless grin. 'You know, living how I do, some priests think I'm challenging them. There were churches in the States where I wasn't allowed to preach. Schools too. I want to be friends with bishops, priests, all kinds of clergy – I'm one hundred per cent Catholic – but this way I can touch more people's lives.' He paused again, grinned again. 'Besides, truly following Jesus' example means being an outsider.'

He had no plans for the future, but would go wherever

the Good Lord sent him. He had no ambitions either, but hoped somehow to meet the Pope.

All day the Old City was crowded, but after dark it cleared. The shops and stalls and temporary cafes closed for the night, while the souks became strip-lit corridors of bolted doors and drawn shutters, every display of fresh fruit and coloured fabric packed away. The scale of the place also shifted, as if leaning back, breathing out. Its passageways were empty now except for the blue air, the bleeding streetlight. No clouds in the sky, no breeze on the ground, and the shadow-cloaked buildings were cool to touch. I was reminded of Istanbul at midnight, that second week of June, and the reeling streets of Thessaloniki, that lonely weekend in May. Of a Good Friday procession in the ruins of the Colosseum, and a circle of shrines at the childhood home of Benoît-Joseph Labre. How far I had come. How many cities I had seen. All waiting for this final journey.

By eleven o'clock the streets were deserted. That was when I began to walk.

I was walking the Via Crucis, the half-kilometre path from the Jaffa Gate to the Holy Sepulchre, following Christ's route to the crucifixion. It was lined with chapels and numbered plaques, counting out the fourteen stations.

The first station was a madrassa, its walled courtyard occupying the space where Herod's Palace once stood. I set off from here, past the Chapel of the Condemnation, where Christ was judged, and the Chapel of the Flagellation, where he was scourged. Inside this church, the second station, a mosaic roof was pieced in a pattern of thorns, crowning the building with barbed branches. But that night the gates were locked.

A doorway opened onto the third station, where a sculpture of Christ knelt to the floor, falling for the first time. The crypt chapel beyond was a dim, sheltered space, bare except for the tabernacle behind the altar. Its ornate case contained a chalice of brassy gold, and beneath the chalice a nun bowed in prayer.

The gate to the fourth station had a lintel carved with an image of Christ meeting his mother; the wall of the fifth was imprinted with a hand, where a thousand thousand pilgrims had touched; the sixth occupied an underground chamber with an icon of Jesus copied from the Veil of Veronica, for this was the place where she cleaned the blood from his brow. Then I came to the seventh station, where Christ fell for the second time. A black double door with red and gold tracery. The eighth station, where he met the women of Jerusalem. Told them, *Weep not for me but for yourselves*. A sheet of coarse stone with the letters *IC XC NIKA* embossed on the one smooth slab. The ninth station. Where he fell for the third time. A corner of the Coptic Patriarchate and a wooden cross left leaning in the shadows. Left there as if forgotten.

At the end of the Via Crucis a locked door led to the Church of the Holy Sepulchre, where the five remaining stations were arranged. A crowd of pilgrims stood outside the door – most of them elderly Russian ladies in ankle-length puffa jackets. They were waiting to join the all-night vigil in the basilica.

Around twelve the door opened and the crowd filed into the forecourt. Despite the darkness, I could just make out a grand bell tower rising to one side, but otherwise the architecture was basic, as if the original facade had been sheered away, leaving the base wall exposed.

Stepping into the basilica, the pilgrims started crossing themselves: blotchy skin and blotchy hands and fingers whispering over synthetic jackets. Then they moved into the rotunda, a grand chamber ringed by a triple arcade, with columned ranks rising towards the dome. The pilgrims did not stop, however, moving on into the Orthodox chapel that formed the basilica nave. This was the Katholikon, a church within a church. Its iconostasis framed a pair of marble thrones, and a marble urn at the front marked the very centre of the world.

On entering the Katholikon the pilgrims began kissing the icons, crossing themselves one two three times, one two three times. A group of nuns were kneeling near the sanctuary, their faces webbed with wrinkles, and a single priest stood at the lectern, reciting the liturgy. Yet I could not tell if the service had started, for the room never seemed to settle. Monks came; they went. The chanting thundered louder; it ebbed towards silence. From time to time an elderly Russian lady would approach the candle stand beside the entrance and balance a stick of wax in the sand. After a while one of the nuns would shuffle over and stub the candle out, collecting the wax in a fold of black cloth. Before long the elderly lady would be back, lighting more candles and setting them in the sand. Then the sister would return, snuffing the flames and gathering the stubs.

This went on for an hour or more, their movements like clockwork, measuring out the night.

At one o'clock the clash of bells interrupted the chanting. A deacon carried a censer from the sanctuary, dousing the Katholikon with incense. Next he marched round the ambulatory and doused the minor chapels too. The censer made a splashing sound as it circled the basilica, tying each room in tatters of scented smoke.

I followed the deacon from the Katholikon and walked a circuit of the church. The layout was confusing, with chapels occupying different levels and a labyrinth of corridors between. And, in the night-time, the whole place looked derelict.

During the next hour the air cooled, the service slowed, and the congregation swayed from one foot to another. Come two o'clock my legs had seized, so I walked a second circuit of the church and went down to the Chapel of St Helena, a pillared room with a domed roof. Oil lamps dangled from the ceiling and a coppery light tainted the air.

More steps led to the Chapel of the Finding of the Cross, where the altar was just a table and the apse no more than a niche. Bare rock bulged from the wall, fringed with the faint residue of fresco.

Sitting in the chapel, I kept telling myself that the pilgrimage was over. But I barely believed it, because I could not imagine a time after the journey. Though I left home in search of healing, only to realize the pilgrimage was hurting me, I never discovered a new reason to walk. Whatever insights I may have gained on the way, I could not summon them now. And, if I was waiting for some final epiphany, that chance was almost over. So instead I thought back to the start of the sickness.

For much of my adolescence, I wanted to be unwell, as it seemed to excuse the sense that I was ill-fitted for this world. At first the drinking blurred this feeling, but over time it made the problem worse. Then, when my thoughts began to craze, it seemed like some deep part of myself set free. I was glad for those wasted days, lying in bed and turned from the window, because it meant that the future was suspended. In my mind death was a release from shame, an escape from regret, and suicide a form of salvation.

As I began to get better, I was drawn towards religion, because it appeared to offer another way of leaving this life. When I set off on pilgrimage, I was bewitched by the stories of surrender, of sacrifice. But in the course of my journey I was shown how sacrifice could mean something much smaller: the habit of kindness, or the discipline of humility, or the steady practice of patience. And looking back on the last ten months, it was not the solitude I remembered, but the charity of so many strangers.

Throughout that time, the pilgrimage provided a sense of purpose. As well as the long march towards Jerusalem, it also knitted my life into the landscape. The months were replaced by the shifting seasons, while the weeks were measured out in rounds of worship. Staying in monasteries and convents, presbyteries and churches calmed what was restless within me, and during the regular services I noticed how the minutes slowed and the silence assembled, until the days were worth more than they had been before.

This was not what I had expected. At the start of the journey, I thought I was walking into the wreckage of Christianity. My impression now was of how much remained, holding tight to its decayed inheritance. Despite the decline of religion in Europe, it was still possible to cross the continent like a medieval pilgrim: travelling on foot, stopping at shrines, and supported by charity. Still possible to find comfort in pilgrim rites, even if the belief was gone. So maybe decline was also evidence of endurance, and loss the price we pay for surviving.

Sitting in the basilica that night, I wondered whether this was true for my own life too. Do we gather up mistakes like mementos, until they form the true texture of experience? And build ourselves stronger from the regrets collected year after year? Perhaps that was the lesson of the pilgrimage, for though I had hoped to heal myself by walking, any recovery came on the far side of collapse. In which case, I should not try to forget what had happened, but remember it. Remember a London bedroom with curtains closed and a rented flat stained with ash. Remember train tracks sunk in shadow and carriages screaming through the night. And that weightless moment when I rose still living from the ground.

It was three o'clock. My legs were aching, my shoulders stiff. The pilgrims were leaving the Katholikon and climbing a narrow staircase near the entrance. There they entered a second, smaller chapel, its corners inky with shadow, its surfaces stained with age. More lamps hung from the ceiling, made of red glass or burnished brass, and lamplight played off the arch of streaked gold behind the altar, framing silver sculptures of Mary Magdalene, the Virgin Mary, and a painted figure of the crucified Christ. Beneath the arch was a gap in the floor where you could touch the bloodied rock on which the cross was raised.

This was it. The twelfth station. Calvary.

Another deacon stood in the centre of the room, wearing a tunic of golden mail. As he recited the liturgy in a trembling bass, his vestments glimmered. My attention was fading, so I do not remember if we stood, or knelt, or touched our foreheads to the cold stone floor. I do not remember if we held candles and watched our fingers flickering, or clenched our hands tight until the knuckles went white. But I remember the young monk who came over before the climax of the service and ordered me downstairs with polite murmurs of apology, citing complicated theological reasons why only Orthodox pilgrims could remain.

I was too tired to protest, so I made my way back to the rotunda. Beneath the dome stood a boxy chapel caged in steel supports: the Edicule. It was a crude structure, the green-grey walls seeming to absorb the gloom. Candlesticks tall as columns flanked the entrance, their candles shedding no light, but when four o'clock chimed from somewhere in the building, the night softened to a mute blue.

An Armenian service was going on inside the chapel. Outside, a fierce-looking Franciscan set up barriers for morning mass.

Over the next hour some thirty or forty people arrived, mostly middle-aged women wearing black dresses, black jackets and mantillas of black lace. James was among them, a supermarket bag hanging from his left hand.

Once the Armenian service was finished, the fierce-looking Franciscan counted half of us into the Edicule. The first room, the Chapel of the Angel, was panelled in folds of stone, reminding me of a mausoleum. A passage led through to the second chapel, the Room of the Tomb, its door just crouching height. I could see little of the space beyond the passage, except for the gleam of plush fabric and polished metal, like the inside of a jewellery box. And a priest conducting mass at a cracked marble slab.

Although the priest was speaking Italian, I struggled to pay attention, his voice too quick and too quiet. Instead I stared at the eager, frightened faces beside me, some biting their lips, others clutching their throats, and one or two pressing their palms into their eyes. We were standing so close that our breathing fell into time, each intake of air rattling round the room, as if the tomb were a body, a corpse – dead no longer, gasping back to life. I kept reminding myself that this was the fourteenth station. Where he dropped into darkness. Where he rose to his feet. Where he stepped once more into the light. This was the end of my pilgrimage too, yet I experienced no sense of triumph, only a weary detachment pierced with regret. During the journey I had found some meaning in pacing slow along sacred paths, and in those lonely shrines where the world felt stilled. But, on reaching Jerusalem, I spent my time surrounded by believers, waiting for a sign that the journey was done. Perhaps I was looking in the wrong place. If I wanted to finish the pilgrimage, I should start walking again.

When the service was over, I followed James out of the tomb. It was not yet six, but more Catholics queued behind the barriers, while a large group of Protestants were gathering in Calvary. The basilica forecourt was empty, however, so we sat near the entrance, watching shadows recede over the flagstone floor.

James asked how it was going, but I could not answer. I was aware only of the bewildered calm that comes after a night without rest.

Eventually I said that, despite all the pilgrims, Jerusalem seemed a lonely place.

'A lot of people visit this city,' he replied. 'Mostly they're just passing through. Sometimes people from America will recognize me – they saw me preaching, saw me on the news – but it's hard to build anything like that. And this way of life – I can't have a spouse or anything—'

He tried again: 'Maybe if there was a community of like-minded people—'

He stopped speaking.

I tried to imagine a religious order founded in James's image, picturing armies of pious young men roaming barefoot between the cities of the world. There was something endearing about this ambition, about its boundless vanity. It made his whole calling seem hopeful, human – like the charmed conviction of a child. So I asked James if he knew the story of Benoît-Joseph Labre, patron saint of pilgrims, and began describing the boy too weak for the monastery, who left his home to wander the shrines of Western Europe. I explained how he refused all offers of kindness and fled from those who might follow him. I mentioned his innocence, his pride, and the devotion that slowly destroyed him.

'You think he was lonely?' James asked.

I wasn't sure. Perhaps he wanted to prove himself, or punish himself, or wanted desperately to feel forgiven. Perhaps this was the relief he sought in faith: from a shame which can never be shed.

James emptied sliced bread and sliced cheese from the supermarket bag and started to make sandwiches. When he offered me one, I shook my head, but he kept offering until I accepted. A man with no money sharing his breakfast with a stranger. Charity that gives before anything is asked and gives without hope of return. I wondered what hurt had driven James from home and carried him across continents. And if, over time, that hurt had become sympathy – for surely this was sacred. But I realized now that his motives did not matter. In the end, the kindness was all that mattered.

He broke the bread and shared it between us. While we ate together, I felt the courtyard opening up, as if there was now more space in the night. Perhaps it was the residue of a dream, a stray figment from the place before waking, yet it seemed more than that. It seemed that the world was stretching wider, or my life uncentred now. I tried to hold onto the feeling, but it was nothing that I could grasp, and then the moment passed and the morning settled.

Six o'clock. The dawn was drawing back, the buildings becoming solid. As the city surfaced from the night, I watched dust streaming off the basilica walls – grey and yellow and sparked with gold. And the sun pouring into the sky, making the courtyard to shine.

My breakfast tasted of paper, of putty, but I swallowed the last few mouthfuls. Then I thanked James for his help and climbed off the floor. Finally I fastened my rucksack onto my back and stepped out into the risen light.

Epilogue

Next morning I wake early and walk from Jerusalem, moving south along Highway 60. The road from the city is lined with modern apartments, shapeless office buildings, and low-rise flats made from concrete boxes. At eleven o'clock an expanse of suburb spills out to my right: range after range of whitewashed neighbourhoods. Then I enter the dusty scenery of the Judean Hills. The far-off hills are cultivated – green strata of orchard and vine – but nearer the soil is spent. Roofless farm buildings cap the nearest hills, and olive trees so twisted they look tortured. Blue road signs point towards Bethlehem, but first I must enter the West Bank.

Around midday I arrive at Rachel's Crossing, the gate on the southern side of Jerusalem. Although the gate is shut to traffic, a hallway of turnstiles and metal detectors forms a passage through the wall. The hallway is empty except for a pair of Israeli soldiers standing guard. When they ask if I am walking to Bethlehem, I tell them I am going to see the desert.

A caged corridor leads out of the checkpoint, chain-link fencing on one side and slabs of concrete on the other. Each slab rises six or seven metres, the lower half covered in graffiti – in flags and slogans and a cartoon image of God letting down a ladder from the clouds – with barbed wire trimming the top. All this I have seen before, in photographs and videos, documentaries and news reports, yet still I am surprised how the barrier splits the town, dividing streets and bordering houses. How close people live to the wall.

Curved roads rise up from the crossing, past souvenir shops selling crates of decorations and an inflated Father Christmas bobbing by the high street, his plastic face puckered in the heat. I keep climbing until I can see the whole town laid out beneath me, churches and religious institutes enclosed by flat houses with untidy roof terraces. A sparse skirt of green circles the town, but beyond that the earth is stale, crumbling like bread.

The Church of the Nativity occupies the eastern end of Bethlehem's main square. Its walls of soft-hued stone have discoloured with age, turning a burnt brown or a cavitied black. The door is a narrow opening no taller than a child, where crowds of people queue to enter. But I do not join them, because I am going to see the desert.

Heading east from Bethlehem, I enter a chain of villages with half-finished houses dragging down the road. No pavements now, so the children play on the trampled ground beside the tarmac. Sometimes they call hello, or run towards me with hands outstretched, tugging the straps of my rucksack or slipping my water bottle from its netting. A few chase after me on bicycles, until their father shouts from a doorway and they scatter.

Then I leave the villages behind and the children's voices fade.

Blunt ridgelines break up the distance. The sun has stripped the earth, revealing the rude geology beneath. No grass, no scrub, not even the chapped lichen that grows on exposed rock – just a ribbon of road unravelling over wasted desert. Hills of limestone, dolomite, clay and chalk mound up next to the road, cliffs grazing their heights and wadis scoring their bases. Animal tracks stitch the slopes, resembling thread veins showing through thin skin, and the hilltops are littered with sediment, pale like sand and powdered like sand. But it is not sand, only baked soil and broken marl.

All afternoon I walk towards the horizon, yet the ridgelines come no closer. The landscape has the texture of old ash, dead snow, and bone polished blue by water. It is a landscape of icons, a supernatural landscape, the most beautiful landscape that I have ever seen. A place never peopled. A country without a past.

Around teatime the road runs out and I enter the Kidron Valley. The valley walls are cut so steeply that I do not notice until I reach its upper rim.

A pair of Byzantine watchtowers stand at the end of the road. One of the towers is ruined, and from here I can see Mar Saba. The monastery is the size of a mountain village, poised above the drop. Every church, chapter house and cellblock is propped on stone buttresses or embedded into the cliffs, and each building has the golden sheen of a locust's shell.

Afternoon now, almost five. I'm hoping to spend the night here, yet when I knock on the door the guest master asks if I have a letter of permission from the Orthodox Patriarch.

I do not.

He shakes his head.

I want to tell him that, in the last ten months, I have visited almost a hundred monasteries and never once been turned away – until I came to the Holy Land. But I say nothing, only stand in the doorway looking disappointed.

Eventually he suggests that I sleep in a cave on the far side of the valley. Then he hands me a pot of honey with Cyrillic lettering on the label.

Natural honey, he tells me. From Romania. No liquid, only natural.

Footpaths etch the valley, descending towards a curtain of reddish rock. The rock is stepped in layers of scree, with caves lodged into the crags. A wrecked chapel occupies the mouth of one cave, while another has a wooden door pitched above a thirty-metre precipice, too high for anyone but climbers and angels. As I approach I realize that they are cells: the whole eastern edge of the valley is riddled with hermit cells.

After crossing the valley floor I climb up to the caves. There are coffin-shaped burrows and cone-shaped hives, chambers with dry-stone walling and warrens several storeys tall. They are all deserted, but some of the floors are inlaid with mosaic and one cell has a shrine cut into its corner. The shrine is spattered with candle wax, the deposits smooth as scar tissue.

I leave the remains of my rucksack by the entrance and duck into the cave. Within, the air smells stale like horded newspapers. Mar Saba is opposite now, and from here it resembles an optical illusion. Turquoise domes, rock-cut steps, open courtyards and overhanging balconies – all perched at that impossible angle. Beneath, the Kidron Valley carves a thirty-kilometre corridor from Jerusalem to the Dead Sea. On the day the world ends, this is where God will sift the saved from the damned.

Evening is coming on, and the sun has hidden behind a hunched shoulder of rock. There is no noise in the valley but the distant whinnying of the wind. When I hold my breath, I can hear boundless silence. When I close my eyes, I can see sparks.

I unroll my sleeping bag and lay my clothes on the floor. After three hundred days of walking – five thousand five hundred kilometres – my arms and legs have burnt a deep brown. New muscle swells at the neck and calves, but otherwise the flesh has been eaten away. The spoke of each rib spreads wide when I inhale, the hips jutting out like handlebars. My waist is dented, my stomach starved, and scars fleck my palms from half a dozen falls: in the woods south of Reims, on the pavements of Thessaloniki, and in the mountains above Lake Karacaören. And there are other, older scars. The kink in my left arm, where the bone was cracked. The seam at my left eye, where the skin was split. Yet, standing above the Kidron Valley, I am thankful for these wounds, thankful for the mistakes that brought me to this place.

The light is failing and the cave beginning to simplify. Watching the valley fill with shadow, I remember that murderers once walked to Jerusalem as penance for their sins, and that suicide was once the gravest sin of all, for it meant despairing of God's grace. After death the body of a suicide was an unclean thing, buried at a place where two roads meet. Buried beneath a crossway. Standing there, watching darkness pour into the valley, I wonder whether a life could be emptied out like the desert. If fear is the shadow the past casts upon the future, would consolation with the past set us free from fear? Is that how it feels to be saved? In which case, resurrection needs no miracle – the dead need not rise, nor Creation burn – only a moment of gladness for the things we have suffered.

Tonight I will try to sleep, yet wake dreaming of firelight in the caves nearby. At dawn I will rise and start hiking, my path pointing east along the valley. Canyons will lift up beside me – two hundred, three hundred metres – the route dropping down a grand staircase of stone and entering the lowest place on the planet. The daylight will wash clean the shadows, the desert bleach white as the sky. The sand will be salt at my feet, the silence fantastic.

Midmorning I will catch sight of a stranger, pacing forwards out of the sun. He will greet me, welcome me, wonder how far I have come. He will ask about my route, ask who gave me shelter. He will want to know why I am walking.

I will look away, telling him it is a long story.

He will turn his face towards mine.

'Speak.'

Acknowledgements

My greatest debt is to the many priests, monks and nuns who housed me during ten months of travel, as well as the countless strangers who offered me food and shelter. Without such kindness, the pilgrimage would have been impossible. In addition, I am grateful for the hospitality of Elena Narozanski and her family, and of Alev Scott, Alex Reddaway, Gypsy McLean, and Claudia Lewis. Also, for the generosity of the HRH Prince Hamzah bin Al Hussein Travel Award, and the company of Charles Marshall.

William Dalrymple and Caroline Finkel provided valuable guidance during the planning of the trip; Habib Malik and Tom Fletcher did the same while en route. During the writing, the feedback of Ed Gorman and Edward Charlton-Jones was particularly appreciated, as was the advice of Henry Hitchings, and the encouragement of the Deborah Rogers Foundation Writers' Award judges.

Special thanks to my agent Zoë Waldie and my editor Kris Doyle, who have given this book all the commitment and care I could have hoped for. And to Kate Mason, first reader and dearest friend.

Above all, thank you to my parents, who supported this journey from the start, and every step along the way.

Select Bibliography

PROLOGUE

Léon Aubineau, *La vie admirable du saint mendiant et pèlerin Benoît-Joseph Labre* (Paris: Société Générale de Librairie Catholique, 1883)

Giuseppe Loreto Marconi, *The life of the venerable Benedict Joseph Labre: who died, in the odour of sanctity, on the sixteenth of April, 1783*, trans. James Barnard (Wigan: William Bancks, 1786)

Jonathan Sumption, *Pilgrimage* (1975; London: Faber, 2002)

PART ONE

Bernard of Clairvaux, *The Letters of St Bernard of Clairvaux*, trans. Bruno Scott James (London: Burns, Oates, 1953)

Janet E. Burton and Julie Kerr, *The Cistercians in the Middle Ages* (Woodbridge: Boydell & Brewer, 2011)

Emilia Jamroziak, *The Cistercian Order in Medieval Europe 1090–1500* (London: Routledge, 2013)

Peter Kropotkin, *In Russian and French Prisons* (London: Ward and Downey, 1887)

—*Kropotkin's Revolutionary Pamphlets*, ed. Roger Nash Baldwin (New York: Vanguard Press, 1927)

Kenneth Scott Latourette, *A History of Christian Missions in China* (London: Society for Promoting Christian Knowledge, 1929)

Claire Marquis-Oggier and Jacques Darbellay, *Le bienheureux Maurice Tornay: un homme séduit par Dieu* (Martigny: Éditions du Grand-Saint-Bernard, 1993)

Thérèse of Lisieux, *Autobiography of a Saint: the complete and authorised text of 'L'Histoire d'une âme'*, trans. Ronald Knox (London: Harvill Press, 1958)

PART TWO

James Glass Bertram, *Flagellation & the Flagellants: A history of the rod in all countries, from the earliest period to the present time, by the Rev Wm. M. Cooper, B.A.* (London: William Reeves, 1877)

Debra J. Birch, *Pilgrimage to Rome in the Middle Ages: continuity and change* (Rochester, NY: Boydell Press, 2000)

Daniel E. Bornstein, *The Bianchi of 1399: popular devotion in late medieval Italy* (Ithaca: Cornell University Press, 1993)

Norman Cohn, *The Pursuit of the Millennium: Revolutionary Millenarians and Mystical Anarchists of the Middle Ages* (1957; London: Pimliço, 1993)

John Henderson, 'The Flagellant Movement and Flagellant Confraternities in Central Italy, 1260–1400' in *Studies in Church History*, Vol. 15 (Cambridge: Ecclesiastical History Society, 1978)

Desmond O'Grady, *Rome Reshaped: Jubilees, 1300–2000* (New York: Continuum, 1999)

Marjorie Reeves, *Joachim of Fiore and the Prophetic Future* (London: SPCK, 1976)

Jacques-François-Paul-Aldonce de Sade, *The Life of Petrarch: Collected from Mémoires pour la vie de Petrarch*, trans. Susannah Dobson (Dublin: John Beatty, 1777)

Philip Ziegler, *The Black Death* (1969; London: Penguin, 1982)

PART THREE

Robert Byron, *The Station: Athos: Treasures and Men* (London: Duckworth, 1928)

Robert Curzon, *Visits to monasteries in the Levant* (London: John Murray, 1849)

Pierre Gilliard, *Thirteen years at the Russian court: A personal record of the last years and death of the Czar Nicholas II and his family*, trans. F. Appleby Holt (London: Hutchinson, 1921)

Loren R. Graham and Jean-Michel Kantor, *Naming Infinity: A true story of religious mysticism and mathematical creativity* (Cambridge, Mass.: Harvard University Press, 2009)

G. M. Hamburg, 'The Origins of "Heresy" on Mount Athos: Ilarion's Na Gorakh Kavkaza (1907)' in *Religion in Eastern Europe*, Vol. 23 (Newberg: George Fox University, 2003)

Malcolm Lambert, *Medieval Heresy: popular movements from the Gregorian Reform to the Reformation* (1977; Oxford: Blackwell, 1992)

Kyriacos C. Markides, *The Mountain of Silence: A Search for Orthodox Spirituality* (New York: Doubleday Books, 2001)

R. I. Moore, *The War on Heresy: Faith and power in medieval Europe* (London: Profile Books, 2012)

Dmitri Obolensky, *The Bogomils: A Study in Balkan Neo-Manichaeism* (1948; Cambridge: Cambridge University Press, 2004)

Edward Peters, *Heresy and Authority in Medieval Europe: documents in translation* (Philadelphia: Penn Press, 1980)

Edvard Radzinsky, *Rasputin: The Last Word*, trans. Judson Rosengrant (London: Weidenfeld & Nicolson, 2000)

Grigori Rasputin, *My Pilgrimage to Jerusalem*, trans. Todd Bludeau (1911; New York: Liberty Publishing, 2013)

Steven Runciman, *The medieval Manichee: A study of the Christian dualist heresy* (Cambridge: CUP, 1960)

The Encyclopædia Britannica: a dictionary of arts, sciences, literature and general information, 11th edition (Cambridge: CUP, 1910–11)

'The Presbyter Cosmas's sermon regarding the newly appeared Bogomil Heresy' in *Monumenta Bulgarica: a bilingual anthology of Bulgarian texts from the 9th to the 19th centuries*, compiled by Thomas Butler (Ann Arbor: Michigan Slavic Publications, 1996)

The Way of a Pilgrim and *The Pilgrim Continues His Way*, trans. R. M. French (London: SPCK, 1954)

PART FOUR

Thomas Asbridge, *The First Crusade: A new history* (London: Simon & Schuster, 2004)

Malcolm Barber, *The Trial of the Templars* (Cambridge: CUP, 1978)

Charles-Louis Cadet de Gassicourt, *Le Tombeau de Jacques Molai: ou, Histoire secrète et abrégée des initiés, anciens et modernes, des Templiers, francs-maçons, illuminés, etc.* (Paris: Desenne, 1797)

Chronicles of the First Crusade, 1096–1099, ed. Christopher
    Tyerman (London: Penguin, 2012)

Anna Comnena, *The Alexiad of the Princess Anna
    Comnena: being the history of the reign of her father,
    Alexius I, Emperor of the Romans, 1081–1118 A.D.*,
    trans. Elizabeth Dawes (London: Kegan Paul, Trench,
    Trubner & Co., 1928)

*Gesta Francorum et aliorum Hierosolimitanorum: The
    Deeds of the Franks and other pilgrims to Jerusalem*, ed.
    Rosalind Hill (Oxford: Clarendon Press, 1967)

Joseph von Hammer-Purgstall, 'Mysterium Baphometis
    Revelatum' in *Fundgruben des Orients*, ed. Gesellschaft
    von Leibhabern (Vienna: Anton Schmid, 1818)

Conor Kostick, *The Social Structure of the First Crusade*
    (Leiden: Brill, 2008)

Helen Nicholson, *The Knights Templar: A new history*
    (Stroud: Sutton Publishing, 2001)

Jonathan Riley-Smith, *The First Crusade and the Idea of
    Crusading* (London: Athlone Press, 1986)

Steven Runciman, *A History of the Crusades: Volume 1,
    The First Crusade and the Foundation of the Kingdom
    of Jerusalem* (Cambridge: CUP, 1951)

*The Rule of the Templars: The French text of the Rule of
    the Order of the Knights Templar*, trans. J. M. Upton-
    Ward (Woodbridge: Boydell, 1992)

Christopher Tyerman, *How to Plan a Crusade* (London:
    Allen Lane, 2015)

PART FIVE

Sacvan Bercovitch, *The Puritan Origins of the American
    Self* (New Haven: Yale University Press, 1975)

'Cambrai Homily' in *Thesaurus Palaeohibernicus: A
    collection of old-Irish glosses, scholia, prose and verse*,

eds. Whitley Stokes and John Strachan (Cambridge: CUP, 1903)

Christopher Columbus, *The Diario of Christopher Columbus's First Voyage to America, 1492–1493, abstracted by Fray Bartolomé de las Casas*, trans. Oliver Dunn and James Kelley (Norman, OK: University of Oklahoma Press, 1988)

— *The Book of Prophecies*, ed. Roberto Rusconi, trans. Blair Sullivan (Berkeley: University of California Press, 1997)

William Dalrymple, *From the Holy Mountain: A Journey in the Shadow of Byzantium* (London: Harper Collins, 1997)

Carol Delaney, *Columbus and the Quest for Jerusalem* (London: Duckworth, 2012)

Early Travels in Palestine: comprising the narratives of Arculf, Willibald, Bernard Sæwulf, Sigurd, Benjamin of Tudela, Sir John Maundeville, De La Brocquière, and Maundrell, ed. Thomas Wright (London: Henry G. Bohn, 1848)

Philip Edwards, *Pilgrimage and Literary Tradition* (Cambridge: CUP, 2005)

The Irish in Early Medieval Europe: Identity, Culture and Religion, eds. Roy Flechner and Sven Meeder (London: Palgrave, 2016)

F. Thomas Noonan, *The Road to Jerusalem: pilgrimage and travel in the Age of Discovery* (Philadelphia: Penn Press, 2007)

John Ryan, *Irish Monasticism: origins and Early Development* (New York: Longmans, Green and Co., 1931)

The Voyage of St Brendan, trans. John J. O'Meara (Dublin: Dolmen Press, 1978)

picador.com

blog
videos
interviews
extracts